72 वर्ष

भारतीय ज्ञानपीठ

णाणं पयासयं

वीर नि.सं. 2470

ई. सन् 1944

भारतीय ज्ञानपीठ

ĀCĀRYA KUNDAKUNDA'S
SAMAYASĀRA

BHARATIYA JNANPITH

(Founded on Phalguna Krishna 9; Vira N. Sam. 2470;
Vikrama Sam. 2000; 18th Feb. 1944)

MOORTIDEVI GRANTHAMALA

Founded by

Sahu Shanti Prasad Jain

In memory of his illustrious mother Smt. Moortidevi

and

promoted by his benevolent wife

Smt. Rama Jain

In this Granthamala critically edited Jain agamic, philosophical, puranic, literary, historical and other original texts in Prakrit, Sanskrit, Apabhramsha, Hindi, Kannada, Tamil etc. are being published in the original form with their translations in modern languages. Catalogues of Jain bhandaras, inscriptions, studies on art and architecture by competent scholars and popular Jain literature are also being published.

ĀCĀRYA KUNDAKUNDA'S

SAMAYASĀRA

English Translation and Commentary based upon
Amṛtacandra's Ātmakhyāti tīkā

by

Prof. A. Chakravarti

BHARATIYA JNANPITH

Moortidevi Grantahmala : English Grantha 1

ISBN 978-81-263-1557-4

Printed at Vikas Computer & Printers, Delhi

SAMAYASĀRA
(Jaina Philosophy)
A Prakrit text of Ācārya Kundakunda
Translation & commentary by : Prof. A. Chakravarti

Published by
Bharatiya Jnanpith
18, Institutional Area, Lodi Road, New Delhi-110 003
Ph. : 011-24698417, 24626467; 23241619 (Daryaganj)
Mob. : 9350536020; e-mail : bjnanpith@gmail.com
sales@jnanpith.net; website : www.jnanpith.net

Sixth Edition : 2017
Price : Rs. 450

GENERAL EDITORIAL

(First Edition)

Kundakundācārya is an unquestioned authority on Jaina dogmatics; and his position, especially among the Jaina Teachers and Authors of the South, is unique. His very name has an auspicious significance, to be enumerated next only to that of Mahāvīra and Gautama Gaṇadhara. All of his works are available in Prākṛit which borders on Śaurasenī and contains some traits of Ardha-māgadhī, and hence called Jaina Śaurasenī. Three of his major works: *Pañcāstikāyasāra, Pravacanasāra* and *Samayasāra* are called *Nāṭaka-traya, Prābhṛta-traya* or *Sāra-traya* reminding us of the term *Prasthāna-traya* of the Vedāntins. The *Samayasāra* is studied with great zeal among the Jainas; and its exposition by Amṛtacandra has made it a fountain of religious inspiration, spiritual solace and universal appeal.

Kundakunda is so popular in the South Indian Jaina tradition that he is mentioned under different names. Some of the details about him need further verification and clarification. In all probability Padmanandi was his name; he came to be called Kundakunda or Koṇḍakunda possibly from the place to which he belonged; and his name reached such an eminence that a line of Teachers originated from him, Koṇḍakundānvaya by name.

Besides the *Sāra-traya* or *Prābhṛta-traya* noted above, some more works (all the available ones in Prākrit) are attributed to him; The *Ṣaṭkhaṇḍāgama-ṭīkā, Parikarma* by name (not available at present); the *Mūlācāra* (Kundakunda's name is mentioned in some Mss. as its author); Ten Bhaktis in Prākrit (*Titthayara-*, *Siddha-*, *Suda-*, *Cāritta-*, *Anagāra-*, *Āyariya-*,

Nivvāṇa- and *Pañcaparameṭṭhi-bhatti*, to which we have to add perhaps *Naṁdīsara-* and *Saṁti-Bhattis* available in prose passages); Eight *Pāhuḍas* (*Daṁsaṇa-*, *Cāritta-*, *Sutta-*, *Bodha-*, *Bhāva-*, *Mokkha-*, *Liṃga-*, *Sīla-Pāhuḍa*); *Rayaṇa-sāra* (its authorship, still *sub judice*); *Bārasa-aṇuvekkhā*; and *Niyamasāra*. Whether all these available works are composed by one and the same Kundakunda; or there were authors more than one bearing the name Kundakunda: this has to remain an open question so far as critical scholarship is concerned (see for instance, W.Schubring : Kundakunda echt und unecht, ZDMG, 107, 3; Dec. 1957; here the full text of the *Bodha-Pāhuḍa* is edited by him). It is more or less accepted now that the *Rayaṇasāra*, as the text stands today, cannot be attributed to Kundakunda, the author of the *Prābhṛta-traya*.

Generally speaking, Kundakunda's works are like small and big *Prakaraṇas* devoted to a specific topic or topics. They are a repository of inherited knowledge which the author has recorded for future generations. Their mode of treatment and discussion have a traditional stamp, and the exposition is systematic. This can be very well seen from the *Bodha-pāhuḍa*, etc. Some of the verses of Kundakunda are almost Sūtras, quite pregnant with meaning and presuming a great inheritance of traditional knowledge.

There are traditional tales recorded in later literature to shed light on the biography of Kundakunda; but their authenticity is of uncertain nature, as long as they are not substantiated by contemporary evidence. So far as his own works are concerned, his name is found mentioned in some Mss. of the *Bārasa-aṇuvêkkhā*; and at the end of the *Bodha-pāhuḍa* it is specified that it was composed by the *Śiṣya* of Bhadrabāhu.

As to the age when Kundakunda flourished, different opinions are held. That is inevitable in the absence of any clear-out evidence given by the author himself. *Paṭṭāvalis* and traditional tales assign him to the first century of B.C. or A.D. Modern scholars have offered their opinions on the date of Kundakunda, but as yet no unanimity is reached. Taking into consideration the history of Jainism in the South, it appears that Kundakunda's age lies at the beginning of the Christian era.

Now-a-days attempts are made to arrive at conclusions in chronological matters from parallel ideas and expressions. But this is not a correct and safe method, because the Indian thought-pattern is made up of much that is traditionally inherited from the past, besides there being many undercurrents and cross-currents the clues of which are not necessarily detected. Secondly, we cannot lay much reliance on the so-called dates given in the *Paṭṭāvalis* and *Prabandhas*, etc., because these are not contemporary records; and further, their details are full of inconsistencies and anachronisms. Lastly, chronology needs a certain type of evidence which we must try to discover before assigning a specific date to any author. Under these circumstances it is safer to put together such data as help us to fix the relative chronology of different authors and their works. Kundakunda's age may also be fixed in this manner.

(1) Pūjyapāda, in his *Sarvārthasiddhi* (II. 10), has quoted five *gāthās* (25-29), in the same order, from the *Bārasa-Aṇuvekkhā* of Kundakunda.

(2) Siddhasena Divākara, as sufficiently indicated by Haribhadra in calling him *Śrutakevalin*, was a Yāpanīya and therefore a native of South India. His *Sanmati-sūtra* clearly shows the influence of the *Pravacanasāra* both in its pattern and even in some expressions. He proposes *Abheda-vāda*, to indicate the relation between the *Jñāna* and *Darśana* of a Kevalin which is, in fact, nearer the *Yugapad-vāda* already put forth by Kundakunda in his *Niyamasāra*.

(3) The South Indian tradition, recorded even in some inscriptions, etc., is quite uniform in mentioning Umāsvāti as a successor in the ascetic line of Kundakunda, though he was Gṛddhrapiccha, i.e., one who carried a bunch of vulture-feathers as against those who carried a bunch of peacock-feathers or a bunch of wooly stuff.

(4) Lastly, there are the Mercara copper-plates of Śaka 388 which mention the Kundakundānvaya and enumerate six Ācāryas of that lineage.

While proposing any date for Kundakunda the facts noted

above should not be ignored or just explained away somehow or the other.

The three major works of Kundakunda have been commented upon in Sanskrit by Amṛtacandra (c. close of the 10th century A.D.) and by Jayasena (c. 12th century A.D.) and in Kannaḍa by Bāḷacandra (c. 13th century A.D.). On the *Niyamasāra* there is the Sanskrit commentary of Padmaprabha Maladhārideva who passed away on Monday, February 24, A.D. 1185. Śrutasāgara has written Sanskrit commentary on Six *Pāhuḍas*, and he flourished at the beginning of the 16th century A.D. Some other Sanskrit commentaries by Prabhācandra and Malliṣeṇa are reported on some or the other of the Prābhṛta-traya.

Among the commentators of the *Prābhṛta-traya*, Amṛtacandra is concerned more with the exposition of the contents in a high-flown style, Jayasena, however, interprets the text word for word and then adds some observations here and there. Bāḷacandra mostly follows Jayasena.

Amṛtacandra's commentary of the *Samayasāra* is full of religious fervour; and the verses composed by him in his commentary are replete with spiritual appeal. They are studied, even to this day, with great zeal. Lately, Muni Śrī Puṇyavijayaji has discovered another work of Amṛtacandra, namely, *Sphuṭatattvasiddhi*, in fluent Sanskrit verses. It is awaiting publication. Amṛtacandra, as observed by F.W. Thomas, 'is an excellent master of Jaina Sanskrit; he employs fullness of phrase which not infrequently gives an impression of enjoyment of sonorous circumlocution and complicated sentences rather than of a simple striving for exactitude, and which renders the work of interpretation and translation extremely difficult; but no special charity is required for recognising in the remorselessness of style the outcome of an inflexible religious faith.'

The works of Kundakunda, especially the three *Prābhṛtas*, have enjoyed unsurpassed popularity. They are translated into many an Indian language; and there have been various editions from different places.

The *Pañcāstikāya* was translated into English by Prof. A. Chakravarti, and the *Samaysāra* by J.L. Jaini; and both of them appeared in the Sacred Books of the Jainas. The *Pravacanasāra* has been translated into English by B.Faddegon and A.N. Upadhye.

The late Prof. A. Chakravarti (Nayanar), (1880-1960), passed his M.A. with distinction, in 1905, from the Christian College, Madras, and took his L.T. in 1909 from the Teachers' College, Madras. For a year or two he worked as a Teacher in the Wesley Girls' School and as a Clerk in the Accountant General's office, Madras. In 1906, he was appointed as Assistant Professor of Philosophy in the Presidency College, Madras, and thereafter he worked as such (having become a Professor in 1917) in the Government Colleges at Rajahmundry, Madras and Kumbakonam (of the then Madras Presidency) from where he retired as Principal in 1938. He was conferred upon the title of Rao Bahadur in the same year.

Prof. Chakravarti was well-versed in the various schools of western philosophy. He brought his wide learning and deep scholarship to bear upon his study of Jaina Philosophy. His introduction to the *Pañcāstikāya* (Arrah 1920) is a valuable exposition of Jaina metaphysics and ontology. In 1937 he delivered Principal Miller Lectures which are published under the title 'Humanism and Indian Thought.' He was a stalwart Jaina Śrāvaka of his times in Tamil Nadu. He was specially interested in 'Jaina Tamil literature' on which he has written a monograph in English (Arrah 1941). He has edited a number of Ṭamiḷ works by Jaina authors with their commentaries and, in some cases, with his learned exposition in English. For instance, Neelakesi, the text and the commentary of Samaya Divākara Muni, along with his elaborate Introduction in English (Madras 1936); *Tirukkural* by Thevar, along with the Tamil commentary by Kavirāja Pandithar (Bharatiya Jnanapith Tamil Series, No. 1, with an English Introduction (Madras 1949); *Tirukkural*, with English Translation and Commentary and an exhaustive Introduction. He has also edited the *Merumandarapuranam* in Tamil. His exposition (described by M.S.H. Thompson, in the J.R.A. Society, London 1955, as 'an indispensable aid to the study of Tirukkural') of the Tirukkural has been hailed both in India and outside as a learned and liberal exposition of the Kural, the

Tamil Bible. His 'Religion of Ahimsa' is published by Shri Ratanchand Hirachand, Bombay (1957). It is a learned exposition in English of some aspects of Jainism.

Prof. Chakravarti, as an authority on his subject, contributed a number of essays and articles on Jainism, *Ahiṃsā* and contemporary thought to various publications such as Cultural Heritage of India, Philosophy of the East and West, Jaina Gazette, Aryan Path, Tamil Academy. He wrote both in English and Tamil. Some of his papers are reprinted in the 'Yesterday and Today,' Madras 1946. He was a member of a number of Associations and Institutions in Madras.

As a pious Jaina and a deep scholar of Jainism, he wrote a commentary in English on the *Samayasāra* of Kundakunda. He mainly follows the Sanskrit commentary of Amṛtacandra. Still his exposition of the *Samayasāra* and his evaluation of its contents clearly demonstrate how ably he has expounded the principles of Kundakunda to make them intelligible to the modern world.

Prof. Chakravarti was a well-wisher of the literary activities of the Jnanpith which are conducted under the patronage of Shriman Sahu Shanti Prasadji Jain and his enlightened wife Smt. Rama Jain. Both of them have encouraged with great self-sacrifice the study and publication of the neglected branches of Indian literature. It is through their generous patronage that the second edition of the *Samayasāra* by the late Prof. Chakravarti is being published here in the Mūrtidevī Granthamālā. There is no change in the contents; but care has been taken to print the Prakrit and Sanskrit texts more correctly and to add diacritical points, etc.. for the Sanskrit words used in this work.

The General Editors remember with gratitude the late Prof. A. Chakravarti who gave this work for publication in this Granthamālā and record their sense of gratefulness to the patrons of the Granthamālā who kindly financed the publication of this second edition.

Mahavira Jayanti.
April 8, 1971

H.L. Jain
A.N. Upadhye

PREFACE

Samayasāra is the most important philosophical work by Ācārya Kundakunda. It deals with the nature of the self, the term Samaya being used synonymously with *Ātman* or *Brahman*. The translation and commentary herein published are based upon Amṛtacandra's *Ātmakhyāti* but some other commentaries are also consulted. Jayasena's *Tātparyavṛtti* and Mallişeṇa's Tamil commentary were also consulted. The extra *gāthās* found in Jayasena's *Tātparyavṛtti* do not give any additional information nor do they affect the general trend of *Ātmakhyāti*. Hence the present English translation confines itself to the gāthās found in *Ātmakhyāti*. It may be mentioned that the Tamil commentary by Mallişeṇa seems to be based upon *Ātmakhyāti* by Amṛtacandra. Since the work deals with the nature of the Self from the Jaina point of view, the introduction also deals with the nature of the self from other points of view. The introduction is divided into three main groups: the nature of the Self dealt with in Western Philosophy, the nature of the Self in Indian Philosophy and the same topic according to Modern Science. A rapid survey of Western thought beginning with the Greek philosophers is given in the first part of the introduction. The second part, Indian Philosophy, begins with a concise account of the Upaniṣadic thought with which Kundakunda appears to be acquainted. The modern scientific approach towards the problem of self is also given in the introduction. It is not a detailed account of modern scientific thought; but here an attempt is made to present the modern scientific attitude which is quite different from that of the latter half of the 19th century. The Scientists and Philosophers of the

Victorian period were not sure about the nature of the self. Orthodox Physicists and Physiologists treated consciousness as a by-product in the evolution of matter and motion. Following this dominant attitude of physical science, psychologists also tried to discuss the problem of consciousness without a soul or self. All that is changed now. Scientific writers mainly influenced by the results obtained by the Psychic Research Society now openly acknowledge the existence of the conscious entity, the self or the soul, which is entirely different in nature from matter; it survives even after the dissolution of the body. Researches in Clairvoyance and Telepathy and veridical dreams clearly support the attitude of modern thinkers as to the survival of the human personality after death. Though nothing definite is established scientifically this change of attitude is itself a welcome one. This change introduces the rapprochement between Western thought and Indian thought as is evidenced in the writings of persons like Aldous Huxley. This must be considered as a good augury, because in the war-worn world bankrupt of spiritual values there is a ray of hope that the Indian thought of perennial nature may feed the spiritually starved world which is in search of some genuine idea serving as a solace and hope for the spiritually famished humanity.

This book is published as the first of the English series in the Bharatiya Jnanpith publications. The publication will reveal to the world what Indian thinkers 2000 years ago had to say about the problem of the Self.

A. Chakravarti

CONTENTS OF THE TEXT

INTRODUCTION

(Contents)

1

2

INTRODUCTION

1. SELF IN EUROPEAN THOUGHT

Man's development in all aspects may be described as an attempt to discover himself. whether we take the development of thought in the East or the West, the same principle 'Know thyself' seems to be the underlying urge. When we turn to the West we find that the beginnings of philosophy are traced to the pre-Socratic period of Greek civilisation.

Greek Philosophy

That was a period of culture where Greeks had a form of religion according to which their Gods, Athene and Apollo, were superhuman personalities trying to help their favourite Greeks by taking part in all their struggles. This naive popular form of religion very soon gave place to a flood of scepticism organised by the school of Sophists. They began to challenge some of the fundamental concepts of religion and ethics. It was, when this process of social disintegration was going on, that we find Socrates appearing on the scene. Though he was one of the Sophists himself, he was actuated by a higher ideal of salvaging what remained of the destructive analysis of Sophism. For this purpose he began to question and to find out the so-called educated individuals of the Athenian society. This process of questioning with the object of discovering whether the opponent knew anything fundamental about religion and ethics was designated as the 'Socratic Dialectic'. He would catch hold of a person from the market-place who was eloquently haranguing about justice or goodness and questioned what he meant by the Just or the Good. When the opponent gives an instance of what is just or what is good and defines the concept on the same principle, Socrates would confront him with an exception to that definition. This would force the opponent to modify his definition. This process of debating will go on till the opponent gets confounded in the debate and is made to confess that after all he was ignorant of the nature of the fundamental concepts. By this process of cross-examination Socrates exposed the ultra vanity and hollowness of the so-called learned Sophists of Athens. Then he realised himself and made others realise how shallow was the knowledge of the so-called scholar. That was why he obtained the singular testimony from the Delphic Oracle that he was the wisest man living because he knew that he knew nothing. This process of dialectical analysis so successfully employed by Socrates resulted in building up of the Athenian Academy which gathered under its roof a number of ardent youths with the desire to learn more about human personality and its nature.

Plato, a disciple and friend of Socrates, was the most illustrious figure of the school. In fact all that we know about Socrates and the conditions of thought about that period are all given to us by Plato through his immortal Dialogues. He systematized the various ideas revealed by his master, Socrates. He constructed a philosophical system according to which sense-presented experience is entirely different from the world of ultimate ideas which was the world of Reals. He illustrates this duality of human knowledge by his famous parable of the cave. According to this parable, the human being is but a slave confined inside a cave chained with his face towards the wall. Behind him is the opening through which all-illuminating sunshine casts shadows of moving objects on the walls of the cave. The enchained slave inside the cave is privileged to see only the moving shadows which he imagines to be the real objects of the world. But once he breaks the chain and emerges out of the cave he enters into a world of brilliant light and sunshine and comes across the real objects whose shadows he was constrained to see all along. Man's entry into the realm of reality and realization of the empty shadow of the sense-presented world is considered to be the goal of human culture and civilisation by Plato. Instead of moving in the ephemeral shadows of the sense-presented world, man ought to live in the world of eternal ideas which constitute the scheme of Reality presided over by the three fundamental Ideas — Truth, Goodness and Beauty. This duality of knowledge necessarily implies the duality of human nature. Man has in himself this dual aspect of partly living in the world of realities and partly in the world of senses. The senses keep him down in the world of shadows whereas his true nature of reason urges him on to regain his immortal citizenship of the ultimate world of ideas. On the basis of this conflict of reason and the senses, Plato builds up a theory of ethics according to which man should learn to restrain the tendencies created by Senses through the help of Reason and ultimately regain his lost freedom of the citizenship in the world of Ideas. The two worlds, which he kept quite apart, the world of ideas and the world of sense-perception, were brought into concrete relation with each other by his successor Aristotle who emphasised the fact that they are closely related to each other even in the case of concrete human life. Hurr an personality is an organised unity of both reason and sense and hence the duality should not be emphasised too much to the discredit of the underlying unity in duality.

A few centuries after Socrates, we find the same metaphysical drama enacted in the plains of Palestine. The Jews who believed to be the chosen people of Jehovah claimed the privilege of getting direct messages from Him through their sacred prophets, the leaders of the Jewish thought and religion. On account of this pride of being the chosen people they maintained a sort of cultural isolation from others whom they contemptuously called Gentiles. A tribe intoxicated with such a racial pride had the unfortunate lot of being politically subjugated by more dominant races such as the Egyptians, the Babylonians, and finally the Romans.

Christian Thought

When Palestine was a province of the Roman Empire ruled by a Roman Governor there appeared among the Jews a religious reformer in the person of Jesus of Nazareth. As a boy he exhibited strange tendencies towards the established religion and ethics which sometimes mystified the Jewish elders congregated in their temples and places of worship. After his twelfth year we know nothing about his whereabouts till he reappears at the age of thirty in the midst of the Jews with an ardent desire to communicate his message. When he began his mission, the Jewish society was marked by an extreme type of formalism both in religion and ethics. The scholars among them who were the custodians of the religious scriptures — Pharisees and Scribes — were so much addicted to the literal interpretation of their dogmas and institutions that they pushed into the background the underlying significance and spirit of the Hebrew thought and religion. In such a society of hardened conservatives, Jesus of Nazareth first appeared as a social curiosity evoking in them an intellectual shock which ended in hatred. Here was a person whose way of life was a challenge to the established traditions of the Hebrew religion. He freely moved with all classes of people, disregarding the social etiquette. The elders of the Hebrew society therefore were shocked when they found the so-called reformer moving freely with the publicans and sinners. When challenged he merely replied that only the sick required the healing powers of a doctor. He was once again questioned why he openly violated the established rules of conduct according to the Hebrew religion. He answered by saying, 'Sabbath is intended for man and not man for Sabbath', thereby proclaiming to the world in unmistakable terms that the various institutions, social and religious, are intended for helping man in his spiritual development, and have no right to smother his growth and impede his progress. He enthroned human personality as the most valuable thing, to serve which, is the function of religious and ethical institutions. He told the Pharisees and Scribes frankly that the kingdom of God is within. Though in this conflict between the new reformer and the old order of Pharisaism the latter succeeded in putting an end to the life of the new leader, they were not able to completely crush the movement. His disciples recruited from the unsophisticated Jewish society firmly held fast to the new ideas of the Master and went about all corners of the country publicising this new message. From the Roman province of Palestine they made bold to enter into Rome, the very capital city of the empire, and ardently preached what they learnt from their Master. They were suspected to be a subversive organisation and were persecuted by the Roman authorities. Undaunted and uncrushed by persecution the movement was carried on in the catacombs till the new idea permeated to a large section of the Roman population. The Romans had hitherto a naive realistic form of religion after the pattern of the Greek Religion of the Homeric Period. The advent of Christianity resulted in the breaking down of these primitive religious institutions of the Romans. This breakdown of traditional Roman religion brought many recruits to the new faith from the upper strata of Roman society, till it was able to convert a member of the imperial household itself. The condition of the Roman society was extremely favourable to this wonderful success of the new faith.

The Roman Empire which had the great provincial revenues pouring into the Imperial Capital converted the Roman citizens from ardent patriots of the Roman Republic into debased and demoralised citizens of the Imperial Capital sustained by the doles offered by the provincial pro-consuls. They were spending their time in witnessing demoralising entertainments and in luxuries. For example, the Roman citizens were entertained in the amphitheatre to witness the slaves being mangled and torn by hungry lions kept starving for this purpose. It is no wonder that such demoralised social organisation completely collapsed when it had the first onslaught from a more powerful idea and certainly a more soul-stirring message.

The Roman Empire became the Holy Roman Empire in

which there was a coalition of the authority of the States with that of the Church. This Holy Roman Empire which had the Church and the State combined had rendered wonderful service to the whole of Europe by taking the barbarian hoardes of various European races and converting them into chivalrous Christian knights by a strict religious discipline imposed on them by the various self-sacrificing orders of the medieval monasteries. This education of the inferior races through strict discipline enforced by the Roman Church had in its own turn a drawback cautioned against by the founder of Cristianity. The Roman Church so jealously guarded its power influence that it did not promote any kind of free intellectual development suspected to be of a nature incompatible with the established traditions of the Church. This process of disciplinary suppression of the development of human intellect went for several centuries which are designated as the 'dark ages' by the historians of Europe. But human intellect can never be permanently suppressed like that.

Renaissance

There were murmurs and revolts within the Church itself. The unwarranted assumption of the priest-craft that it formed the intermediary between man and God was openly challenged. This movement of reform within the Church had strange co-operative forces from other sources. In the field of astronomy, Copernicus introduced his new and modern conception of the constitution of the Solar system which completely displaced the old Ptolemaic astronomy accepted by the Church. The earth which was considered to be the centre of the Universe around which the heavenly bodies moved for the purpose of shedding light on the earth's surface, was relegated to a minor planet among the several planets revolving round the sun which forms the centre of the Solar system. This astronomical revolution suddenly introduced a new angle of vision opening up immense possibilities of research revealing the wonders of an infinite Universe.

Similarly the discovery of the new world by Columbus introduced a revolution in geographical knowledge revealing new routes of travel and conquest unknown to Alexander the Great, who had to turn back from the banks of the Indus because his army would not move any further, as they thought they were approaching the ends of the earth. To add to these two discoveries there was the flight of the Greek scholars towards Rome as a result of the conquest of Constantinople by the Turks. These Greek scholars carried with them rich treasures of Athenian culture, which was revelation to the starved intellect of the medieval Europe, an intellect which had nothing but the Christian Bible and Aristotle's logic to feed upon. This wonderful Athenian culture and civilisation had produced a fervour of enthusiasm among the few thinking individuals of medieval Europe who devoted themselves to the development of the new arts such as architecture, sculpture, painting, music etc. The whole movement is called Renaissance or the rebirth, when man discovered his true nature. This movement of Renaissance incorporated with the religious Reformation ushered in the new world of Europe which was so fruitful of important results, such as the origin and growth of modern science, a new intellectual development which completely transformed the modern world. The growth of modern science resulted in a conflict between the established religion and the new Thought.

The intellectual development just after the Renaissance took two different forms, one associated with Francis Bacon who emphasised the importance of the experimental method adopted by science, and the other associated with Descartes who emphasised the mathematical method as the necessary intellectual discipline for the reconstruction of philosophy.

Bacon and Scientific Method

Francis Bacon who felt the inadequacy of the old

Aristotelian method of intellectual discipline proposed a new method suitable for modern scientific research in his book called 'Novem Organon' — The New Instrument. This new method suitable for scientific research, Bacon describes in detail. According to him it should neither be purely imaginary as the spider's web spun out of its own body nor should it be merely mechanical collection of facts by observations like the ant. Scientific method must adopt the way of the honey-bee which collects material from various sources and transforms them into useful honey. Such an intellectual transformation of facts observed will ultimately unlock the secrets of Nature for the benefit of man. Such a discovery of Nature's secrets for the purpose of utilizing them for social reconstruction ought to be the ideal of science according to Bacon. In order to successfully apply such a scientific method, Bacon prescribes certain conditions as a necessary intellectual preparation. Generally the mind of a scientist may be crammed with certain traditional beliefs and superstitions. Such preconceived notions which Bacan calls 'Idola' should be entirely got rid of and the student of science should approach Nature with an unbiased open mind which alone will give a correct insight into the Laws of Nature. This experimental method prescribed by Bacon, if adopted by a student of science, will give inductive generalisations relating to the constitution of Nature and her Laws- generalisations which would be of a certain amount of high probability. Though the inductive generalisations arrived at by scientific research do not have the absolute certainty, characteristic of mathemetical propositions, they were considered by Bacon to be of great practical value for the benefit of mankind. The attitude has been perfectly justified by the development of modern science with the practical application of scientific generalisations which have transformed the life of man in the modern world. Such a reconstruction of human society based upon scientific achievements was foreseen by Bacon in his essay on the New Atlantis. This new experimental approach to Nature has conquered for science, realm after realm, departments of Nature as Astronomy, Physics, Chemistry, Geology, etc. This successful conquest of the realms of Nature by science resulted in complete elimination of mind of man as a factor for interpretation of natural events. This elimination of consciousness, completely, from the field of research ultimately resulted in scientific reconstruction of Nature as a huge mechanical system in which the Law of Causation was the only principle of operation. In this mechanical system all events are guided by necessary causal conditions. There is no scope of intellectual interference either to modify or to suppress the occurrence of natural events according to the desires of man. The old thought which entertained the possibility of intereference with the natural events by supernatural agancies was completly discredited as a pure mythology having no place in the realm of Nature, whose constitution is revealed to the student of Science. This inductive method adopted by modern science finally resulted in the generalisation of conservation of mass and energy as the basis of nature and in relegation of consciousness to an extremely subordinate place as a sort of by-product in the operation of natural events. Such a generalisation suggested by the physical science was also adopted by Charles Darwin to explain the phenomena relating to the animal kingdom. He also fell in with the general trend of physical science and formulated his famous Law of Evolution, based upon natural selection and survival of the fittest. This principle of explanation of the origin of species also relegated consciousness as an unnecessary factor not required for the explanation of life- phenomena which he considered to be quite intelligible on the same principle of mechanical Law of Causation. This intellectual attitude which attemped to explain both the organic and the inorganic realms of nature purely on the principle of mechanical Law of Causation was designated Naturalism as contrasted with pre-scientific thought which introduced supernaturalism. Such was the state of modern thought at the end of the 19th century. But this triumph of Naturalism was openly challanged in the beginning of the 20th century especially by Biologists and

Psychologists who exposed the inadequacy of the naturalistic method of interpretation of dealing with biological and psychological phenomena. This open challenge to Naturalism which started in the beginning of the present century had led to the recognition of consciousness as an important factor in the evolution process of both the biological and psychological realms and restored consciousness to its own status of dignity and importance. Such challenge and the consequent recognition of the importance of consciousness which is relevant to our general enquiries regarding the nature of the self will be dealt with later on.

Cartesianism : Mathematical Methods

In the meanwhile let us turn to Descartes. He was a mathematician and philosopher and he formulated another method necessary for the reconstruction of philosophy. Being a mathematician he wanted to reconstruct metaphysics on certain foundation. Just as Euclid started with certain undeniable and axiomatic propositions on the basis of which he raised the whole structure of mathematics, Descartes attempted to examine human experience and discovered some absolutely certain and undeniable propositions as the foundation for metaphysical reconstruction. Like Bacon he also prescribes certain preliminary conditions as necessary preparation for such a course. He examines the contents of human experience in order to find out whether there is anything of the nature of mathematical certainty, which cannot be challenged by anybody. All the traditions and principles accepted on the authority of a great person or of the Church, principles and beliefs on which the religious and moral aspects of human life are based, he found to be open to challenge and denial. The very fact that every religious dogma or moral principle has a rival or an opponent in another system reveals the inadequacy of such religious beliefs. Since they lack the absolute certainty of mathematical propositions they could not be taken as the basis for philosophical reconstructions. Even the sense-presented world, Descartes finds to be inadequate, as the world of sense-presented experience is liable to illusions and hallucinations and hence the object of the sense-presented world cannot be taken to be one of absolute certainty. Thus step by step he clears that the whole of human experience is inadequate foundation for philosophy according to his mathematical principle. Is there no intellectual salvation? Does such a sceptical analysis of our experience leave nothing to the student? Descartes says there is one thing which is absolutely certain. Even if we doubt every item of experience the act of doubt cannot be denied. That there is thought even when in the process of challenging experience must be accepted as an undeniable fact. If we accept thinking as an undeniable fact we have necessarily to accept some entity which is responsible for such a thinking. Thus he arrived at the famous conclusion Cogito Ergo Sum — I think, therefore, I am. Such a sceptical analysis through which Descrates approached the problem of metaphysics led him to the thinking self as an absolute certainty whose reality cannot be doubted at all. This principle of Cogito Ergo Sum forms the foundation of what is known as Cartesianism, a philosophical reconstruction just after the Renaissance in Europe.

Because thought exists therefore the soul exists, is a proposition which emphasises the relation between a substance and its essential attribute. The principle of cogito is an inference from the reality of an essential attribute of the substance in which the attribute inheres. The metaphysical bedrock on which Descartes wanted to raise a superstructure was thus arrived at through a sceptical analysis of human experience. Having arrived at this inevitable conclusion Descartes tries to bring back all those ideas which he dismissed as improbable and unreal. When he examines the contents of thought he is able to perceive certain ideas entirely distinct in nature from the ideas acquired through sense-perception. The latter are only contingents whereas the former are found to be necessary and certain. All ideas relating to mathematics are such necessary ideas. These cannot be contradicted; hence they are absolutely certain. Such necessary ideas which he calls 'innate' must be traced to a different origin altogether. One of such ideas which he chooses for investigation is the idea of a perfect and infinite Being, God. Man could not have acquired this idea through sense perception. Nor is it possible for him to construct such an idea from elements supplied to him by the senses. Hence he concludes that this idea of a perfect and infinite Being must be an item of thought from the very beginning of man. Man from the very moment of his origin should have started with this idea and hence Descartes infers that this idea necessarily leads to the conclusion that there is a real being who is the origin of this idea — God. He stamped his own mark on man from the very beginning. By such an argument Descartes emphasises the reality of a perfect and infinite Being, God, besides the thinking substance, Soul, whose reality he established through the famous cogito. Given the reality of Soul and God, the rest of experience which he dismissed as an unreal position that it might be due to sense deception is now recognised to be real, for sense deception would be a blot on the character of the Creator — the Perfect Being. Such a being cannot indulge in deceiving his creatures. Hence the external world must be accepted to be real. The reality of the external world though admitted to be real is considered to be entirely distinct from the soul. The external world which consists of material objects is made up of a different substance altogether — matter, whose essential attribute is extension. Thus Descartes recognises two distinct substances, the thinking thing and the extended thing. These two substances constitute the whole of reality. The physical realm made of extended things is entirely based upon the mechanical principle of causation. Any event in this physical world is necessarily conditioned by appropriate physical antecedents. Human body as a part of this realm of extension is controlled by the same physical law of nature, whereas the soul and its behaviour, since they are guided by a different system of laws, are not subjected to the operation of physical laws. This duality consisting of thinking things and the extended things forms the main characteristic of Descartes' philosophy. Though he recognises that these two substances are present in a human being, his body a part of physical realm and his soul the thinking substance related to his body; he does not consider that the rest of the animal kingdom is of this type. The animals have no soul. The animal body, being thus unrelated to the thinking substance, is considered to be purely a mechanical apparatus, unguided by a thinking thing. The animal is a soulless physical automation. The Cartesian belief persisted till the end of the second half of the 19th century when the Biologists proclaimed the fundamental unity of the animal kingdom and emphasised the kindred nature of the man and the animal. Once again we have to emphasise that the thinking substance or the soul is the central doctrine of Cartesian philosophy, and this is relevant to our study of the self.

His successor Malebranche took up the problem relating to the nature of man. According to Descartes man has a dual nature, his body belonging to the realm of extension is associated with the soul which belongs to another realm altogether. Each is a closed system controlled by the operation of distinct laws. Inspite of this distinctness the behaviour of man illustrates the strange phenomenon that a particular change in the mind produces a corresponding change in the body and *vice versa*. How could there be such a relation between two things which are absolutely distinct from each other in nature and attributes. The body is subject to the laws of the external world, the mind is subject to the psychological laws and strangely these two appear to be related in the human being. This is a problem for Malebranche to explain. How could there be a correspondence between an event in the physical realm and an event in the mental realm when they belong to the isolated systems. The solution offered by him consists in his throwing the responsibility on the shoulders of God for maintaining such a correspondence between events belonging to two different and isolated systems of reality.

According to Malebranche, God so arranges things that there is a parallel and harmonious correspondence between events in the physical realm and events in the psychical realm. Such a solution of a harmony secured through divine intervention was found inadequate. His successor Spinoza, the famous God-intoxicated philosopher took up the trend of thought as left by Malebranche and developed it to a wonderful pantheism. He found the dualism of substances, thinking thing and the extended thing, which was the legacy of Descartes to be an inadequate explanation of experience, necessitating the intervention of a third substance to make the relation between the two intelligible. Spinoza thought such a multiplication of substances to be purely unnecessary. According to Spinoza, there is only one substance, God, endowed with a number of attributes of which the extension and thought are but two important attributes. All physical objects in the external world are but modifications of this ultimate substance through the attribute of extension, and all the living beings, the souls, are again the modifications of the ultimate substance through the other attribute of thought. The theory of harmony through divine intervention introduced by Malebranche for the purpose of explaining human behaviour was considered to be quite irrelevant and unnecessary by Spinoza. Man being a modification of the ultimate substance must exhibit corresponding changes both in extension and thought, the ultimate substances being the necessary condition for corresponding changes. Thus the thinking substances with which Descartes started passed through the two-natured man of Malebranche and ended with the all-absorbing pantheism of Spinoza. The Spinozistic pantheism though extremely fascinating did not last long. It reduced human personality to an entirely inadequate and unimportant position. Whenever there is such a deterioration of human personality there is always the inevitable reaction. The Spinozistic pantheism which absorbed all thinking things and reduced them to non-entities was followed by Leibniz, Monadism.

Leibniz wanted to restore the reality of individual personality. He did not relish the theory of an all-devouring ultimate substance. Hence according to Leibniz the whole system of reality consisted of manads or individual units, some of which are thinking monads and others, with a dormant thought. Thus though thought is the necessary characteristic of all monads; it was explicitly present in some monads and in others it existed in a latent form. These latter monads whose thought was latent practically appeared to be unthinking substance and thus constituted the physical realm. The unity emphasised by Spinoza between the external world and the thinking souls was thus retained by Leibniz, though he threw overboard the ultimate God substance which Spinoza introduced to bring about the unity. According to Leibniz the unity is the identical nature of the monads throughout the realm of reality, though some of these constituted the apparently unthinking physical objects as contrasted with the thinking monads or souls. Thus at one stroke, the ultimate God-substance of Spinoza was split up into an infinite number of monads, all identical in kind though they appeared with different degrees of development. This theory which reduced the world to an infinite number of monads has introduced a problem in itself. Leibniz' monad was considered to be completely self-sufficient. Development of thought was purely an internal affair. Even in the matter of sense - presentation Leibniz does not believe that the monad has an access to the external world. The monad is windowless and completely shut up within itself. There is no external world or internal world in the case of monads. The monads being completely windowless and shut up, how could they have a common object of perception? Several individuals may perceive the same tree or stone in the external world.. Monad being windowless, the common perception of a single object in the external world will remain unintelligible because there is no perception at all, much less a common perception. Perception is an inner development in the monad and hence the supposed common perception of the same thing in the external world could only be interpreted as a correspondence in the perceptive consciousness of the various windowless monads unrelated to one another. Here Leibniz introduces his theory of pre-established harmony which is merely a modified form of Malebranche's theory of divine intervention. When the monads were first created they were so arranged that each developed in its own way and maintained a correspondence with the other monads which developed in their own ways. In order to illustrate this pre-established harmony, Leibniz compares Monads to several clocks which may show the same time though unconnected with one another. The different clocks may be wound up and may be set up at a particular time and they will all show the same time at subsequent periods, not because they are connected with one another, but because their mechanism is so constructed that they are bound to show an inevitable correspondence. This he calls pre-established harmony which he introduced for the purpose of explaining the mysterious correspondence in experience among the various windowless monads.

The English Empiricism

Let us turn to the empirical philosophy of Locke, Berkeley and Hume. Here we have a complete change of attitude. Instead of trying to understand the nature of the substance, the Ego, the English empirical philosophers confined themselves to the analysis of human understanding. Technically there is a shift from the ontological point of view to the epistemological point of view. Here is an attempt to comprehend the nature of the self by trying to analyse the nature and the process of knowledge and by examining the nature of the contents of knowledge. We saw that the Cartesian philosophy was based upon what is called the innate idea, the idea of the Supreme and the infinite Being. The Cartesians recognised the importance of such necessary ideas besides sense perception. But the

English empirical philosophers start with this assumption that there is nothing in the mind which is not obtained through the senses. Hence all the contents of the human understanding may be traced to sense perception. The mind itself is compared to a sort of photographic camera with the sensitive plate inside the mind on which the sense impressions are created by the stimuli from the environment. What the mind perceives is just the impression on this sensitive plate caused by the objects in the extrenal world. The mind itself being a passive receptacle of impressions from outside and the contents of the mind must be ultimately traced to the impression caused by external objects. Starting with this assumption Locke tries to make a distinction among the impressions so created by external objects. Some of the characteristics of these sense impressions or images in the mind such as colour, taste, smell, etc., are dependent upon the nature and function of the sensory organs. These qualities are referred to by the mind to the external objects. These are called secondary qualities as constrasted with the primary qualities of extension etc. The spatial object perceived by the senses thus appears to be a complex constituted by the spatial properties of extension, solidity etc., and the sense-created properties of colour, taste, smell etc. According to Locke, the latter secondary qualities are purely mental and are present in the mind alone though they are referred to external objects. The object existing in space has only space qualities without these secondary qualities. Thus the external object is analysed into two groups of properties, the primary properties residing in the object in the external world and the secondary qualities as colour, taste and smell which are really present in the mind though referred to the external object by the mental habit. By this analysis Locke emphasises the importance of the stimuli from the external world and reduces the mind or the self to a *tabula rasa*, an inactive receptacle for impressions and converts the objects of the external world into colourless entities though endowed with spatial properties. This bifurcation of experience partly consisting of colourless external objects and partly consisting of mental impressions inside the consciousness is taken up by his successor, Berkeley.

Berkely, being a clergyman is influenced by his religious predilections. He is not satisfied with Locke's classification of properties as primary and secondary. Even the spatial properties which Locke considers primary and which are supposed to reside in the external world are really dependent upon the nature and function of the perceiving agent. Intrinsically there is no distinction between the spatial qualities of the object and the properties of colour, taste and smell. The whole group of properties thus being taken to be mental images the only form of reality consists of a number of perceiving spirits for there is no external reality of objects. The spirit and its ideas constitute the experience of the individual self and the whole world and the nautre is but the perceived body of the supreme spirit, God. Just as one individual spirit appears to another individual spirit as an embodied entity so the supreme spirit of God appears to the individuals as the world of Nature which is really the body of God. Thus according to Berkeley, the external objects cease to exist and the reality consists of individual spirits presided over by the Supreme Spirit. One spirit appears to another in the form of body whereas the body itself is really the mental image in the mind of the perveiving spirit. What we are sure about is our own self. Our knowledge of the external world is based upon an inference from the directly perceived ideas or images inside the mind and even that inference is unwarranted and erroneous. What we surely know is our own spirit and the ideas present in mind which we wrongly assume to be the objects of the external world. This empirical idealism of Berkeley is taken up by the Scottish philosopher, Hume.

Hume is not influenced by religious bias. He carries the empirical analysis rigorously to its logical conclusion. He accepts Berkeley's analysis of the external world as sound. The contents of the mind are but ideas. Imagining them to be objects in the external world is certainly unwarranted and erroneous as is maintained by Berkeley. But Berkeley's certain assertion about the nature of the spirit is but the result of religious prejudices. Berkeley must have directed his attention towards this nature of spirit. If he had done so he would have obtained a different result. "For whenever I turn my attention inwards", says Hume, "I stumble upon some idea or other and what they call the Soul I am not able to perceive." Thus when experience is thrown into the crucible of philosophical analysis by Hume, not only the external world disappears but also the supposed undoubted entity called the spirit or the self which could not withstand the logical analysis of experience. According to Hume therefore consciousness consists of successive ideas or images, a stream of psychic entities and nothing more. Belief in the spirit or the soul is as unwarranted as belief in the external objects. Belief in these instances is but a psychological habit which could not stand the test of rational analysis. The popular assumptions of the external world and the existence of a self are thus dismissed to be unwarranted social prejudices by Hume, social prejudices which cannot be accepted as philosophical truths. Thus Locke's empiricism ends logically in Hume's Nihilism according to which there is no reality except the stream of conscious ideas. As a result of this nihilistic conclusion Hume is bound to discard even the Law of Causation which is the bedrock of modern science. The belief that events in nature are inevitably determined by their antecedent causal conditions is also taken to be purely a habit of the mind having no rational foundation. The fact that A precedes B on so many occasions creates in the mind the habit to expect B whenever A occurs, and on account of this habit A is called the cause of B. Beyond this mental habit of expecting B whenever A occurs there is no rational connection between A and B. There is no reason why B may not occur after X or Y. There is no fundamental reason to prove that B will occur only after A and not after any other events X or Y. Therefore the Law of Causation which is made so much of by modern science is also converted by Hume's analysis to be a popular prejudice based upon the mental habit having no rational foundation. This nihilistic conclusion of Hume is exactly parallel to the Buddhistic conception of experience in Indian Thought. Buddhism also is a sort of Nihilism for which neither the external world nor the Self or *Ātmā* has any reality. What really exists is a stream of momentary and mental impressions and nothing more. Thus the English empiricism practically ends in the denial of both the self and the external world.

The German Idealism

Hume's sceptical analysis resulted in reducing the Law of Causation not only to an empty mental habit but also in rejecting all propositions such as mathematical ones which are considered absolutely certain and unchallengeable. Propositions in mathematics, according to Hume, depend upon the same mental habit which is the foundation of the Law of Causation. We have been accustomed to observe, for example, that the angles of a triangle are together equal to two right angles. Merely because of the fact that this proposition has been observed to be true in the past in all cases that we examined, it does not follow that it would be true in other cases. Thus even mathematical propositions according to Hume are only highly probable statements but not necessarily binding on the human intellect to be absolutely true. This sceptical result obtained by Hume was the starting point of idealism. Immanuel Kant, the great German philosopher admits that he was roused from his dogmatic slumber by Hume. According to Kant, Hume's result though logically inevitable from the empirical assumptions shows the frustration of reason. Neither the dogmatic philosophy of Descartes nor the sceptical philosophy of Hume would be a satisfactory solution of the metaphysical problem. Kant therefore attempted to reconstruct metaphysics in such a way as to avoid both these extremes. As he himself confesses, "The starry heavens above and the moral law within always fill me with awe and reverence", his task as a philosopher therefore is to explain nature and constitution of the cosmos and understand

and explain the significance of the moral Law. The former he takes up in his first book of Pure Reason and the latter he takes up in his second book of Practical Reason. His attempt to salvage metaphysics from Humean secpticism constrains him to examine first the foundations of mathematics. Are the mathematical propositions really necessary and true or are merely contingent and probable stataments? He is not prepared to accept the latter alternative. Hence he concentrates his attention to find a suitable explanation for the necessary truth of mathematical proposition. According to Kant, the typical mathematical proposition is associated with geometry. Hence for him space is the foundation of mathematics. The problem therefore resolves itself into the study of the nature of space and its properties. Locke's attempt to give space an independent existence in the external world proved to be futile in the hands of his successors, Berkeley and Hume. If space, therefore, is assumed to be an external entity then we have to get ourselves entangled in the inevitable scepticism of Hume. Hence Kant is compelled to adopt a new method. The external world no doubt is the region of sense stimuli. But the object perceived by the sense is the result of a combination between the stimuli supplied from the external source and the shape given to it by the mind itself. The contribution which the mind makes in the process of perception is the form of space. Space and time according to Kant are the forms contributed by the mind while it is engaged in the process of perceiving external objects. The external world as seen by us is thus the result of two different factors: one the sense stimuli from an external source, the other the space which the mind impresses upon these sense stimuli. Thus no object can become an object of perception for us unless it is compelled to take the form of space. Since it is the combined product of sense stimuli and space-form, it necessarily follows that all objects perceived by us must necessarily have the form of space impresed on the materials by the mind itself. Spatial quality therefore becomes a necessary property with all perceived objects in our sense-presented experience. This world of experience therefore must necessarily conform to spatial form, and hence the objects of experience must necessarily be in conformity with spatial properties. If spatial form is an indispensable and necessary concomitant of physical objects, the space properties are similarly inevitable and necessary in a sense-presented experience. It automatically follows according to Kant that spatial properties, which are necessary and inevitable, form the foundation of mathematics. Hence mathematical propositions, since they are based upon the properties of space, must also share the nature of space and thus must be necessary and inevitable. Thus having secured a safe foundation for mathematical propositions, Kant next goes to further examine the implications of human understanding.Just as in the process of perceptual activity mind contributes the forms of space and time so also in the higher intellectual activity of understanding mind contributes certain other elements which he calls categories, the most important of which is Causation. Since the construction of experience is to be in conformity with the categories of human understanding they must be according to the pattern of causation which happens to be the framework of the whole edifice according to Kant. Hense causation is the inevitable and necessary framework of human experience and events therein must necessarily happen according to this causal sequence on which the whole structure rests.

Thus after securing a foundation for the principle of causation in the very structure of human experience, Kant surveys the whole of experience which is the result mainly of the activity of the mind in contributing the forms and categories according to which the sense-materials are shaped and arranged. The sense-material which is thus fashioned into human experience by the mind comes from beyond. What is the source from which this sense stimulus comes to the mind? Have we any access to this? Kant frankly admits that this 'Beyond' from which sense stimuli proceed is inaccessible to the mind and therefore not known. For, according to him, anything that is to be known by the mind must become a part of human experience, and hence must already be subject to operational activity of mind and must bear its impression. Hence what is not so subjected to the intellectual operation must necessarily be unknown. This thing which is outside our experience and which is unknown and which is the source of sense stimuli, Kant calls the 'Thing-in-itself'. Similarly the mind we are aware of is the one engaged in its operational activity in the experience. What the mind is when it is not so engeged in the fabrication of human experience is unknown, since it is also outside the human experience. Therefore the Ego-in-itself also is beyond knowledge as the Thing-in-itself. The Ego-in-itself and the Thing-in-itself, since both lie outside our experience must necessarily be unknown to us and hence we cannot state anything about them. Nevertheless we are certain of their existence, though we are not aware of their nature. This unknown region of the Thing-in-itself and the Ego-in-itself is the region of real existence according to Kant, and which is the 'Noumenal' region as contrasted with the phenomenal nature of our experience. Thus our experience is confined to the phenomenal region whereas the Ultimate Reality is the region of Noumena of the thing-in-itself and the ego-in-itself. This result obtained by Kant is rather unsatisfactory. The ultimate region of reality remains unknown for ever and what we know is the phenomenal one which is merely an unimportant appearance resulting from the operation of the mind upon the stimuli supplied by thing-in-itself.

Thus we are destined to be shut up within the phenomenal experience never hoping to come out beyond this magic circle. Kant's attempt to salvage metaphysics from Humean scepticism thus results in an inevitable agnosticism according to which man can never know the nature of reality and must be satisfied with the unimportant illusory appearance of the phenomenal world. In spite of this unsatisfactory conclusion, Kant proceeds with an undaunted spirit to reintroduce some of the important moral concepts which get exploded in the first part of his Critique of Pure Reason. The conclusion of the critique of Pure Reason does not permit Kant to speak with any amount of certainty as to the nature of Ego, whether it is mortal or immortal, whether its ultimate destiny is to achieve the combination of virtue and happiness. He frankly says that according to pure reason we can never be certain about this. In his Critique of Practical Reason many of these concepts are admitted by the back door which were driven out by the front door. He proceeds with the assumption that virtue must necessarily be associated with happiness. If virtue is not associated with happiness ultimately, there can be no moral foundation at all. But in ordinary experience, virtue is not always associated with happiness. That is why in cases of weak men they forsake virtue in pursuit of pleasure, because they find that virtue is not always rewarded with happiness. This contradiction of moral experience, Kant attempts to solve by his metaphysical suggestion, the ultimate summum bonum of life necessarily be the combination of virtue and happiness. This would happen though not now, ultimately in some far off future. If this proposition is accepted, it necessarily follows that the short span of life which man enjoys in the phenomenal world persists beyond the phenomenal birth and death and hence the immorality of Self should be accepted, if the moral proposition that virtue and happiness coincide somehow is to be accepted.

Thus according to Kant in order to justify moral life of our existence we are bound to accept the reality and immortality of the self which could not be guaranteed according to the pure reason of his first book. Thus in spite of the Agnosticism in his first book he attempts to restore the centre of gravity in the second book, the Practical Reason, where he tries to explain the reality and immortality of the Self and provides rational justification of his moral pursuit in search of happiness. In spite of his service to religion and morality his metaphysical system as a whole remains unbalanced since it rests upon a meaningless dualism of Noumena, the Unknown Reality and the phenomena, the unimportant illusory experience, which is the only source of knowledge for us.

Kant's philosophy is taken up by his successor Fichte. Fichte directs his attention to the criticism of the Thing-in-itself. The Noumenal world which was considered to be the Ultimate Reality by Kant and which was also said to be unknown and unknowable Fichte considered to be an unnecessary metaphysical encumbrance. Why speak about the thing which is unknown and unknowable? What is the value of your statement as to the existence of such a reality? Since nothing is known as to its existence and its nature, Fichte dismisses that as unworthy of metaphysical consideration and confines himself to what Kant called the phenomenal world of appearance. Therefore Fichte recognised the ego and the phenomenal world which it constructs. He does not worry himself as to the source of the sense stimuli. What we are searching about is the world of the objective reality. This world of objective reality is the result of the activity of the ego. Why should the ego or the self indulge in creating such a phenomenal world of experience? According to Fichte this is necessary because of the full moral growth for the self. The self creates the world of experience, a sort of moral arena in which it struggles in order to gain moral strength and to grow to its full stature of moral personality. Thus with Fichte there is nothing more than the self and the phenomenal world of experience which it creates for its own purpose; there is no other reality besides this. Thus Kantian idealism in the hands of Fichte turns out to be merely the self and the phenomenal world of experience which it creates, a result more or less the same as Berkeley's idealism in English empiricism. This dismissal of the foundation of external reality and converting it into merely an appearance created by the self was considered to be extremely unsatisfactory and it was rejected by his successor Hegel.

Hegel is one of the great world-thinkers. He saw how a careless analysis led to an unsatisfactory and incomplete system of metaphysics. He was not satisfied with Fichte's moral idealism. Nor was he satisfied with Kant's bifurcation of reality into a thing-in-itself and the phenomenal world of appearance.

The whole attempt of Hegel is to restore the ultimate unity of reality and to avoid the inconvenient corollary of mistaken bifurcation. He does not like to postulate the reality as unknown and unknowable, far off from the world of experience. He can't think of a reality detached from the world of experience. The reality must be in the world of experience and there must be an intimate relation between this reality and what Kant called the phenomenal appearance. The thing-in-itself dissociated from the world of appearance and appearance dissociated from the underlying reality, both are meaningless abstraction according to Hegel. The appearance is just the appearance of the reality and the reality cannot exist apart from and independent of its appearance which is but its manifestation. The contradiction between the reality and appearance is but the result of mental abstraction, and as such has no basis in a genuine metaphysics. The function of metaphysics is to understand the significance of our great experience, and any conclusion that nullifies the reality of our experience must be self-condemned. Hence Hegel tries to bring back the reality which was located in a far off 'beyond' by Kant and restore it to its legitimate place in the world of experience. According to Hegel the great world of experience consists of organic entities which are characterised by continuous growth and development. Organic development is significant and symbolic of the nature of reality itself. What do we find in the nature of organism? What is the process of growth of a particular tree or a plant? A seed that does not sprout out must be considered to be defunct and worthless. If it is to grow into a plant it must somehow change its nature as a seed breaking itself up so that the seedling may sprout out. The tender plant that comes out of the seed must also change its nature and put on foliage. Further growth must necessarily depend upon sprouting out of the new leaves and shedding of the old ones. Thus the growth of an organism consists in a process of dying in order to live, a combination of two opposite processes united and integrated in the life of the organism. This process of organic growth which contains within itself the process of breaking up and building up while maintaining its intrinsic identity and unity is the central idea of Hegel's thought. He calls that 'dialectic'. According to this dialectic we have the thesis, the antithesis and synthesis. Thesis refers to the postulation of affirmation of characterising this. Antithesis is just the opposite, negation of this characteristic, and synthesis is the combination of the two processes in the same nature of organic identity. The growth of organism is the illustration of this dialectical process. If you fix your attention to a particular stage in its growth you have to postulate its nature at that moment. If what is true at that moment does not change but perpetuates itself, then the plant will practically die. If it is to live it must give up its nature and change into some thing else. It must shed off its own leaves and put on new sprouts. It must change. It must be displaced by antithesis. Without antithesis there cannot be growth, no reality. Yet the change must be consistent with its thesis. A margosa plant all of a sudden will not put on the characteristics of a mango tree. That will be a mass self-destruction. No reality in nature behaves in this erratic fashion. Even while the old leaves are shed off and the new sprouts are springing up, the intrinsic identity of the plant is not destroyed. There is a mysterious process of synthesis which maintains the ultimate identity and unity throughout the process of this change. This dialectical process which we found illustrated in the life of a single organism is taken to be a symbolic process of the whole of Reality. Viewed from this point of dialectic, the whole of reality of our experience is characterised by this process of change, a change which is held together by an underlying inevitable identical unity. Identity in the midst of difference, unity in the midst of multiplicity, reality in the midst of appearance are the significant phrases used by Hegel in describing the nature of Reality. To speak of identity in isolation from the diversity or unity apart from multiplicity or of a reality apart from appearance should be said to be an empty abstraction in the place of reality and these empty abstractions can never sustain their stability long, even though they are set up in metaphysical throne by careless thinkers. They must quit the realm of abstraction and come back to the world of experience where alone they can live and have significance. This realisation of reality in its proper place in the realm of experience and the recognition of its importance in the midst of appearance and diversity must be considered to be the greatest contribution of Hegel to modern philosophy. He accepts the Kantian doctrine that experience is the result of the activity of mind, though he rejects Kantian abstraction of reality. When viewed from his own dialectical process this world of experience is but the appearance and the manifestation of the Ultimate Reality. The whole is an organic process of development, the underlying reality being spiritual. He calls this Ultimate Reality, the Idea. The great world of experience is the dialectical manifestation of this Ultimate Idea. This Ultimate Idea is also called the Absolute, a term which has become more popular among the philosophers. The Absolute is Ultimate Reality, the manifestation of which is experience of this great world. The great world of experience, therefore, is considered by Hegel as an organic growth. Hegelianism became very popular throughout the thinking world and practically all the European thinkers have been influenced by Hegel's metaphysics. Absolutism of Hegel became a dominant world- concept. It immensely influenced the world in all the fortunes of life. Universities in England and in the continent of Europe and even in distant America were subject to the influence of Hegelian Absolutism, and thinkers began to introduce Hegel's point of view and the dialectical development as a necessary panacea for the intellectual troubles created by the earlier thinkers. Besides its influence directed in the face of metaphysics which completely brushed aside the other forms of thought as English Empiricism, Kantian idealism etc.

Hegel's influence was felt in two important directions which led to the complete transformation of the concept of State and concept of the society. When Hegel postulated that the Ultimate Reality is Absolute and the whole of our experience is the manifestation of this Absolute, every department of human activity including religion and morality is given a subsidiary place in this development of the Absolute idea. The most important manifestation of this Absolute according to Hegel is the state organisation. The state is the greatest and the highest manifestation of this absolute idea, and every other social organisation must be subordinate to this. Even the Chruch must be subordinate to the State and religion becomes an instance in the manifestation of the state organisation. The ultimate result of this state absolutism of Hegel reduced human personality to the status of building material for raising the edifice of a state. Man is but a brick to be utilised for constructing the state edifice, and besides this function there is no justification for the existence of man. This result is unfortunately the contradiction of the noble idealism of 'man' by Kant who declared that man is an end to himself and should not be reduced to a means for any end. Hegel's Absolutism completely changes this picture and reduces man to be merely the material for building up the state. Man derives his significance and importance only because of his services to the state. Apart from the state organisation he has no significance and no right of independent existence. Thus from a genuine metaphysical contribution, a perverse political philosophy is developed which pervaded the whole European culture and civilisation and resulted in the two destructive world wars.

The other development of this Hegelian Absolutism is in the economic direction. Karl Marx, the founder of Communism claims himself to be a disciple of Hegel. His materpiece "The Capital" is the Bible of the Communist. He postulates that the socio-political development is according to the process of the Hegelian dialectic-materialism. Tracing the growth of economic development up to 19th Century, he points out the intrinsic contradiction between capital and labour and emphasises the intrinsic identity and unity of both. The capitalist who controls the productive machinery is but the creature of labour and as such should be made subordinate to labour which is the ultimate creator of wealth. The economic organisation which allows the concentration of wealth in the hands of a few capitalists who happen to control the productive industries and who engage thousands of labourers to run the machinery, according to Marx, is an iniquitous economic system.

Hence the restoration of the economic organisation according to Karl Marx must consist in restoring the true controlling agency to that power which creates wealth, i.e., the labour which creates wealth must necessarily be controlling agency of the capital and must run the industrial organisation. The creator of wealth must have the right to control it and to enjoy it. This economic revolution is also the result of Hegelian Absolutism in subjugating the organisation of society. Thus the modern civilisation of Europe which started with Hegelian Absolutism exhibits both the beneficial influence as well as the baneful influence of the Hegelian Absolutism.

2. SELF IN INDIAN THOUGHT

Before we begin the systematic study of the *Darśanas* let us try to acquaint ourselves first with the general tendencies of Indian thought prior to the rise of Buddhism. All the available information is to be gathered from three sources: (1) The later Saṁhitās, the Brāhmaṇas, and the Upaniṣads. (2) Jaina literature, secular and religious. (3) Buddhistic literature, secular and religious. A broad survey of the first group certainly indicates the existence of a rival school of thought side by side with what may be considered the main current of orthodox thinking. This early protestant school among the Āryans had its important influence in moulding the thought of the Āryans in general, sometimes because of its strong opposition and sometimes because of sympathetic reconciliation. Roughly speaking this school of Āryan Protestantism may be associated with the Kṣatriyas of the Ikṣvāku line whereas the Āryans of the Kurupāncāla may be identified with the orthodox school. In this connection it is better to remember that the term orthodox simply means implicit acceptance of the ritualism of Vedic sacrifice whereas protestantism merely means opposition to the sacrificial ritualism either in a complete or a partial form. This Ikṣvāku house of Kṣatriyas is associated with Ayodhyā, in the country of Kośala. Purāṇas as well as the literature of the Jainas and the Buddhists, all vie with one another in singing the praises of the kings of the Ikṣvāku line. It is enough to mention the fact that one of the two great epics of India is about an Ikṣvāku hero. The Ikṣvāku heroes have so much dominated the thought of the later Vedic period that about the time of Purāṇas, some of the members of the Ikṣvāku line were elevated to the avatāraship of Viṣṇu. In describing generally the characteristics of the Raghus, Kālidāsa says, "The Raghus during their youth are engaged in study, during the period of manhood are engaged in their daily household life, in old age they renounce the household life and become Munis and finally relinquish the body after performing Yoga."

In Saṁhitās the Self or *Ātman* only means that Self is existing in free form of Spirit. It is the Life of all lives and the moving power of all things. This idea of the *Ātman* is further elaborated in the Brāhmaṇas and the Upaniṣads until it is made to absorb all the other ideas and it means the only real existence. In the beginning the world was the *Ātman* alone. There was nothing else near to it. It thought, "let me create the universe" and the universe was created. Here also *Ātman* figures as the Lord and king of all. "As the spokes of a wheel in the chariot so all the souls of the world are fastened in one, that Soul the Gods adore as the light of all lights. That Divine Self is not fully grasped by tradition nor by understanding nor by all revelation. It is he whom the Self chooses. By him alone is the Self to be grasped". Spiritual immortality consists in the perceiving of the Divine Self, the *Ātman* as the only existing thing. The other conception, that runs parallel to this until it finally becomes identified with it, is the *Brahman*. In the *Ṛg* hymns *Brahman* signifies force or will. It means the sacred hymn or prayer invoking the aid of Gods. This hymn or Prayer is endowed with a mystic power, an occult force which inevitably binds the Gods towards men. This meaning of the word *Brahman* slightly changes and becomes applicable to the magic utterance at the sacrifice. Thus the term gets a new connotation, and the term itself most probably was derived from a different root *Bṛh* which means to grow or spread. Finally it came to signify the priest who uttered the sacrificial *mantra*. Thus the term *Brahmaṇa* became identified with the sacrificial priest. Finally this term is used to designate a person of a particular community whose general occupation would be sacrifice. The term now becomes a term of masculine gender and that is the present significance in as much as it refers to a member of a particular caste. But from the original Vedic meaning of prayer or magic power of prayer there is another line of connotation ending with Upaniṣadic *Brahman*. The term *Brahman* in the sense of prayer is constantly used in the Vedic hymns and in the Brāhmaṇas. This magic power denoting some thing of spiritual order behind the visible universe forms the foundation or *Brahman* in the sense of God, though this import is not quite prominent in the period of the *Ṛg Veda* until it is explicitly present in the *Brāhmaṇas*. *Brahman* is spoken of as a God dwelling in the highest place whose head is the sky, whose measure is the Earth, and it is this significance which becomes prominent in the Upaniṣadic period. Throughout the Upaniṣadic texts we find this as the ruling conception. Towards the close of the Upaniṣadic period there is the Identification of *Brahman* with *Ātman*. These terms are indiscriminately used to refer to the Ultimate Reality of which man and the nature are but the special manifestations. "From Him the universe springs, to Him it returnes." "Thou art the Self of all and Maker of all." In Maxmuller's words, "It was an epoch in the history of the human mind when the identity of Self with the neuter *Brahman* was for the first time conceived though the name of the term, the Ultimate Reality, which is the import of both is very often referred to as Sat—Existence. *Tattvamasi*—That thou art. This famous Upaniṣadic formula represents the development and the final identification of the terms *Ātman* and *Brahman*. Then it becomes a Transcendental concept thereafter. The significance of personality which was associated with *Ātman* gets submerged in the neuter concept of *Brahman*. The Upaniṣadic *Brahman* is said to be beyond description. It can be described only negatively. It is not man or woman, nor is it neuter. It is without breath without mind, higher than the Highest, the Imperishable. The only adequate description we can have of this is *Neti Neti* — not this, not this. When we go to study the Upaniṣads in detail we shall see more of this.

The Age of the Upaniṣads— The Upaniṣadic age has certain marked characteristics peculiar to itself and not found either in the Saṁhitā or Brāmaṇa period. During the Ṛg Vedic period the Āryans were mainly of a homogeneous society. Their Gods were magnified human beings actuated by human sympathies and sharing even human failures. The Vedic singer invoked their aid both in war and peace to fight the enemy and to promote his own prosperity. This age corresponds to the Homeric age in the Greek civilisation. All this primitive simplicity disappears when we enter into the Upaniṣadic period. Here we have a different order of society. We are no more with the Āryans whose life was mainly pastoral whose wealth was cattle and who spent most of their time in offering sacrifices to Indra or Agni and drinking their favourite *soma*. To bring the Greek parallel once again we are quitting the world of Agamemnon and Odysseus and entering the world of Socrates and Euripides. Now we are concerned with a people already divided into different sects and we are face to face with a race highly contemplative. Sacrifices and rituals do not retain their importance though they are still extant. These persist merely as vestigial institutions preserved by tradition and custom. They ceased to be the genuine ideals of religion. The intellectual atmosphere is surcharged with sophistical idealism. In short, we are in the centre of the world of Indian sophists who are actuated by theoretic curiosity as to the nature of man and the universe. With such a change in the body-politic of the Āryans. the old order must have elapsed. We have already noticed the internal social differentiation even during the period of the Brāhmaṇas. The Vedic bard has somehow lost his enthusiasm for life. The joy of living present is somehow surreptitiously replaced by the *ennui* of life. Life in this world is nothing but a link in the endless chain of births and deaths. Link after link may come and go but the chain will go on for ever. This mysterious whirling of life, endless and aimless rotation of births and deaths is considered by the Upaniṣadic thinkers as an evil to be avoided. The theory of transmigration and the corollary of *karma* have somehow taken possession of the thought of this age. Further the social organisation has resulted in the establishment of certain religious customs as well. Besides the differentiation into several castes the Upaniṣadic society recognised four distinct stages of individual development. This evidently refers to a process of spiritual probation and development to which every one irrespective of birth was entitled. The period of youth is to be spent as a *Brahmacāri* when the young man is to be educated under the personal guidance and supervision of a master. During this period he has to live away from his home in his master's *āśrama*. Learning and service are the only two occupations for him. Intellectual development of the highest order associated with personal humility would equip the individual to discharge his duties in the best possible manner. So equipped the *Brahmacārī* after education returns home and enters into the second stage of *gṛhastha* life. Now he becomes a householder and looks after his personal property, gets married and lives as a husband and father. As a member of the society then he does not forget his obligations. He fulfils socio-economic duties and thus contributes to the general welfare of society. But he is not to be here for ever. He has to enter the third stage of his life. He is to become a *parivrājaka* or a religious mendicant wholly devoted to the spiritual affairs. Having served society well and to the best of this ability he now depends upon society for his maintenance devoting his whole time to philosophical research. Now he spends most of his time outside the *Grāma* or *nagara* staying in the adjoining *vana* or woodland. On account of this habit of dwelliing in the *udyānas* or *vanas* outside the city, the third stage is very often referred to as the stage of *Vānaprastha*. This is to be followed by complete renunciation which is the last stage —*Saṁnyāsa* which marks the close of the spiritual development. The Upaniṣadıc and their associated *Āraṇyakas* perhaps refer to the third stage, *Vānaprastha*. It calls to our mind a picture of life closely akin to that of St. Francis of Assissi in the medieval Europe. His associates were the beasts and the birds of the forest. He had untrammelled spiritual peace, that passeth understanding in the undisturbed solitude of forest full of charm. It is something like this that we have to imagine as the characteristic of the Upaniṣadic period. We are ushered into a world of congregations of preachers and disciples, the former elaborately expounding, the latter reverently listening to the theosophic *rahasya* otherwise known as Upaniṣadic secrets. The change from the world of sacrificial ritual to the world of philosophic speculation brought with it new claimants to honour and Truth. The sacrificial *mantras* and the sacrificial procedure were mainly cultivated and prectised by the priestly class during the earlier period. But the *Brahma vidyā* or *Ātman* cult of the Upaniṣads has nothing in common with the recitation of sacrificial *formulae*. This new philosophic speculation seems to have had its origin in the king's courts. It is associated with the Kṣatriyas on account of peace and prosperity or perhaps the fruits of life are eaten to surfeit by them. The Kṣatriyas were the first to experience the emptiness of life and to turn their attention inwards in search of the underlying spiritual principle, *Ātman* or *Brahman*. Whatever be the social conditions that brought about this new outlook on life this much is certain that the Kṣatriyas of the Upaniṣadic age were mainly engaged in the speculation about man and the universe whereas traditional sacrifices were still important to the priestly class. Perhaps this is not quite an accurate description. Even the priests could not escape the influences of this new thought. We see them therefore disturbed by this new discontent. They go about from place to place, from thinker to thinker, with the object of getting initiated into the new wisdom, the *Ātma vidyā*. This craving for the *Brahma vidyā* becomes almost universal. The whole age is thrown into feverish activity intellectually and every one desires to participate in the new knowledge —*par excellence* as against the earlier learning associated with ritualism. Like a pillar of light this new *parāvidyā* was leading the Āryans into the promised land of wonderful philoshophical wisdom which constitutes the treasure of Āryan learning and to which all the later systems of Indian thought point out with pride as the source of authority and inspiration.

The Meaning of 'Upaniṣad' — The term as used in the Brāhmaṇas normally denotes the secrets of some word or text. But in the *Bṛhadāraṇyaka* it is already used in the plural as the designation of a class of writings, no doubt actually existing. Thus the term came to be used to denote the writing containing the secret doctrine. The exact primary sense of the term is doubtful. The natural interpretation of the world adopted by Max Muller makes the word mean first a session of pupils, hence the secret doctrine communicated to a select number of disciples. Secondly, it is the title of a work on such a secret doctrine. Oldenberg traces the word to the original sense of worship. According to this interpretation Upaniṣad primarily means a secret form of worship. Deussen combines both these interpretations when he explains the meaning of the word. For him the word originally meant a secret word or a secret text. Then it came to refer to secret import of secret doctrine. This order of meaning is improbable as is suggested by McDonald. The term is explained by Śaṅkara in his commentary as that which destroys ignorance or that which leads to the knowledge of *Brahman*. Indian writers use the term in the sense of secret doctrine or *Rahasya*. Upaniṣadic texts are generally referred to as *Parāvidyā*, the great secret. The Indian usage distinctly implies something secret. Further as Deussen points out it was an ancient custom all over the world to preserve certain important spiritual truths as a secret and to communicate them only to the initiated few. Among the Pythagoreans the philosophical doctrines were confined only to the members of that order. Similar was the case during the medieval age. Numerous passages from the Upaniṣads point to the same reference. There is internal evidence to show that Upaniṣadic truths were communicated to others with great discretion and very often with great reluctance. The father would select his eldest son as his fit disciple. If the disciple is a stranger to the master the applicant has to serve several years of probation before he can be initiated into the mysteries. Even among the learned men evidently all were not acquainted with the Upaniṣadic truths. These facts go to support the traditional meaning of the term Upaniṣad that it is a secret doctrine — that it is a *Rahasya,* and sometimes in the primary sense of secret doctrine. These differences do not matter much. When the initiated talked to one another they must indicate their meaning only by signs which would be understood only by the initiated. This fact explains why the term is used in the sense of a secret word or text.

The Date of the Upaniṣads — 1000 to 500 B.C.:— The Upaniṣads do not form the composition of a single author. They are many in number. Most probably even a single Upaniṣad is due to the co-operation of several persons. The Upaniṣads taken as a whole collection would cover a period of several centuries. Some of the earliest Upaniṣads take us to the period of Vedic thought and rituals and some of the latest ones exhibit distinct traces of modern thought and would even bring us to the period of Mohammedan rule in India. To ask for a chronology of the composition stretching across so many centuries would be neither scientific nor useful. Indian commentators such as Śaṅkara recognised certain Upaniṣads as genuine and wrote commentaries on them. Scholars generally confine themselves to such Upaniṣads as are recognised by the well-known commentators. Even here there is no consensus of opinion. Tradition speaks of ten Upaniṣads; whereas different commentators mention different numbers. If we confine ourselves to the most important and the recognised ones we can say this much about their period of composition. They are distinctly anterior to the rise of Buddhism. So we can safely mention that the Upaniṣads, the important of them at least, must be placed earlier than the 5th Century B.C. Can we say anything as to the beginning of these Upaniṣads? The period generally accepted by Orientalists is about 1000 B.C. Hence the duration from 1000 to 500 B.C. would probably represent the period when the Upaniṣads were composed.

The Origin of the Upaniṣads — An interesting controversy is associated with the origin of the Upaniṣads. We need not emphasise the fact that the *Brahma vidyā* of the Upaniṣads is quite opposed to Vedic ritualism based upon sacrifice. The question therefore arises, "How could this theosophic speculation be logically connected with the Vedic form of ceremonialism?" Many important passages in the earlier Upaniṣads supply us with a clue. Thus in the Chāndogya we find five learned Brahmins requesting one Oudgalya to instruct them concerning the *Ātman*; he, confessing inability, takes them to Aśvapati Kaikeya to whom all the six appeal for initiation into the *Ātmavidyā*. Again in Bṛhadāraṇyaka the famous scholar Gārgya offers to expound the knowledge of *Brahman* to the king Ajātaśatru of Kāśī. But his explanation is rejected by the king as erroneous whereupon the Vedic scholar presents himself as a disciple to the king to be instructed in the knowledge of *Ātman*. The king does accordingly prefacing his exposition with the remarks that it is a reversal of the rule for a Brahmin to enter himself as a pupil under a Kṣatriya in order to have *Brahma* knowledge expounded to him. Again in the Chāndogya, a king figures as the teacher to a priest whom he addresses as follows :— "Oh Gautama! This doctrine has never, upto the present time, been in circulation among the Brahmins. Therefore in all the world the Government has remained with the warrior caste." From these passages scholars like Deussen and Garbe conclude with a very high degree of probability that the doctrine of the *Ātman* standing as it did in such sharp contrast to all the principles of Vedic ritual was taken up and cultivated primarily not in the Brahmin but in the Kṣatriya circle and was adopted by the former in later time. As against this view it is contended that *Brahma vidyā* had its origin in the earlier Vedic literature itself and that the Brahmins themselves have as much to do with it as the Kṣatriya. In order to understand the full significance of this controversy we have to remember certain important and relevant facts.

Even earlier than the Upaniṣadic period, in the period of Brāhmaṇas we have traces of rivalry between Brāhmins and Kṣatriyas. We need not go back to the legendary period of Vishvāmitra vs. Vaśiṣṭha, when the former asserted his equality of status with the latter. What is contained in the Brāhmaṇa literature is much more historical than such legendary anecdotes. We have a reference to an Āryan tribe in the countries of Kāśī, Kosala, Videha and Magadha. The term Kāśī is used in plural to denote the people thereof. The Kāśīs and the Videhas were closely related because of their proximity, sometimes the Videhas were clubbed with the Kosalas. These were always considered by the Kurupāñcālas as a hostile group. It is a fair conclusion that between these two groups of people there did exist some political conflict, probably based upon some difference of culture. The Śatapatha *Brāhmaṇa* in which occurs the story of the advance of Āryan civilisation over Kosala and Videha, preserves a clear tradition of its time and furnishes a piece of evidence that in the Kurupāñcāla country lay a great centre of *Brāhmaṇa* cult. From these it appears to have been brought to the countries of Kāśī and Kosala probably by the settlers of a later date. It is probable that the Eastern Countries were less Āryan than the Western ones as they were less completely brought under Brahmin supremacy as the rival systems of Jainism and Buddhism indicate. Among the Kosalas, Videhas and Magadhas the Kṣatriyas were ranked above the Brahmins. The social supremacy of the Kṣatriyas in these countries is further corroborated by the fact that the later Vedic texts display towards the people of Magadha a marked antipathy which may be reasonably explained by those people's lack of orthodoxy which may perhaps be traced as far back as Vājasaneya Saṁhitā. In this Saṁhitā (the earlier of the Ṛg Saṁhitās) we have a contemptuous reference to the current language used by the Magadhas which perhaps indicate the use of 'Prākṛta' in those parts. Even in the *Brāhmaṇa* period there is reference to a prevalent unbelief which is deplored. "Then the unbelief took hold of men, those who sacrificed became more sinful and those who sacrificed naught became more righteous." "No sacrifice then came to the gods from the world." The gods thereupon said to Bṛhaspati Aṅgirasa — "Verily unbelief has come upon men. Ordainst thou the sacrifice to be done." This Bṛhaspati Aṅgirasa seems to have accepted and thus revived the sacrificial culture. The Kṣatriyas referred to in the Upaniṣads as the custodians of Upaniṣadic *Rahasya* are all of the Kosala— Videha country. Ajātaśatru is the king of Kāśī, Janaka, the king of Videha. The other important names mentioned therein also appear to be Kṣatriya names. In Śatapatha Brāhmaṇa there is a reference to the fact that king Janaka became a convert to Brahminism— a fact which indicates the traditional Brahminical lore reasserting itself.

The founder of Buddhism was himself a Kṣatriya of the Magadha country. He was a contemporary of Mahāvīra. The latter is claimed by the Jainas as the last of religious teachers. Orientalists generally accept this claim and suggest that his predecessor Pārśvanātha was the real founder of Jainism. Leaving open the question of the origin of Jainism we may note the interesting fact about Mahāvīra's predecessor. According to Jaina tradition Pārśvanātha belongs to the ruling family of Kāśī. His father was the ruler and his name was Viśvasena. The relevant fact for us here is that one of the Kṣatriya founders of Jainism belonged to Kāśī. If we remember that the central doctrine of Jainism, Ahiṁsā originated as a protest against Vedic sacrifice, then we may not be far wrong if we maintain that the "Kṣatriya heretics" referred to in the Brāhmaṇa literature were probably the earlier founders of Jainism. The Brāhmaṇa literature as we already saw had a sinister reference to the people of Kāśī and Videha. The country of Videha also had a religious importance for the Jainas. Jaina tradition speaks of Videha as a *Nityapuṇya bhoomi*, a place where *Dharma* is always flourishling. The Jaina teachers who succeeded Mahāvīra, whenever they had any doubt on scriptural matters, went to Videhakṣetra to clear these doubts. The very place which is pointed as the abode of heterodoxy is held in high esteem according to Jaina and Buddha traditions. The unbelief referred to in Satapatha Brāhmaṇa, the unbelief which manifests in opposition to the Brāhmaṇas, must therefore refer to some sort of Kṣatriya movement that must have been prevalent in the countries of Videha and Magadha even prior to the rise of Buddhism. All these facts constitute strong circumstantial evidence supporting the theory that *Ātma vidyā* —the central doctrine of Upaniṣadic culture first arose from the Kṣatriyas as a sort of protest against the Vedic sacrificial ritualism, jealously defended by the Brahmins. Upaniṣadic thought is mainly influenced by the Ahiṁsā cult associated with Lord Ṛṣabha, a cult prevalent in India even prior to the Ārya invasion. Since the Upaniṣadic thinkers have accepted this *Ahiṁsā* doctrine as superior to Vedic ritualism there was a spirit of compromise at that period. Except for rival claims for social domination there was most probably no great difference between the Brahmins and the Kṣatriyas of those ages. Both were Āryans and both defended their culture and civilisation from non-Āryan inroads. This is substantiated by the fact that many learned Brahmins welcomed the new movement of *Ātma vidyā* and were willing disciples under Kṣatriya teachers to learn the new truth. If they had any antipathy to the new form of faith they would have exhibited it. They would not have manifested so much eagerness to assimilate it. In fact about the time of Bṛhadāraṇyaka we find the tables are completely turned. Yājñavalkya a great teacher in Bṛhadāraṇyaka figures as the towering personality. He, a Brahmin, becomes the instructor now and Janaka the king places himself as his disciple. This represents a later stage in the development of Upaniṣadic thought. Yājñavalkya being a master-intellect successfully incorporated the new doctrine into the old. Kṣatriya protestantism in the reform of *Ātma-vidyā* was so completely assimilated that it ceased to exist as an independent movement, a phenomenon which is often repeated in the later history of Indian thought; for example Śaṅkara completely assimilated Buddhism which led to its extinction. This conjecture is further supported by the nature and development of the Upaniṣadic thought itself. On account of reconversion of Janaka to the old orthodox ritualism which evidently implies an effected compromise between two rival schools, radical reformers of the extreme left had to recede entirely from the orthodox centre. They persisted in their protestantism and emphasised their opposition to sacrificial ritualism as a result of which we have the birth of Buddhism. Reading facts in this light would agree well with the theory suggested by some oriental scholars on the evidence of the Upaniṣadic passages themselves that the Upaniṣadic doctrine of *Ātma-vidyā* first started in the Upaniṣads as a protest against the sacrificial rites of the *Vedas* and thereafter assimilated and recognised by the priestly class as well.

The Fundamental Doctrine of Upaniṣads— We have already noticed the Vedic concept of *Ātman* or *Brahman*. We have to touch upon two other doctrines, Transmigration or metempsychosis and *Karma*. The latter is in a way the corollary of the former. The doctrine of metempsychosis is peculiar to the age of the Upaniṣads. There is no trace of it in the Vedic period. So much so scholars are of opinion that the Āryans must have borrowed this from the non-Āryans. We know the Egyptians believed in the doctrine. It is certainly a difficult question to settle whether the Upaniṣadic thinkers borrowed this doctrine from non-Āryans or the Egyptians. Probably the truth is that they borrowed from non-Āryans who were living in the land at the time of the Āryan invasion. They were evidently having a higher form of culture and thus they were champions of a more satisfactory doctrine of Self. The value of any theory depends upon its offering satisfaction to intellectual curiosity. Any theory of creation, any philosophy that retains the importance of human personality and maintains it to be an eternal principle will be forced not only to look forward to an infinite future but also to trace back to an infinite past. The human personality that is associated with the short span of the present, must somehow be related to a hoary past as well as a glorious future, making the present but a step in this spiritual evolution. It is this process of spiritual development that is the inner meaning of the doctrine of transmigration. It is bacause of the truth of this principle of spiritual progress that the Indian mind persists in tenaciously clinging to that doctrine. If this is remembered then we can very well understand that the attitude of Gough and others is more guided by inborn prejudice than by an endeavour to intellectual appreciation. Upaniṣadic thought is not the babbling of a primitive race but it marks an important stage in the philosophic development of Indian culture. Associated with this doctrine of metempsychosis is the doctrine of *Karma. Saṁsārà,* the cycle of births and deaths, is supposed to be the result of *Karma*— as a man soweth so doth he reap. *Saṁsāra* for the Upaniṣadic thinker meant a meaningless chain of births and deaths heralding a gloomy prospect. The *summum bonum* of life for the Upaniṣadic thinker therefore consisted in liberation from this chain. The very term Mokṣa implies 'Deliverance', 'Liberation.' Pessimistic aversion may be present with an inborn optimism of the future, the inherent evil of *Saṁsāra* and the implied possibility of *Mokṣa.* These constitute the correlative doctrine to that of *Brahman* which together form the message of Upaniṣadic thought. All the latter Indian systems in spite of their mutual differences are permanently based upon these ideas. This fact stands as an evidence of the unity of their origin, i.e., all the Indian systems are born of the Upaniṣadic speculations.

The Upaniṣads and the Western thinkers— The first knowledge of the Upaniṣads gained by European scholars is an interesting historical fact. a Mogul prince, one of Shah Jehan's sons, evidently influenced by Akbar's dream of universal religion attempted to bring about a union between Hinduism and Islam. With this purpose he translated the Upaniṣads into Persian for the benefit of his co-religionists. A copy of this Persian translation was presented to a French scholar who was interested in the study of Zoroastrianism. This French scholar translated the Upaniṣads from Persian to Latin. This Latin version fell into the hands of Schopeuhauer, who by personal temperament and philosophic tradition was eminently fit to appreciate the philosophy of the Upaniṣads. It was he who first popularised its study among German students. He himself used them as a Bible. "It has been the solace of my life and I hope it will be the same in my death." The Upaniṣads peculiarly appealed to the German students, because they themselves at the time of Schopenhauer were in possession of a philosophy quite analogous to this.

Deussen on the Upaniṣads— Speaking of the concepts of the Upaniṣads in their relation to philosophy, Deussen writes : "The whole of religion and philosophy has its root in the thought that the universe is only appearance and not reality. This fact that philosophy has from the earliest times sought to determine the first principle of the universe proves that it started from a more or less clear consciousness that the entire empirical reality is not the true essence of things, that, in Kant's words, is only appearance and not the thing-in-itself. There have been three occasions on which philosophy has advanced in a clearer comprehension of its recurring task and of the solution demanded. First in India in the Upaniṣads, again in Greece in the philosophy of Parmenides and Plato and finally at a more recent times in the philosophy of Kant and Schopenhauer". Deussen adds : "All great religious teachers therefore, whether in earlier or later times, nay even all those at the present day whose religion rests upon faith are unconsciously followers of Kant. The new testament and the Upaniṣads, the two noblest products of the religious consciousness of mankind are found, when we sound their deeper meaning, to be nowhere in irreconcilable contradiction but in a manner the most attractive, serve to elucidate and complete one another." The purport of these words of Deussen is that Kant's philosophical agnosticism is the last word in philosophy and that a religion not associated with Kantian metaphysics is far from being a genuine religion. It places the philosophy of the Upaniṣads on a *par* with that of Kant and Plato. If he wants to express his admiration of the philosophy of the Upaniṣads by comparing it to his own national philosophy we have nothing to quarrel about. He is at liberty to choose hiw own method of critical appreciation. He may quite well regard the philosophy of Kant and Plato as the only genuine philosophy. But when he says that the philosophy of the Upaniṣads is the same as that of Plato we have to protest. This is an unwarranted philosophical attitude with certain European scholars who started the study of Indian thought with the unwarranted assumption that the Advaita Vedānta was the one fruit to produce which the whole of Indian life and culture conspired. This bias was further strengthened by the tendencies of European thought moulded by such German thinkers as Kant and Hegel. It requires no serious argument to show how unfounded the assumption is even if we admit for the sake of argument such an interpretation of the Upaniṣadic philosophy. We cannot consistently explain the claims put forward by other systems of Indian philosophy that they are also resting on the Upaniṣadic authority. The real fact is that all the Indian systems whether orthodox or heterodox are based upon fundamental concepts of Upaniṣadic thought and that all have the right to claim the authority of their source. This simple fact of History cannot be denied in the face of so much preponderating evidence. To maintain that the Upaniṣadic thought is the Indian counterpart of Plato or Kant is quite an unwarranted dogma sustained more by personal predilection than by objective evidence. Further Prof. Deussen is justified in maintaining that Plato-Kantian idealism is the best system of philosophy. In spite of the beauty of conception and grandeur of diction Plato's idealism is but a temporary aberration of Hellenic thought which was brought to its equilibrium by his friend and disciple Aristotle. Similar is the case of Kant's transcendental agnosticism. It is but an episode in the career of modern thought quite unconnected with the course of modern culture. As against Deussen's *obiter dictum* we take the liberty to state that the idealism of Plato or Kant is distinctly of a modern thought and marks but the refuge of the defeated intellect sustained more by personal mysticism than by logical necessity. Champions of such a philosophy of the type of Deussen always make the mistake of believing that any other form of philosophy will be incompatible with the highest aspirations of religious and moral culture. In short, they think that the only alternative to such an effective idealism is an impossible materialism. It is because of this assumption that they try to escape into some form of idealism. The birth of idealism is very often due to such intellectual confusion. In order to safeguard the eternal values of life from the alleged menace of materialism some thinkers propound the doctrine of idealistic metaphysics which ultimately results in nullifying the very eternal values. It ends in repudiating the distinction between truth and error, good and evil and beauty and ugliness. Let us go back to Deussen. He makes the astounding proposition that the true religious philosophy must have as its backgroud something of the Kantian transcendentalism. He says in so many words that the value of a religion consists in its allegiance to a philosophy to which the concrete world is an illusion or māyā and life is but a mockery. There may be some kind of religious satisfaction resting on such a metaphysics. But we doubt very much if the Upaniṣadic religion is of much value only because of this attitude. Again he seems to think that modern Christianity has its value because of its metaphysical idealism which he assumes to be its foundation. We are quite sceptical about this. Neither the founder of Christianity nor his followers ever believed that the concrete world of reality is but an illusion or an appearance. We rather think that the success and popularity of Christian religion are entirely due to its grasp of concrete life and its emphasis upon the value of human personality. Take away these, it would cease to have any value and with that perhaps it would cease to be a religion. We can only look with dismay when Deussen connects modern Christianity with Kantian idealism. His congratulations on Upaniṣadic thought because of its similarity to Kantian Idealism we are rather prone to decline because his attitude is corroborated neither by historical development nor by phisolophical evidence of later thought in India.

The Chāndogya Upaniṣad — The Upaniṣad belongs to the *Sāmaveda* as evidence by '*Chandas*'. It is one of the oldest Upaniṣads and is divided into eight parts of varying lengths. The first two are related to rituals which go to show that this Upaniṣad was once a Brāhmaṇa treatise dealing with ritualistic procedure. The really Upaniṣadic or philosophic portion is very interesting mainly in the form of dialogues reminding one of Platonic dialogues. This Upaniṣad may be taken as a typical of the Upaniṣads in general. Some of the important characteristics of the Upaniṣadic thought are found here. The fundamental concept of the Upaniṣad has been mentioned as *Brahman*. This concept is introduced in the very beginning of this Upaniṣad. Even in the ritualistic chapter it is not forgotten. Some of the syllables of the *mantras* uttered are identified with *Brahman* or *Ātman*. This attitude of philosophical interpretation of even dry ritualistic formulae is a distinct mark of Upaniṣadic period. The spiritualistic interpretation has replaced the materialistic interpretation of the Ṛg Vedic Period, for example "Self transcends all magnitude. He is myself within the Heart, smaller than the canary seed or the kernel of a canary seed. He also is myself within the heart, greater than the earth, greater than the sky, greater than heaven, greater than all these worlds." There is no physical measure which is able to comprehend the non-physical. The Self is completely incommensurable with anything physical. The Upaniṣadic truth relating to the *Brahman* or *Ātman* was considered to be a secret by the teachers and was communicated to others with great caution. This aspect is well brought out by the legend of Satyakāma who goes to a teacher with the idea of becoming his disciple. "I will lead the life of a student of the sacred knowledge, I will lead the life of a student of sacred Self." Thus he addressed himself to Gautama. "Of what family art thou my dear?" asked Gautama. In reply to this Satyakāma said, "I do not know sir, of what family I am. I asked my mother. She answered in this manner: 'When I went about a great deal serving as a maid I got you. So I do not know this of what family you are. However I am Jābāla by name and you are Satyakāma by name. So I am Satyakāma, son of Jābāla Sir." The teacher was attracted by the frankness of the boy and admitted him as a disciple "I will receive you as a disciple for you have not deviated from the truth." His discipleship consisted of tending the master's cows for a number of years and such patient service was finally rewarded and he obtained the knowledge of *Brahman.*

In chapter V an allegorical representation of Life is given. The several senses quarrel among themselves saying "I am better—I am better." They all went to the great father—The All Creator and asked Him "Sir, who is the best of us?" He replied, he by whose departure the body seems worse than the worst, is the best of you. Then first, speech departed from the body. Returning after some time it found the person still alive though mute, Convinced of its own importance according to the criterion proposed by the All Creator, speech returned the wiser. The eye went off : Having remained a year away it came round again and said, "How have you been able to live without me?" Like the blind people not seeing but breathing with the Breath, speaking with the tongue etc. Thus have I been able to live." The eye entered in. Next was the turn of the ear. The person though deaf nevertheless lived. Then the mind tried its worth. Nevertheless the person lived mindless. Lastly it was the turn of thr vital breath. Now the breath, when on the point of departing, torn up the other sense as a horse going to start might tear up the pegs to which he is tethered. Then they all came to it and said "Sir, remain, thou art the best among us. Be thou our Lord. Do not depart from us." This allegory distinctly implies that the spiritual principle on account of whose presence the senses function is the *Ātman* or Self. It is the life-principle itself that is the foundation of existence. This vital breath is certainly more than the material conception of the Ṛg Vedic period. It is identical with that which makes all sense-activities possible.In the same V chapter again we have an important dialogue indicating the nature of the problems especially discussed in the Upaniṣad. A young man by name Śvetaketu Āruṇeya goes to an assembly of scholars from Pañcālas. The boy is subjected to severe cross-examination, when he told the assembly that he had been fully instructed. He was asked, "Young man, has your father instructed you?" "Yes Sir." "Do you know where men go to from here?" "No Sir." "Do you know the parting of the ways, one leading to the God and the other to the Fathers?" "No Sir." "Do you know how the yonder world is built up?" "No Sir." Then the teacher scolds him : "Why do you say you were instructed?"

This dialogue is instructive and points out the nature of the topics dealt with and studied in those days. The study of the traditional type was confined to the Vedạs and the Vedic rituals. Besides this traditional course there was the characteristic interest of the age centering round the philosophical studies as to the nature of the Self. It was the latter which was prized and coveted by the scholars of the age. Of course the dialogue ends with the boy returning to his father to ascertain the answer to the above questions. The father also has to confess his ignorance. The lad and his father returned to the king for the information.

The Gautama went to Janaka's court when the king offered him proper respect. In the morning the king went up to the assembly and announced, "Ask of me such a boon as men desire." Gautama replied, "Such things as men possess may remain with you, Sir. Tell me the speech which you addressed to the boy." The king was perplexed and said "Wait a while." Then the king said, "As to what you have said to me, oh Gautama, this knowledge did never yet come to any Brahmin before you and in all the world the truth belonged to Kṣatriyas only."

Two points may be noticed from this interesting dialogue. (1) The new thought, the knowledge of the *Ātman* was considered to be richer than the richest possession in all the world. (2) It originated among the Kṣatriyas and was preserved as a secret doctrine for some time. The very same fact is emphasised in another section of the same chapter. Five great theologians held a great discussion as to what is Self and what is Brahman. After a few days' deliberation they go to a great scholar Uddālaka who is reputed to be in possession of the knowledge of the Self. But the great scholar promises to enlighten them on the matter and asks them to accompany him. He takes them to a king Aśvapati Kaikeya. This king also offers them rich presents which they decline begging him to impart the much prized knowledge of Brahman. In the VI chapter several illustrations are given to explain the nature of Brahman.

The scene is as follows:

The boy is given a small seed and asked to break it open. Then the father asks the boy, "What do you see there?" "Nothing inside it, Sir," replied the boy. Then the father said, "the central essence you do not see there. Of that central essence this great tree exists. But it is in the essence of it. In it all that exists has its self. This is the truth. It is the Self and That thou art." Similarly the all pervading nature of this principle is taught to the boy in the following way : The boy is asked to dissolve a little salt in a cup of water. He is then asked to take a sip of it from different parts. He finds it everywhere saltish. Then the boy is instructed :

"Though the thing is not perceived by the senses, still the salt is there. That which is the finest essence of the world is the soul of reality. That thou art." The boy who wants further instruction is taught by the father that life here is one of bondage and escape from it is the form of realisation of Self. But as one might tread his way home even if he be stranded in a foreign country, so can we individuals tread our way back to the Universal Being. Towards the close of the Upaniṣad the scene is placed in Devaloka. The thirst for knowledge possesses even the gods. Nārada goes to Sanatkumāra with this appeal : "Sir, teach me the doctrine." Narāda is asked to give a list of all the sciences he learned. After enumerating the names of different sciences, such as the four Vedas, mathematics, astrology and so on, he addresses Sanatkumāra thus : "but Sir, with all this I could not know the Self. I have heard that he knows the Self who overcomes sorrow. I am in grief. Do help me to overcome the grief." Then Brahma-knowledge is imparted to Nārada by Sanatkumāra and he realizes his Self. Nārada is then progressively instructed by Sanatkumāra as to the nature of Self. Finally, the chapter concludes with the following words : "The soul is indeed below, the soul is above, the soul will be in this whole world. Verily he who sees this, who thinks this, who understands this, who has pleasure in the soul, who has delight in the soul, he is autonomous. He has Svarājya. He has unlimited freedom in all the worlds. But they who know otherwise than this are without Svarājya. They have perishable worlds. In all the worlds they have no freedom."

The True way to Brahma World — The way to realise the true self and to enjoy the spiritual bliss is not by following the traditional rituals but by purity of conduct. "Now what people call sacrifice, *Yajña* is really the chaste life of a student of sacred knowledge. For only through the chaste life of a student of sacred knowledge does he who is a knower find that world. Now what people call what has been sacrificed is really the chaste life of a student. Now what people call the propriety of a sacrifice is also the chaste life of a student. Now what people call silent asceticism is really the chaste life of a student. Now what people call hermit life is really the chaste life of a student."

Next we have the instruction of Indra by the Lord of Creation. Indra is actuated by the desire for Brahman-knowledge. He goes to the Lord of Creation to beg of him the same knowledge. The Self which is free from evil, ageless, deathless, sorrowless, hungerless, thirstless, whose desire is Real, whose conception is the Real. It is such a Self that Indra wants to realize. The Indra here is quite different from our old friend of the Ṛg Veda. Indra here seeks to obtain a knowledge of the Brahman which is the ultimate principle both of the individual and the world. He is told that even the gods in Brahmaloka reverence their selves shaking off evil, shaking off the body as the moon shakes itself from the mouth of Rāhu, a perfected soul passeth off into the uncreated world of Brahman and into it, it may pass. Such is the consolation of the perfected soul which has become perfect by knowing its own Self. Thus we have a complete change of intellectual attitude. Life in the world according to ceremonies and customs is looked down as a source of misery. It is merely to sell one's birth-right of freedom, to be ruled over by anything other than our own Self. The true relief from grief is to secure the freedom from the danger of the non-self. This is the fundamental truth of the new thought. This seems to have actuated both men and gods. The reference to the Devas, the mythological personalities which we have in the Upaniṣadic writings is really interesting. We find in Vedic period, for example, Indra who wanted casks of wine to infuriate the strength of him in the battlefield is now met with as a docile disciple of the samite in his hand begging to be instructed in this new knowledge of the Self. Here heroes are not measured by physical prowess. Self-control and purity of thought constitute the real worth of life both for men and gods. This aspect will become more and more prominent as we go to study the other Upaniṣads.

Kaṭha Upaniṣad — This belongs to Yajurveda. It is mainly associated with a particular kind of sacrifice called Naciketas.

But the Upaniṣad is interesting for us not because of this sacrifice but because of the important problem discussed therein — The great problem of the Hereafter. What is the nature of the soul? Does it survive death? If it does whither does it go? These are the questions which are discussed in this Upaniṣad. These questions have occupied the serious attention of thinkers all over the world. In fact these problems form the pivot of religions and philosophy. Socrates, Plato, Buddha and Christ have all had their attention to these facts and the very same problems are here discussed by the Upaniṣadic thinkers who were evidently the fore-runners of the above mentioned great world teachers. The Upaniṣad opens with a simple household scene. A Brāhmaṇa wants to obtain certain benefits by offering sacrifices. He promised to offer all his valuable possessions for sacrifice to seek his end. He was offering his cows and sheep and other things of great value. He had an intelligent boy who was watching the whole thing. His name was Naciketas. The sacrifice mentioned in this Upaniṣad is named after him. It means the sacrifice of Naciketas. This boy perhaps in a scoffing mood reminded his father that he did not offer his most valuable thing referring, of course, to himself. The boy importunately asked his father, "Whom are you going to offer me to?" When this question was repeatedly put, the father got angry because of this disturbance during the sacrifice and he answered in a rage, "To Yama, thou shalt go, thou art offered to Death." Before his father could revoke his command the boy started on his journey to Yama's land. Having reached that place he could not meet the Lord of Death, for he was not at home. The boy had to wait three nights without being attended to. Yama returned on the fourth day, and he regretted very much for the neglect shown to the Brāhmaṇa boy waiting as a guest at his door. As a compensation Yama offered three boons to the boy and he was asked to chose any three. As his first boon the boy cleverly asked that he might rejoin his father and that his father should forgive and forget and welcome him to his household. This was granted by Yama. As his second boon the boy chose to be instructed in the well-known sacrifice Naciketas leading to heavenly bliss. Yama initiated the boy into the mysteries of the desired ritual and honoured the boy by naming the sacrifice after him. The boy had this third boon still left. When Yama asked him to choose the third, the boy said, "When a man is dead where is this doubt about him—some say that he is and others that he is not. Let me know the truth and let this be the third boon." When the boy asked Yama to lay open the door of Hereafter there was a good deal of hesitation and reluctance on the part of the teacher. Whenever the great religious teachers of the world are asked about the Hereafter, they offer only an evasive reply. Yama too wanted to avoid this question and tried to turn away the boy's curiosity from awful and sublime. He says, "The gods themselves have been perplexed about this. It is no easy thing to discover." Hence he asked the boy to choose an alternative boon. The evasive answer only whetted the curiosity of the boy. Yama himself admitted that the problem was very important and subtle and that it perplexed even the minds of the gods. Certainly such a thing is worth knowing, and if knowledge is to be had at all it must be from the Lord of the Great Hereafter. The boy would not lose this golden opportunity. Hence he insisted on getting an answer. But Yama tempted his disciple's youthful imagination. Like the great temptation of another Personality this youth Naciketas had the sovereignty of the world, human and divine, placed at his feet. The whole aggregate wealth was at his disposal. He was promised heavenly damsels. He had the chance of being feasted with their divine music. But none of these things appealed to him. He would not budge. Like Gautama Buddha this boy spurned the pleasure of the world as worthless. He must have that one priceless boon the knowledge of the hereafter from the only person who had an authority to speak on the matter. Man is not to be satisfied with wealth. Wealth we shall obtain ourselves. Tell us about that life that gods themselves do not know. Thus the boy would not have any other boon but would rent the veil which hid Yama. Thus the strength of will exhibited by the boy ultimately succeeded in eliciting the sympathy of Yama who was willing to offer the truth. Thus there is the revelation of the Upaniṣadic teaching as to the nature of the soul and its survival after death. The teaching begins with the good and the pleasurable. Both these engage a man though the ends are diverse. Of these it is well with him that takes the good. He that chooses the pleasurable is tied to the wheel of life dwelling in the midst of illusions infatuated by the pleasures of the world. These fools are subject to repeated births and deaths and go round and round like the blind led by the blind. He is even under the subjugation of Yama. But the path of good leads to the Self. Wonderful is he that teaches and wise is he that attains it. This goal is attained only by renouncing the other path leading to the misery of *Saṁsāra*. Thus we notice in this teaching of Yama the emphasis on Self-realization as the goal of life. This goal is to be obtained only by self-renunciation, freedom from the allurement of the environment. The cult of sacrifice is subordinated to this path of spiritual discipline. Here we notice the movements of great religious thought. Continuing this teaching, Yama describes the nature of the *Ātman*. The Self is not born and it does not die. It is omniscient. It is not created and it creates nothing. It has no beginning nor end. It perishes not even when death overtakes the body. If the slayer thinks that he slays and the slain thinks that he is slain, neither of them knoweth the Self for the Self neither slayeth nor is slain. It is bodiless and yet is in all bodies unchanging and yet in all changing things. The sage that knows the infinite, the all-prevading self no longer has any grief. The nature of the soul is therefore distinct from that of the body. Apprehension of this truth is the gate to wisdom. But this great self lies in the midst of different senses which lead him astray towards the worthless treasures of the world. This self is not to be obtained by mere learning or even by much sacred lore. It is obtainable only by the grace of the great self. It is by a process of minute spiritual development that spiritual freedom is to be acquired. The allegory of the chariot is introduced here. Yama continues his teaching and compares the soul to the chariot and the senses to the restive horses. Only by controlling the senses the self gains freedom. We are reminded here of the same allegory in Plato. He compares the soul to a chariot dragged by horses. In the case of the gods the winged horses are good and controllable, and they never lead reason astray but in the case of man one of these horses is restive and is dragging the other one. Hence the ethical conflict in man's nature is due to the conflict between reason and the senses. The same analogy is obtained in Yama's teachings. The release from the chain of births and deaths is to be had only through spiritual purity. Here again we notice the subordination of the sacrificial cult to moral discipline. Then Yama comes to the point which started the discussion. "Oh Gautama, I will proclaim again this mystery : The everlasting self and his hereafter. Some souls pass to other births. Some to enter into other bodies according to their worth and knowledge." Hence we have the emphatic sanction of the doctrine of metempsychosis. Souls after death pass into another birth determined by their own *Karma* and *Jñāna*. This is the basic principle on which the future Indian systems arose. The self that is still after pleasures is tied to the wheel of births and deaths; some going up and some going down; some endowed with happiness and others with misery, but all sharing the universal merry-go-round of *Saṁsāra*. But only that self which realizes its true spiritual nature, only that which saves itself from the allurements of the world and imposes on itself the rigorous spiritual discipline can know the truth, can escape from the illusion and attain that never-failing bliss of true freedom.

Muṇḍaka Upaniṣads — This Upaniṣad belongs to Atharvaṇa Veda. It is divided into a number of *Khaṇḍas*. Its main purpose is to teach the knowledge of Brahman. Hence it may be taken as the farthest limit of the anti-Ritualistic culture of the age. This Upaniṣad starts with the distinction between the two kinds of knowledge. Lower knowledge consists of the study of the Vedas and the secular sciences such as grammar, astronomy, astrology etc. The higher is the knowledge of the indestructible Brahman. It is this indestructible Brahman that is the source of all things. Its nature is described thus. "That which is invisible, unseizable, without family or caste, that which has no eyes, no ears, no hands, nor feet, the Eternal, the omnipresent, Infinitesimal and imperishable. That it is which the wise regard as the source of knowledge. As the spider sends forth and draws in its thread, as plants grow on earth, as the hairs of the head shoot forth from every person, thus does everything arise from the imperishable." These two verses clearly illustrate the spiritual nature of Brahman and he is the root principle of all existence. What is the value of the lower knowledge of the traditional religion of the sacrificial *Mantras* and the skill in arranging sacrifices, but frail in truth are those boats (the sacrifices). Fools are they that praise this as the highest for they are subjected again and again to old age and death. Fools who hold this Vedic scholarship or rituals wise in their own conceit and puffed up with vain knowledge go round and round staggering to and fro like blind men led by the blind. If at all it is of any use to a person who offers sacrifice, it will lead him to *Svarga* which is merely a kind of lower happiness since that state of existence is also included in the *Saṁsāric* cycle. How is the higher knowledge to be obtained? "By truthfulness, by penance, right knowledge and abstinence must that Self be gained." The Self whom spotless anchorites gain is pure, and is like a light within the body. Further the Upaniṣad emphasises that *Ātman* cannot be gained by the Veda nor by understanding, nor by much learnig, nor is that Self to be gained by one who is destitute of strength or without earnestness or without right meditation. Having well-ascertained the object of the knowledge of the Vedānta, having purified their nature by Yoga or renunciation, all anchorites, enjoying the highest immortality become free at the time of the great end in the worlds of *Brahma*. This imperishable *Brahman* is the soul and the goal of all beings. He is the supreme person who is the source of human personality as well as the cosmic universe. He is in short the source of the world and the individual. Because of him the senses are active, all doubts are cut off and one's *Karmas* cease when He is seen. The highest golden sheaf is Brahman without stain, without parts. The sun shines not there, nor the moon and the stars. There lighnings shine not, much less this fire; when He shines then everything shines after him. This whole world is illumined with His light. That immortal *Brahman* is before, is behind, is right and left, is below and above. *Brahman* indeed is this whole world; it is indeed the excellent. Not by sight is it graphed, not even by speech, nor by another sense-organ, austerity or work. By the light of the knowledge of one's nature becomes purified in that way, by meditating one does not behold Him who is without parts. The cause of rebirth and *Saṁsāra* is said to be desire, those who attain to the *Brahma-Jñāna* are free from these desires and pass beyond the seed of rebirth. But he who is still in the meshes of desires is born again here. The reward of attaining this *Brahma-Jñāna* is to assume the nature of *Brahman* himself. He who knows that supreme *Brahman* becomes the very *Brahma.* He crosses all sorrow. He corsses all sin — so liberated, he becomes immortal. This is the truth. So ends this short Upaniṣad.

Bṛhadāraṇyaka Upaniṣad — This perhaps represents a later stage of the Upaniṣadic culture. In this we have an attempted reconciliation between the traditional ritual cult and the new thoesophic wisdom of *Brahma-vidyā.* We referred to the implied rivalry on a former occasion between the Kurupāñcālas on one hand and Kosalas and the Videhas on the other. The latter countries were associated with heretical anti-sacrificial civilisation. In an interesting chapter in the Śatapatha Brāhmaṇa there is mentioned an attempt by the Kurupāñcālas to reconvert the Kosalas and the Videhas to Vedic tratitioins. Such a successful reconversion most probably marks the period of the Bṛhadāraṇyakas. One of the champions of the old traditional culture studies the new thought successfully and finally assimilates it so completely that the theosophic *Brahma-Jñāna* once originated by the rival school dominated by the Kṣatriyas ceases to have an independent existence. This personality who contributes to the complete annihilation of the rival school by the successful assimilation of the same by the old culture is Yājñāvalkya. From the point of view of culture and philosophic insight he is head and shoulder above his contemporaries. He is looked upon with awe and reverence by other priests. He is welcomed and honoured by kings. Having studied the new thought and made it his own, he is able to reassert the supremacy of the traditional Vedic cult thus in this Upaniṣad. We have all the characteristic conflicts symptomatic of a transition period. The Upaniṣad begins with the conception of Aśvamedha. Here it has only a symbolic meaning. The whole world is compared to one grand process of cosmic sacrifice. There is an account of the creation which starts from *asat*. After comparing the evolution of the world to the grand horse-sacrifice, the Upaniṣad goes to describe the nature of human personality. Breath or *Prāṇa* is said to be superior to the other bodily functions. This leads indirectly to a glorification of chanting the Vedic hymns which is possible only because of breath. In the next section there is another account of the creation of the world. Starting with the lonely *Puruṣa* who is the beginning of all things, the narrator proceeds to describe the appearance of a mate from himself. From these primeval pair the whole of the human race is supposed to have originated. But the primitive mother all of a sudden develops a resentment to the unconventional matrimonial alliance and tries to hide herself from her companion. Thus she becomes a cow but he became a bull and thus originates another species of animals. Then she changes herself into other animals and the primitive *Puruṣa* longing to meet his mate undergoes a corresponding transformation. Thus are created the different species of animals. In the next passage there is an interesting and novel version of the hymn of Puruṣasūkta of the Ṛgvedic hymns. In the Ṛg Veda there was a description of the origin of the four castes. Here is a different account. Puruṣa exists originally as Brahman. Being lonely it was not developed. It created still further a superior form of the

Kṣatrahood even those who are Kṣatras, rulers among Gods. This higher principle of Kṣatrahood is represented by Indra, Varuṇa, Soma, Rudra, Yama and Īśāna. Therefore there is nothing higher than Kṣatra. Therefore at the Rājasūya ceremony the Brāhmaṇa sits below the Kṣatriya. Upon Kṣatrahood alone does he confer his honour. Yet this same thing viz; Kṣatrahood has as its source Brāhmaṇahood. Therefore even if the king attains supremacy he rests finally upon Brahminhood as his source, so whoever injures Him (that is a Brahmin) attacks his own source. He fares worse in proportion as he injures one who is better. This passage is characteristic of the spirit of compromise. Kṣatriyahood and Rājasūya sacrifice are clearly acknowledged to be super-eminent and at the same time the rank is derived because they originate from Brāhmaṇahood. Unlike the *Puruṣasūkta* of the Ṛg this account suggests a caste organisation even among the Gods. Brahman's manifestation was not yet complete. Then he produced the Vaiśya element which is represented among the gods by the Rudras, Ādityas, the Maruts, and the Viśvadevas and among men by the Vaiśya. Brahma was not yet developed and he created the Śūdra-varṇa of which caste the divine representative is Pūṣan identified with the Earth the-all-nourisher and among men the same is represented by the fourth caste. The process of creation is not yet complete. Then Brahma created a still further form in the shape of *Dharma* or Law. It is the source of all. This is the power of the Kṣatriya caste. Therefore there is nothing higher than Law. Verily that which is Law is truth. This law is higher than Gods as well as men. It is because of this Law and in conformity with it the world-order subsists. The Kṣatriya-order on earth is but an aspect of the sovereignty of Law over all. In this interesting passage we have several instances. We are distinctly in a philosophical age when an intrinsic principle of Law of *Dharma* is recognised as the highest to which even the traditional gods are subordinated. This reminds us of the corresponding period of the Hellenic civilisation represented by the age of Eurepides. Just as the conception of Law in Greek thought formed the central doctrine of the later Stoic Philosophers so the conception of Law is to be elaborated by the later Buddhistic schools in which it would occupy the central position in the shape of the doctrine of *Karma*. But we quit the age of an intellectual conflict and enter into an age of compromise. The old rivalry and struggle between the two rival communities are in abeyance. There is a spirit of mutual give and take. From the one point of view, the Rājasūya sacrifice associated with the Kṣatriyas is the highest, and from the other point of view the Vājapeya-sacrifice associated with the Brahmins is the highest. Kṣatriya is taken to be superior because of his strength and Brahmin is equally powerful because of his religious inspiration. Thus we have a note of compromise indicating that both the aspects are necessary and important from the point of view of social economy.

In the II *Adhyāya* we are introduced into the scene in Ajātaśatru's court. A learned priest by name Gārgya Balāki goes to Ajātaśatru, King of Benares and offers to expound the doctrine of Brahman. The king was very much pleased and promised to give him a present of a thousand cows for such a speech before him, for it was a general fashion among the philosophers in those days to run to the Court of Janaka of Videha; then Balāki narrates his views about Brahman. He identified Brahman with the sun, moon, lightning, ether, air, water, fire and so on. He even suggests the identity of Brahman with the image in the mirror. All these things are rejected by Ajātaśatru as inadequate. Is that all? Asked Ajātaśatru. Gārgya replies "That is all". Oh! With that much is not known. Gārgya : Let me know.

Ajātaśatru : Verily it is contrary to course of things that a Brahmin should come to a Kṣatriya with the object of gaining Brahma-knowledge! But anyhow Gārgya was willing to be instructed by Ajātaśatru. Balāki was taken to a man who was asleep. But when he was touched with the hand he arose. From this object-lesson Ajātaśatru drew the following conclusion. When this man was fallen asleep thus then the person who consists of intelligence having taken to himself, the intelligence of these senses rests in that place which is within the heart. When that person restrains the senses he is said to be asleep. The breath, the voice, the eye, the ear and the mind are all restrained. When he draws in his senses the worlds are all in him. Then he becomes a great Brahman as it were. Verily as a youth, as a great king, or a great Brahman when he has reached his summit of bliss, so he rests now. As a spider might come out with its thread, as small spark come out from the fire, even so from this Soul comes forth all vital energies all worlds, all gods, all beings. The mystic meaning thereof is the real of the real. Breathing creatures are really the Real, but He is their Real. Thus according to Ajātaśatru the self in the movement of sleep is not only the custodian of the senses of the individual but is also indentical with the soul of the world. All breathing things are real but He is their Real. Continuing the discourse Ajātaśatru speaks of the two forms of *Brahman-Mūrta* and *Amūrta* —the formed and the formless— the mortal and the immortal, the actual and the beyond. This doctrine of duality of Brahman is interesting in this way. The ultimate reality includes both the actual concrete experience and the transcendental principle which expresses itself in this. The transcendental is described by negatives. The actual and the normal portions of reality are recognised to be real and are described by the positive designation. This section lends support to that particular school of Vedānta —Viśiṣṭādvaita. The organic world consisting of breathing things is real and not *Māyā*. It represents the *Mūrta* form of Brahman but this does not exhaust the complete Brahman because there is the *Amūrta*, the formless aspect of that on account of which he is called the real of the real.

Next we find ourselves in Yājñavalkya's household. The scene is laid in his home. Yājñavalkya proposes to take leave of his wife and retire from the householder's status. Yājñavalkya wants to make a final settlement of his property but Maitreyi asked Yājñavalkya whether by possession of wealth one would obtain immortality. This interrogation perturbed the philosopher a bit and he had to answer the question in the negative. Maitreyī would not be satisfied with anything else than that which lead to the highest bliss, "What you know, Sir, that indeed tell me" Then we have Yājñavalkya's teachings as imparted to his wife Maitreyī. The only thing in the universe which has intrinsic value is *Ātman* or Self. It is this that is dearest to us. Everything that we desire to have obtains a derivative value from this *Ātman*. This is the end in itself. This is associated with the unconditioned and absolute value. Domestic life, worldly possessions, social status and even religious ceremonials and national traditions have their value only so long as they serve us as means to the realization of the *Ātman*. A Brahmin who prides on his birth without knowing this ceases to be a Brahmin and the same is the case with the Kṣatriya. One may possess riches. One may carry out every commandment of his religion and all this would be of no avail if the knowledge of the self is not the guiding star of life. Conventional notions of value of social status and rank are all things that dwindle into insignificance by the side of this — One truth, the Great Puruṣa. Communion with this is the only safety for and the only guarantee of true life. Even the much prized Vedas and the other sciences owe their origin and importance to this one. It is this one inspiring principle the unitary Puruṣa that lends lustre to anything that is shining. From Him comes the elements, into them also they vanish.

After death there is consciousness. Thus say I, says Yājñavalkya. This doctrine that after death there is consciousness bewildered Maitreyī. She demanded an explanation. Accordingly Yājñavalkya said thus:

Consciousness is entirely based upon the subject-object duality 'Dvaita'. On account of this dualism we have an agent who has an object, presented to him who hears a sound, who speaks to another person, who thinks of another thing, but if this subject-object dualism is transcended and if we are left with one only without a second, then whereby and whom one would hear and whereby and whom one would speak to, whereby and whom one would understand. Naturally all objects of thinking and consciousness would cease to be because consciousness implies duality. Unity cannot therefore accommodate consciousness. Thus we have not only the identification of subject-object into one soul but the identification of the universe with the one soul. Thus we obtain an unqualified Advaita, an uncompromising advaitism diametrically opposed to Ajātaśatru's doctrine of the two kinds of Brahman. This conflict only proves that we don't have s systematic doctrine worked out in the Upaniṣads but we have embodied therein the germs of all possible speculations. Next we are in Janaka's court, and we meet there the great Yājñavalkya again. Janaka was going to perform a great sacrifice. Several learned Brahmins were assembled. Janaka had a desire to know which of these Brahmins was the most learned. He offered a tempting prize of 1000 cows with ten gold coins tied to each horn. "Oh the venerable Brahmins! Let him who is the cleverest among you drive these cows." No one came forward. Yājñavalkya said to his disciple "Drive these cattle home." This excited the other Brahmins who challenged him to a metaphysical discussion. He proved himself more than a match to these rivals. Several eminent scholars tried their strength with Yājñavalkya. But no one of them could stand his cross-examination. Finally it was the turn of a lady philosopher— Gārgī. She proposes three important questions as to the nature of the Imperishable and the Ultimate. The way in which she addresses Yājñavalkya is expressive of her real greatness. She announces that if Yājñavalkya answers all her questions then they must all recognise and acknowledge that they are vanquished and disgraced. Three questions proposed by Gārgī were all about the self indestructible both in the individual and in the Universe. Yājñavalkya answered all of them to the great satisfaction of the questioner. The whole physical universe ultimately depends upon space and space itself ultimately depends upon the *Ātman*. This is the meaning of his answers. Yājñavalkya makes out that the soul is transcending all notions of humanity and devoid of all sense-qualities. {Thou shalt not see the seer nor hear the hearer. That is the self that is within all. It is above the heavens beneath the Earth, and embracing past, present and future. Whosoever not knowing the indestructible offers oblations and performs penances even for one thousand years is a miserable slave, whereas he who knows the self as imperishable is real *Brahmàn*. This indeed is the true form free from evil. This is filled with bliss and is free from sorrows. Yājñavalkya explains the different stages of consciousness, a doctrine which becomes more prominent in later metaphysics. The first stage is waking-consciousness. The second is sleep where we have dream-consciousness. Third is the dreamless stage of deep sleep, and the fourth stage beyond which we reach the inmost self. According to Yājñavalkya the true nature is identical with the fourth or the Turīya state. This may be spoken of as the "Ego in itself," Self which is distinctly metempirical and transcendent.

The next scene is where we see Yājñavalkya again in the court of Janaka of Videha who asked Yājñavalkya the purpose of his visit whether it is for philosophical disputation or for rich presents. Yājñavalkya is shrewd enough to answer that his aim is both. Then begins the discussion. Jamaka is asked to expound all that he learned about the doctrine of Brahman. The king narrates the different doctrines of *Brahman* which he learnt from various scholars. He tries to identify *Brahman* with sight, speech, hearing, mind etc. All these doctrines are recognised by Yājñavalkya to be only partially true. He completes the teaching by supplementing Janaka's doctrine of the self.

According to Yājñavalkya the *Ātman* is the condition of the operation of the different senses as well as *manas*. As conditioned by *Ātman*, these sense-activities may reveal in their own way the nature of the underlying *Brahman*. But to identify consciousness or any one of thr senses with Brahman would be unjustifiable and erroneous. The soul is what subserves these functions though it is not identical with any one of these. Its true nature lies far beyond the strata of consciousness. We should have to dive deep into consciousness in order to have a glimpse of this Brahman. In his teaching, Yājñavalkya exhibits a width of learning quite manifest from his discussion. We can also point out that this is corroborated by modern psychical research. What we are aware of as consciousness is but a fractional aspect of our true personality, a great portion of which lies hidden in the depths of subconsciousness. Yājñavalkya's teaching therefore rightly and justifiably repudiates this shallow intellectualism and tries to bring to the forefront of discussion the magnitude and the importance of the subconscious self which more than anything else determines the conduct of the individual and contributes to his worth. This subconsciousness of our personality is always felt by the conscious individual as something other than ourselves which makes for righteousness. It is this sublime mysticism that forms the solid contribution of Yājñavalkya's teaching in Janaka's court. No wonder that at every stage of discussion his speech is punctuated with a present of 1000 cows. This time Yājñavalkya leaves Janaka's court with his well-earned present of several thousands of cows, a good fee for a noble work.

Janaka is the examiner in another occasion and Yājñavalkya the examinee. Consistent with his antecedents here also Yājñavalkya surprises Janaka with his sublimity of thought and intensity of philosophical insight. It is here that Yājñavalkya describes in suggestive verses the true nature of *Brahman.* This is indeed in true form free from desires, free from evil, free from fear, knows not anything within or without. This indeed is his true state. There is no wish in him left unfulfilled and hence is he free from sorrow. In that state ordinary relations of social life have no meaning, a husband is not a husband, a mother is not a mother, the cāṇḍāla is not a cāṇḍāla, saint is not a saint, it is a state beyond Good and Evil. Then we have transvaluation of all values. From Him proceedeth all that has value, Himself being beyond all valuation. Side by side with this uncompromising pantheism Yājñavalkya propounds the doctrine of *Karma*. A person is after all a bundle of desires. His desires determine his conduct and according as one acts so doth he become. The doer of good becomes good, the doer of evil, evil. One becomes righteous by righteous action and bad by bad action. He does not accept that desires have no connection with acts. Some say that man is judged by his desires and not by acts. Yājñavalkya rejected this erroneous notion. The springs of desires are in the action. What a man desires that he tries to achieve. Hence there is no discrepancy between desire and conduct and each person is the architect of his own. The true meaning of salvation consists in getting rid of desires which drag the soul along all points of the compass. Man free from desires has but one desire to realise his true nature or to become the released person. He verily becomes the Brahman. As the slough of a snake lies on an ant-hill, dead and cast away, even so is it with this body. But this incorporeal immortal life is Brahman indeed, is life indeed. The rest of the Upaniṣad is concerned with Yājñavalkya's attempts as justifying the rituals symbolically by giving them metaphorical interpretation. He tries to identify the Vedic conception of diversity of Gods with the supreme concept of *Brahman*. This part of the Upaniṣad is characteristic of the attempt to reconcile the *Ātmavidyā* with the traditional Vedic culture. Yājñavalkya by embracing this new philosophical doctrine was not evidently prepared to snatch himself away from the traditional Vedic rituals. We may also note here that Yājñavalkya probably did not belong to the orthodox Brahmins of Kurupāñcāla and hence was looked with an amount of suspicion by the latter. This is quite evident from Yājñavalkya's conversation with lkalya who resents to Yājñavalkya's reference to the Brāhamaṇas of Kurupāñcāla and retorts "Yājñavalkya! because thou hast decried the Brahmaṇas of the Kurupāñcāla what Brāhmaṇa dost thou know." We see Yājñavalkya throughout this Upaniṣad mustering all his resources to prove that in the various rituals there are the same tendencies, the same doctrines, embodied in the Upaniṣads.

The General Tendencies of the Upaniṣadic Period —The study of these important Upaniṣads has revealed to us some main characteristics of this age. The most prominent idea is the *Brahma*, the ultimate principle in the universe as well as in the individual. This is represented in various discussions where the self is identified with *Prāṇa* or *Ākāśa* or sometimes with Vedic gods such as Sūrya, Soma, and Indra. Many of the Vedic terms are used synonymously to denote this new Upaniṣadic concept of *ātman*. But all these synonymous terms are brushed aside as inadequate. Brahma is identified as the principle of Cetanā or the ground of consciousness which manifests in various forms of activities. That is the truth revealed by Ajātasatru. that is the truth learned by Nārada from Sanatkumāra. That again is the teaching of the celebrated Yāgñavalkya. Brahma is consciousness or Cetana plus something more than that. Hence it cannot be identified with any particular aspect of experience. He, being the knower, cannot be one of the known. He is within the heart of man and yet has his abode in far off Heaven. He is neither the sun nor the moon of the Vedic thought but he is the Puruṣa. He is quite near us and yet not seen by us. He is within us and yet illuminates things outside of us. This is the message of the Upaniṣadic thinkers. The identity between Brahma as the cosmic principle and ātman as individual personality is generally acknowledged by all the Upaniṣads. Is the identity contemplated here of the nature of absolute identity? Is it one or many? Are the objects of the world real or illusory? Is there existence besides the Self? These are some of the questions for which we have no unanimous answer. Some passages in the Upaniṣads emphasize the identity of the Brahma and the individual, whereas many of the important passages tend towards pantheism. Everything in the universe is maintained and sustained by the Brahma. This Upaniṣadic pantheism does not contemplate the unreality of the external world. The process of evolution, the birth and growth of the world from this spiritual principle according to this Pantheism is compared to the spinning of cobwebs by the spider. Besides this, pantheistic tendency there is also a clear idealistic note sounded by Yāgñavalkya. His doctrine (Bṛhadāraṇyaka Upaniṣad) may be taken as the basis of Advaita. According to Bṛhadāraṇyaka the *Brahma* is shown to be the transcendental Identity beyond the knower and the known. Hence it is metempirical and beyond consciousness. He is to be described only by negatives because no category of our experience can truly explain this transcendental Idea. Besides this advaitic attitude there are also symptoms of theistic tendency. *Brahma* is spoken as identical with Rudra and Viṣṇu. He is spoken of as the creator and sustainer of the Universe. The individuals are to look up to him for spiritual guidance and help and for final emancipation from *Saṁsāra*. Besides these general tendencies there are other characteristics of the Upaniṣadic Age.

(I)The Upaniṣads are mainly antiritualistic. Since they are antiritualistic they are in a sense anti-Vedic also. Internal evidence indicates that the new thought had its origin mainly among the Rājarisis.

(II) Asceticism and the practice of Yoga seems to be the characteristic institution of the Upaniṣadic age. The practical course of realising the *Brahma* contemplated by the Upaniṣads involves an elaborate process of self-discipline. As against the older forms of fire sacrifice the Upaniṣads contemplate a new kind of sacrifice- sacrificing one's own attractions towards the world. "These two are unending immortal oblations referring to the sacrifice of speech and other sense-qualities. Whether waking or sleeping one is sacrificing continuously uninterruptedly. Now whatever other oblations there are, they are limited, for they consist of works-*Karma māyā*. Knowing this very thing verily indeed the ancients did not sacrifice the agnihotra sacrifice" (*Kauśitaka Upaniṣad* II *Adhyāya*). This passage indicates that Yoga or Tapas is considered as an ancient institution and has taken the place of the traditional agnihotra about the time of the Upaniṣads. This is further strengthened by circumstantial evidence that the Upaniṣadic age must be of very long duration comprehending within itself an earlier conflict between anti-ritualism and ritualism and a later attempted reconciliation of some sort. Asceticism of the type of spiritual agnihotra must necessarily imply what is elsewhere called the other-worldliness. The concrete of our everyday life is associated with evil and suffering. The goal of life is emancipation from saṁsāric cycle. The means of attaining this goal consists in eradicating all desires by performing Tapas. All that is of the nature of evil in Life must be burned in the spiritual fire of the Ātman. This is the path of self-realisation. Instead of the sacrifice of various animals to realise the aim of one's life one has to offer one's own desires as the sacrificial victim in his higher agnihotra. The Yāgakuṇḍa of the Upaniṣadic age is in the very heart of one's own self. It is a sort of crucifying the old Adam in man for the glorification of the new one. Thus we have in this age of theosophic wisdom all the terms of a later systematic philosophy. Here we find the traces of all theistic tendencies in India. We have also in the same age the ground of the intellectual condition that ultimately developed into the religion of peace and harmony which preached the glory of renunciation. Max Muller says, "The Upaniṣads are to my mind the germs of Buddhism while Buddhism is in many respects the doctrine of the Upaniṣads carried out to its last consequences. The doctrine of the highest goal of Vedānta, the knowledge of the true self is no more than the Buddhism- the common property of the Saṅgha fraternity open alike to the young and old, to the Brāhmaṇa and the Śūdra the rich and the poor, the literate and the illiterate." In the Upaniṣads we have the germs of all the philosophical systems not only of the Vedic and the orthodox but also those religio-philosophical systems which are non-Vedic such as Jainism and Buddhism. We may repeat our statement that it was an age of general philosophical outbursts in which there were several tendencies with multifarious characteristics. Crystalisation of these tendencies and forces ultimately resulted in the rise of several systems of Philosophy which adorned the succeeding period.

The Rudiments of Upanisad thought in the Samhitas and the Brahmanas

Upaniṣadic literature practically forms a part of Vedic literature in general. Thus it is a part of Śruti as opposed to Smṛti. When we spoke about the various Brāhmaṇas we saw what these Brāhmaṇas treated about. The Brāhmaṇas are associated with different Vedic groups, i.e., we have the Brāhmaṇas belonging to Ṛg, Yajur and so on. Thus we have the mantras or the sacrificial hymns constituting the Saṁhita portion of a particular Veda followed by the Brāhmaṇas which explain the sacrificial procedure. These Brāhmaṇas contain what are known as āraṇyakas or forest-treatises and Upaniṣads, a sort of philosophical discourse. These Upaniṣads constitute the last of the śruti or Vedic literature. Hence they are sometimes known as Vedānta, the last of the Vedas which name was specialised to represent a particular school of Philosophy later on. Now we have to consider this third stage of Vedic literature known as the Upaniṣadic literature. It is here we have the origin of genuine philosophy. There are two fundamental conceptions implicitly present throughout the early Vedic literature which finally become the central ideas in the Upaniṣads. These are ātman and Brahman. *Ātman* is derived from a Saṃskrit root meaning Breath, It implies soul or spirit of the individual and indirectly of the universe as well. In a verse of the Ṛg Veda it is used in the sense of Life. "Increase or Bright Indra this our manifold food thou givest us like sap." This life-principle was early recognised to be inside of and different from body. The next step in the history of Vedic thought is to recognise the soul or life of the universe. Just as there is a non-material principle constituting the essence of man, there is an essential principle at the centre of the universe. This spiritual principle at the core of the universe is also designated by the same term ātman. Another verse of the Ṛg Saṁhitā runs thus; where was the life, the blood; the soul of the universe who went to ask this avocations, in their old age all take to Saṁnyāsahood or to use his own words become Munīs and finally give up their bodies through the performance of yoga or tapas. Thus taking to the life of a munī and performing tapas or yoga was considered the general career of the Kṣatriyas of the Ikṣavāku family. Further we have to notice this fact that the Ikṣavāku line is traditionally traced to series of Manus who were a sort of mythic rulers and organisers of humanity. Reference to the same house is made by the Jaina writers relating to the origin. The founder of Jainism according to their own tradition was one Vṛṣabha, king of Ayodhyā belonging to the Ikṣavāku line and a descendant of the Manus. After ruling the country for some time he abdicated the throne in favour of his son, Bharata and became a munī engaged in tapas or yoga. This Vṛsabha is supposed to be the founder of the doctrine of *Ahiṁsā,* that it is wrong to inflict pain on any living thing on any account even in the name of religion of God. From this Vṛṣabha the tradition speaks of a succession of Jaina prophets ending with the last and the twenty-fourth Mahāvīra Vardhamāna, an elder contemporary of Gautama Buddha. The date of His *nirvāṇa* is fairly well determined to be 527 B.C. The Jaina tradition associated his immediate predecessor Pārśvanātha with Kāśī. He was the son of the king of Kāśī, whose name was Viśvasena. The interval between Pārśva and Mahāvīra is 250 years and this would place him about 777 B.C. This date is recognised to be fairly accurate and the personality of Pārśva is accepted to be quite historical. The fact we have to notice in connection with this Jaina tradition is this. Of the 24 Jinas nearly 20 are associated with the Ikṣavāku house and all of them are connected with the Royal houses of Kāśī, Kosala, Videha and Magadha. Throughout the sacred Jaina writings, the country is referred to as a sacred land, *nityapuṇyabhūmi*, where the *Dharma* never dies—*Dharma* referring to the doctrine of *Ahiṁsā*. The importance of Videha, we shall know in another connection also. The Upaniṣadic thought mainly centred round Janaka of Videha and Yāgñavalkya, also of Videha. Perhaps we have to make a slight distinction between Eastern Videha and Western Videha. The portion bordering on Magadha, what is known as Pūrva Videha, evidently retained the anti-sacrificial culture whereas the north-west part of Janaka's country finally accepted a sort of compromise between these sacrificial ritualism and the anti-sacrificial protestantism. The same importance of the Ikṣavāku house we find in Buddhistic literature. The very first chapter of Rockhill's life of Buddha contains an acount of the life of the Śākyas clan to which Gautama Buddha of Videha belongs. In this account we find the Śākya clan traced to the house of the Ikṣavākus. This evidently implies the general belief in those days, that to trace their lineage to the Ikṣavāku house was considered to be a proud distinction among the Kṣatriya clans. Such a distinction could be claimed by this Ikṣavāku house only because of the solid contribution they made towards the culture and the civilisation of the early Āryans, and yet these Ikṣavākus are hardly known and rarely mentioned in the Ṛg veda period. Hence we have to think of the two different schools of culture even among the fold of the Āryans and we are constrained to accept Bloomfield's hypothesis that the Āryans of the Eastern countries in the Gangetic plain mainly dominated by the Kṣatriyas constitute an early group of Āryans who migrated into India much earlier than the Āryans of the Kurupāñcāla whose ritualistic culture was dominated by the priests. Rivalry between the two, not merely in culture but in political relations, there must have been; for we have constant references to expeditions of the Kurupañcālas into the countries of Kosala and Videha which appear to be partly for the purpose of proselytisation and partly for the purpose of political aggrandisement, the spirit of the conquest being associated with the missionary spirit a frequently found phenomenon in modern history. One other thing we have to notice and that is about the sacred language of the respective clans. The Eastern Āryans mainly used a form of Prakrit as their language, a corrupt and an easier form of Sanskrit a fact very often referred to by the Kurupañcālas. The Kurupañcālas sneered at the Eastern Āryans because of their incapacity to pronounce accurately many of the Sanskrit names. But the language sneered at by the priests of the Kurupañcālas, was not only the language of the masses among the Eastern Āryans but also the medium of this sacred literature. The Jaina and Buddhistic scriptures were all written in the form of Prākṛit language, for Pāli the language of the Buddhist scriptures was but a slight modification of prakrit. We cannot have a clear history of the beginning of this protestant school among the Āryans till we are able to understand the several obscure references which are scattered in the later Saṁhitās as well as in the Brāhmaṇa literature. It is enough to mention only two. The institution of Yatis and Vrātyas constitute extreme obscure topics of the Vedic literature. The term Yati occurs in the *Saṁhitās* literature where they are said to be destroyed by Indra by offering them to the wolves of the forest. These Yatis are described to be Saṁnyāsin who did not accept Indra worship, who would not chant the vedic mantras and who were opposed to the Brahmavādas. The description is quite clear and it implies that the yatis were a group of ascetics quite opposed to sacrificial ritualism for which they were evidently punished and persecuted by the more dominant branch of the ritualistic Āryans. The school of the yatis must have been at a certain period more influential and consequently more popular— a fact indicated by the Brāhmaṇa literature, which speaks of the giving up of Indra worship and the Soma sacrifice for several years. It is very significant to note that the reason giving up the Indra beginning with the slaughter of Vṛthra ending with that of the yatis. Does it not suggest that at a certain period of the later Saṁhitās and at the early Brāhmaṇa period tha anti sacrificial school was more popular than the other which led to the discarding of Indra worship and of the consequent sacrificial ritualism? The same note of opposition is associated with the institution of the Vrātyas. The Vrātyas are sometimes extolled for their virtues and very often condemned for their anti-sacrificial unconventionalism. In an important book of the Atharvana Veda the traditional deities of the Vedic pantheon are made subordinate to him and they go about as his attendants.

He is the greatest and the highest among the Gods and yet he is described as a wandering mendicant, an ascetic who has to occasionally visit a house-holder for his good, a description quite in keeping with later Jaina and Buddhistic accounts. A Jaina yati or Buddhistic bhikṣu of a later period had to live mainly in the outskirts of his city and had to go in the streets of the city only during the time of meals and that too occasionally. The description of Vrātya is almost identical with a wandering ascetic. He is one who had given up the traditional rituals of a Brahmin, the saṁskāras of a brahmacārin. In spite of this fact they are not considered as complete alien racially because the orthodox fold devised ceremonies as a sort of prāyascitta after the performance of which the Vrātya could be taken back into the Brahmanical fold. This fact completely rejects the hypothesis suggested by some scholars that the Vrātyas were some sort of aboriginal nomads living in the midst of the Aryans. The orthodox literature even while condemning the ways of the Vrātyas never speaks of them as non-Āryans. They are only corrupt Aryans speaking a corrupt language found in Magadha and the surrounding districts. Magadha was the seat of Jaina and Buddhistic cultures. Taking all these into consideration it is not an implausible hypothesis to suggest that long before the rise of Buddhism there was liberal school of thought existing side by side with the orthodox Vedic school. To stop here with the suggestion that the protestant school was dominated by the Kṣatriyas just as the other was by the Brāhmins would rather be inaccurate. There must have been militant proselytising on either side and also dominant free thinking. So much so we find several schools led by Vedic ritualism and the Kṣatriyas just as Janaka accepting a modified form of ritualism. Among this school of protestantism we are able to recognise through the hazy past two inner currents one indicating the origin of Vaiṣṇavism and the other of Jainism. Vaiṣṇavism to be accurate is a mixture of several currents of thought and culture with a Vedic nucleus is well brought out by Dr. Bhandarkar in his monograph on the 'History of Vaiṣṇavism'. The Vedic nucleus is associated with Nārada, a disciple of Sanatkumāra. Nārada must have been one of the great opponents of the sacrificial cult involving Hiṁsā as was Viśwāmitra of the Ṛg vedic period. This Nārada school of the Upaniṣadic period constitutes the Vedic nucleus for later Vaiṣṇavism characterised by the full recognition of the doctrine of *Ahiṁsā* except in the Chāndogya where the qualifications of a person who reaches the Brahma world are given. After mentioning the condition of Vedic study the following is added. "He who has concentrated all his senses upon the *ātman*, He who practises *Ahiṁsā* all elsewhere than at Tirtha who indeed lives thus throughout the length of life reaches the *Brahma-* world and does not return again." This verse indicates a spirit of compromise. We see a split in the very body of the anti-ritualistic school, the right one representing the Upaniṣadic thought. This thing must have gone on for some centuries when there was the necessity and the occasion of a more radical school—Buddhism which threw open the gates of *Dharma* to all irrespective of the distinction betwen the Āryan and the non-Āryan. Many of the schools or *darśanas* must have been codified just after the time of Buddha.

Sāṁkhya Philosophy : Kapila— The Sāṁkhya system propounded by Kapila is perhaps the oldest of the trasitional systems of philosophy. It is referred to both in the Jaina and Buddhistic sacred literature. Jaina work describing the origin of Jaina Dharma associates the origin of Sāṁkhya school with one Mārīci who was a grandson of Vṛṣabha, the founder of Jainism according to Jaina tradition. This grandson of Vṛṣabha even during his grandfather's life-time is said to have started a rival school, though based upon the fundamental doctrine of Ahiṁsā. The difference between Mārīci and Vṛṣabha's school is in the philosophical background of each, and Kapila is referred to as one of the disciples of Mārīci. This suggestion is borne out both from internal and other references. From internal evidence Sāṁkhya school clearly appears to be a revolt against the Vedic sacrificial ritualism in unmistakable terms. Further, Guṇaratna in his commentary on Haribhadra's *Ṣaḍ-darśana*

Samuccaya refers to the Sāṁkhya school thus. Sāṁkhyas were opposed to the Vedic doctrines of Hiṁsā and were interested in *Adhyātmavāda*. Again this Kapila, the reputed author of Sāṁkhya, is referred to in the Buddhistic account as to the origin of the Sākya clan of Kṣatriyas to which Gautama Buddha himself belonged. We referred to the fact that the Sākyas claimed to be descendants of the Ikṣavāku family. One of the kings of the Ikṣvāku Viruddaka declared his youngest son as his successor and exiled his four other sons by his first wife. The princes accompanied by their sister and a great many people travelled towards the Himālaya mountains and reached the hermitage of Kapila. The Ṛṣi showed them where to build a town and they built it according to his directions. The Ṛṣi Kapila having given the soil 'Vastu' of the place they called the town the soil of Kapila—Kapilavastu; and this Kapilavastu is the birthplace of Gautama Śākya Muni, son of the ruling prince Śuddhodana. According to this account, Kapila is an ancient ṛṣi much earlier than the rise of Buddhism. In the purāṇic literature he is sometimes referred to as the son and sometimes as the avatār of Viṣṇu. Kapila is also referred to in the Mahābhārata and Rāmāyaṇa. The Bhagavata Gītā which is a part of the Mahābhārata is mainly based upon Kapila's Sāṁkhya philosophy and distinctly mentions the name of the Philosopher as well as the philosophy. By the time the Mahābhārata was composed Kapila's Sāṁkhya system must have been prevalent and was probably very popular. Kapila again figures in the Rāmāyaṇa. He is associated with King Sāgara who wanted to perform an Aśvamedha. The horse let loose by him to have its triumphant march was stolen by a Rākṣasa. It was taken to the nether-world and tied to a tree close by which Kapila was performing tapas. The persons sent out to search the animal found it by the side of the ṛṣi. Mistaking the ṛṣi to be the culprit they began to molest him. Enraged at this he punished them by burning them all to ashes through his mystic powers. Again Kapila is referred to in the Upaniṣads. Here not only the name of the author but also several characteristic doctrines of the system are also mentioned. This reference in the Upaniṣads indicates that Sāṁkhya school was one of the dominant schools of revolt against Vedic ritualism. The literary references cast a good deal of mystery round the personality of Kapila referred to with great awe and reverence, and in Sanskrit Literature he has the unique distinction of owning the title Paramarṣi. This unique title of Paramarṣi is a clear evidence to show his importance in the early philosophical literature of India. The followers of Sāṁkhya school are called after the founder's second name Paramarṣi. But at present this school is not represented by distinct followers. Most probably all the Sāṁkhyas were absorbed into the fold of later Vaiṣṇavism; for it is clear from the introductory remarks of Guṇaratna that they were the worshippers of Nārāyaṇa. This absence of a school claiming a number of devotees is sometimes explained by the fact of the anti-ritualistic and antitheistic tendencies of the system. Because of these tendencies Kapila's teaching according to some European scholars never secured a good following. This view of European scholars cannot be accepted. Though at present there are no representatives of the Sāṁkhya school, still we have evidence to show that in earlier period of Indian history about the time of Guṇaratna there were a number of devotees professing the Sāṁkhya faith. Therefore it is not quite accurate to state that Kapila "Left no traditions and found no school." (David's *'Sāṁkhya Kārikās.'*) In Guṇaratna's commentary we find the following introductory note to the chapters on Sāṁkhya . "In order to distinguish who the Sāṁkhyas are I mean to describe certain of their characteristic marks and habits of dress. They carry three sticks but some of them carry only one. They all had red-coloured clothes and carried with them deerskins, as their *āsanas.* whenever they met each other they saluted *namo nārāyaṇa* which would be returned *nārāyaṇa namāḥ.* These were called Parivrājakas." From this description we have to admit that at one time there were a large number of Sāṁkhya ascetics in the country, which belied *obita dicta* of the Orientalists who believe that there were no schools of the Sāṁkhyas. Most probably these Parivrājakas were absorbed into the general Hindu fold as was suggested. From the characteristic salutation referred to by Guṇaratna we can infer that Sāṁkhya Parivrājakas had something to do with the growth of modern Vaiṣṇavism which is a result of several tendencies of Thought.

(1) The Upaniṣadic doctrine of Brahman which is closely allied to the Sāṁkhya doctrine of Puruṣa or Ātman. (2) The Vāsudeva cult and the traditions which have grown aroung the Yādava prince Kṛṣṇa. (3) The traditions associated with the Pre-Rāmānuja period represented by the aḷvārs of the South. From Tamil literature two things are quite evident. (1) The great aḷvārs— the religious devotees of the Dravidian country were worshippers of Nārāyaṇa. (2) The earliest Tamil reference Tolkapyam speaks about the religious faiths. It is impossible for us to say with any amount of exactitude when the Kṛṣṇa cult came to the South. This much we can assert that it must be several centuries before the Christian era much earlier than the introduction of Buddhism. This suggestion is borne out by the fact that some of the founders of Vedic schools Āpastamba and Kātyāyana are spoken of as Dravidian and the Tamil work already referred to also speaks of the prevalent Indra worship in the South. Taking all these facts we have to assign the Āryan migration somewhere about the 7th Century B.C. The migration of Āryans with their characteristic Indra worship must certainly have been associated with the Sāṁkhya school which was mainly opposed to Indra worship and animal sacrifice, that is the two schools of thought must have come down to the South almost simultaneously. Another thing we may notice in this connection is this. The school of revolt against Brahminical ritualism must generally be more liberal in its social aspect. This is clearly borne out in the case of Jaina and Buddhistic schools. The Sāṁkhya school was evidently at one with these two schools in removing the social barriers against religious devotees. Such an assumption well borne out by sister schools of thought would explain the fact that among the aḷvārs of the

south we find representatives from among all strata of society irrespective of the distinction of Ārya and Draviḍa. The Vaiṣṇava tradition is confirmed even by Rāmānuja's teachings, though by a strange irony of fate his followers at present represent the most bigoted form of orthodoxy.

Sāṁkhya Philosophy— The term Sāṁkhya according to European scholars is derived from *Saṁkhyā* or number, because Kapila enumerates a number of *Tattvas* as constituting elements of reality. The term is supposed to be related to number. But according to Indian thinker the term is synonymous with discrimination. This is the meaning in which the term is used in the Mahābhārata. Vijñānabhikṣu a famous writer of the Sāṁkhya school also explains the term as discrimination or setting forth the distinction between spirit or *ātman* on the one hand and matter or Prakṛti on the other. Śaṅkara also adopts the same interpretation. Hence the traditional meaning may be accepted as more correct and the other one suggested by European scholars has to be rejected as far-fetched. Some of them even go to the length of connecting the Sāṁkhya system with the Pythagorean school. Pythagoreanism is also connected with the mystic doctrine of numbers. Reality is some how constituted numbers according to Pythagores. It is scarcely necessary to point out how unfounded such a suggestion is. It is a sample of that method which very often builds up fantastic theories merely on the strength of verbal analogy.

Sāṁkhya Method— The philosophical method adopted by the Sāṁkhya school is just the method of discrimination or vivekajñāna. This method of discrimination is expounded as a means of salvation from *Saṁsāra*. By the way, we may point out that this is the motive of all the Indian systems of thought— how to obtain liberation from the Saṁsāric cycle of births and deaths. Such a freedom according to Sāṁkhya philosophy is to be obtained by "discrimination" or knowledge of the distinction between the spiritual principle or Puruṣa and the environmental existence of Prakṛti.

The Sources of Sāṁkhya— The existing works through

which we can have an idea of the Sāṁkhya system are mainly the following : Some of these are in the sūtra form and the others in the form of commentaries. (1) *Sāṁkhya sūtras* or otherwise known as *Sāṁkhya-pravacanasūtra* is traditionally ascribed to Kapila himself. But this belief is quite unfounded. There is clear evidence to show that this is quite a modern work. Śaṅkara and Vācaspati Miśra, the great philosophical commentators, never refer to this work at all. Guṇaratna, the commentator on *Ṣaḍdarśanasamuccaya* while mentioning several other works on Sāṁkhya, does not refer to this work even by name. Hence this is considered neither important nor an authoritative work on the Sāṁkhya school of thought.

(2) *Tattvasamāsa*: This work also is erroneously attributed to Kapila. Max Muller elaborately argues that this work is a genuine work of Kapila. His arguments are far from convincing and hence his view is not accepted by modern scholars. (3) *Sāṁkhyasāra*: This is by Vijñānabhikṣu who wrote a commentary on the Sāṁkhyapravacanasūtra. Hence this work is a compendium of his commentary. (4) *Sāṁkhya-Kārikā* of Iśvara Kṛṣṇa: This work contains a clear exposition of the Sāṁkhya system. It is a small work of 72 couplets and may be considered as an early authoritative work on the Sāṁkhya system. This work is referred to by several philosophical writers. Guṇaratna bases his commentary on the chapter on Sāṁkhya mainly on this work from which he freely quotes. This may be taken as an evidence of its antiquity as well as its authoritativeness. Besides this work Guṇaratna speaks of a number of other Sāṁkhya Treatises many of which are not available.

The Sāṁkhya System— The chief purpose of philosophical study in ancient India was to get rid of the sorrows of life. This ideal is stated at the very beginning of the system. Life according to Kapila is subject to three kinds of sorrow. *Mokṣa* or liberation consists in the extinction of pain and misery originating from these three sources. The three sources of sorrow according to Sāṁkhya are: (1) *ādhyātmika*, that which is dependent of self (2) ādhibhautika, that which is dependent on the environment (3) ādhidaivika, that which is dependent on supernatural and divine influences. *Ādhyātmika Duḥkha*, sorrow dependent on self may be due to two reasons: (a) bodily conditions or *Śārīrika* (b) mental conditions or *Mānasika*. Sorrow due to bodily condition relates to suffering pain due to diseases, etc., which pertain to the body. Sorrows due to mental conditions are the unpleasant experiences associated with certain emotions such as anger, fear, etc. The second class of sorrows known as *Ādhibhautika* is due to environmental conditions. The interference from environmental source may be from fellow human beings or animals or birds or other natural conditions. The third kind, *Ādhidaivika*, refers to sorrow originating from the influences of supernatural agencies. The wrath of the deities, adverse conjunction of planets, the mischief of the Yakṣas and Rākṣasas would all come under this head. The *summum bonum* for life is to escape from these kinds of *Duḥkha* or sorrow. This escape from suffering and pain is to be achieved by the knowledge of the several *Tattvas*, and hence the desire to know the *Tattvas*. All souls long to escape from such misery and to seek liberation. The Sāṁkhya method propounds the means of escape from sorrow and of the attainment of the consequential bliss. The Sāṁkhya method of liberation is quite different from the traditional Vedic method which was by sacrifice. Kapila condemns the sacrificial cult. The revealed Vedic method is quite useless according to Kapila because of its defects which are three.

Impurity— Destruction and excess or enormity. The Vedic method of sacrifice is impure because it is caused by bloodshed due to slaughter of animals. This method of sacrifice though supposed to expiate all sins even *Brahmahatyā* is rejected by Kapila, for all such rites according to him are impure. Further it leads to mere destruction. The method of sacrifice instead of leading to complete liberation from *Saṁsāra* merely leads to another state of *Saṃsāric* existence. The end aimed at is happiness in *Svarga* and certainly this is not *Mokṣa*. Hence the path of sacrifice is the path of destruction and not of salvation. The traditional method is excessive or unequal. Sacrifice generally involves a lot of expenditure, e.g., in an *Aśvamedha* sacrifice sometimes hundreds of horses have to be sacrificed. Hence this method is not within the reach of all. Therefore as against such an impossible way to escape Kapila proposes a method which is quite adequate and feasible to all. The path to liberation according to Sāṁkhya philosophy consists in the progress of acquiring discriminative knowledge of the nature of the self from its environmental existence. This discrimination that the spirit or *Puruṣa* is quite different from *Prakṛti* or matter leads to self-realisation which is the true *Mokṣa*. The material environment which practically imprisons the spirit is called by Kapila *Prakṛti*. Hence the discriminative knowledge also meant the knowledge of the number and the nature of the several *Tattvas*— ultimate principles. The problem relating to the path of *Mokṣa* resolves therefore into the problem as of the nature of the *Tattvas*. The next question therefore is what are the Sāṁkhyan *Tattvas*? Kapila starts with the assumption that the self or *Puruṣa* is quite distinct from *Prakṛti* or the ultimate matter. The former is the spiritual principle in man whereas the latter, the primeval basic principle of the material universe. The cosmos is evolved out of this *Prakṛti*. In the midst of this unfolding and developing *Prakṛti* the several Puruṣas are situated. According to Kapila the *Puruṣas* are infinite in number. Thus in the technical language of modern metaphysics the Sāṁkhya system may be said to be dualistic as well as pluralistic: Dualistic because it postulates two classes of reals *Cetana* and *Acetana*, spiritual and non-spiritual and pluralistic bacause it postulates an infinite number of Puruṣas or souls. Each Puruṣa is encircled by *Prakṛti* or *Pradhāna* which is another name for describing matter. In the earlier form of the Sāṁkhya system each *Puruṣa* was supposed to have his own peculiar and individual *Prakṛti*. But later schools of Sāṁkhya maintained that all the different *Pradhānas* relating to different *Puruṣas* are really one in nature since they are all evolved from one and the same *Prakṛti*. The

Puruṣa who is encircled by an alien and extraneous matter forgets its true nature and pristine purity, and identifies itself with bodily activities and conditions. This ignorance of its true heritage is the real cause of human misery. Hence the realisation of the true nature of the *Puruṣa* as distinct from the material conditions is the ideal to be aimed at.

Evolution of the cosmos from the Primeval Prakṛti— This Prakṛti is uncreated and self-existing. It is from this *Prakṛti* all other things emanate except the Puruṣa. This primeval matter or *Prakṛti* is endowed with three guṇas or qualities. Whenever the harmonious equilibrium of the quality in the *Prakṛti* is disturbed it begins on the career of manifestation or differentiation. This process of differentiation really constitutes the process of the building up of the Cosmos. The first thing that emanates from this unmanifested Prakṛti is Buddhi or Mahat— the Great. The term Buddhi is sometimes translated as intellect but we should remember this fact that it is mainly of the nature of matter since it evolves from acetana reality— *Prakṛti*. Intellect in modern psychology suggests a relation to a mind or self but Prakṛti in Kapila's system corresponds to Descarte's unthinking thing. Therefore Buddhi which is evolved from this *Prakṛti*, subtle though it be, is still a material mode. This Buddhi or Mahat must therefore mean in the Sāṁkhya system some sort of subtle material environment quite in the proximity of the *Puruṣa* or self. It is only through the medium of this Buddhi that *Puruṣa* has knowledge of the external world. Sāṁkhya writers compare Buddhi to a sort of mirror which reflects the knowledge of the external world for the benefit of *Puruṣa*. On the one hand, it reflects the outer world and on the other it reflects also the *Puruṣa*. *Buddhi* is that peculiar medium in which the *Puruṣa* and his material environments are brought into relation which is the ultimate source of *Saṁsāra*. It is because of this relation of Buddhi between the self and the non-self that there is a chance for the *Puruṣa* to mistake his true nature and to identify himself with *Prakṛti* and thus to imagine that he is responsible for all the changes in the material environments.

The next step is the birth of *ahaṃkāra* from *Buddhi.* It is the I or the Ego which is the ground of our personal identity. Here also we have to notice that *ahaṃkāra,* the Sāṁkhya ego is not quite identical with the conception of the Ego or self of modern psychology. The ego of modern psychology corresponds to *Puruṣa* whereas the Sāṁkhya *ahaṃkāra* merely means some further modification of the subtle *Buddhi* which itself is a modification of acetana *Prakṛti.* The Sāṁkhya Ego probably refers to a process of individuation, a process culminating in organic body. The self or *Puruṣa* becomes an organic individual through the means of *ahaṃkāra.*Next we have the origin of the five senses known as the *Tanmatras.* This term is a technical term of the Sāṁkhya school meaning the sense qualities. these subtle sense-qualities emanate from that principle of individuality known as *ahaṃkāra.* The *Tanmātras* are five in number, sound, touch, smell, taste and visibility. Even these *Tanmātras* we have to remember are material categories. These sense-elements or *Tanmātras* form the primary basis for the evolution of the grosser matter. This grosser matter which is derived from these *Tanmātras* is again of five kinds, the *Pañcabhūtas. Akāśa* (Ether), air, earth, water and fire. Ether arises from sound, air from touch, earth from smell, water from taste and fire from visibility or light. Thus the five *bhūtas* are respectively derived from the five *Tanmātras,* the basic categories of the physical universe. This line of development from ahṃkāra to the world of physical things represents only one side of the process. There is another process of development from the same source— from *ahaṃkāra* or the principle of individuality. We have the principle of building up the organic. This process of building up the organic body consists in the evolution of the five buddhīndriyas or organs of sense-perception and five *Karmendriyas* or the organs of activity and *manaindriya*— the organ of thought. The five organs of sense-perception are the five familiar sense organs— Eye, ear, nose, tongue and the skin. These sense-organs acording to the Sāṁkhya system are evolved out of the principle of individuality, ahaṃkāra. So also are the five *Karmendriyas* which are the vocal organs for speech, the hands, the feet, the organs of excretion and the generative organs. These five *Buddhīndriyas* and the five *Karmendriyas* together with the manas are the eleven Indriyas derived from *Ahaṃkāra*. Thus the primeval cosmic principle *Prakṛti* evolving upto *ahaṃkāra* branches off into two lines of development one leading upto the cosmos and the other to the building up of the body which serves as the temporal tabernacle for the *Puruṣa*. Thus the Sāṁkhya Tattvas which are derived from *Prakṛti* are 24 in number. These together with *Puruṣa* constitute the 25 Sāṁkhya *Tattvas*.

The Nature of Prakṛti— Prakṛti is otherwise called Avyakta or the unmanifest or *Pradhāna* or the primary basis of existence. When we look to the process of evolution of the different *Tattvas* enumerated above we find this *Prakṛti* as the fountain source of not only the elements that go to build up the physical universe but also of those that lead to the origin of organised living bodies. This primeval subtle matter- *Prakṛti* may be some kind of Ether which early Sāṃkhyas may be said to have imagined. This is the connecting link between the gross matter on the one hand and life-activity on the other, the fountain source of both the inorganic and the organic. Even according to modern Science Ether is the primeval source of matter. According to what is known as the electron theory of matter, the physical atom is a complex system of electrons. Thus the physical basis of matter is traced to Ether which is the basis of forces like electricity, magnetism, light, heat, etc. The process of development of physical science is interesting in this respect. Towards the close of the 19th century there was the wonderful analysis of the physical realm into a definite number of chemical elements out of which the whole cosmos was built. Science then recognised two fundamental concepts mass and energy as constitutive of matter. The speculation of Maxwell and Thompson ultimately indicated that Mass was but a derivative concept, Energy being the primary one. The next step was reached when the electrical theory of matter was propounded.

This leads to the complete identity of all forms of physical energy, heat, light, magnetism and electricity. The next and most important step of advance is marked by the discovery of radio-activity. On the one hand it discovered the extremely complex nature of the atom which resembles the Solar system in miniature inasmuch as it contains a nucleus around which a number of negative electrons revolve with incredible velocity. The second result of this discovery is equally important. The chemical elements which were considered to be completely isolated are now shown to be merely of quantitative differences brought about by the electronic changes in the intra-atomic constitution. The dream of the alchemist that all the chemical elements had a common basis and hence transmutable is no more a matter of historic curiosity suggesting merely how men went wrong in their early scientific speculations. It becomes a matter of scientific possibility for unquestionably it is indicated that all the elements have a common source. If this theory as to the constitution of the cosmos is accepted and there is evidence enough supporting it then Ether becomes the primeval fountain source of all energy constituting the physical realm. This again conversely implies that due to the intra-atomic changes the physical universe may altogether get dissolved and then disappear into the very same primeval Ether. On the side of the organic world we have had a similar development pointing towards some such source as the Ether. We are all acquainted with the Darwinian conception of biological evolution which traces the diversity of animal life to a single source of organised protoplasmic matter. No doubt modern science has not been able to bridge up the gulf between the inorganic and the organic. Nevertheless the life-activity in protoplasmic matter which is the ultimate source for the wealth and richness of animal life may be this very intra-atomic energy, probably controlled and guided by a higher category not yet fully known to modern science, and most probably indicating to the same source of Ether. Towards the side of psychology many an abnormal phenomenon such as telepathy and clairvoyance are supposed to be due to some kind of Ether which is capable of transmitting thought-waves. Thus from every direction speculation leads to the same kind of origin. When different departments of modern science agree to postulating a common entity—Ether, for the purpose of explaining their respective phenomena we may very well imagine that Kapila contemplated some such ultimate basis which would account for the evolution of the cosmos as well as the organic world. Kapila's system not only describes the building up of things living and unliving from a primeval *Prakṛti* but also contemplates the possibility of their losing their concrete form and thus disappearing into the original Prakṛti. Thus as a tortoise throws it limbs backwards so also will the universe retract all its emanations and evloving things back to its own bosom. This in short is the account of the evolution of the world according to Kapila.

This primeval *Prakṛti* of Pradhāna is considered to be the substratum of the three *guṇas*—Sattva, *Rajas* and *Tamas.* The Sāṁkhya system emphasises the importance of the three guṇas of Prakṛti. *Sattva* means good or Truth; *Rajas* means activity or passion. *Tamas* means darkness or inertia. This conception of guṇas is really an obscure doctrine in the Sāṁkhya system. These three guṇas are supposed to inhere in the primeval matter-*Prakṛti.*These do not belong to *Puruṣa.* The uncreated and indestructible *Pradhāna* which has the potency of life and consciousness has also this privilege of owning these three *guṇas* which somehow are interested in the evolution of the Cosmos. The interplay of the three *guṇas* in the Prakṛti forms the starting point in the evolutionary process. When the three guṇas are harmoniously settled there is a sort of internal equilibrium and peace within the *Prakṛti.* Somehow this primeval harmony is disturbed when one of the guṇas gets predominance over the rest and this starts the process of evolution. On account of this original and unexplained disturbance, the *Prakṛti* enters into a sort of creative evolution though itself is not created. Thus it carries in its bosom in a latent form the richness and multiplicity of the well ordered universe. The original disturbance of harmony which is the beginning of the process of evolution remains an ultimate metaphysical assumption on which Sāṁkhya system rests. Why there should be a disturbance at all in the primeval peace, Kapila does not trouble to explain. But this is an assumption without which subsequent changes would remain inexplicable. By some mysterious internal disorder, *Prakṛti* is set moving and then follows change after change and at each step the progressive making of the universe. In the fully evolved universe Kapila assigns each *Guṇa* its respective region. The *Sattvaguṇa* which is associated with light, fire or flame is the symbol of purity. The spotless shining quality of *Sattva* is present in the ordinary fire and flame. The presence of this quality makes the flame turn skywards thereby indicating its divine origin from above. In air there is the predominance of *Rajoguṇa*. Hence it is marked by its violence. It roams about horizontally in the middle region of the universe. Solid and liquids stand for *Tamoguṇa*. Hence their opacity to light, and hence their inert and impervious nature, and hence their tendency to sink downwards is there. Thus the evolution of the denser and grosser matter is the result of the precipitating of the *Tamoguṇa*. Thus the three *guṇas* have their part to play in the origin and growth of the organic world. Organisms are but the modifications of the same *Prakṛti*, and hence they are also subject to the influence of the three guṇas. The living world is divided into the upper, the middle and the lower. The upper region of the cosmors traditional *Svarga* is the abode of the devas. The lower one is associated with the animal and trees whereas the middle region is the natural habitation of man. The *Svarga* abode of happy divine being is also the place where Brahmā and Indra reside. The elemental beings like Gandharvas and Yakṣas also reside there. These beings of the higher regions have in them the *Sattvaguṇa* in abundance. Hence they are marked by mutual goodwill and general happiness. In man there is a predominance of *Rajoguṇa*. Hence arise the feverish activity of man who is destined to eat the fruits of his *karmas*. His life is marked by the dominant note of struggle, the misery, and the few cases of momentary happiness which he now and then manages to experience only go to accentuate his general unhappiness and misery. The last is the region of the animals. This has the maximum of *Tamoguṇa* or darkness. Hence all the inhabitants of this region are marked by general unconsciousness and stupor. All these regions of the world constitute the one whole world of *saṁsāric* cycle according to Kapila. The same chain of births and deaths binds the three kinds of beings animals, men and Devas. Even the prominent residents of *Svarga*, Brahma and Indra who generally enjoy unalloyed happiness throughout their lives have to meet with death. Hence their life is equally subject to the vicissitudes of *Saṁsāra* and suffers from the bondage of births and deaths. Theirs is not the life of pure and liberated *Puruṣa*. Thus not only in the building up of the inorganic world but also in the evolution of the organic one including the super and subhuman regions, the part played by the three *guṇas* of *Prakṛti* is felt in no mean degree. These *guṇas* are invoked by the Sāṁkhya thinkers to explain the birth of the world and the process of *Saṁsāra*.

Mokṣa or liberation : According to Sāṁkhyas *Mokṣa* or liberation consists in getting rid of all the root causes of Saṁsāra which are the three kinds of bondage, mentioned above. Kapila curiously expects the means of salvation from the very *Prakṛti* which is the original source of the bondage. The intelligent Puruṣa is inactive by nature and hence is incapable of being the architect of his own destiny. *Acetana*—the unenlightened—*Prakṛti* has all activity and force in itself and is quite blind by nature. The *Puruṣa* is intelligent but inert and *Prakṛti* is all activity but blind. The union of the two—the blind and the cripple—leads to living. It is that soul may be able to contemplate on its own nature and entirely separate itself knowing that the union is made as of the halt of the cripple and the blind and through that union the universe is formed. It is *Prakṛti* that is privileged to carry the *Puruṣa* to its final goal. It is through the manifestation of *Prakṛti* that the soul acquires discrimination and obtains *Mokṣa.* Is there any conscious co-operation between *Puruṣa* and *Prakṛti*? No, that cannot be for *Prakṛti* is *Acetana* and the *Puruṣa* cannot live in peace with it, and yet there is this union between the two. Kapila vehemently protests against postulating a higher intelligence than *Prakṛti,* Īśvara, in order to explain the union between the two. He advances arguments to show that there can be co-operation even in the region of the unconscious. Purposive adaptation according to Kapila need not necessarily imply the operation of an intelligent agent. Secretion of milk from the cow is no doubt necessary and useful for the calf. This secretion is no doubt a case of purposive adaptation, but all the same the cow is not consciously responsible for this. Similarly the relation between *Prakṛti* and *Puruṣa* is a case of purposive adaptation without the necessity of an intelligent adjuster. *Prakṛti* unconsciously itself operates for the benefit of *Puraṣa* and is a case of unconscious inner necessity to serve the purpose of the soul. The adaptation between the two is absolutely unconscious thought suggestive of an intelligent designer. Again through the help of *Prakṛti, Puruṣa* is able to obtain discriminative knowledge about his true nature. The *Puruṣa* is able to realise himself to be absolutely independent of and uninfluenced by the *Prakṛti* activities. He knows he is different from the senses, *Buddhi* and *ahaṃkāra.* This realisation of independence from the environment including his own psychophysical mechanism leads to perfect knowledge. Then the *Puruṣa* is able to perceive that the activities are all due to *Prakṛti* while he himself remains in unruffled peace. *Prakṛti* ceases to affect him. *Prakṛti* retires from the stage saying "I have been seen. I can no more please the *Puruṣa*" and then the Puruṣa remains calm and peaceful saying "I have seen her; no more can she please me." This discriminative knowledge and the consequent retirement of the *Puruṣa* from the cosmic stage is an interesting philosophical metaphor. *Prakṛti* or nature continues to spin round on account of its own original impulse even after

Puruṣa's liberation. But this activity can no more influence the liberated *Puruṣa* because through knowledge he has obtained freedom or *Mokṣa.*

The main objection is that Kapila starts his system as a panacea for the evils in this world. He thereby recognises at least to some extent the importance of ethical value. But the system as finally wrought out by him is incapable of accommodating any such moral value. Human volition and consequent human conduct as such are said to be the effects of acetana *Prakṛti* virtue and vice are alien to the *Puruṣa.* They are associated with the non-spiritual *Prakṛti* and hence they do not affect the soul and yet with a strange inconsistency it is the fate of *Puraṣa* to enjoy the fruits pleasurable and painful of the *karmas* directly and immediately due to the activity of *Prakṛti.* Why it is the fate of *Puruṣa* that he should vicariously suffer the consequences of an alien being in life is entirely unexplained. To be consistent with his own presuppositions he ought to have made *Puruṣa* indifferent to the consequential pleasure or pains of conduct. But that would have made the *Puruṣa* an altogether unintelligible shadow of reality. It is this inherent paralysis of his system that strikes us as an important defect. In spite of the various defects we have to pay our homage to the great ancient thinker for the courageous application of the rational method for the problem of life and reality. In a remote age of Indian thought when customary dogmas played the dominant part in the explanation of philosophical problems it is really a matter for admiration to see such a rigorous and rational thinker as Kapila. In philosophical study the method is more important than the results. The results may be modified but the method leaves a permanent impression and contributes an endowing value in creating the right intellectual attitude. If the method of analysis and explanation is admitted to be of greater philosophic value than the actual doctrine obtained thereby, Kapila, judged by this standard, must occupy a place on a par with the world's greatest thinkers.

It was stated in a previous section that the doctrine of *Ahiṁsā* was prevalent even before the time of the Ṛgvedic period, probably due to the influence of the Lord Vṛṣabha of the Ikṣvāku clan. This school of thought continued to have a parallel existence to the Vedic culture of the sacrificial tenets. There must have been mutual influence between these two schools, one emphasising sacrifice and the other condemning it. That there were such counter currents of thought is obvious from the conflicting passages found in the Ṛgvedic literature. It sometimes emphasises sacrifice, in such passage as *Ajena Eṣṭavyaḥ*, and sometimes condemns sacrifice—*Mā-hiṁsyāt.* In this struggle between the two schools of thought, we find the rival school to Vedic sacrifice becoming more dominant now and then, leading to giving up of sacrifice and Indra worship. But about the time of the rise of the Upaniṣadic literature the schools standing for *Ahiṁsā* championed by the succession of Kṣatriya teachers became quite supreme. The sacrificial cult championed by the Priests evidently gave up the struggle as hopeless and entered into a compromise. They recognised the new thought characterised by *Ahiṁsā* and *Ātmavidyā* as distinctly superior to their own sacrificial cult which they accepted to be distinctly inferior. This compromising effect by welcoming the new thought as *Parā-vidyā* and assigning an inferior to the sacrificial cult as *Aparā-vidyā* must have secured intellectual peace and harmony only for some time. Because in the later Upaniṣadic literature while accepting the new doctrine of *Ātmavidyā* they surreptitiously smuggled into the Upaniṣadic cult the doctrine of sacrifice as a specially exempted one. Thus we find in Upaniṣadic literature an open recognition of the doctrine of *Ahiṁsā* and at the same time introducing a clause except in the case of religious sacrifice. This ingenious method of smuggling into the new thought, the old objective doctrine of sacrificial ceremony was evidently virulently protested by the rival schools. The struggle continued with increased strength, because by that time, the old Vṛṣabha thought of *Ahiṁsā* gained additional strength by the rise of Buddhism and also from the co-operation of the Sāṁkhya and Yoga schools which crystalised out of the Upaniṣadic cult itself. Strange to say there was the unexpected co-operation from free thinking school of Cārvākas, when they joined the struggle—a school of thought identical with school of modern materialistic philosophy. Though the Cārvākas did not believe in the existence of *Ātmā*, or in the future world, they were opposed to the Vedic culture as an ineffectual waste. In this renewed struggle abounding in destructive criticisms against Vedic sacrifice there must have been a distinct damage caused to the traditional edifice. Hence the orthodox thinkers were bound to reconstruct the cultural edifices and re-habilitate the same from the destruction caused by the rival intellectual bombardment. They had to re-examine the notion of Dharma as well as the notion of *Ātmā.* As a result we have the two schools of thought the Pūrvamīmāṁsā and Uttaramīmāṁsā or Vedānta.

The Pūrvamīmāṁsā school concedes many of the points of the rival school in order to safeguard its main doctrine of Vedic sacrifice. They openly reject the doctrine of Vedic sacrifices. They openly reject the doctrine of creation and the existence of Īśvara or *Sarvajña.* They don't recognise anything higher than the human personality itself, the point emphasised by the Jainas, Sāṃkhyas and the Bauddhas. In spite of this concession they try to maintain with elaborate arguments that Dharma means the Vedic Dharma in the sense of sacrificial ritual. Thus it is an enquiry into the nature of Dharma and hence the work begins with the sūtra *Athāto Dharmajijñāsā.*

Uttara Mīmāṁsā or Vedānta : Who are qualified to *Brahma Vidyā*—Surprisingly in conflict with the Upaniṣadic tendencies the Brahma-sūtras take the attitude that only the Dvijas are eligible. As a matter of fact about the period of the *Sūtras*, caste conservatism was rampant. That is the reason which explains the retrograde tendency herein implied. The critical examination and representation of Sāṁkhya is again taken up. *Pradhāna* as the basic principle of the Universe is rejected. The scriptural terms *Aja*—'non-generated'—cannot refer to *Avyakta pradhāna*. It must imply Brahman who is the author of all. He is the only Aja. Brahman is not only the guiding intelligence of cosmic evolution but also is the constituting substance of the cosmos. Brahman is not only the *Nimittakāraṇa* but also the *Upādānakāraṇa*, the material cause of the universe. Brahman is the stuff of which the world is made. All that exists partakes of the nature of Brahman. It is the beginning as well as the end of things. It is the origin as well as the goal of individual souls. Here ends the first book.

The second book also begins with the same topic, Yoga is taken up for criticism. According to Yoga there is a controlling Īśvara superintending the cosmic evolution proceeding from *Pradhāna*. This Īśvara of Yoga is said to be identical with Brahman. It is said to represent only an inappropriate and imperfect aspect of Truth. Consequently Yoga Īśvara is taken to be an incomplete description of the ultimate reality which is Brahman. Incidently there is an attempt to answer several Sāṁkhyan objections against Īśvara. The author formulates his own doctrine of causation. Vedāntic view of causation does not recognise any cause or effect. *Kāraṇakāryābheda* is their characteristic doctrine. The Sāṁkhya concept of causation is therefore rejected as unreal. According to Vedānta cause and effect are identical. This is corroborated both by Vedic authority and concrete experience. The cause of cloth is thread. There could be no quarrel about this that yarn in a particular arrangement constitutes cloth.

Responsibility of the Creator—Sāṁkhya emphasises the fact that an Īśvara, being an intelligent cause of the universe, must be responsible for the whole of the cosmos including the faults thereof. The defence put in the *Brahma-sūtras* is something obscure. Here the author takes his stand on the separateness of Brahman from *Jīvātmā*. According to the Sāṁkhya view activity implies desire and motive in the agent.

The desire of Brahma to bring about the world, cannot be a desire to help various beings, for they are still uncreated and non-existent. If there is a motive for the activity, the motive must imply some sort of want in the creator. The answer is that there is no genuine motive for the creator. According to the Vedāntic defence Brahma creates the universe merely out of sport or *Līlā*. But the next is the more important objection. It relates to the responsibility of the creator for uneven distribution of pleasure and pain. The answer offered by Vedānta is a bit strange. The act of creation is not said to be quite arbitrary but takes into consideration the merit and the demerit of the individual soul. This defence naturally implies that individual souls should have their separate and independent existence and that they are not really created though they are destined to undergo a periodic cosmic slumber from which they get awakened at the beginning of creation. How such a doctrine of individual selves could be reconciled with Vedāntic monism is not clearly shown. Neither the sūtra nor the great commentary of Śaṅkara is helpful. The latter part of the second book is devoted to the refutation of the other theories such as Vaiśeṣika, Bauddha, and Jaina. The author again and again returns to the criticism of Sāṁkhya. There is an interesting point to be noticed before we take leave of this. Buddhism is condemned to be unreal. We shall be surprised to see both the Sūtrakāra and the commentator Śaṅkara reject the Bauddha conception for this reason that according to Buddhistic view the world of external reality is purely mental and unreal. This reason offered for rejecting the Buddhistic view is certainly perplexing. The Bauddhas are found fault with because they annihilate the fundamental distinction between the concrete world of reality and the dream world of unreality, and they believe that the world is made of such stuff as dreams are made of. And yet this is the very conclusion to which Vedānta is striving. This surprising philosophical attitude has a parallel in western thought. Kant establishing the phenomenality of the external world to his satisfaction gives vent to righteous indignation at Berkleyan idealism to refute which he devotes one full chapter. Berkley would be much more akin to the ordinary view, and yet Kant in the West and Śaṅkara in the East claim the privilege of protesting against their own conclusions, when they are heard from alien quarters. To us it is interesting in this way. Idealism which is considered to be the claim of philosophic thought even in its most triumphant existence has an unconscious desire to hide its true identity from the ordinary world and attempts to appear as something different.

The latter part of II *Adhyāya* again takes up the discussion of the doctrine of creation. According to Vedāntism, there is no process of creation at all. The evolution and involution of the world during periodic *Kalpas* is but an appearance. If creation is a real process of evolution then they cannot reasonably object the Sāṃkhya evolution. The *Avyakta* unmanifest of Kapila is the primeval matter. But the Vedānta takes this *Avyakta* to be his intelligent Brahma. From *Avyakta* proceeds *Akāśa* or ether. From this proceeds Vāyu, then Agni, and then water and then the earth. This description of creation occurs both in the Vedic texts of the *Mantras* and Upaniṣads. The elements created out of the Brahma get reabsorbed by him in the reverse order. Thus describing the process of creation the scriptural texts demand an explanation from the *Brahma-Sūtras.* According to the Vaiśeṣika view *Akāśa* or space is eternal or uncreated. It is the substratum of *Śabda* or sound. This Vaiśeṣika doctrine will conflict with ultimate concept of Brahma. There would be two eternals, *Ākāśa* and Brahma. Hence the Vedānta school is constrained to show that the Vaiśeṣika doctrine of infinite space is unique and they must show that space is created by Brahma. According to Sāṁkhya the starting point of evolution is *Acetana Prakṛti.* The Vedānta school emphasises the psychical nature of Buddhi and *Ahaṃkāra.* But these according to Sāṁkhya are derived from Acetana *Prakṛti.* Brahman-sūtras therefore rightly criticise that Sāṃkhya view of deriving Cetana entities from *Acetana*

Prakṛti. Buddhi and ahaṃkāra are therefore considered as the manifestation of Brahma or Sat. Similarly the Nyāya and Vaiśeṣika view of self is rejected by *Brahma-Sūtras.* Nyāya-sūtras maintain that the individual souls are uncreated. In this respect the Vedāntic doctrine conflicts with Nyāya and Vaiśeṣika views. Though the Vedānti accepts the uncreated and eternal nature of individual selves in a way still he does not recognise the substantiality thereof. Individuality is an illusion for him. Birth and death, creation and destruction of the individual souls are all due to the body. The self-in-itself is beyond birth and death. Its essence is *Cetana.* Hence the view of the *Brahama-sūtras* is different from that of the Vaiśeṣika school according to which consciousness is an accidental quality of the self brought about by its contact with manas or mind.

The doctrine of the size of the *Ātman* is next criticised in the Brahmasūtras. The atomic size of *Ātman* is as old as the Upaniṣad. This doctrine is accepted by the Vaiśeṣikas. The Brahma-sūtras reject this view in spite of the Upaniṣadic authority. To speak of the size of soul or *ātman* is to confound its nature with body. The categories of spatial magnitude are inadequate to describe the soul which is intrinsically of the nature of thought and the spiritual entity may be spoken of either as an atom or as an infinite. It may be both infinitesimal as well as infinite. The individual self is also a *Kartā* or agent. He is able to act and thus he is able to produce karma. Being the author of *karma* he is obliged to enjoy the fruits thereof, *Kartā* must be *bhoktā* also. In this respect the Vedantic view is different from the Sāṃkhyan system where Puruṣa is merely the enjoyer and not an actor. But when we examine more closely the Vedāntic View the *prima facie* objection disappers. Activity is not the intrinsic quality of the soul. Activity is due to its accidental conjunction with the body. In the technical language of Vedānta *Ātmā* becomes a kartā only because of the physical conditions or Upādhi. On account of the same upādhi it becomes a *bhoktā.* Thus action and enjoyment are both due to exraneous conditions. The so-called *upādhis* are constituted by the several indriyas or sense-organs. In this respect many docrines are common to Sāṃkhya and the Vedānta. The activity of the individual self though appearing as a difference between the two schools does not constitute a real difference. The activity is explained away ultimately in the *sūtras*. Activity in the individual is really due to Brahma himself or the *Antaryāmī*. Hence the individual soul is not a free agent. He acts because of the Iśvara in him. But this control exercised by Iśvara is assumed to be entirely consistent with the *karmas* of the individual. The inference of an Iśvara is not an instance of an arbitrary act. He is himself determined by the karmas of the individual self.

The third chapter of Brahma-sutras contains the same topic about the soul. Transmigration is taken up. The soul retains its manas and sūkṣma śarīra after death. Hence it is not free from *Upādhi*. It is still subject to decay and death. It is still tied to the wheel of *Saṁsāra*. After death it may have its sojourn in different lokas. But nevertheless the individual must come back to the world because it is from here that it has to obtain final liberation.

A discussion of Dreams and Hallucinations—The doctrine of the four stages of the Self mentioned in the Upaniṣads finds a place here. The two kinds of knowledge are; absolute and relative *Parāvidyā* and *Aparāvidyā*. The lower knowledge or *aparāvidyā* refers to the sacrifice and it is supposed to be related to Saguṇa Brahma whereas the higher knowledge leads to *Nirguṇa Brahma*. The last and fourth chapter lead to *Mokṣa*. The two *Vidyās* lead to two different paths. The lower associated with worship of *Iśvara* leads to Svarga whereas the higher one resting upon the contemplation of *Nirguṇa Brahma* leads to Self Realisation and identification with Brahma. There is no distinction between the individual and the absolute. The upādhis being eliminated, the conditions being destroyed, the individual self finds the absolute.This is known as *Mukti*. It is direct immediate realisation of the Self, whereas the former path through lower knowledge may ultimately lead to Mukti though not directly and immediately. The realisation of the self and the consequent liberation is brought about by *Samyagdarśana*, the true path. There is true knowledge of the self. It is the state of perfect *Nirvāṇa*. All qualities have withered away from Brahma. It is *nirguṇa, nirviśeṣa*. Thus it is qualityless and formless. He is beyond description—*anirvacanīya*. Thus ends the *Brahma-sūtras* indicating the true nature of ultimate reality—the unconditioned Brahma.

Saṅkara and Vedāntism—Saṅkara represents a stage in the development of Vedāntism. He lived about the 8th century, a contemporary of Kumārila Bhaṭṭa, a student of Govinda, who was a disciple of Gauḍapāda. Śaṅkara's Vedāntism is expressed in his great commentaries on the Upaniṣads as well as *Brahma-Sūtras*. His advaita is the logical outcome of Gauḍapāda's advaitism. It is most influential among the current schools of Indian thought. In this introduction to the great *Bhaṣya* on the *Brahma-Sūtras* he says "It is a matter not requiring any proof that the object and subject whose respective spheres are the notions of Thou and Ego and which are opposed to each other as light and darkness. The two cannot be identified. Hence it follows that it is wrong to superimpose on the subject the attributes of object and *vice versa*." Thus he starts with a sufficient warning that the subject and object are quite distinct and they should not be confounded with each other. He warns against the suprimposition of attributes—*Adhyāsa*. The subject should not be associated with the attributes of the object, nor the object with those of subject. The two are distinct in kind. One is a *cetana* entity and the other an acetana thing. Śaṅkara starts just where Sāṁkhya started. There also *Cetana Puruṣa* is different from *acetana Prakṛti*. Again the starting point of modern thought in Europe was the same. Descartes started with the distinction between the thinking thing and the extended thing. Yet by an inscrutable logic adopted by both Descartes and Śaṅkara the goal reached by them is fundamentally different from the starting point. Cartesianism ends in Spinozistic monism where the ultimate substance engulfs all things, *Cetana* and *Acetana* within itself. And similarly Śaṅkara ends with an all-devouring absolute which could not brook by its side any other entity. Śaṅkara in the same introductory passage suggests that this *Adhyāsa* is a common vice of our experience and is due to our ignorance or *avidyā*. The only way to get rid of it is by *Vidyā* or knowledge. Thus *Adhyāsa* or mutual confusion of self and nonself is the result of ignorance. It is on ignorance that all the duties enjoined in the scriptures are based. Hence the doctrine of *Pramāṇas* includes perception and inference. Several Vedic texts enjoining various religious duties all have for their objects the world which is the resultant of the *avidyā* or ignorance. The world of objective reality is thus due to ignorance and even the Vedic rites and injunctions are not excepted. These have no value for one who possesses real knowledge. Distinctions of caste. status in society, etc. are all due to *adhyāsa*. The conception of Vedic Dharma has meaning only with reference to *Adhyāsa*, accidental conjunction of the true self with the extraneous caste, birth, etc. But for this false conception Vedic Dharma could have no meaning and no validity for Dharma pertains to *Varṇa*, which in turn depends upon the body and not upon the soul. Because of the false identity between soul and body we speak of one as a Brahmin or a Kṣatriya. These attributes are true only of the body and yet are falsely associated with the self. Thus Saṅkara not only indicates the truth that the self and the environment are distinct but also suggests that the confusion and false identity is due to avidyā. From a thinker who emphasised the danger of this philosophical error we should naturally expect consistently a system of philosophy strictly maintaining the opposites. On the other hand, Śaṅkara offers just the reverse. He dismisses the distinction between self and non-self as unreal and unphilosophical. What is the nature of the external world according to Śaṅkara? Gauḍapāda already compared it to a dream. Śaṅkara accepts the same without question. The diversity and objectivity of the world of things and persons are all illusory. The objective world around is but the *māyā* of the juggler, the juggler in this case being *Atman* himself. Since the juggler himself is not a victim to his own illusion, so the highest self is not affected by the world-illusion, The whole of the external world is but the manifestation of Brahma or *Atman*. The substance of which this world is constituted being *Centana* is genuinely akin to dreams. That it is a dream will not be evident to us so long as we are dreaming, so long as there is *avidyā*. When we wake from this dream to another world then the dream-world will vanish. When the individual wakes up into highest selfhood, then he will understand the dreamlike illusory nature of his former experience. When he rids himself of over-powering *avidyā* the multiplicity and objective will automatically disappear.

Is the individual *ātman* real according to Śaṅkara? The individual self shares the same fate as the objective world. All the other Indian systems of thought recognised individual *ātman* to be eternal and uncreated. But in the hands of Śaṅkara the individual soul dwindles into a shadow of a higher reality. In the passages emphasising his own advaita view he rejects the panthetistic view according to which the objective world and the individual self can be real and yet subsisting in the same universal. Several passages in the Upaniṣads compare the Brahma to a tree and the individuals to various branches thereof. Unity and multiplicity are both real in organic life. So is the ocean though the waves are many. So the clay is the same though the pots are many. These Upaniṣadic passages do not and need not necessarily imply the doctrine of the illusoriness of the world and individual selves. But such an interpretation Śaṅkara does not want. He sternly rejects that as erroneous. He emphasises the unity as absolute. If the phenomenal world and individual souls are unreal, then it would be against the practical notions of ordinary life. Such consequences are not disconcerting to Śaṅkara. Such objections do nto damage his position, because the entire complex of phenomenal existence is still true to a person who has not reached the true knowledge and realised his true self. As long as one is in ignorance the reality of the world and self is vouchsafed for him. He may behave as if these were true and his life will not be affected by the higher philosophical doctrine. Śaṅkara's self is thus an absolute—a sort of Parmenidean absolute—eternal and unchanging.

What has Śaṅkara to say about the several passages in the Vedic scriptures which speak of the creation and evolution of the world? If the world of concrete reality is illusory the Vedic doctrines of creation would have no meaning. This objection he wards off with the remark that the creating qualities of Brahma depend on the evolution of the germical principles *Nāma* and *Rūpa*. The fundamental truth that we maintain is that the creation, destruction and sustenance of the world all proceed from an omniscient and omnipotent principle and not from an unintelligent *Pradhāna*. While maintaining absolute unity or Advaita of self how can the above be maintained? The longing of the self—the name and form are the figments of Nescience. These are not to be either as being the same or different from it. The germs of the entire phenomenal world is called in the *Śruti, Māyā* or Illusion, *Śakti* or Power, *Prakṛti* or Nature. Different from these is the omniscient world. Hence the Lord depends upon the limiting adjuncts of *Māyā* and *Rūpa,* the products of the *avidyā* out of which *Īsvara* creates the world. He being a creator, His omniscience and omnipotence all depend on the limitations due to those very adjuncts whose nature is *avidyā.* From these passages extracted from *Śaṅkara Bhāṣya* we have an idea of Śaṅkara's philosophy. Ultimate reality is undivided and undivisible unity same as Upaniṣadic Brahma. The several Vedic gods are but fractional aspects of this. Śaṅkara wants the reader not to confound his system with the Vedic theology. He clears away *adhyāsa* or error. His system is a streneous attempt at an accurate definition of *ātman.* Through a very skilful dialectic all the qualities of the external world are shown to be alien to Brahma. Spatiality, objectivity, colour, sound, etc. all are with a psychological insight shown to be non-spiritual. By this process of elimination the essential nature of ātman is clearly defined as *Ātman*. It is the only thinking thing, *Cetana dravya*. Thinking is not merely an attribute of the Self. Self is thought. *Ātman* is Cit. Having gone thus far Śaṅkara is tied down to a philosophical doctrine which appears to be inconsistent with his own standpoint and also with thought and general tradition. Such a result is probably due to the following reasons. The Upaniṣadic writers spoke of the Brahma as the spiritual essence, the leaven which leavens all things. In these passages the doctrine of *ātman* exactly corresponds to Cartesian thinking substance. The Upaniṣadic passages did not negate the reality of the phenomenal world. When Śaṅkara took up the doctrine he was confronted with a difficulty. Śaṅkara could not accept the naive Upaniṣadic pantheism. He wants a clear definition of *ātman*. This naturally widened the gulf between subject and object. While these according to Upanisadic writers had vague common substratum. Not satisfied with this philosophic vagueness Saṅkara wanted to shift reality to the side of the subject or Cit. Hence Śaṅkara not only finds *ātman* identical with Cit but it is also identical with existence or Sat. If the Brahma is the soul and if the soul is the Brahma then the Sat must be Cit-existence and thought must be identical. If existence and thought are absolutely identical then anything other than thought will be unreal or *Asat*. The objective world is not Cit or thought. Hence it cannot be real or *Sat*. Śaṅkara is compelled to propound the doctrine of the unreality of the objective world. What is the justification for such a conclusion. There is no doubt he is supported by certain Upaniṣadic passages as well as by some of his predecessors like Gauḍapāda. But we have to remember that many Upaniṣadic passages that declare the external world as unreal do so only metaphorically and comparatively. Thus Upaniṣadic doctrine compares with the Cartesian doctrine of gradation. The ultimate substance has the maximum of reality whereas man has less of that. But with Śaṅkara it is otherwise. For him a thing must be Sat or an Asat. To be real, a thing must be *cit* and what is not *Cit* must necessarity be *Asat.* Thus after establishing the reality of ātman and the illusoriness of the rest Śaṅkara is confronted with an extraordinary difficulty to reconcile his philosophy with the common-sense view on the one hand and the traditional Vedic religion on the other. He manages this by his distinction between *Vyāvahārika* and *Pāramārthika* points of view. For all practical purposes and for the ordinary affairs of religion the world may be taken as real though philosophically it is no more than the phantom of a deluded personality. Many Vedāntins bring in the parallel of Kant who also has a duality. The world is empirically real but transcendentally ideal. But we should protest against such a comparison. For Kant recognises the so-called thing-in-itself which is the ultimate source. The phenomenal world is the resultant of the interaction between thing-in-itself and Ego-in-itself—the one supplies the stuff and the other the form. That is one of the reasons why Kant protests against Berkeley and wanted to keep his philosophy entirely different from that. Saṅkara's advaitism is fundamentally different from Kant's phenomenonalism. He is more akin to Fichte's. Even this resemblance is superficial for the monistic idealism of Fichte is only a metaphysical explanation of moral value. According to Fichte it is only a metaphysical explanation of moral value. According to Fichte the world of objective reality is a stage or an arena created by the Ego for its own moral exercise. Moral value is the pivot on which Fichte's monism revolves. But for Saṅkara all these values have reference to human life and human personality and therefore must be relegated to the realm of illusions from the higher point of views. In his own words "The external world as well as individual personality are mayā, asat, nothing else."

Śaṅkara and the doctrin of Māyā—Speaking of the

External world Śaṅkara says it is all *māyā* or illusion and yet he with other Vedāntins repudiates the doctrine of Buddhism that the external world is purely psychical and as such has no substantiality of its own. What is the significance of this paradoxical attitude? According to the Sāṅkhyan doctrine as to the origin and nature of the world the External world is evolved out of *Prakṛti* which being opposed to *Puruṣa* is *Acetana*. It is more or less similar to the modern scientific 'Matter' Besides this *Prakṛti* Sāṁkhya postulates the existence of the *Puruṣas*. Now for the Vedāntin everything existing is the manifestation of Brahma. The Brahma being *Cetana* entity it is not difficult to derive individual souls thereform. But the Vadāntin derives the external world also from the same. But the external world is an *acetana* entity and is therefore opposed to thought. Hence it cannot be easily derived from Brahma. Śaṅkara certainly has recognised the fundamental difference between the two *Cetana* and *Acetana* and warns the reader against confusion. Yet he wants to logically maintain that every thing living and non-living is derived from the same Brahma. He tries to reconcile the two irreconcilable doctrines. First he maintains that the subject is quite independent of the object and the two have nothing in common and that all ills of life are due to confusion between the two. Secondly he wants to show that there is only one existence ultimately, the real and that all else is purely derivative. If he is successful in establishing the former doctrine (the distinction between the subject and object) he cannot at the same time maintain the latter. The actual result is he introduces a sort of make-believe reconciliation. The objective world is something derived from *māyā*. *Māyā* is the substantial and constitutive of the external world. The stuff of which objective world is made is variously described as Māyā *Prakṛti* and *Pradhāna*. He thus introduces Sāṁkhyan terminology in order to emphasise its distinction from *Puruṣa*. Pursuing this line of thought he ought to have got the conclusion that the external world is constituted by a substance fundamentally distinct from and incompatible with self or Brahma. This would have landed him in a dualism which he streneously tries to avoid. Thus the problem with him was to retain the Sāṅkhyan dualism just to emphasise the distinction between the subject and object and at the same time to maintain Vedāntic monism. In this attempt at a compromise his language becomes ambiguous and his own attitude wavers between Dualism and Monism. He satisfied himself by introducing two kinds of existence or *Sat* corresponding to *Puruṣa* and *Prakṛti* and yet these two kinds of *Sat* he wants to derive from the Cetana Brahma. Beyond the Brahma there could be no existence, he being the only *Sat* as well as the only *Cit.* Hence the *Prakṛti* which Śaṅkara requisition to explain the external world is not only *acit,* non-thought, but also *asat*—non-real. Being *asat* inasmuch as it is distinct from Brahma, it must be identical with mere nothing and yet it must be substantial enough to be the basis of objective world. It is such an impossible function assigned to *Māyā* by Śaṅkara. He cannot condemn it altogether to be nothing for he expects real work out of it and so far it must have some causal potency. But on this account he dare not recognise its reality lest it should set up an imperium in imperio a rival claimant to the throne of Brahma. Therefore Śaṅkara relegates *Māyā* to the metaphysical purgatory where it is expected to live the life of something midway between absoulte being and absolute nothing. What he further means by this curious amalgam of something-nothing we do not clearly appreciate. It is because of this precarious reality of *Māyā* that he is able to make his readers believe that in his monism the objective reality maintains a greater dignity than assigned to it by the Buddhists. In short to avoid the *śūnyavāda* Śaṅkara invents the impossible doctrine of *Māyā* which lends plausibility to his system which would otherwise be untenable and also indistinguishable from Buddhistic nihilism. It was because of this indistinguishability between Buddhism and advaitism that Indian critics condemned advaita as Buddhistic nihilism in camouflage and called Śaṅkara a Pracchanna

Bauddh, a bauddha in disguise.

Brahma : Sat as well as Cit, Existence and Intelligence, but for Vedāntin it is something more. It is not merely the substratum of the concrete world, it also stands for the transcendental goal of life. It stands for the other world to which every Indian thinker looks forward. It is that higher reality which the Indian aspires to as a haven from the ocean of *Saṁsāra*, a place of rest from the toils of transmigration. It corresponds to Buddistic *Nirvāṇa*, the *Samādhi* of the Yogin, the Liberated Puruṣa of the Sāṁkhyas and the God Īśvara of Nyāya Vaiśeṣikas. If it is to be the negation of the ennui of *Saṁsāra* to be the end of the misery of concrete life, to be the place from where there is no return, it must embody in itself something unique and that is absent in the world of *Saṁsāra*, an unalloyed and unchanging Bliss which knows not its opposite. The Brahma therefore besides Sat and *Cit* is *Ānanda* as well. It represents that transcendental bliss which no man has tasted here and which everyone is entitled to have if he walketh the path of liberation. Such a transcendental bliss is entirely different from the ephermeral pleasure of the world. Else it would not be sought after by the wise. Hence the Brahma must also be *Ānanda*, Bliss or Joy. This absolute reality Sat *Cit Ānanda* is the ultimate concept of Vedāntism. It not only serves as the metaphysical cause of things existing, but also the end of things. Climbing the pinnacle of Metaphysical monism Śaṅkara finds it hard to recognise the claims of ordinary mortals in his system. He cuts the Gordian knot by invoking the aid once again of the doctrine of the distinction between the relative and the absolute points of view. There is no justification for the demands of either religion or morality in an absolute monism. In the ratified atmosphere of monism neither morality nor religion can breathe and live. The inevitable conclusion of his logic may not be realised by the ordinary man nor accepted by the orthodox scholar. The Vedic scholars have faith in the injunctions of the Vedas and may still believe in the beneficial effect of sacrifice. The unsophistical man of the religion associates with absolute reality, the object of his religious adoration and worship and maintains that to be the fountain head of all good and valuable. The metaphorical conception of Brahma, therefore, must live side by side with popular religion and must live in accordance with Vedic ritualism. Śaṅkara manages to satisfy all these demands by postulating the fictitious deity of a lower Brahma who may be considered real from the practical and relative point of view though he cannot hide his real inanity from the vision of the enlightened. The ordinary man may continue his traditional worship, the orthodox Vaidika may perform his usual sacrifies quite unperturbed on the assumption that there is an object of devotion and worship in his *Īśvara.* In this matter, Śaṅkara seems to take a lesson from the Mīmāṁsaka teacher and lets alone the traditional ritualism unhampered by metaphysical speculation. It is a peculier mentality the like of which we have in Hume. After proving the unsubstantiality of human personality and the external world Hume exclaims that the world will go on, neverthless, as if these things were quite real. This kind of estrangement between life and metaphysics, life getting on in spite of metaphysics, would only establish the undeniable truth that life is more than logic. To allow concrete life to exist by sufference, to recognise its reality from the *vyāvahārika* point of view may, instead of proving the reality of the concrete world, really establish the bankruptcy of the underlying Metaphysics.

Jainism, its age and its tenets

The term Jainism which means faith of a Jaina is derived from the world Jina which means the conqueror or the victorious. Jina means who conquers the five senses, destroys all the *karmas* and attains Omniscience or *Sarvajñahood.* The person who performs tapas or *yoga* attains such a self-realisation and omniscient knowledge or *kevalajñāna.* After attaining self-realisation and after acquiring Omniscience, the Jina spends the rest of his time in *Dharmaprabhāvanā* or preaching the *Dharma* to the mass of human beings. Not satisfied with his own self-realisation, he engages himself in the noble task of helping his fellow-beings with his message of *Dharma* which would enable the ordinary mortals to reach the *summum bonum* of life and attain the same spiritual status of perfection which he himself has acquired. Because of this noble task of showing the path of spiritual realisation or *Mokṣamārga*, Jina is also called Tīrthaṅkara. This term Tīrthaṅkara means one who helps human beings to cross the ocean of *Saṁsāra* by providing them with a vessel to sail with in the form of *Dharma*. Jinadharma is the boat which is provided for the human beings for the purpose of crossing the ocean of *Saṁsāra* and because of this noble task of helping the mankind Jina is also called Tīrthaṅkara. The divine personality Jina, who by his act of benevolence is called Tīrthaṅkara is therefore called *Arhanta* which means one worthy of adoration and worship. *Arhat Parameṣṭhī* is therefore the Lord worshipped by all the Jains. He is represented by a pratibimba or image which is installed in a Caityālaya or a Jain temple built for the purpose. The pratibimba is always of the form of a human being because it represents the Jina or the Tīrthaṅkara who spent the last portion of his life on earth in the noble task of proclaiming to the world *Mokṣamārga* or the path to salvation. The idol will be either in a standing posture or *Kāyotsarga* or in the posture of *Padmāsana*-sitting—technically called *Palyaṅkāsana*. Whether standing or sitting it represents the Divine Lord absorbed in the self-realisation as a result of *Tapas* or *Yoga*. Therefore the facial expression would reveal the intrinsic spiritual bliss as a result of self-realisation. People who worship the Jina in this form installed in a Jinālaya or the Jain temple and who follow the religious tenets proclaimed by the Jina are called the Jainas and their religion is Jainism.

The same faith is also designated by the term *Ārhatamata*,

which means religion followed by *Ārhatas* or Jainas, since the term *Ārhata* means one who follows the religion of the *Arhat Parameṣṭhī*. The terms Jina, Tīrthaṅkara and *Arhat Parameṣṭhī* all refer to the divine person or *Sarvajña* who lived in the world with his body, and it refers to the period after attaining *Sarvajñahood* or Omniscience the last period of the *parinirvāṅa*, when the body is cast away and the self resumes its own intrinsic pure spiritual nature and it becomes *Paramātmā* or *Siddha*. This is the last stage of spiritual development and is identical with the Self completely liberated or *Muktajīva* or the self which attained *Mokṣa*. This Siddhaparameṣṭhī is identical with the Vedāntic conception of *Parabrahma* or *Paramātmā*, which terms are also used by the Jaina thinkers. This *Siddhasvarūpa* or *Paramātmā Svarūpa* is without body—*Aśarīra*, and without form—*Arūpa*. Hence its nature can be understood only by yogic contemplation for which the individual must be fit and highly qualified. Ordinary people who are not endowed with the capacity of realising the nature of the pure self *Paramātmā* or *Siddha Parameṣṭhī* whose pratibimba is installed in Jaina temples for worship for the ordinarly people who were expected to concentrate their attention on the image of Jina or *Arhat Parameṣṭhī* corresponds to the Vedāntic attitude, which while recognising that the highest state of spiritual development is represented by the *Parabrahma*, provides for the ordinary man something lower than this as the object of worship, or what is called the popular or *Vyāvahārika* point of view. As a matter of fact, it may be said without contradiction that this distinction between *vyāvahārika* and *pāramārthika* points of view was adopted by the great commentator Śaṅkara who took the suggestion from the earlier Jaina thinkers, especially Srī Kundakunda. This term *Siddha*, since it implies the complete destruction of all the karmas which enshroud the intrinsic purity of the self is also called *Nirgrantha*, who is devoid of all attachment. The term Kandazhi which occurs in the Tamil work Tholkpya means the same thing as *Siddha* or the self which is completely liberated from all the shackles of karmas. Though the temple-worship is associated with *Arhat Parameṣṭhī* or Tīrthaṅkars, Jainas have not forgotten the fact that the *Siddha* represents the highest spiritual development. Hence the practice of silent salutation, *Namaḥ Siddhebhyaḥ* or *Siddham Namaḥ* is a common practice among Jaina whenever they begin any good work either literary or of ordinary kind. Probably this practice of beginning with adoration of *Siddhaṁ Namaḥ* or *Namaḥ Siddhebhyaḥ* was prevalent among the non-Jainas also especially in South India where the people when they begin their daily work in school are taught to start with this salutation *Siddhaṁ Namaḥ*.

The Age of Jainism—There is a good deal of incorrect views prevalent among even educated people as to the age of Jainism. It is an unfortunate fact that Indians had to learn their history from foreign scholars. Foreign writers with incorrect and insufficient knowledge of the Indian historical background wrote textbooks on Indian history which provided the historical background, wrote taxtbooks on Indian history which provided the historic information to Indian students in schools. These history text-books were mainly responsible for a good deal of erroneous views prevalent among the educated Indians as to the past history of their land. One of these deplorable errors is the view that Jainism is an off-shoot of Buddhism and Hinduism. This error we are glad to say is no more prevalent among the oriental scholars both in the West and East, though the error persists among the educated Indians whose knowledge of history is not uptodate. The origin of this error is to be found in the fact that the founder of Buddhism Gautama Śākyamuni and Mahāvīra Vardhamāna the last of the Jaina Tīrthaṅkaras were comtemporaries. Buddhistic literature contains references to Mahāvīra and his followers, and similarly Jaina literature composed at time of Mahāvīra contains cross references to the Buddha and his religion. Persons who studied first the Buddhist literature and who had no knowlegde of Jaina scripture came to the hasty conclusion that Jainism must have been a branch of Buddhism. Later on when oriental scholars came to study the subject they corrected their erroneous views and were constrained to call that Jainism must have been earlier than Buddhism. As a matter of fact, the Buddha was a younger contemporary of Lord Mahāvīra. The Buddha himself in his conversation with this friend and disciple Sāriputta, narrates the fact that he himself in his earlier days was adopting Jaina practice of austerity which he had to give up because of the rigorous discipline which he did not like. The date of Mahāvīra's parinirvāṇa, 527 B.C. is accepted as a land-mark in the history of India. According to Cambridge History of India, the 23rd Tīrthaṅkara, Lord Pārśva who lived 220 years prior to Lord Mahāvīra is also considered a historical personage. According to the view Jainism must have been prevalent in India nearly three centuries prior to Gautama Buddha, the founder of Buddhism. Though writers of Cambridge History of India did not go beyond Lord Pārśva, we can point out the fact that Jainism was in existence even prior to this period. The Tīrthaṅkara prior to Lord Pārśva, the 22nd Tīrthaṅkara, according to the Jaina tradition is Lord Ariṣṭanemi, who is said to have attained his *Nirvāṇa* on the Mount Girnār in Junāgaḍha State, which is a place for pilgrimage for the present-day Jainas. This Ariṣṭanemi was a cousin of Śrī Kṛṣṇa of Mahābhārata fame and the name Ariṣṭanemi occurs in Vedic literature as one of the great Ṛṣis. This Jaina tradition circumstantially supported by non-Jaina Vedic literature may also be accepted as having some historical basis. If Śrī Kṛṣṇa of Mahābhārata war is accepted as having some historical basis then we have to accpt the history of Ariṣṭanemi also. According to the Jaina tradition, there were twenty-four Tīrthaṅkaras beginning with Lord Vṛṣabha and ending with Mahāvīra Vardhamāna. Of these the last three may be taken to be personalities of the historic period. The rest are persons of prehistoric age and we need not trouble ourself about their history till we know something more than mere tradition. The first of these Tīrthaṅkara Lord Vṛṣabha who is considered by the Jainas to be responsible for revealing *Ahiṁsā Dharma* for the first time to the world seems to be a very interesting personality. According to the Jaina tradition, he was a hero of the Ikṣvāku family. His father was Nabi mahārāja, the last of the Manus and his mother Mārudevī. Vṛṣabha's period represents a complete change of world conditions. Prior to this the country was called *Bhoga Bhūmi* where the people were satisfied with all their wants by the mere wish through the help of the traditional *Kalpakavṛkṣas*. During the time of Lord Ṛṣabha these happy conditions completely disappeared and the people were in a perplexity as to the way of life which they were expected to carry. Then they all went to Lord Ṛṣabha praying for help. He is said to have consoled them by showing the way of life. He taught them how they could obtain food by tilling the soil, that they should take to agriculture for the production of food, which they could obtain in plenty by their own toil in spite of the fact that the *Kalpakavṛkṣas* disappeared. He taught some other people to carry their agriculture-produce to different people and supply to those that were in need. He again set apart a number of able-bodied men for the purpose of defence. Thus the first social organisation owes its existence to Lord Vṛṣabha who divided the society according to its functions into three groups, agriculturists, traders, and soldiers. After ruling over his kingdom for several years, he abdicated his throne in favour of his son, Lord Bharata and went into the forests to perform tapas. After the practice of tapas for several years he attained *Kevalajñāna* or Omniscience : then he went about from place to place preaching his *Ahiṁsā* dharma to the people of the land, so that they may also have spiritual relief. Thus Lord Ṛṣabha is known among the Jainas as Ādijina, Ādi Bhagavān and so on, This first Tīrthaṅkara's life is repeated verbatim also in non-Jaina Purāṇas, for example the Bhāgavatapurāṇa (V. skandha). The same story is repeated in the Viṣṇupurāṇa and the Vāyupurāṇa also. All these Hindu *purāṇas* maintain that Lord Ṛṣabha preached the doctrine of *Ahiṁsā* after performing yoga for several years. He went about from place to place completely discarding all ornaments and clothes, and hence he was misunderstood by the people to have gone mad. The repetition of this life history of Lord Ṛṣabha in non-Jaina *purāṇas* can only be explained by the fact that at one time when the story was a common property to both Jainas and non-Jainas the hero must have been considered as worthy of worship by all.

According to Jaina tradition when Lord Ṛṣabha attained his *Nirvāṇa* from Mount Kailash, his son and the ruling emperor of the land, Lord Bharata built a temple at the place of *Nirvāṇa* and installed an image of Lord Ṛṣabha for the purpose of worship for himself as well as for the general public. This worship of Lord Ṛṣabha's idol must have been prevalent throughout India from far-off ancient period of the Indian history. That it was so prevalent in ancient India we may infer from certain facts available in the Vedic literature. The Vedas constitute the earliest record available. They form three distinct groups, the Saṁhitāa, the Brāhmaṇas and the Upaniṣads. The Saṁhitās are four in number: The Ṛg Veda, Yajur Veda, Sāma Veda and Atharvaṇa Veda. The Ṛg Veda mantras are uttered for the purpose of invoking the aid of the Vedic Gods. Indra is the most important of the Vedic deities. The religious life of the Āryans in the Ṛg Vedic period centred round the personality of Indra, the Vedic God. His aid is invoked by the Aryans of the Ṛg Vedic period to obtain prosperity in their agriculture and also in their cattle wealth. His aid is also invoked for the purpose of destroying the enemies— the people of the land, who resisted their advance. Thus the Āryans had to encounter opposition from among the people of the land whom they considered their enemies, and who strongly resisted the invading Āryans. The Ṛg Vedic hymns composed with such a back-ground of racial conflicts furnishes us with certain interesting facts as to the life and characteristics of the people of the land who violently opposed the incoming Āryans. These hymns referred to a section of the Ikṣvākus or Puruṣa who were in existence in the land long before the Āryans of Ṛgvedic period came into the scene. These Ikṣvākus are recognised to be of the Āryan race and they are referred to in terms of respect and adoration. This Ikṣvākuvaṁśa otherwise called the Raghuvaṁśa, evidently was an important and a famous ruling dynasty of ancient India, which must have been in existence even prior to the Āryans of the Ṛgvedic period. That this Ikṣvākuvaṁśa otherwise called the Raghuvaṁśa, evidently was an important and a famous ruling dynasty of ancient India, which must have been in existence even prior to the Āryans of the Ṛgvedic period. That this Ikṣvākuvaṁśa was famous is borne out by the fact that most of the ancient Kṣatriya families traced their origin to these Ikṣvākus and even the Śākya clan to which Gautama Buddha belonged claimed its origin from Ikṣvākus. The heroes of this family are celebrated in Kālidāsa's Raghuvaṁśa. According to Kālidāsa, these heros began their life in early childhood as students, then they lived their household lives, after which they completely renounced their worldly attachment and roamed about in the forests performing Tapas or Yoga and then finally discarded their bodies after realisation. This description in full corresponds with the life history of Lord Ṛṣabha, the greatest hero of Ikṣvākus and the first revealer of Ahiṁsā to the world and the importance of tapas or yoga for the purpose of self-realisation. We suggest that this Ṛṣabha cult must have been prevalent even before the advent of the Āryans and the Ṛg-vedic tradition. In support of this thesis we note the following facts revealed by the Vedic literature. The Āryans of Ṛg Vedic period it is stated, were resisted by the people of the land who were called Dasyus. The term Dasyu is interpreted sometimes as an enemy and sometimes as a slave. These two interpretations represent two different stages. First when the people of the land resisted they were called the enemies, and when the enemies were subjected after a military conquest and taken as prisoners and made to work as slaves, the same Dasyus became slaves. Facts that deserve emphasis in this connection are the descriptive terms used by the Āryans to describe these enemies, the people of the land. These Dasyus are described as Ayajña, Anindra, Avrata, Anyavrata and so on. These terms respectively mean those that are opposed to *Yajña*, Indraworship, those that observe a different religious practice, and those that do not practise the religions of the Āryans. From these descriptive terms it is quite clear that the people of the land were deadly against the Vedic institution of *Yajña* or animal sacrifice. Their opposition to the invading Āryans must therefore be due to two factors. The people of the land politically resisted the invading foreigners, and secondly because the people of the land were afraid of the fact that their culture would be destroyed by the invaders whose culture and religion were entirely different from their own. These Dasyus, the people of the land, are also described to have been of dark skin and to have been speaking a different tongue. Therefore they must have been the early Dravidians who were present all over India at the time of the Āryan invasion. After describing the practice of these Dasyus in negative terms, the Vedic literature uses a very significant term to describe their religion. The early Dasyus, the enemies of the Āryans, who were opposed to *Yajñas* and Indra worship were worshippers of Śiśnadeva. This is a very interesting revelation. European oriental scholars translate this term Śiśnadeva as worshippers of Liṅga. The Sanskrit term Siśna is not identical with the Liṅga which is now worshipped by the Śaivites. Śiśna represents the male sex organ whereas the Liṅga designates both Siśna and Yoni. Hence the term Śiśna cannot be interpreted in any way to mean the Liṅga which is a combination of Śiśna and Yoni of phallic worshippers. Therefore the only interpretion that we could have is our theory that the ancient Dasyus who were the people of the land and who resisted the invading Āryans were in the habit of worshipping a nude idol as their God, which can be called consistently as Śiśnadeva. If the prergvedic people of the land had for their worship a nude male image called Śiśnadeva by the Āryans, all the other descriptive terms may fit in with this theory. If you take that this Śiśnadeva worship must have been the characteristic of the Ṛṣabha cult introduced by Lord Ṛṣabha, the first Tīrthaṅkara, and encouraged by his son Bharata in the form of a temple-worship. The excavations of Harappā and Mohenjodaro circumstantially corroborate our theory, because among the discoveries resulting from the excavations we have nude images of a yogi considered to be idols used for worship by the people of the Indus Valley civilisation and the symbol of the bull is found in abundance in coins and seals belonging to that period. Hence it will be consistent to maintain that the religious life of the people of the Indus Valley civilisation must have been associated with the Ṛṣabha cult which must have been prevalent throughout the land from Himalayas down to Cape Comorin and further south in Laṅkā. After some time when the invading Āryans completely conquered the whole of Northern India, the people of the land who were called Dasyus must have withdrawn to the south. viz., to this side of the Vindhya hills. That there must have been such a withdrawal by the people of the land to the South is corroborated by the traditional account both in Jaina purāṅas, and Hindu purāṇas. According to the Jaina tradition the Northern India was completely occupied by five Kṣatriya dynasties, namely, the Ikṣvākuvaṁśa, Harivaṁśa, Kuruvaṁśa. Ugravaṁśa and the Nāthavaṁśa. These five Kṣatriya groups completely occupied the whole of Northern India and the people of the land who are called Vidyādharas, by the Jaina tradition, had to be satisfied with the peninsula to the South of the Vindhyas. These Vidyādharas are represented by two important dynasties of ruling families, one of which was more powerful to which Rāvaṇa the emperor of Laṅkā belonged. The other group was represented by Vāli, Sugrīva and Hanumān. According to Jaina tradition, these Vidyādharas were highly cultured people, in fact more cultured than the rest, and they were specially skilful in applied science, or Vidyās, on account of which they were called Vidyādharas. They had the privilege of travelling in air by some sort of aerial vehicles or vimānas which they were skilful enough to build for themselves. Since they were skilful people of very high culture, the ruling chiefs of the Ikṣvāku family very often entered into matrimonial alliances with those Vidyādhara families, in fact, the Jaina tradition mentions that Lord Ṛṣabha himself married a Vidyādhara princess by whom he had his son Bharata, the first ruler of the land and who gave his name to the land, Bhāratavarṣa. These Vidyādhara rulers who were designated as Rākṣasas by their political enemies, Āryans, are recognised to be highly cultured by the Āryans themselves. The Jaina tradition makes these Vidyādharas followers of Ṛṣabha cult, strictly practising *Ahiṁsā Dhrama* and sternly opposed to Vedic Yajña. There is an interesting chapter in Jaina Rāmāyaṇa, Padmapuāṇa of the Jainas, which narrates the life story of Śrī Rāma. The chapter refers to the elaborate preparations made by one Kṣatriya prince called Marutha for the purpose of Vedic sacrifice. The chapter is called *Maruthayajñadhvaṁsa sarga*. These preparations for the performance of *yajña* are made on the borders of Rāvaṇa's territory. Nārada who happens to pass by that way observes these elaborate preparations. According to the Jainas, Nārada is considered to be a champion of *Ahiṁsā*. He advised the Kṣatriya prince Marutha not to perform the sacrifice. Nārada's advice was rejected. He then goes to Rāvaṇa straight and informs him of the vast preparations made by a Kṣatriya prince quite in violation of Ahiṁsā. Rāvaṇa sends a few officers to stop these preparations. These officers were sent away unceremoniously by the prince Marutha. But Rāvaṇa himself appeared in person officially with his soldiers. Then Marutha confessed that he was instructed by the Vedic priests to perform this *yāga*, though he was not very well informed about this. Then Rāvaṇa rebukes him, stops the preparations, releases all the animals intended for sacrifice and threatens the priest. Then Marutha was initiated to the practice of *Ahiṁsā Dharma* and he was made to give a solemn promise that he would be no more a party to animal sacrifice or *yajña*. This story found in Jaina Rāmāyaṇa clearly indicates that the Vidyādharas since they were followers of *Ahiṁsā* cult were sternly opposed to any performance of *Yāga* within their borders. Perhaps that explains why according to the Vālmiki Rāmāyaṇa, the Rakṣasas were always bent upon preventing the performance of yāgas and whenever an attempt is made to perform yāga the parties had to seek the aid of military protection before they could carry on the ceremony. This is illustrated in the Rāmāyaṇa where Viśvāmitra takes the military aid of the royal princes, Rāma and Lakṣmaṇa, before he starts the rituals. Thus the circumstantial evidence goes to support the theory that the people of the land were all followers of Ṛṣabha cult and they were staunchly defending their cult of *Ahiṁsā* whenever there was an interference from outside. This theory implies that even before the advent of the Ṛṣabha cult of *Ahiṁsā* is further borne out by an evidence supplied by the later Brāhmaṇas and the Upaniṣads. When the Āryans of the Ṛgvedic period prominently settled in Northern India, their Vedic culture of *Yāgas*, must have been prevalent side by side with the religious practice associated with the earlier Ṛṣabha cult. The royal families representing the Ikṣavāku clan and other clans must have been driven towards the East by the conquering hoards of the Ṛgvedic Āryans who came and settled in the Punjab. The earlier Āryan families who adopted the *Ahiṁsā* cult of Lord Ṛṣabha must have been opposed to this new cult of the Āryans. Therefore we have a reference to the Prācyadeśa, the Eastern countries, in the Brāhmaṇas. The most important of these the Śatapathabrāhmaṇa refers to the people of these Prācyadeśas which include, Kāśī, Kośala, Videha and Magadha as Āryabhraṣṭas. The orthodox Brāhmins of Kurupañcāladesa are advised not to travel in the Eastern countries. Because the corrupt Āryans completely gave up the performance of *yāga*;

they adopted an opposite *Dharma* altogether. They hold that not- performing *yāga* is their *Dharma* and performing *yāga* is a contradiction to Dharma, or Adharma. Further these people of the Eastern countries do not recognise social eminence of the priests. Socially the Kṣatriyas claim to be superior to the Brāhmaṇa priests. Hence the orthodox priests, if they travel in the Eastern countries will not be respected according to their social status. These reasons given in the Śatapathabrāhmaṇa clearly indicate that the people of the Eastern countries of Gangetic valley were all opposed to the Vedic culture of the *yāga*, and were followers of *Ahiṁsā Dharma*. The intellectual leaders of the Eastern countries of the Gangetic valley were all Kṣatriyas. All the twenty four Tīrthaṅkaras of the Jainas and the founder of Buddhism Gautama Buddha all claimed to be Kṣatriyas; that the Kṣatriyas were champions of Ahiṁsā Dharma that they were opposed to vedic sacrifice, *yāga* championed by the priests of the Kurupañcāla countrey is further corroborated by the Upaniṣadic literature which forms the Vedānta or last form of vedic literature. When we turn to Upaniṣadic literature we observe a complete change in the intellectual attitude towards life and problems. Prior to that the whole of Vedic culture is *Svargakāma Yajetavyaḥ*—if you want happiness in *Svarga* you must perform sacrifice. But when we turn to the Upaniṣadic period the idea is entirly different. We notice that the intellectual leaders of the Upaniṣadic period do not attach any importance to the utilitarian idea. Prosperity here and *Svarga*-happiness hereafter are considered both as worthless acquisitions. One is advised to look to something far more valuable than this. That Naciketa rejects the blessings of prosperity offered by Yama, that Maitreyī, the wife of Yājñavalkya refused the offer by her husband of all his riches show clearly that the ideal of the Upaniṣadic principle is far higher than that presented by the previous age of the Vedic culture. Spiritual *yāga* is considered to be inferior. The Upaniṣads emphasise a metaphorical *yāga* of kindling the spiritual fire by yoga in which all the impurities associated with the self are to be burnt for the purpose of self purification and spiritual realisation. The priests of Kurupanñcāla countries throng to the royal courts of the Prācyadeśa with a request to be initiated into this new culture of *Ātmavidyā* which is championed by the Kṣatriya scholars of the land. What is the origin of the new change of the attitude in the Upaniṣadic culture? The only answer that we can think of is the Kṣatriya intellectuals of the Eastern countries of the Gangetic valley staunchly defended their *Ahiṁsā* cult given to them by Lord Ṛṣabha till they were able to convince the priest of Kurupañcāla that their sacrifice was distinctly inferior to this cult of *Ahiṁsā* or *Ātmavidyā.* Thus we have the Jaina tradition fully corroborated by non-Jaina Vedic literature in these three distinct historic groups of the Saṁhitā, the Brāhmaṇas, and the Upaniṣads. These facts supplied by the Vedic literature taken in conjunction with the evidence supplied by the excavations of the Indus valley civilisation will constrain us to believe that the Ṛṣabha cult of *Ahiṁsā* and the practice of tapas or yoga must have been the ancient cult of the Indians throughout the land prevalent even before the advent of the Āryans who sang the hymns of the Ṛgveda. Thus the *Ahiṁsā* cult revealed by Lord Ṛṣabha was the most ancient of the religious cults which must have been prevalent in the Northern India and which must have been the practice in religion of the people of the land at the time of Āryan invasion.

Mokṣa Mārga : What is the *Mokṣamārga* which is peculiar to Jainism? What are its special features? How is it different from the religious principles associated with the other Indian Darśanas. *Samyak-Darśana-Jñana-Cāritrāṇi Mokṣamārgaḥ* : Right faith, right knowledge and right conduct, these three constitute the path to salvation. This is the first *Sūtra* of Umāsvamī's monumental work called *Tattvārtha Sūtra.* The emphasis is laid on all the three only; when all the three characteristics are combined they can constitute to *Mokṣamārga.* Each by itself is imperfect and therefore insufficient. To depend entirely on faith as is maintained by some Hindu Darśana will not lead one to happiness or *Mokṣa*. Similarly *Jñāna* or knowledge alone cannot lead one to happiness. Nor can *Cātritra* by itself, however admirable the conduct be sufficient to lead to the desired goal. Hence faith, knowledge, and cunduct must be presented together by an individual if he is to walk the path of righteousness. Further it is emphasised that these three—faith, knowledge and conduct must be of the right type. Hence it is called right faith, right knowledge and right conduct alone when combined together would constitute the *Mokṣamārga*. Mere faith which is not of the right type will not be founded upon the ultimate nature of reality. Similarly right knowledge and not any other knowledge will constitute the *Mokṣamārga*. Right knowledge will therefore exclude all incorrect attitude and disruption of the nature of reality. Hence that prefix *Samyak* is used in each of the terms. The commentator of the *sūtras* gives an interesting metaphor to bring out the force of the *sūtra*. A person suffering from a disease, say fever, if he desires to cure himself of the disease must have faith in the capacity of the doctor and must know the exact nature of the medicine prescribed by him for his disease and must drink the medicine according to the instructions of the doctor. Mere faith in the doctor will be of no use. Faith in the capacity of the doctor and the knowledge of the nature of the medicine would equally be useless unless the patient takes the medicine. The person who expects to be cured of his disease must not only have faith in the doctor's capacity, and full knowledge of the nature of the medicine but also take the medicine according to the prescription. In this case beings in the world of *Saṁsāra* are assumed to be patients suffering from a spiritual disqualification or disease who desire to get rid of this disease and to attain perfect spiritual health. Thus for the purpose of helping such persons this *Mokṣamārga* is prescribed as a spiritual remedy and the spiritual remedy therefore must be associated with all three characteristics of right faith, right knowledge and right conduct in order to be effective. These three constituent elements of the path to salvation are called *Ratnatraya* or the three jewels. These *Ratnatraya* or the three jewels of the Jaina Dharma should not be confounded with the three jewels of the *Ratnatraya* of the Bauddhas, where they mean three different things—The Buddha, founder of Buddhism and *Dharma*, the message revealed by Buddha, and the Saṅgha, the social federation organised by him. Therefore the three jewels of the Bauddhas are Buddha, Dharma and Saṅgha which are quite different from the Ratnatraya of the Jainas, which constitute the *Mokṣamārga*.

What is *Samyak Darśana* or Right faith? *Samyak Darśana* is defined in the following sūtra :

Tattvārtha Śraddhānaṁ Samyak Darśanam : Faith or belief in the nature of the reality is right faith or *Samyak Darśana.* Belief in the *Tattvas* or the reals as they exist forms the foundation of Jaina faith. What are these Tattvas? Belief in these is emphasised as the important foundation of Jainism. These tattvas or the reals are said to be seven in number. Jīva- the living entity, *Ajīva— the* non-living entity, *Āśrava, Bandha, Saṁvara, Nirjarā* and *Mokṣa. Āśrava* means flow of karmic matter into the nature of self or soul. *Bandha* implies the mixture of the *karmic* matter into the nature of self or soul. *Bandha* implies the mixture of the karmic matter with nature of the soul on account of which the soul loses its intrinsic purity and brilliance. *Saṁvara* represents the act of preventing the inflow of the *karmic* matter, and hence it is the blocking of *Āśrava. Nirjarā* represents the act of destroying the karmic matter which may adhere to the soul. As a result of blocking up the flow of fresh *karmic* matter and destruction of the old *karmic* matter clinging to the soul you have the emergence of the soul in its pure form, free from *karmic upādhis*, whose state is represented by the term *Mokṣa.* These are the several fundamental realities proclaimed by the Jaina Darśana, which every Jaina is expected to believe. Of these the first two— Jīva and *Ajīva*, the living and the non-living, form the primary categories and the others are only secondary. The third and fourth represent the association of the first and the second. The fifth and the sixth represent partial dissociation of the first (*Jīva*) from the second *Ajīva* or matter. The seventh represents the complete dissociation of the first from the second.

Before examining these categories in detail let us explain some of the fundamental philosophical doctrines associated with Jaina Darśana. Let us take first the doctrine of Sat or Reality. The definition of Sat given in Jaina Metaphysics is that it is a permanent reality in the midst of change of appearance and disappearance. *Utpāda-vyaya-dhrauvya-yuktaṁ sat.* This conception of reality is peculiar to Jainism. The only paralle that we can think of is the Hegelian conception of reality in Western thought. The real existence is not merely the state of static and permanent existence. An existing reality in order to maintain its permanent and continued existence must necessarily undergo change in the form of appearance and disappearance. This may appear to be apparently a paradox. But when we appreciate the significance of this description of reality, it may be found that it is the most accurate description of reality in the actual state of things. Everywhere we find growth and development and this is manifest in the organic world. Whether we look to the world of plants or of animals, the field of botany or biology, this description of reality is clearly borne out. Let us confine ourselves to the life history of a plant. It begins itself in the form of a seed. The seed which is planted in the soil must necessarily break the shell and sprout out. That is the first step in its attempt to grow. If the seed remains as a seed without this change there will be no growth and no plant; the seed will be condemned as a lifeless one. Hence it is necessary that it should change its own form and assume a new form which is the necessary stepping stone for the growth of the plant. This sprouting seed must further undergo change and some portion of it must come out seeking the sunlight and another portion of it must go down into the earth in order to obtain nourishment from the soil. That portion of the sprouting which goes down into the soil will undergo enormous changes into the root system, all engaged in acquiring nourishment for the mother plant. Similarly the portion that shoots up into the air and sunlight will undergo enormous change, of sprouting out in tendrils and leaves finally resulting in branches and stem of the plant all engaged in the task of procuring nourishment with the help of sunlight, from the chemicals available in the atmosphere, such as carbondioxide. At every stage thus we find change, the old leaves being shed off and the new sprouts coming in. This seems to be the general law of Nature by which life maintains its identity and permanence, because without this change life will cease to be life and organism will die. What is true of a plant is equally true with the life history of an animal. The life history of a mammal or a man may follow the same principle with similar process of growth, starting with a single cell organism with fecundated ovum in passing through the multiplicity of cells constituting a mass undergoing elaborate anatomical change within the uterus of the mother till the time of the birth, when it comes out as fully constituted body waiting to grow further in the outer environment. Here also the same principle is maintained, i.e., identity in the midst of change-appearance and disappearance, the old disappearing and the new appearing in the organism. Every part of the physiological system of the body of the child will thus undergo change till the child grows into an adult and a full-grown individual. It is this Law of Nature that is observed to be prevalent in the world of reality. That is implied in the definition of reality given above. The apparent paradox thus reveals the intrinsic nature of reality and we find it illustrated everywhere in the world of nature. It is this very same principle that is associated with the great German philosopher Hegel, who spoke of the dialectical nature of reality, dialectic implying thesis passing to its opposite, the antithesis, and both the opposites being comprehended under the general principle of synthesis. What are apparent contradictions are but two essential aspects of the same higher reality which comprehends within itself two conflicting principles. The general biological conception of life in the form of metabolism may be taken to be a fit illustration of this Hegelian dialectic, as well as the Jain conception of Reality—sat. Life activity or what is called Metabolism implies conflicting process of anabolism and catabolism which are the two necessary aspects of life-activity and the healthy balance between these two conflicting activities is the general characteristic of metabolism. In this respect Jaina conception of reality is different from the other Indian Darśanas, because the other Darśanas, some of them, would emphasises permanency alone as the nature of reality; while some others, would emphasise change alone as the characteristic of reality. Vedāntism may be taken to be an example of a philosophical system which emphasises permanency as the characteristic of reality and dismisses change as sheer illusion. Similarly Buddhistic *Kṣaṇikavāda*—the theory of momentary change, over-emphasises change to the utter neglect of the underlying permanency. The one sided emphasis either of permanency or change is rejected by Jaina thinkers who condemn such systems as *Ekāntavāda*, a system which clings to a partial aspect of the reality. It neglects to note the other aspects which are also necessarily present in the system of reality. After rejecting the non-Jaina systems as a group of Ekāntavādins, the Jaina thinkers call their own system as *Anekāntavāda*, a system of philosophy which maintains that reality has multifarious aspects and that a complete comprehension of such a nature must necessarily take into consideration all the different aspects through which reality manifests. Emphasis on one particular aspect of reality and building up the system of philosophy on that alone would be similar to a fable of blind men attempting to describe the nature of an elephant. A clear and correct description of the animal, elephant, would be accurate only when you take into consideration all the descriptions which the blind men make by their partial contact with the real animal. Hence the Jaina Darśana is technically called *Anekāntavāda* as it attempts to apprehend fully the whole of reality by taking into consideration the different aspects through which this reality manifests.

The Concept of Dravya—This conception of Sat or the existing reality that is a permanency in the midst of change leads us to another philosophical concept associated with the Jaina Darśana, the Concept of *Dravya.* The term *Dravya* is generally applied to different classes of objects that constitute the whole of reality. The term *Dravya* itself is derived from a root which means the flow. Any object of reality which persists to exist in the midst of continuous disappearance and appearance may be described to be a flow of reality just like a stream of water. This autonomic fluidity of an object of reality is what is implied by the technical term *Dravya* which is applied to any class of objects constituting the Reality. This *Dravya* is defined thus : *Guṇa-paryayavat Dravyaṁ*—that which has characteristic qualities and that which is undergoing constant modifications is what is called *Dravya.* The general illustration of a dravya given in textbooks is the substance, gold. This *dravya*—gold—has got its characteristic quality of yellowness, brilliance, malleability, etc., and it may be made into several ornaments. One ornament of gold may be changed into another ornament, if the owner so desires. The changing form into which this substance, gold, shall be constituted is its mode. The substance, gold, out of which these ornaments are made is the *Dravya* and the characteistic attributes of yellowness, etc., constitute its *Guṇa.* Here also the conception of *Dravya* is peculiar to the Jaina Darśana, and to a very large extent differs from the conception of *Dravya* found in the other Non-Jaina Darśanas. The substance and its qualities cannot be separated. *Dravya* and *Guṇa* are inseparable and yet the substance is not the same as its attributes nor the attributes same as the substance, though it is a fact that it is the substance that manifests this nature through its attributes. Substance without attributes and attributes dissociated from the underlying substance would all be meaningless abstractions. Guṇa cannot exist apart from the *Dravya,* nor the *Dravya* apart from the guṇas. A real *Dravya* is that which manifests through its *Guṇas* and real guṇas are those that have their roots in the underlying *Dravya.* Guṇas which are not based upon the underlying *Dravya,* whose manifestations they are, would be merely sensory illusions having no claim to the status of reality. Hence in the world of reality there can be no separate existence either of *Dravya* or *Guṇa* from each other. It may be clearly seen that, according to Jaina Darśana, the systems which speak of a real existence without *Guṇas, Nirguṇa* or of *Guṇas* existing separately from the substance till they are brought together by a third entity called *Samavāya,* are erroneous philosophical views not corroborated by facts of reality. As we shall see later on, according to this conception even Cetana or Soul or *Ātmā* cannot separate its quality of *Cetana* or consciousness, but some other philosophical systems do maintain that the *Cetana* quality and *Ātamadravya* are two different entities occasionally brought together by extraneous circumstances. These two doctrines as to the nature pertaining to reality—Sat, and *Dravya* lead us to the consideration of fundamental and logical doctrine which is also peculiar to Jainism.

Asti-Nāsti-vāda—According to this doctrine every fact of reality is capable of being described in two logical propositions—one affirmative and the other negative. This paradoxical logical doctrine of *Asti-Nāsti-vāda* has perplexed many non-Jaina thinkers including even the great philosopher Saṅkara. Apparently this conception will be meaningless. How could the same fact be described by two contradictory logical propositions? How can we say that it is and at the same time it is not? *Asti-Nāsti* literally means the thing is and is not. If we remember the two previous philosophical doctrines of Sat and Dravya and if we remember that the ultimate reality is a permanent and changing entity manifesting through constant change of appearance and disappearance, then we can understand that a fact of reality when looked at from the underlying permanent substance may be descrined to be unchanging and permanent, where as from the point of view of the modes which appear and disappear, the thing may be described to be non-permanent and changing.This difference of aspect is called *Naya* technically by the Jaina thinkers. Describing a thing from the aspect of underlying substance or Dravya is called *Dravyārthika naya,* wheras the description based upon the modifications or changes is called *Paryayārthika naya.* Thus the same fact of reality may be apprehended and described from the *Paryayārthika naya* or from *Dravyārthika naya.* From the point of view of the former it may be called an ever-changing fact, whereas from the latter point of view it may be said to be an unchanging permanent entity. Hence these two apparently contradictory logical propositions, though applicable to the same fact of reality, are predicated with a view to two distinct aspects, one emphasising the underlying substance, the other emphasising the changing modes. If we recognise that the conflicting predications are logically possible and fully significant since they refer to two different aspects of view, the logical doctrine of *Asti-Nāsti-vāda* loses much of its mystery and apparent contradictory nature. This *Asti-Nāsti-vāda* doctrine is further elaborated by Jaina Logicians. Take the case of a piece of furniture, the chair or the table before us. If we enquire into the nature of the material, the timber, the same piece of furniture admits of two different logical propositions, one affirmative and the other negative.

If the chair is made of Rosewood then it is capable of being described as furniture made of rosewood. Can we describe the same chair as made of teakwood? Certainly not. We have to say emphatically that it is not made of teakwood. The same piece of furniture therefore admits an affirmative proposition that it is made of rosewood, when you take into consideration the actual timber out of which it is made, and a negative proposition that is it not made of teakwood when you take into consideration some other timber alien to its own nature. Similarly when we want to know whether a piece of furniture is in the drawing room or in the verandah of your house, and if it actually exists in the drawing room, we have to say that is in the drawing room and it is not in the verandah. It is according to this doctrine of *Asti-Nāsti Vāda* as elaborated by the Jaina logicians every fact of reality may be described according to four different conditions—*Dravya, Kṣetra, Kāla* and *Bhāva*—nature of the substance, the place where it is, the time when it exists, and the characteristics intrinsically present in it. Every object from its own *Dravya* or substance admits of an affirmative predication, and looked at from the paradravya, alien substance, admits of a negative predication. The example of a chair given above from *svadravya*, rosewood, admits of affirmative predication, it is made of rosewood; and from the point of view of *paradravya*, alien substance, negative predication. Similarly from *svakṣetra* it is said to be in the drawing room and from *parakṣetra* it is said it is not found in the verandah. This principle of predications may be extended to any object of reality. When we say an animal Cow, and when the question arises what kind of animal it is, we have to say affirmatively it is a cow and negatively it is not a horse. If the question is where is the cow and if it is actually grazing in the compound, we have to answer the cow is in the compound and it is not in the cattleshed. Affirmative predication is from the *svakṣetra* and negative predication, from *parakṣetra* where it is not. Similarly historical proposition may be said to be true in its own period, not true in another historical period. Alexander's invasion of India is an event which took place before the beginning of the Christian era and therefore cannot be associated with the historical period of the Christian era. Hence we have to say that the invasion took place in B.C. and not in A.D., from the point of view of *kāla*. So this doctrine becomes an obvious statement according to common sense point of view and need not be considered to be an exremely intricate philosophical doctrine. Yes, in spite of its obvious nature based upon commonsense point of view, it has been misunderstood by many non-Jaina thinkers and even the great Śaṅkara dismisses The doctrine as prattlings of a mad man. With this short account of philosophical background of Jaina Darśana, we may go to examine some of the important categories in detail.

Jīva or Soul : The term *Jīva* represents a living being. It denotes a spiritual entity. Its essential nature is *Cetana* or thought. *Jīva* is defined by the Jaina thinkers as an entity which lived in the past, which continues to live in the present and which will certainly live in the future also. From this definition it is clear that the term *Jīva* or soul is an entity which had no beginning and which will have no end. It is beginningless and unending continuous existence of a spiritual nature. This *Jīva* or soul is mainly of two kinds—*Saṁsāra* Jiva and *Mokṣa Jīva*. The soul that is embodied, life in the concrete world of biological kingdom associated with the *karmic* bondage is the *Saṁsāra Jīva*; the soul that is free from such *karmic* bondage and which transcended the cycle of *Saṁsāra* and which had attained its nature of intrinsic purity as a result of liberation from *karmic* bondage is *Mokṣa Jīva*. This conception of *Jīva* may be said to be the central doctrine of Jaina philosophy, all the other categories being merely secondary and subsidiary to the central entity. The *Saṁsāra Jīva* itself is divided into four main classes, or Gatis as they are technically called *Catur Gatis*. These *Gatis* are *Devagati, Manuṣyagati, Triyaggati* and *Narakagati*. The first represents the class of devas living in what are called devalokas. The second term *Manuṣyagati* refers to the human being living in this world. The third term refers to the sub-human creatures or lower animals of the zoological and botanical kingdoms which are found with mankind in this world. The fourth term refers to the beings in the hell or the *Naraka*—Netherworld.

The Devaloka or the upper world and *Narakaloka* the world of hell are recognised in Jaina cosmology, according to which the concrete world of living beings—men and lower animals—is called the madhyama loka, the middle world. All beings of these four different groups are called *Saṁsāra Jīvas*, that is a *Jīva* which is subject to the cycle of birth and death, which cycle is denoted by the term Saṁsara. All *Saṁsāra jīvas* are embodied according to their individual spiritual status. Each *Saṁsāri* soul is born with a body and continues to live as embodied soul subject to growth, old age, decay and death; when it has to quit its body in search of another body it acquires another body consistent with and determined by its own karmic conditions. Throughout the series of births and deaths, thus associated with the appearance and disappearance of the corresponding body the underlying *Jīva* or the soul is a perpetual entity serving as a connecting thread of unifying the various births and deaths associated with that particular Jīva. This *Saṁsāra Jīva* associated with its own karmic bondage and its own corporeal existence is considered to be uncreated and therefore beginningless. For the Jaina metaphysician the question when did the soul get associated with material body is a meaningless question, because they say *Saṁsāra* is *anādi*. The cycle of births and deaths has no beginning. Whatever may be the difference of opinion between Jaina metaphysics and the other schools of Indian thought, in this particular point all agree. All maintain that the *Saṁsāra* is *Anādi*. Hence no school of Indian thought would allow the question when did *Saṁsāra* begin to be a sensible question. While all the systems maintain that *Saṁsāra* is beginningless—*Anādi*, all of them do maintain that this series of *Saṁsāra* will come to an end. At the time of liberation of the soul from material and karmic bondage it is said to attain *Mokṣa* or liberation. In this respect also they are at one with the Jaina thinkers that the *Saṁsāra Jīva* is capable of liberating itself ultimately from the *Saṁsaric* cycle of births and deaths and of obtaining its form of intrinsic purity when the soul is called *Mukta Jiva* or *Parmātmā*. The two are one and the same. The doctrine that maintains that the *Jīvātmā* and *Paramātmā* are intrinsically identical is the fundamental Jaina doctrine of Advaitism, which is also the fundamental doctrine of Advaitism of Śaṅkara of latter days. In fact Śaṅkara dismissed all the other systems which do not accept this doctrine as erroneous ones to be discarded, and emphasises this doctrine of identity between the *Jīvātmā* and *Paramātmā* as his own *Siddhānta*. The nature of *Jīva* is *Cetana* or thought, and is therefore quite different from all the other categories which are not so characterised by *Cetana* or thought. The other *Acetana* categories are called *Ajīva* in Jaina metaphysics. This term *Ajīva* includes *Pudgala* or matter. *Ākāśa* or space and two other principles called *Dharma* and *Adharma*-principles of equilibrium and motion which are peculiar to Jaina physics.

The four categories which are grouped in the *Ajīva* class are distinctly non-spiritual and hence incapable of consciousness or thought. They are grouped under *Acetana*. All *Ajīva* categoreis are called *Acetana*. It is only the *Cetana* entity, *Jīva*, that is associated with the consciousness. This consciousness or thought which is the characteristic of *Jīva* may manifest in three distinct psychological activities of cognition: the process of knowing, emotion—the process of feeling pleasure or pains, and conation—the process of activity culminating in voluntary activity. All *Jīvas* therefore are associated with these three different forms of psychic activity of consciousness which are technically called *Cetana Paryāyas*—awareness of the environment, hedonic reaction to the objects so cognised and the characteristic activity manifesting as a result of this feeling of pleasure or pain. This *Jīva* is intrinsically the Knower, the Enjoyer and the Actor. Every soul according to its own status in the course of evolution is thus capable of being in its own way the knower, the enjoyer and the actor—*Jñātā*, *Bhoktā* and *Kartā*. This process of knowing may be limited according to the biological conditions of the individual being. Knowledge may be wider or narrower according to the scale of evolution. The environment and knowledge expected of a lower animal will be much narrower than that of a human being, and the environment and knowledge of a cultured individual will be very insignificant when compared to the knowledge of a person who by *yoga* or *tapas* acquires super-sensual knowledge whose extensity would be very great. Thus the growth of knowledge is conditioned by the spiritual growth of the individual soul or *Jīva.* In the case of *Mokṣa Jīva* the knowledge becomes infinite comprising within itself all the three worlds, when he becomes the knower par-excellence who acquires the nomenclature of *Sarvajña*, the Omniscient and whose extensity is limitless in space and powers. This *Paramātmā* is *Jñānī*, par-excellence. This Jaina conception of *Jīva* though fundamentally identical with the concept of *Jīva* in other Indian systems of thought, still differs with the concept of *Jīva* in other Indian systems of thought, still differs from the other view in certain respects. For example, Sāṁkhya Puruṣa which corresponds with the *Jīva* of the Jaina mataphysics is slightly different from the Jaina concept of *Jīva.* The Sāṁkhyas thought that Puruṣa is a *Cetana* entity, but *Puruṣa* is the knower and the enjoyer, *Jñātā* and *Bhoktā,* but he is not active. He is not a *Kartā.* All activities in the concrete world according to Sāṁkhya school are associated with body, which is called a material entity which is called *Prakṛti* in the Sāṁkhya school and which is called *Pudgala* in the Jaina school of thought. Since all activities associated with non-thinking *Prakṛti* in Sāṁkhya system, the Cetana entity Puruṣa is not connected with any kind of activity. Then why should he be responsible for the activity carried out by some other entity? He is really non-active *Akartā.* The Jaina thinkers object to this Sāṁkhya view. They say that if the *Puruṣa* is *Akartā* or non-active and merely a spectator of an activity carried out by another agency, there is no moral justification in maintaining that he is the *Bhoktā* or the enjoyer of the fruits of such an activtiy. The fruits of an activity are either pleasurable or painful, and why should an entity which is not responsible for the activity be destined to enjoy the result of pain or pleasure. Similarly the other schools of thought such as the Mīmāṁsakas and the Vaiśeṣikas maintain that Jñāna— the knowing capacity gets associated with the soul which is by nature intrinsically devoid of this *guṇa* or quality. The knowing capacity or *Jñāna* which is a distinct entity from the soul is brought in association with the soul or *Jīvātmā* by combination; then the soul becomes the knower. This doctrine also is rejected by the Jaina thinkers as most contradictory, because it would reduce the *Ātmā* or the soul to a non-thinking entity before it has the good fortune to be combined with *Guṇa* or quality of knowledge or *Jñāna*. The knowing capacity or *Jñāna* is intrinsic manifestation of the spiritual entity *Cetana dravya* or Jīva. To imagine that the quality or *guṇa* can exist separately from the *Jīva* or the *Ātmā* is according to Jaina metaphysics quite impossible and meaningless, because according to this central doctrine of Jainism *Guṇa* and *Dravya* cannot be separated and when so separated each becomes a meaningless abstraction incapable of existence in reality. Hence the triple psychic characteristics of knowing, feeling and action are considered inalienable qualities of the *Cetana* entity, *Ātmā* or *Jīva*, and they should not be considered to be of independent existence brought together by combination or association. Each quality may vary in intensity or in extensity. But all the three characteristics must be present in every *Jīva*, however high or low it be in the scale of development. The process of *Jñāna* being an intrinsic quality of the *Cetana* entity or *Ātmā* introduces a peculiar attitude in the matter of epistemology according to Jaina thinkers. The basic principle of knowing process of the Jīva or the *Ātmā*, and the variations in the knowing process of a particular *Jīva* are due to associated conditions. An ordinary living being has access to the environmental objects through sense-perception. Sense perception is through the medium of sense-organs of the body. Since they are parts of the body, physical and physiological the sensory-organs are distinctly material in nature and thus distinct from the nature of Jīva or the *Ātmā*. Sense-perception therfore according to Jaina epistemology is the knowledge which the *Ātman* acquires of the environment through the intermediary of material sense-organs. Since it is through the intermediary of physiological organs of sense, perceptual knowledge cannot be considered to be immediate access of the soul to the environment- objects. Hence sense-perception becomes mediate and not immediate. Direct contact of *Jīva* with the object is what is called pratyakṣa by the Jaina thinkers. Since the sense-perception is conditioned by physical sense-organs, it is not immediate. Sense-perception becomes *Parokṣa*, mediate knowledge, according to Jaina epistemology. In this respect the terms *Pratyakṣa* and *Parokṣa* are completely reversed in Jaina epistemology. What is directly in contact with the soul is *pratyakṣa* and what the soul acquires through the intermediary agent is *parokṣa*. Hence the sense-perception is a *parokṣa* knowledge and not *pratyakṣa* as described by the other Indian systems. But Jaina epistemology recognises two kinds of supersensory knowledge, (1) awareness of objects in distant places and times and (2) contact with thought present in other individual beings. The former is called *Avadhijñāna* which may be translated as clairvoyant knowledge, and the latter is called *Manaḥparyaya Jñāna* which means telepathy in the language of modern psychology. These two features of supersensory knowledge, *Avadhi* and *Manaḥparyayajñāna*, clairvoyance and telepathy are recognised to be knowledge of immediate type or *pratyakṣa*, since they do not depend upon any intermediary of sensory-organs. Of course, the real *pratyakṣa* knowledge is the supreme knowledge of *Paramātmā* when he gets rid of *karmic* bondage and when he attains *Kevalajñāna*—the knowledge par- excellence. This knowledge is infinite in nature and unlimited by spatial and temporal conditions. In this belief that the *Jīvātmā* is capable of becoming *Paramātmā* or the *Sarvajña*, we find similarities and divulgence between the various other Indian systems. The Mīmāṁsakas whose fundamental doctrine is that the Vedas are eternal and *apauruṣeya*, not revealed by any individual person, do not believe in any *Sarvajña* or Omniscient being. In this respect the Mīmāṁsaka system is wholly opposed to Jaina system of metaphysics and also to the Vedāntic school of thought. The Mīmāṁsakas who deny the reality of the *Sarvajña* also go to reject the doctrine of a creator and the doctrine of creation—*Īśvara* as the *Sṛṣṭikartā*. In this respect the Mīmāṁsakas entirely agree with the Jaina and Sāṅkhya systems in rejecting the creation theory. The *Sarvajña* or *Parmātmā* in Jaina system is not a Sṛṣṭikartā or the creator. As a matter of fact, the doctrine of creation may be said to have been completely rejected by all the Indian systems and not merely by the Jaina school of thought. No Indian system, not even the Vaiśeṣikas and Naiyāyikas who speak of an *Īśvara* as the *Sṛṣṭikartā* accept the doctrine of creation as bringing into existence of non-existing entity. That form of creation is entirely foreign to Indian thought. This doctrine is vehemently opposed and rejected by the Mīmāṁsakas as most ridiculous contradiction. All systems begin with the uncreated *Ātma* or soul and the uncreated world of physical objects. Transformation in these objects, conjunction and separation between the living and the non-living in various forms are accepted and described by the Indian thinkers as the primary entities, so combined or so undergoing transformations are all postulated to be uncreated and indestructible having a permanent existence of their own. In this respect also the Jaina philosophy agrees with the other Indian systems in maintaining that the *Jīva* and *Ajīva* categories are permanent and uncreated and indestructible.

Self in Modern Science

Even the biological developments of lower organism may be

said to be a preparation for building up a vehicle for the self to express itself. From the lowest mono-cellular organism and ameaba right up to man, the process of evolution is a process of building up the body enabling the self to express its nature and characteristics fuller and fuller. Psychological devlopment of man illustrates the same point of view.

Further cultural development involving socio-political organisations and metaphysical evolution all point to the same end. It is now a recognised fact that the character and behaviour of living organisms are entirely distinct from that of the inorganic things. Life's activity is characterised by an underlying purpose. Purposive behaviour of organism marks the distinguishing characteristic of the biological kingdom. No biologist now-a-days has faith in famous Belfast declaration by Professor Tyndall that matter contains the promise and potency of life and consciousness. The mechanical aspect of the physical realm is recognised to be different from the teleological aspect of the kingdom of life. Even the case of ameaba which consists of protoplasmic matter covered by the cellular wall containing inside it a nucleus behaves characteristically in a purposive manner. This monocellular organism is able to recognise in a mysterious way the difference between friend and foe. It is able to run away from a powerful enemy. It is able to attack and defeat an enemy of modest intensity and power. It is able to stretch out pseudopodia from the cell-wall to capture food-stuff and assimilate it. Thus it has in its own way the glimpse of sensitive awareness to help its behaviour. It exhibits the main functions of life such as motion and locomotion, digestion and assimilation and even reproduction by a process of germination. This acquatic mono-cellular organism does not carry on with this mode of life and character for long. Nature seems to be dissatisfied with this process of evolution. Then begins the process of building up a colony of cells clinging together with a sort of co-operative purpose of common life. Thus arises the beginning of multi-cellular organism. The mother cell separates into two cells which are brought about by a processs of germination. These clinging together resulting in the constitution of the colony of cells, form the multi-cellular organism. The change naturally brings about a change in the characteristics of the behaviour of the organism. The cells in the outer periphery of the organism have the chance of coming in contact with the environment whereas the cells inside the mass have no such chance. This necessarily brings about a division of labour in order to promote the common life of the colony of cells. The outer cells are practically specialised to perform the function of awareness of the environment and also the function of motion and locomotion, whereas the cells inside the mass specialise in the function of digestion and assimilation. In order ot facilitate this functional differentiation the colony of cells provides a central channel through which food is shoved in which is assimilated by the inner cells and circulated to the cells in periphery also. This central channel is a representative of the future digestive system of the major organisms and also the circulatory systems. The cells in the periphery get on specialised further into sensory-motor systems of the higher organism. The front opening of this colony of cells represents the primitive mouth of the organism. It is this side of the colony that approaches and catches foodstuff which are shoved into the central channel for purpose of digestion and assimilation. Hence the multi-cellular organism develops tentacles at the frontal orifice for the purpose of capturing food-stuff and shoving them in. Some cells at the frontal orifice futher specialise into different types of sensory awareness while the ameaba had the privilege of contact awareness only, the multicellular organism develops in addition, the sense of taste and the sense of smell, the former to distinguish food from the non-edible objects and the latter to recognise the approach of an object whether it is friend or foe through scent. Thus the cells of the periphery near the central orifice must further specialise another functional structure some devoted to the awareness of taste and others to smell. This form the beginnings of the sensory systems in the organism. Even an organism of this type which is merely a mass of cells with the central orifice with the tentacles near the orifice is able to express its characteristics in a significantly purposive manner.

Professor Loeb conducted certain experiments to determine the behaviour of such primitive organisms. He introduced pieces of bread near the mouth, the tentacles caught these pieces and examined these and shoved them in. When the experiment was repeated the tentacles were eargerly waiting for small bits of bread and the moment these pieces were introduced without further examination they were pushed in. When this behaviour was fully developed, he introduced pieces of card-board, the first piece of cardboard was eagerly caught and shoved in. After a little while this was brought out without being digested and kicked away by the tentacles. Afterwards this primitive organism was able to recognise the difference betwen the piece of bread and piece of cardboard. The latter when introduced would be kicked away without ceremony—a characteristic behaviour fully illustrative of the purposive nature of life-activity.

The next stage in the sensory development consists in the appearance of the beginnings of eye which will be sensitive to light. Certain other cells about the frontal orifice develop a sensitiveness to light which is the primitive representative of future-eye of the higher organism. The differentiation of cells thus responding to different sensory stimuli constitutes the origin of the different sense-organs, which naturally must get coordinated by interconnections, if they are to subserve the general purpose. Such interconnections of these sensory regions from the primitive nervous system form the brain of the higher organism.

Let us pursue the development of the sensory organism and the other systems in the higher organisms. All this development in the multi-cellular organism is associated with acquatic organisms. When these animals become amphibians partly living on earth and water, then there is the scope of further sensory development of hearing. The latter evolution branches off in two directions one towards the fowls of the air and the other towards the beasts of the earth.

Confining ourselves to the career of the quadrupeds we find a wonderful development of the nervous system and specially the brain. Examination of the brain of the lowest types of quadrupeds, say the rabbit, we find that the whole mass of the brain consists of the sensory centres connecting with the peripheral sensory organs, such as taste. smell, touch, sight and sound. Besides these central sensory organs and the brain, there are what are called motor regions of the body, some controlling the movements of the hind legs, some controlling the movements of the front legs and so on. When we follow the development of this brain in the mammals, we find the appearance of some brain regions which are not characterised either by sensory functions or motor functions. These areas of the brains were called silent areas, because the physiologists were not able to determine their function accurately by experiment. Later on it was discovered that these silent areas perform a very important function of co-ordinating the different elements of sensory awareness with appropriate mascular reactions controlling the general behaviour of the animal and these serve as the fundamental basis of the origin and development of consciousness. This hypothesis is fully corroborated when we watch the development of these silent areas in the brain surface of the mammals.

When we come to the simian type of quadrupeds, we find a critical and interesting turn in the brain development. Probably frightened by the pre-historic giants, certain quadrupeds had to take up to arboreal life by climbing up the trees and living there the major part of the time in order to preserve themselves, from the danger of the enemies below. This necessarily resulted in the liberation of the front legs which were converted into hands capable of grasping things with the flexible fingers and so on. This liberation of the front leg led to immense possibilities of future developments found in man. Beginnings of the human culture and civilisation may be traced to this critical turn in the evolution of life where the front legs changed into hands and which again led to an erect posture of the animal standing on the hind legs alone, thus assuring in the advent of man in the world. We now perceive the subordination of the sensory areas of the brain and the major portion of the surface of the brain assigned to motor functions to the functions of the association of different centres. Thereafter we find that the so-called silent centres otherwise called association centres of the brain becoming the dominant area of the brain, and they are at the maximum in the human brain, thus indicating that they form the functional basis of consciousness which is the fundamental characteristic of man. Thus the process of building up the body for the purpose of serving as a vehicle for the expression of consciousness, which seems to be the guiding principle in the whole process of evolution. This principle is generally recognised by modern biologists who refute the inadequacy of Darwinian theory of natural selection based upon mere mechanical environment.

Let us confine ourselves to human brain. Here you have the centres representing the various sense-organs of the periphery, the motor centres controlling the various systems of the body and besides these large tracks of association centres which cover the major portion of the brain area. Modern physiologists recognise the importance of their association areas and they believe that the same form the physiological basis of conscious activity. But the psychological development and especially the study of abnormal psychology brought to the forefront certain important facts, which necessitate the modification of the theory postulating that conscious activity is generally based upon physiological functions of the different centres of the brain, sensory and motor. Since these facts indicate that sometimes consciousness functioning in a mysterious way completely transcends the activity of the brain. This result is obtained from two independent sources. Mental disorders brought about by violent shock or accident are observed in cases where the medical men were not able to detect any injury to the brain. A person falling from his dogcart, was found to be completely devoid of his past memory. He was not even able to speak. His condition was just like that of a baby incapable of uttering coherent words and incapable of rcognising familiar objects. In this case, the medical men were not able to find any damage to the brain and they were in a fix to account for this tragic wiping out of past memories. The case was finally taken up by a psychologist. He began to teach this patient a few words and made him understand few objects in the environment. Thus he was equipped with a few words to carry on conversation. Then he was subjected to hypnotic treatment and, to the great surprise of the psychologist, the patient when in hypnotic sleep remembered all his past experience which he vaguely as if in a dream. Feeling glad that the past memory is not altogether wiped off, the treatment was continued for some time, the patient was given the post-hypnotic suggestion that he would remember all the past experiences which he vaguely recognised as dreams in the hypnotic trance. When the patient woke up to normal conciousness from the hypnotic sleep, to his great joy, he remembered the whole of his past experience which was temporarily wiped out, and became his former self once again. Such cases were numerous during the last war, when men in the front through shellshock suffered such mental aberation. All such cases were treated by the psychologist and restored to normal life to the joy of the patient.

It is clear that verdict of modern psychology is that the human personality is distinct from the material body with which it is associated and that it survives even after death.

Śaṅkara and Kundakunda

Śaṅkara's introduction to his *Bhāṣya* is a philosophical masterpiece by itself. There he gives his own personal opinion without being constrained to follow the text of the sūtras. Hence he freely expresses his views on life and things. First he maintains that the Self and the Non-Self are two entirely distinct entities. He begins his introduction with the following words :

"It is a matter not requiring any proof that the object and the subject whose respective sphres are the notion of the 'thou' (the Non-Ego) and the 'Ego' and which are opposed to each other as much as darkness and light are, cannot be identified. All the less can their respective attributes be identified. Hence it follows that it is wrong to superimpose upon the subject—whose Self is intelligence, and which has for its sphere the notion of the Ego—the object whose sphere is the notion of the Non Ego and the attributes of the object and vice versa to superimpose the subject and the attributes of the subject on the object."

From this it is clear that these two distinct entities the Self and the Non-self, have no common nature and no common attributes. One is *Cetana* and the other *Acetana*. The attributes of the one cannot be superimposed upon the other. Such a confusion is a distinct philosophical error and correct knowledge necessarily demands complete escape from such an error. Otherwise it is not possible to realise the true nature of the Self which is the ultimate object of all philosophical and religious discipline. "In spite of this it is on the part of man a natural procedure which has its cause in wrong knowledge—not to distinguish the two entities (object and subject) and their respective attributes, although they are absolutely distinct, but to superimpose upon each the characteristic nature and the attributes of the other, and thus coupling the Real and Unreal, to make use of the expressions such as 'That I am.' 'That is mine'."

The second point which he brings out in the introduction is the distinction between the two points of view, *Vyavahāra* and Paramārthic, practical point of view and the absolute point of view. The confusion of attributes referred to above is brought about by Nescience or *Avidyā*. The discriminating knowledge of the true nature of the Self is therefore to be obtained by the opposite *Vidyā* or knowledge. He maintains that the concrete life in this world is vitiated by Nescience and is real only from the practical point of view. "The mutual superimposition of the Self and the Non-Self, which is termed Nescience, is the presupposition on which there base all practial distinction—those made in ordinary life as well as those laid down by the Veda—between means of knowledge, objects of knowledge and all scriptural texts, whether they are concerned with injunctions and prohibition (of meritorious and non-meritorious actions) or with final release." Thus he points out that in ordinary life, every individual has to operate only through his body and sense without which life itself would be impossible in the concrete world. Even the cognitive process of knowledge depends upon sense-perception and intellectual activity which naturally presupposes the organic body. Even when the individual is looked upon as an agent carrying out the injunctions religious and eithical an organic body must be presupposed for carrying out all those injunctions. His conduct as the social being in the world is therefore inextricably mixed up with bodily behaviour, without which he can neither discharge his duties as a social being nor as a religious devotee. In this respect he is of common nature with other animals, who also behave in an identical manner in reacting to the environment. In the presence of an enemy, the animal tries to run away and escape and in the presence of a friendly environment it feels happy. Thus this concrete world of natural experience which is common to both men and animals though philosophically supposed to be the result of Nescience, is to be considered real and important from the practical point of view. In this concrete world which is real in its own way, the social distinctions based upon rank and birth hold good. That one is a Brahmin and another is a Kṣatriya, one is a master and another is a servant, are all distinctions based upon the body and hold good only in the empirical world.

The third point which he emphasises is that this empirical world resulting from the non-distinction between the Self and the Non-Self exists without beginning and without end. This natural world, which is without beginning and without end is produced by the Nescience or wrong conception which is the cause of individual souls appearing as agents and enjoyers in the empirical world or *Saṁsāra,* is influenced by this wrong knowledge which identifies oneself with external objects.

"Extra-personal attributes are superimposed on the Self, if a man considers himself sound and entire or the contrary, as long as his wife, children and so on are sound and entire or not. Attributes of the body are superimposed on the Self, if a man thinks of himself (his Self) as a stout, lean, fair as standing, walking or jumping. Attributes of the sense-organs, if he thinks I am mute or deaf or one eyed or blind. Attributes of the internal organs when he considers himself subject to desire, intention, doubt, determination, and so on."

Lastly he indicates the true nature of the Self which should be discriminated from the Non-*Cetana* bodily attributes as free from all wants and raised above all social distinction as Brahmin and Kṣatriya and so on, and entirely transcended the empirical *saṁsārika* existence to whom even Vedic injunctions will cease to be operative, because he is placed in a region from where he does not want to achieve anything more, because he is completely self-sufficient.

This introduction of Śaṅkara may be taken to be an introduction to Śrī Kundakunda's *Samayasāra* also. The philosophical work of Samayasāra deals with all these points and practically adopts indentically the same attitude. Śrī Kundakunda begins his work with the distinction between the two points of view *Vyāvahārika* and *Niścaya*, practical and real. He describes the empirical world where the individual identifies himself with the characteristics of the external objects as a result of the absence of true knowledge. The course of conduct prescribed by practical ethics is said to have only a secondary value as a probation for the higher class. Bodily characteristics, instincts, and emotions and the various psychic states of the individual Self are all dismissed to be the result of the operation of the erroneous identification of the Self or *Paramātmā.* Thus without changing the words, Śaṅkara's introduction may be considered to be a fitting introduction to Śrī Kundakunda's *Samayasāra.* We shall later on point out the various points of similarity between the two, Śaṅkara and Śrī Kundakundā, which would constrain the reader to accept the suggestion that Śaṅkara was well acquainted with Kundakunda's philosophy either in the original or in the Sanskrit commentary by Amṛtacandra.

Śaṅkara and his Points of View

The distinction between *Vyāvahārika* and *Pāramārthika* points of view which Śaṅkara makes throughout his commentary is said to have been copied from the Buddhistic philosophy. A writer in the Journal called '*Achūta*' referring to this says, that Śaṅkara must have copied this from the Buddhistic metaphysics because the distinction is not found anywhere else. This writer evidently is not acquainted with Jaina philosophy. If he were acquainted with the Jaina philosophy, he would not have made such a sweeping statement that the distinction is not found anywhere else. In fact the doctrine of *Naya* or the points of view is peculiar to Jaina metaphysics, which maintains that knowledge is to be obtained from *Pramāṇas* and nayas. *Pramāṇa-Nayādhigamaḥ*—is the fundamental Jaina doctrine of knowledge. Following this Jaina tradition Kundakunda starts his work Samayasāra by mentioning this distinction between *Vyāvahārika* and

Pāramārthika points of view in his study of the nature of the real Self or Samayasāra. He justifies the adoption of the *vyāvahārika* point of view even in the approach of a student towards the ultimate reality of the Self, as a preparatory method of his adopting the *Niścaya* or the *Pāramārthika* point of view. According to him all persons are not capable of understanding the real nature of the ultimate Self. Therefore the information must be conveyed according to the capacity of the student; just as it is necessary to adopt as a means of communication the language with which the student is acquainted, so also it is necessary to adopt a method of instruction which will be within the reach of the individual student. When a guru teaches an individual not acquainted with Saṁskṛta language through the medium of Saṁskṛta it would not be intelligible to the person concerned, the instructor would defeat his purpose. Hence it is absolutely necessary to speak to him in the language which is his mother tongue and which may be some vernacular other than Saṁskṛta. Similarly it is necessary to adopt *vyāvahārika* point of view in communicating metaphysical truths to ordinary people. With this justification Śrī Kundakunda examines every problem from these two points of view, practical and real, the practical point of view in dealing with problems of an empirical life, and the real point of view in dealing with supreme reality transcending limitations of the empirical life. In this respect, as was pointed above, Śaṅkara closely follows Kundakunda's method, with which obviously he was familiar when he began his *Bhāṣya*.

The Individual and the Saṁsāra

Both Śaṅkara and Kundakunda adopt identically the same attitude as to the nature of the individual self. Both maintain that the individual soul is identical with the ultimate reality, the Supreme Self. Śaṅkara, following the traditional language of Jaina metaphysics, calls this ultimate reality *Paramātman*, or the Supreme Self. Even according to Śaṅkara the Brahma and *Paramātma* are synonymous and interchangeable. Both the thinkers maintain that the individual self in the concrete world is ultimately identical with this absolute reality or *Paramātmā*. The nature of the individual self in concrete experience is the result of limitations imposed upon the ultimate reality, *Paramātmā*. The limiting conditions are very often spoken of as *Upādhi*, which is responsible for clouding the true nature of the ultimate reality. Kundakunda compares the ultimate reality with the shining sun in all his brilliance, and the individual self is compared to the sun hidden by a dense layer of clouds which hides the sunshine. According to the variation in the density of the cloud, the rays of the sun will permeate through the clouds and make the sun visible in varying intensity. These variations in the appearance of the sun correspond to the various stages of spiritual developments of the individual soul. When the clouds completely get dispersed the sun begins to shine in all his glory without any intervening interruption. Exactly in a similar manner, *karmic upādhis* of different density obstruct the self-shining Supreme *Ātman* where the Self will shine in his pristine purity and glory when all the *karmic upādhis* are destroyed and got rid of. The doctrine of indentifying *Jivātmā* and *Paramātmā* is common to both Śaṅkara and Kundakunda. In this connection it is worth pointing out that both Kundakunda and Śaṅkara in their commentaries used the word 'Advaita' -the indication of the oneness of *Jīvātmā* and *Pramātmā*, a term which becomes the central doctrine of Śaṅkara's philosophies. It only means that the doctrine is common to both the Upaniṣadic thought and the Jaina thought. This individual self which is merely the *Paramātmā* limited by *aupādhic* conditions is subject to transmigration, the cycle of births and deaths. This career of births and deaths which is the peculiar property of the individual self is a result of the ultimate self-forgetting its own nature and identify in itself with the external objects of the non-Self. This confusion between the nature of the Self and non-Self is pointed out as the ultimate cause of transmigratory existence of the individual soul both in the Jaina system as well as in the Vedāntic systems. The initial error or *Adhyāsa* or *Mithyā* is recognised to be the cause of *Saṁsāric* existence by both the thinkers. Both maintain that this Saṁsāric existence is without beginning-*Anādi*. *Mokṣa* or Liberation consists in getting rid of this transmigratory existence through the discriminating knowledge of the self as distinct from the external objects. The individual self in this transmigratory existence or *Saṁsāra* is determined by its own *karmic* activity at every stage. If this conduct is good he is destined to have happiness as the fruit of *karma*; if otherwise, misery. The variation in the individual hedonic experience is thus attributed to the individual's own action, good or bad. Even here both the thinkers are at one. Śaṅkara in spite of his enthusiatic advocacy of unqualified monism concedes this point that the individual souls are determined by their respective karmas, good or bad, and that the ultimate Brahma is not responsible for such individual conduct.

Answering to the objection that the creative Brahma must be responsible for the inequalities among the individual souls, Śaṅkara writes :

"The Lord, we reply, cannot be reproached with inequality of dispensation and cruelty 'because he is bound by regards.' If the Lord on his own account, without any extraneous regards, produced this unequal creation, he would expose himself to blame; but the fact is, that in creating he is bound by certain regards, i.e., he has to look to merit and demerit. Hence the circumstances to the creation being unequal it is due to the merit and demerit of the living creatures created, and is not a fault for which the Lord is to blame. The position of the Lord is to be looked as analogous to that of Parjanya, the Giver of rain. For as Parjanya is the common cause of the production of rice, barley and other plants, while the difference between the various species is due to the various potentialities lying hidden in the respective seeds, so the Lord is the common cause of the creation of gods, men, etc., while the difference between these classes of being are due to the different merit belonging to the individual souls." In this passage Śaṅkara appears to drop out the Advaitic doctrine that the Brahma is the material cause or the *Upādāna Kāraṇa* of the individual souls. The individual souls are assumed to subsist with all their individual merits and demerits irrespective of the occurrence of Pralaya and fresh creation. By bringing in the analogy of *Parjanya*, he converts the first cause of Brahma to *Nimitta Kartā* like the potter making a pot out of clay. This attitude is in conflict with the general advaitic attitude. In order to save the Brahma from the responsibility of being the author of inequality existing in the world, he has to assume the independent reality of the individual souls. So far Śaṅkara entirely agrees with the Jaina attitude represented by Kundakunda.

While maintaining that the confusion of the Self with the Non-Self constitutes the initial *mithyā* or the error, both the thinkers part company in further elaboration of their systems. It is certainly an error to identify the self with the sense-characteristics which are peculiar to the physical body because the sense-qualities of colour, taste and smell have nothing to do with the nature of the self. Birth, old, age, decay and death are all characteristics alien to the conscious Self. Social and economic distinction in the individual also pertain to the body and cannot be transferred to the Self. In short the Self is a *Cetana* entity and the non-Self is an *Acetana* entity, which is the object of sense perception. Both Śaṅkara and Kundakunda therefore maintain, one following the tradition of Vedāntism and the other following the tradition of Jainism, that is is *mithyā* to speak of the body as Self. Kundakunda stops with this statement of Śaṅkara and goes beyond this. For the latter it is not only an error to confuse Self with the body, the body itself becomes *mithyā* or illusion. Therefore Kundakunda has to call, Halt! It is only the false identification that is error. The non-self is not mithyā or illusion. This is the fundamental difference between the two systems of metaphysics, Śaṅkara's advaitism and Śrī Kundakundra's Jaina metaphysics. Śaṅkara seems to forget his own statement in the introduction of the fundamental distinction between the Self and the Non-Self, when he comes to propound his theory of unqualified monism by denying the reality of external world itself.

Nature and the External World

The reality of the external world is admitted by the Jaina metaphysics as in the case of Sāṁkhya philosophy. The Upaniṣadic thought also maintains the reality of the external world inspite of its pantheistic monism. The other commentators of Vedānta *Sūtras*, besides Śaṅkara also maintain the reality of the external world. Śaṅkara himself while contradicting the Buddhistic school of Vijñānavāda accepts the doctrine of the reality of the external world in refuting the Buddhistic school. The Vijñānavāda school of the Buddhistic philosophy which maintains that the external reality is merely a manifestation of consciousness is condemned by Śaṅkara by pointing out the difference between the purely imaginary world of dream and the concrete world of sense-perception. There he maintains that the difference in the psychic ideas are intelligible only on the supposition that the psychic images are direct effects of a permanent object in reality. This faith in the reality of the external world which he employs in refuting the Buddhistic metaphysics, he drops out completely when he tries to propound his own theory of *Māyā* according to which the whole of the external reality is converted into a dream-world of unreality. This particular doctrine of Śaṅkara is incompatible with the Jaina metaphysics.

The Origin of the concrete world—The popular view as to the origin of the concrete world that it is due to the creative activity of an Íśvara is rejected by Jaina philosophy. It is also rejected by Sāṁkhya, Yoga and Mīmāṁsā systems of thought.

Śaṅkara also rejects this theory when he criticises the Vaiśeṣika system and the Pāsupata system. The concrete world from the creator or an Íśvara as a result of his creative Will is thus completely discarded by Śaṅkara also. He maintains that it is a result of the manifestation of the ultimate reality, Brahma. In order to establish this doctrine that the world is the result of the manifestation of the Brahma he elaborately discusses the Sāṁkhya view of deriving cosmos from *Prakṛti*, the *Acetana* root cause of the concrete world according to the Sāṁkhya school. Sāṁkhyas and the Jainas staunchly maintain the difference between the *Cetana* Self and the *Acetana* Non-Self. *Prakṛti* of the Sāṁkhyas exactly corresponds to *Pudgala* or matter of the Jains. Since this is contradictory to the nature and attributes of the Self both the systems maintain that it is impossible to obtain one from the other. Therefore they regard both the Cetana and *Acetana* entities as not only distinct and independent of each other, but both are ultimate realities existing peramanently uncreated and indestructible. But Śaṅkara in order to defend the Vedāntic doctrine of the Brahma has somehow to derive the *Acetana* entity also from the same first cause, Brahma. Kundakunda clearly points out that this is impossible. If the doctrine of the identity of the cause and effect is accepted—Śaṅkara also does accept this doctrine—these two contradictory effects, the *Acetana* Non-Self and the *Cetana* Self, cannot be produced by the same cause, the Brahma, which is taken to be a *Cetana* entity according to the Upaniṣadic thought. How can the *Cetana Brahma* produce *Acetana* effect-matter, is the objection raised by the Sāṁkhyas as well as the Jainas. Śaṅkara himself concedes to the fundamental difference between the two in his introduction when he speaks about the *Adhyāsa* which is the root cause of *Saṁsāra*, himself concedes to the fundamental difference between the two in his introduction, when he speaks about the *Adhyāsa* which is the root cause of *Saṁsāra* and yet since he has to defend the Vedāntic pantheism he seems to forget his own doctrine and uses his ingenuity to prove that it is possible to derive *Acetana* non-Self from the *Cetana Brahma*. How far he succeeds in his attempt is certainly an open question to be decided by the readers of his commentary.

The Doctrine of Causation

Kundakunda, following the tradition of Jaina metaphysics, speaks of two different causes, *Upādāna kāraṇa* and *Nimitta kāraṇa*- material cause and instrumental cause. For example, clay is the material out of which the jar is made. In this case the material out of which the thing is made is the *Upādāna kāraṇa*. For tranforming the clay into the jar you require the operating agent, the potter, the potter's wheel on which the clay is moulded, and the stick with which he turns the wheel and so on. All these come under the *Nimitta kāraṇa* or the instrumental cause. This distinction is considered very important in Jaina metaphysics. The *Upādāna kāraṇa* or the material cause must be identical with its effect. There can be no difference in nature and attributes between the material cause and its effect. From clay we can only obtain a mud-pot. Out of gold you can only obtain a golden ornament. Out of gold you cannot obtain a mud-pot nor out of clay can you obtain a golden ornament. The relation between the material cause and its effect is exactly corresponding to the modern conception of Causation, that wherever the cause is present the effect would be present, and wherever the effect would be present the cause must have been present. Again negatively, if the cause is absent the effect must also be absent and conversely if the effect is absent the cause must also be absent. Following this doctrine of identity between the cause and effect, Kundakunda maintains consistent with the Jaina metaphysics, that the Cetana cause can only produce *Cetana* effects, and that non-Cetana cause can only produce non-*Cetana* effects. Accordingly he has to reject the Vedāntic doctrine of deriving both *Cetana* and non-*Cetana* effect from the real cause of

Brahma which cannot contain in himself the contradictory causal potencies to produce two contradictory effects. Strangely the Vedāntic doctrine which maintains the Brahma to be the ultimate cause of all reality also maintains the non-difference in cause and effect.

Commenting on these *sūtras*, Śaṅkara writes, "For the following reason also the effect is non-different from the cause, because only when the cause exists the effect is observed to exist and not when it does not exist. For instance, only when the clay exists, the jar is observed to exist. That it is not a general rule when one thing exists, another also is observed to exist, appears for instance, from the fact that a horse which is other or different from a cow is not observed to exist only when a cow exists. Nor is the jar observed to exist only when the potter exists. For in that case the non-difference does not exist, although the relation between the two is that of an operating cause and its effect."

Again he writes "Ordinary experience teaches us that those who wish to produce certain effect such as curds, or earthern jars, or golden ornaments employ such (things) as milk, clay and gold. Those who wish to produce sour-milk do not employ clay, nor do those who intend to make jars employ milk and so on. But according to that doctrine which teaches that the effect is non-existent (before its actural production) all this should be possible. For if before their actual origination all effects are equally non-existent in any causal substance, why then should curds be produced from milk only and not from clay also, and jar from clay only and not from milk as well.

Again he writes, "As the ideas of cause and effect on the one hand and of the qualities on the other are not separate ones, as for instance the ideas of a horse and a buffalo, it follows that the identity of the cause and the effect as well as of the substance and its qualities has to be admitted.

From these quotation it is quite clear that Śaṅkara's conception of cause and effect is the same as Kundakunda's.

The former following the traditions of Vedāntism and the latter, the tradition of Jaina metaphysics. Both maintain that the cause and the effect are identical and that particular cause can produce an effect entirely identical in nature with the cause. They both reject the view that the effect is non-existent in the cause and occurs as a new thing just after the cause. And therefore they both maintain that the effect is present in the cause though only in the latent form. Clay is shaped into a jar and gold is transformed into an ornament. The jar as such is not present in clay already, nor is the ornament as such present in gold. Therefore the effect is the result of causal manifestation. Thus according to Jaina Metaphysics, the effect is identical with the cause and yet the effect is slightly different from the cause. From the point of view of the underlying substance the effect and cause are identical. From the point of view of manifested form and change, the effect is different from the cause. Thus cause and effect may be said to be identical in one sense and different, from another point of view. In the last quoted paragraph Śaṅkara applies the same doctrine of identity and difference also to the relation between substance and its qualities. The substance and its qualities are inherently identical though they are different in another aspect. This attitude of Śaṅkara is identical with the Jaina attitude as to the relation between *Drayva* and *Guṇa*, substance and attributes. Both Śaṅkara's Vedāntism and Kundakunda's metaphysics are at one in rejecting the Vaiśeṣika doctrine that substance and qualities are two different distinct categories brought together by a third category *Samavāya* which conjoins the two. Rejecting this Vaiśeṣika view of the difference between substance and qualities it is maintained by both Śaṅkara and Kundakunda that they are identical in nature.

One and the Many

To speak of a thing as one or many is entirely dependent

upon the point of view you adopt. The same material clay may be transformed into various clay vessels and the same material substance gold may be transformed into various kinds of ornaments. If you emphasise the underlying substance the mud-pots and jars will be identical in the same nature. They all belong to one class, and similarly ornaments may be said to be golden since they belong to one class. But if you emphasise the ornaments or the pots, they are many in number. Or take the case of a tree. It may be spoken of as one or many. It is one when taken in its complex as a whole, and it will be many when you emphasise the number of branches in it.

"We point out that one and the same thing may be the subject of several names and ideas if it is considered in its relations to what lies without it. Devadatta although being one only forms the object of many different names and notions according as he is considered in himself or in his relations to other; thus he is thought and spoken of as man, Brāhmin, learned in the Veda, generous, boy, young man, old man, father, son, grandson, brother, son-in-law, etc. etc."

This last passage from Śaṅkara completely coincides with the Jaina point of view that any assertion about a thing would take different forms according to the relations of the thing to other things. A person is said to be father when he is taken in relation to his son, as the son when the same is taken in relation to his father. Therefore the question how can the same man be father and son would entirely be meaningless, and it will only exhibit the ignorance of the logical theory of predication. The same principle is extended by the Jaina metaphysics to other relations, such as space, time, substance and modes. This obvious truth forms the basis of the Jaina logical doctrine of predication—*Astināstivāda.* That you can have two assertions about a thing, positive and negative, according to the relation of the thing to other things. Strangely this principle thus accepted by Śaṅkara is forgotten by him when he goes to criticise the *Sūtra* relating to Jainism, that two contradictory things cannot exist in the same. This inconsistency is probably due to the fact that he was only a commentator of an already existing work.

Śaṅkara comments on the first *sūtra 'Athāto Brahma-jijñāsā'*, let us then enquire into the nature of the Brahma or the Self. Where is the reason why such an enqiry should be taken up? he says, since there are various erroneous things as to the nature of the self held by different schools of thought, it is necessary to clear up the errors and to establish the correct notion of the self." He enumerates various schools he consders to be erroneous as Buddha, Sāṁkhya, Yoga, Vaiśeṣika and Pāsupata etc., etc. It is strange that he does not mention the Jaina account of self as one of the erroneous views. Probably the reason why he omits this is his own *siddhānta* which is identical with the Jaina concept of self that the *Jīvātmā* and *Paramātmā* are identical. This exactly is Śaṅkara's considered view. Hence he cannot condemn this as one of the erroneous views, for this forms the foundation of Advaita, which forms the central doctrine of his commentary.

Śaṅkara and Amṛtacandra : We mentioned above that Śaṅkara was acquainted with Śrī Kundakkunda and Amṛtacandra. We refer to this fact in connection with Śaṅkara's distinction between the *Vyāvahārika* and *Pāramārthika* points of view. We have here to mention the fact that the doctrine of *Adhyāsa* is also peculiar to Śaṅkara. *Adhyāsa* is the technical term he used to denote the confusion between self and non-self, a confusion due to *Avidyā* or *Ajñāna*. This term *Adhyāsa* is not found in any of the philosophical writings prior to Śaṅkara. Probably Śaṅkara took a hint from Amṛtacandra who freely uses this concept in his commentary called *Ātmakhyāti* on Śrī Kundakunda's Samaysāra. Probably Amṛtacandra and Śaṅkara must have lived in the same century, Amṛtacandra being slightly older than Saṅkara. The language of *Ātmakhyāti* is very similar to Śaṅkara's Bhāṣya. This suggestion is made because Śaṅkara himself speaks on one occasion that he is influenced by one Draviḍ Ācārya. Probably this refers to Amṛtacandra—the great Commentator of *Samayasāra.* The following quotations from *Ātmakhyāti* will clearly bear out our suggestion that Śaṅkara and Amṛtacandra were of the same age and that the former was acquainted with the writings of Amṛtacandra especially with his commentary *Ātmakhyāti.*

"*Ajñāna* or ignorance causes *Adhyāsa* or confusion of the intellect. On account of this, thirsty animals run towards mirage to quench their thirst thinking it is a lake full of water."

Again the same *Adhyāsa* or confusion caused by ignorance frightens men is dusk at the sight of a rope and makes them run away from it thinking it is a snake.

"Similarly on account of this confusion caused by ignorance men falsely identify their pure and unruffled nature of the Soul with the body and imagine that they are the author of the various psycho-physical activities caused by impure *karmas,* just as the numerous waves in the ocean are caused by atmospheric pressure while the ocean itself remains calm and unruffled. But *Jñāna* or knowledge produces discrimination between the self and the non-self just like the 'haṁsa' bird which is able to separate water from milk unruffled self firm in its pure nature is able to understand that it is not the author of the various impure psycho-physical changes caused by an alien agency."

SAMAYASĀRA

SAMAYASĀRA

CHAPTER 1

JĪVA-PADĀRTHA OR CATEGORY OF THE SOUL

वंदित्तु सव्वसिद्धे धुवम[1] चलमणोवमं गदिं पत्ते।
वोच्छामि समयपाहुडमिणमो सुयकेवलीभणियं॥ १॥

vaṁdittu savvasiddhe dhuvamacalamaṇovamaṁ gadiṁ patte,
vocchāmi samayapāhuḍamiṇamo suyakevalībhaṇiyaṁ (1)

वन्दित्वा सर्वसिद्धान् ध्रुवामचलामनुपमां गतिं प्राप्तान्।
वक्ष्यामि समयप्राभृतमिदम् अहो श्रुतकेवलिभणितम्॥ १॥

1. Bowing to all the *Siddhas* who have attained a state of existence, permanent, immutable and incomparable, I will speak of this *Samayapāhuda* which has been uttered by the all-knowing Masters of Scripture.

Commentary : The author begins the work with the worship of the *Siddhas*, The term *Siddha* implies the Supreme Self which has realised its true nature. He uses the word *savvasiddhe*— all the *Siddhas*, probably to distinguish the Jaina conception of *Mokṣa* from the non-Jaina conceptions. Jainism recognises plurality of selves not merely in the world of *Saṁsāra* but also in the liberated state or Siddhahood

१. Other reading धुवममल-

which is a sort of divine republic of Perfect Souls, where each Self retains its individual personality and does not empty its contents into the cauldron of the Absolute as is maintained by some other systems of philosophy. It is but proper that the work should begin with the worship of the *Siddhas*, since the author is going to discuss the true nature of the Self in this treatise. In the first line of the *gāthā*, he mentions the various attributes of the *Siddha*, the Perfect Self. The attribute *dhuvaṁ* implies an unchanging permanency because, the self, after achieving its true nature on the destruction of all *karmic* shackles, is not subject to any further manifestation and hence is characterised by unchanging permanency. The term *acalaṁ* implies the complete cessation of transmigratory existence. The Self in the world of *Saṁsāra*, determined by its own *karmic* conditions, roams about in the empirical world, being born in any one of the four *gatis*, or major organic classes as determined by one's own *karma*. When *karmas* are completely destroyed, when the Self achieves his true nature and becomes a *Siddha*, this roaming about in the transmigratory world comes to a full stop. This is what is implied by the attribute *acala*. If the other reading, *amala*, is accepted then the attribute would refer to complete absence of *karmic* impurity which is the *sine qua non* for achieving Siddhahood. The next attribute is *anupama*, having no parallel or comparison. This characteristic naturally follows like a corollary because the excellence of the Siddhahood far transcends the excellent things of the concrete world. Hence Siddhahood cannot be indicated by comparison with any concrete object of the empirical world, however great and good it may be. After offering his obeisance to *Siddha* of such characteristics, the author addresses the faithful ones, for whose sake he composes the work called *Samayapāhuḍa*.

The first part of the word *Samaya* means the Self, the

knower, the latter part of the word *Pāhuḍa* is interpreted to mean the essence or *Sāra*. Further, he declares that the treatise which he is going to compose is in confirmity with what is taught by The Śrutakevalīs, the omniscient masters of the scriptures. The author mentions this fact not merely to defend his own work as consistent with the revealed Word of the Lord, but also to imply that what is not so based upon such divine revelation is neither worthy of speaking about nor worthy of listening to.

In the next *gāthā*, the author takes up for discussion the two kinds of Self, the Pure One which is termed as *svasamaya*, and the Impure One which is designated as *parasamaya*. The latter refers to the empirical ego and the former, to the pure ego which transcends the empirical conditions.

जीवो चरित्तदंसणणाणट्ठिदो तं हि ससमयं जाण।
पोग्गलकम्मुवदेसट्ठियं च तं जाण परसमयं॥ २॥

jīvo carittadaṁsaṇaṇāṇaṭṭhido taṁ hi sasamayaṁ jāṇa
poggalakammuvadesaṭṭhiyaṁ ca taṁ jāṇa parasamayaṁ

जीवश्चारित्रदर्शनज्ञानस्थित: तं हि स्वसमयं जानीहि।
पुद्गलकर्मोपदेशस्थितं च तं जानीहि परसमयम्॥ २॥

2. Know ye that the *Jīva* which (in its intrinsic purity) rests on Right Conduct, Faith and Knowledge is the real Self. But that which is conditioned by *karmic* material is other than the real.

Commentary : This *gāthā* states the fundamental problem of philosophy which is discussed by all the systems of thought, both in the East and in the West. The term *Svasamaya*, Ego-in-itself is the pure and ultimate reality which is considered to be the ideal aimed at by all the Indian *Darśanas* and also by some of the western schools of thought. This Ego-in-itself is characterised by the three qualities of *Darśana*, *Jñāna*, and *Cāritra*—Belief, Knowledge and Conduct. These three attributes are also associated with the ordinary human personality in the empirical world. In the latter case the terms have quite intelligible significance in as much as the activity of the ordinary human personality manifests through his own body. The threefold characteristics of *Darśana-Jñāna-Cāritra* are to be understood in relation to the body. But in the case of the Ego-in-itself, which is entirely free from *aupādhic* conditions, the ordinary significance associated with the terms will not hold good. Here we have only to consider the nature of the Pure Self and hence these terms must be interpreted consistent with the state of the Self which is free and pure from *aupādhic* conditions. *Cāritra* cannot therefore mean the same thing as conduct associated with an ordinary man. It must imply the pure and intrinsic activity of the spiritual entity which goes by the name of *Paramātmā* or the Ego-in-itself. Similarly the other two characteristics must imply the intrinsic vision and knowledge which are associated with the Pure Self which has destroyed all the *aupādhic* conditions constituted by *karmic* matter.

After stating the characteristics of *sva-samaya* the author indicates the nature of the empirical ego by stating that it is in association with the very *aupādhic* conditions of *karmic* matter which are absent in the case of the Pure Self. The Self in association with the *aupādhic* conditions is not an entirely different entity from the Pure Self which is designated as *svasamaya*. If the two are identical in nature, the question naturally arises, how does the Ego-in-itself which is pure in nature and which is free from extraneous contamination of *karmic* material, become degraded to an empirical ego entirely enmeshed in *karmic upādhis*. Here is a distinct deterioration in the nature of the Self which may be termed as the Fall of Man. This Fall of Man, as is already stated, is the central theme of religious philosophy all over the world. The self in its pure nature is recognised to be entirely free from *karmic* shackles and yet in the concrete world he is found always in chains. He is by nature free and yet he is everywhere found in chains. What is the explanation of this great spiritual degradation? The Semetic religions, Judaism and Christianity, conveniently answer the question of the Fall of Man by the hypothesis of the original sin. But the Indian systems of thought do not adopt such a cheap and convenient hypothesis. The explanation offered by the Jaina system of metaphysics, places the association of the Self with extraneous matter in the beginningless past. The empirical Self in *saṁsāra* is assumed to be in association with *aupādhic* conditions and it is said to struggle to extricate itself from the shackles of *karmic* conditions in its attempt to realise the ideal and goal—the Liberated Self. The problem, therefore, for the Jaina metaphysician is not the problem of the Fall of Man and the Lost Paradise. On the other hand, it is the reverse of this. It is a grand pilgrimage to the spiritual goal, a noble excelsior towards the hilltop of the Region of Peace and Purity towards which the whole creation moves. This conception in some form or other is accepted by the other Indian systems also. Śaṅkara in the very beginning of his Bhāṣya enumerates the various hypotheses as to the nature of the Self which he rejects as incorrect and finally states his own position which is the identification of Brahma or *Ātmā*, the Ultimate Reality, with the empirical ego in the concrete world. In describing the nature of the latter, empirical ego in *Saṁsāra*, he also speaks of Saṁsāra being *anādi* without a beginning and that the career of the empirical Self is also *anādi* without a beginning. Why is the Self found in association with *upādhis* in its empirical form? Śaṅkara distinctly mentions that the Self builds a tabernacle of *upādhis* by its own *karmas.* The building up of the *karmic upādhis* takes the form of its corporeal existence where the Self, through its own body as its vehicle, is able to enjoy the fruits of its own *karma*, good or bad, in the form of happiness and misery.

This association of the Self with the extraneous material *upādhis* is thus explained to be the result of *avidyā* or ignorance which is present in the empirical self from time immemorial. The attempt to get itself liberated from the bondage of *upādhis* or *karmic* shackles must begin with getting rid of the *avidyā.* When once this *avidyā* is got rid of, the *karmas*, good or bad, are got rid of and the individual soul realises its own pure nature in the form of *Paramātmā* or *Brahma*, as it is generally designated by the Vedāntic writers. This career of the individual Self sketched by Śaṅkara is exactly parallel to the sketch given by Jaina metaphysics and this theory is quite unaffected by the Vedānta theory that the *Brahma* is the ultimate cause of things and persons. The similarity is much more marked when we turn to the Mīmāṁsā conception of the Self. This is not encumbered with the Vedāntic hypothesis of *Brahma* as the original cause. It freely assumes the Self to be eternal and uncreated. It postulates a plurality of Selves each having its own individual career. This individual Self is present in the beginningless *Saṁsāra* in association with *karmic upādhis* which are material in nature. This association with material *upādhis* is determined by the Self's own conduct according to *Dharma* or *Adharma.* Hence, liberation from the *upādhis*, must be obtained through discarding both *Dharma* and *Adharma.* Thus the association of the Self with *karmic upādhis*, its liberation from the same, are both explained without bringing in the aid of any extraneous causal agency. In fact both the Mīmāṁsakas and the Vedāntins stoutly repudiate the hypothesis of a creator or an Īśvara put forward by the Nyāya-Vaiśeṣika systems in order to explain the association of the Self with material *karmic upādhis* resulting in the corporeal existence of the empirical self.

Our author therefore starts with the central theme of the association of Self with *karmic* material, and his work is an elaborate explanation of the problems as why the individual Self is found in *karmic* chains and how it can break the shackles and assume its own true nature, pure and free. This is the aim of *Samayasāra.*

एयत्तणिच्छयगदो समओ सव्वत्थ सुंदरो लोए।
बंधकहा एयत्ते तेण विसंवादिणी होइ॥ ३॥

eyattaṇicchayagado samao savvattha sundaro loe
baṁdhakahā eyatte teṇa visaṁvādiṇī hoi (3)

एकत्वनिश्चयगतः समयः सर्वत्रसुन्दरो लोके।
बन्धकथा एकत्वे तेन विसंवादिनी भवति ॥ ३॥

3. The Self which has realised its oneness (uncontaminated by alien conditions) is the beautiful ideal in the whole universe. To associate bondage with this unity is therefore self-contradictory.

Commentary : The author further emphasises the greatness and sublimity of the Ego-in-itself or *sva-samaya.* This is said to be the sublime and the beautiful in the whole world. The whole of the organic world from the one-sensed organism right up to man is viewed from this angle of vision. It is this sublime and beautiful Ego-in-itself that constitutes the inner reality of every organism. That being the ultimate goal, recognition of this Ego-in-itself as the object to be aimed at is, therefore, the most desirable thing. This ultimate ideal is so far removed from the concrete world of the empirical reality that it would be erroneous to associate *aupādhic* shackles with the sublime and beautiful entity of the Ultimate Self. It is difficult to understand what the author has exactly in his mind, when he says that it is erroneous to predicate bondage of this reality. Neither of the commentators is of any help to us. When he says that it is erroneous to associate bondage with *Paramātmā*, the author must be thinking about some rival theory which in his opinion makes that mistake. To predicate a further career for the *Paramātmā* leading to a further manifestation would certainly be considered by our author as an erroneous hypothesis. Probably he is thinking of the Upaniṣadic system which not only presupposes that *Ātmā* or *Brahma* is the original cause of the world but also postulates the periodic evolution and involution in the life-career of the ultimate *Brahma* which our author evidently thinks reduces the *Brahma* to a *Saṁsāric* entity and therefore amounts to predicating bondage to the *Paramātma-svarūpa*. It would probably be more plausible to suggest that he was thinking of the popular deities of the Purāṇic Hinduism. But such a suggestion would be an anachronism, because Purāṇic Hinduism and Purāṇic deiteis were not fully developed about the Ist century B.C., which is the date of our author. Internal evidence clearly shows that he was fully acquainted with Upaniṣadic literature; hence our suggestion that the author was having in his mind the Brahma's periodic career of manifestation and dissolution, an idea prominently present in the Upaniṣadic thought. This Upaniṣadic Brahma, which is also designated as *Paramātmā*, is the same as our author's *sva-samaya*—the Ego-in-itself; but the Vedāntic Brahma or *Paramātmā* is credited with periodic manifestation and dissolution, a characteristic entirely foreign to our author's concept of *sva-samaya*. This is offered only as a suggestion of a probable implication of the author's intention and we cannot assert anything dogmatically about that.

Next, the author goes to show that of these two Egos, the empirical Ego and the metempirical Ego, the former is easily apprehended whereas the latter is very difficult to realise.

सुदपरिचिदाणुभूदा सव्वस्स वि कामभोगबंधकहा।
एयत्तस्सुवलंभो णवरि ण सुलभो विभत्तस्स॥ ४॥

sudaparicidāṇubhūdā savvassa vi kāmabhogabaṁdha-kahā
eyattassuvalaṁbho ṇavari ṇa sulabho vibhattassa (4)

श्रुतपरिचितानुभूता सर्वस्यापि कामभोगबन्धकथा।
एकत्वस्योपलम्भः केवलं न सुलभो विभक्तस्य ॥ ४॥

4. The proposition that all living beings are characterised by desire for worldly things, enjoyment of the same and consequential bondage has been heard, observed and personally experienced by all. But the realisation of the unity of the Higher Self which is free from all such empirical conditions, by our own personal experience, is not easy of achievement.

Commentary : Here the author frankly states in the beginning that it is extremely difficult to apprehend the nature of the metempirical Self or the Ego-in-itself. He contrasts it with our knowledge of the empirical Ego. The nature of the empirical Self can be easily apprehended from the concrete world of living beings. The behaviour of a living organism is a clear indication of its nature. The instinct of self-preservation in an organism is the main motive force of its behaviour. Every animal has to seek its food from the environment to appease its hunger, to search for water to quench its thirst, and to roam about in search of a mate to satisfy its sex desire. This tendency to seek objects from the environment, to acquire them and to enjoy them is a common characteristic of the behaviour of all living beings from the lowest to the highest. This knowledge we obtain from our observation of other animals and by the study of books on natural history describing the behaviour of animals in general. The information so gathered by observation and study is further corroborated by our own personal experience since our own behaviour as an organic being is no exception to the general law of animal behaviour. The information thus obtained from different sources gives us a fairly accurate knowledge of the nature of the empirical Ego. But when we begin to talk about the metempirical Ego we feel extremely helpless. None of the above sources of information are available to us. The reality which we try to apprehend has nothing in common with our empirical reality. That is why the Upaniṣadic thinker frankly states that it can be described only by negative attributes. We can only speak of it as *neti neti*, not this, not this. That is exactly why Gautama Buddha kept silent whenever he was asked by his disciples to give some information about the Self or *Ātmā*. Again, that is exactly the reason why the founder of Christianity always emphasised that the Path leading to the Kingdom of God is extremely narrow and steep. It is this very truth that is communicated to us by our author in this *gāthā*. Instead of taking refuge in a cheap agnosticism that the Ultimate Reality is unknowable, he merely states that it is exremely difficult to apprehend. Then he promises that one who has the courage and conviction to plod along the steep and narrow path can, however, reach the Summit, the spiritual hilltop, and thus have a complete view of the sublime reality, a privilege not available to the ordinary mortals roaming about in the valley below.

तं एयत्तविभत्तं दाएहं अप्पणो सविहवेण।
जदि दाएज्ज पमाणं चुक्किज्ज छलं ण घेत्तव्वं ॥ ५॥

taṁ eyattavibhattaṁ dāyehaṁ appaṇo savihaveṇa
jadi dāyejja pamāṇaṁ cukkijja chalaṁ ṇa ghettavvaṁ

तमेकत्वविभक्तं दर्शयेऽहमात्मनः स्वविभवेन।
यदि दर्शयेयं प्रमाणं च्युतो भवामि छलं न गृहीतव्यम्॥ ५॥

5. That Higher Unity differentiated from alien real conditions, I will try to reveal as far as I can. Accept it if it satisfies the condition of Truth or *Pramāṇas.* But if I fail in my description, you may reject it.

Commentary : It is a general belief among Indian thinkers that the metempirical Self or the Ego-in-itself is to be approached only through undergoing a special kind of spiritual discipline called *yoga* or *tapas.* This discipline opens up a new door-way to approach the Ultimate Reality which cannot be apprehended through ordinary sense-perception. Such a super-sensuous faculty of apprehending the inner Self is the privilege of those few who by the practice of *yoga* successfully obtain it. Such a supersensuous experience of metempirical Reality must have been obtained by our author through the practice of the spiritual discipline of Yoga which is the necessary condition for such an acquisition. Otherwise he would not make bold to promise that he would reveal the nature of that Ultimate Reality—the Metempirical Self. But when he begins to translate this spiritual intention in terms of ordinary vocabulary for the benefit of his readers, he is not sure about the adequacy of language to express the complete implication of his inner vision. Therefore he cautions the reader to test the message offered to him according to the canons of *pramāṇa* or correct knowledge before accepting it.

If it does not stand the test, then it need not be accepted. That would only prove the inadequacy of language to express accurately the knowledge obtained by supersensuous experience. The term *pramāṇa* is to be interpreted in this context not in the ordinary sense of sense-perception, inference, etc. As a matter of fact, the Jaina thinkers, when they speak of *pratyakṣa*, do not mean sense-perception, which is the meaning given to the term by the other Indian systems. Sense-perception or *pratyakṣa* according to the ordinary meaning is called *parokṣa* by the Jaina thinker because such knowledge is obtained through an intermediate instrument of sense-organ and not directly by the Self. It is the latter that is called *pratyakṣa*, what is directly present before the Self without the mediation of any external instrumentality. It is such a *pramāṇa*, the supersenuous perception of the Self, that the author must be thinking of when he enjoins the reader to test his message before accepting it.

One other point we have to notice is this. Though he says that he is going to follow the footsteps of the Masters of the scripture who went before him, and who themselves had the information directly from the Omniscient Lord, the Sarvajña, still he does not want to impose this on the reader on the authority of the Revealed Word of the Lord. His frank advice to the reader to submit this message to the touch-stone of *pramāṇa* clearly implies two things. He does not want to adopt the method adopted by those thinkers whose systems of thought are based upon the authority of the Vedas. These philosophers, whenever they are confronted with intellectual difficulties imcompatible with the Vedic traditions, reject these, even though they are ordinarily in conformity with the usual *pramāṇas*. To them, the *pramāṇa* of the Veda is the most important and, before that, the other *pramāṇas* become inadequate and hence lose their value of authority. The attitude adopted by our author is entirely different from the Vedic tradition. The other point to be noticed here is the implication that such an inconvenient situation will not arise here, that is the conflict between what is revealed by the Divine Word and the value of the *pramāṇas.* The bold suggestion that his information should be tested before acceptance expresses his complete confidence that what is revealed by the *Sarvajña* and what is also experienced by his own supersensuous method will stand the severest test when critically examined by the canons of Truth. He is sure that his message will certainly pass through the ordeal of critical examination and he will not need to take refuge in some kind of authority, superhuman and unchallengeable. Thus in short the author expresses the nature of Truth as he understands it, and how it is different from Truth resting upoin the authority of the Vedas which is alleged to be superhuman and therefore above criticism.

Next the author describes the nature of the Pure Self which is free from the impure psychic states such as desire etc.

णवि होदि अप्पमत्तो ण पमत्तो जाणगो दु जो भावो।
एवं भणंति सुद्धा णादा जो सो दु सो चेव॥ ६॥

ṇavi hodi appamatto ṇa pamatto jāṇago du jo bhāvo
evaṁ bhaṇaṁti suddhā ṇādā jo so du so ceva (6)

नापि भवत्यप्रमत्तो न प्रमत्तो ज्ञायकस्तु यो भाव:।
एवं भणन्ति शुद्धा: ज्ञाता: य: स तु स चैव ॥ ६॥

6. That real being who is of the nature of the Knower, is neither identical with *Apramatta* nor *Pramatta* beings. His nature as the Knower is unique and self-identical. Thus declare the thinkers who adopt the pure (absolute) point of view.

Commentary : The terms *apramatta* and *pramatta*, (vigilant of duties and non-vigilant of duties) are used as representative terms to denote the various shapes of spiritual development which are implied by the technical term, *guṇasthānas*, which are gradations based upon ethico-spiritual development. Human beings are classified according to the principle of such a development and arranged according to various classes of ascending gradation beginning with *mithyādṛṣṭi* upto *Ayogakevalī*, from the one in whom right faith is absent upto one who has attained spiritual perfection through liberation from karmic *upādhis*. *Apramatta*, which is the seventh stage in the gradation, stands for the eight upper stages. whereas *pramatta*, which is the sixth in the gradation, represents the six lower stages. Thus the author emphasises the fact that the characteristic brought about by the association of the Self-with *aupādhic* conditions,—the *guṇasthāna* being based upon such qualities—must be understood to be entirely alien to the nature of the Pure self.

The author, who proposes to investigate the nature of the True Self, thus starts with the thesis that his nature is distinct from modes and characteristics resulting from its combination with the *upādhic* material condition whose nature is entirely distinct from that of the Ego-in-itself. The intellectual atmosphere about the time of our author was pregnant with certain fundamental truths accepted by the various systems of thought then prevalent. There were thinkers paying allegiance to the Upaniṣadic movement, there were the Bauddhas and the Sāṁkhyas, besides the Jainas. There were also the materialistic free-thinkers about that time. All these different systems accepted certain principles in common. All started with the concrete world of experience as the point of departure for their investigations. In this concrete world they recognised the proud distinction between the organic and the inorganic, the living and the non-living, *jīva* and *ajīva.* They also noticed the fundamental difference between the behaviour of the living thing and that of the non-living thing. The behaviour of a living organism, however rudimentary in development, always indicates a purposive activity capable of spontaneous manifestation, whereas such a purposive spontaneous activity is entirely absent in the inorganic world. The physical object inert and incapable of spontaneous movement will only move when hit by a moving object—the speed and direction of motion being determined by the original impact. Besides the purposive behaviour of the living organism, they possess also certain other characteristics which are altogether absent in the inorganic world. The characteristics are birth and growth, decay and death. Every living being must be born from living parentage, must have development upto a certain stage and then decay and end in death. These characteristics were carefully noticed by the Indian thinkers who postulated a life-principle which was supposed to be present in all organic bodies capable of purposive activity. The behaviour of organic bodies as contrasted with other non-living physical bodies was thus explained by the presence of this life-principle which operated through the living body which is also constituted by various inorganic elements. Thus as far as the organic body is concerned, they recognised two distinct entities. The constitution of the organic body is explained by the combination of various inorganic elements and its purposive intelligent behaviour being credited to the operative life-principle called *Ātmā* or Soul. The materialist saved himself from the trouble of metaphysical investigation by a summary disposal of the problem. For him there was no entity called *Ātmā* which is postulated by others in order to explain this purposive intelligent nature of animal behaviour. The organic body is constituted by the inorganic element constituting the organic body. The other systems rightly rejected this view as erroneous because of its inadequacy to explain satisfactorily the purposive and intelligent behaviour of animals: Hence the other systems are at one in postulating a separate entity besides the body which is constituted by inorganic elements, in order to explain the purposive behaviour of the organism. This entity which is so postulated is assumed to be a *cetana*, being of the nature of intelligence as contrasted with inorganic bodies which are said to be *acetana* and non-intelligent. Thus all the systems reduced the organic beings, including man, to a combination of two distinct entities *cetana* and *acetana*, intelligent and non-intelligent. Their whole philosophical attempt is directed to a clear determination of the nature of this intelligent principle which is supposed to be present in all living beings. Again, all these systems, minus the materialistic one, agree in maintaining that this life-principle or *Ātmā* should not be identified with the body or any organ of the body, though it is the operative principle responsible for the activity of the organic body as a whole or of the various organs, sensorial and motor. Thus the philosophical investigation as to the nature of the life-principle of *Ātmā* or Self, by a careful elimination of all that pertains to the body as alien to its nature. So far the systems agree in their ultimate aim as well as their method of investigation, though the conclusion reached is different in each case, thus resulting in different philosophical systems. Thus we see our author stating the nature of the Pure Self by a process of elimination of all those characteristics which result from its association with inorganic material elements which are designated technically *upādhis*.

The author goes to point out next, that even in the case of the Self free from *aupādhic* conditions, certain diverse qualities ordinarily associated with it such as Darśana etc. when viewed from the absolute point, can be differentiated only verbally and not really.

ववहारेणुवदिस्सदि णाणिस्स चरित्तदंसणं णाणं।
णवि णाणं ण चरित्तं ण दंसणं जाणगो सुद्धो॥ ७॥

vavahāreṇuvadissadi ṇāṇissa carittadaṁsaṇaṁ ṇāṇaṁ
ṇavi ṇāṇaṁ ṇa carittaṁ ṇa daṁsaṇaṁ jāṇago suddho

व्यवहारेणोपदिश्यते ज्ञानिनश्चारित्रदर्शनं ज्ञानम्।
नापि ज्ञानं न चारित्रं न दर्शनं ज्ञायक: शुद्ध: ॥ ७॥

7. From the *vyavahāra* point of view, conduct, belief and knowledge are attributed (as different characteristics) of the Knower, the Self. But from the real point of view there is no (differentiation of) knowledge, conduct, in Pure Self.

Commentary : Jaina metaphysics always emphasises the nature of reality to be identity-in-difference and unity in the midst of multiplicity. This characteristic which is assumed to be present in reality in general is associated in a marked dgeree with the Self. The Self in association with material *aupādhic* conditions is said to be born in the world of *saṁsāra* with various organic bodies in various places and various times. The various births associated with a particular Self will be practically infinite in number when the beginningless *saṁsāric* career is taken into consideration. All these various forms are considered to be *paryāyas* or modifications of the self-same unitary ego. The Self is one and its modifications determined by *aupādhic* conditions are infinite in number. It is in this sense that the saying that the *Ātmā* is one and the ṛṣis call it many is interpreted by the Jaina metaphysics is the relation between the substance and its qualities. The complex nature of the substance with its qualities is also interpreted to be identity-in-difference. The qualities cannot be considered as entirely distinct from the substance. It is the same identical substance that expresses its nature through qualities. No doubt the qualities may be spoken of as different from one another and all from the underlying substance. Such consideration of the quality in abstract is only verbal differentiation. But really the qualities cannot exist independent of the substance, nor the substance independent of its qualities as is maintained by the Vaiśeṣika school of thought. It is this latter point that is emphasised in this *gāthā*. The self in its pure nature, which is entirely free from *aupādhic* conditions, must be considered as an indivisible unity in spite of the different attributes associated with it ordinarily. The characteristics, *Darśana, Jñāna*, and *Cāritra* are only verbal differentiations employed to explain the complex nature of the unitary self. This point that the qualities can only be differentiated verbally from the substance is illustrated by Jayasena in the following manner. We may speak of fire that it burns, that it cooks or that it shines, when we consider the various purposes for which it is employed. Burning, cooking and shining are spoken of as the various properties of fire, because of its relation to other things, based upon different purposes. In spite of the various descriptions of its properties, fire is one and the same. Similarly the Self is one individual identity and unity in spite of the various descriptions of its nature in terms of *Darśana, Jñāna* and *Cāritra*. The same point is illustrated by Amṛtacandra in the following manner. When an able teacher wants to inform his student about the nature of an extremely complex reality possessing innumerable properties, he will proceed cautiously in choosing one property after another in order to instruct the student accurately. Confronting him with the whole complex reality at the same time will only confound the student and the teacher's aim will be defeated. This process of selecting one characteristic after another in order to produce a clear understanding in the mind of the student of the extremely complex nature of the reality which is the object of study will not in any way really tamper with the identical unity of that object. In the same way the self which is a complex reality may for the purpose of instruction be described in different terms, but in spite of the variety of these descriptions it does not lose its ultimate identity and unity. These two *gāthās* (6 and 7) may be taken to be an implied refutation of the Upaniṣadic pantheism, Buddhist *Kṣaṇikavāda* or momentariness of the Self, and the Vaiśeṣika theory of the distinction between *dravya* and *guṇa*, as distinct categories.

1. Though the Jaina view recognises the identical unity of the Self throughout its career of transmigratory existence, still it does not reduce all the concrete personalities and organisms as the modifications of one and the same *ātmā* as is maintained by Upaniṣadic pantheism and later Vedāntism.

2. The *Kṣaṇikavāda* of the Bauddhas is also rejected by the Jaina metaphysics. The Bauddhas, like the western philosopher Hume, rejected a permanent objective reality as well as the permanent identity of the Self. This goes by the name of *Kṣaṇikavāda* or momentariness which is also designated by the term *Anātmavāda*. While the Bauddhas do not accept any individual identity of the Self besides and beyond the series of psychic states, Jaina metaphysics emphasises that these series of psychic states cannot be adequately explained without the postulate of a permanent *ātmā*.

3. We have indicated before, the Jaina conception of the relation between dravya and its *guṇas* and how this account is different from the Vaiśeṣika one. Hence there is implicit refutation of the Vaiśeṣika theory also.

If the real nature of the Self is obtained only by adopting the *pāramārthika* point of view, what is the use of adopting the inferior *vyavahāra* point which is able to give only a partial and incomplete account of the ultimate reality. The answer is given in the next *gāthā*.

जह णवि सक्कमणज्जो अणज्जभासं विणा उ गाहेदुं।
तह ववहारेण विणा परमत्थुवदेसणमसक्कं ॥ ८॥

jaha ṇavi sakkamaṇajjo aṇajjabhāsaṁ viṇā u gāheduṁ
taha vavahāreṇa viṇā paramatthuvadesaṇamasakkaṁ (8)

यथा न शक्योऽनार्योऽनार्यभाषां बिना तु ग्राहयितुम्।
तथा व्यवहारेण बिना परमार्थोपदेशनमशक्यम्॥ ८॥

8. Just as a non-Āryan (foreigner) cannot be made to understand anything except through the medium of his non-Āryan language, so the knowledge of the Absolute cannot be communicated to the ordinary people except through the *vyavahāra* point of view.

Commentary : Here the author enunciates an important principle of education which must be adopted by every teacher in instructing his pupils. The teacher must take into consideration the understanding capacity of the pupil and he must adopt a method of instruction suitable to the situation and present the matter of instruction so as to be easily understood by the pupil. He illustrates this by pointing out how it is absolutely necessary when talking to a foreigner to converse with him only through his own foreign language, in order to make him understand what he wishes to communicate to him. This is given as a justification for adopting the *vyavahāra* point of view which is recognised to be different from and inferior to the *pāramārthika* point of view. This distinction between the *Pāramārthika* Naya and the *Vyavahāra Naya*, the two intellectual methods of approach towards the comprehension of reality, is adopted by the Jaina metaphysicians as a very important one. Our author adopts these two methods throughout the work as the occasion demands. Since Jaina metaphysics assumes the reality to be a complex entity it is bound to adopt both these points of view. The ultimate reality must be subjected to an intellectual analysis and the constituent elements so obtained must be selected and emphasised according to the interest of the student and also consistent with the purpose of the discussion. The variations in the context and the intellectual aim will naturally determine the nature of the descriptions adopted with reference to the reality studied. The method of selective description to suit the purpose of the context is the method adopted by the ordinary man who is engaged in his pursuit in life. Since the method is determined by a purpose of practical interest, the investigation will be relevant only to that purpose and the conclusion obtained must be therefore partial, since it is not concerned with other aspects of the reality which are left out as of no concern, being irrelevant to the purpose in hand. This process of investigation goes by the name of the *Vyavahāra Naya* or the practical point of view as contrasted with the other method, *Pāramārthika Naya.* The term *Paramārtha* refers to the ultimate and implies a philosophical attempt to probe into the inner core of reality with the object of comprehending the intrinsic nature of reality, whole and complete. It is also called *Niścaya Naya*, real point of view, since it is not concerned with the various aspects, partial and purposive, relevant only to the practical man and not to the philosopher. This distinction between the *pāramrārthika* view and the *vyavahāra* is also adopted by Śaṅkara in his *Bhāṣya* on the Vedānta Sūtras. Since Śaṅkara came several centuries after Kundakunda, since he was also of South India, probably he was also of South India, probably he was aquainted with Kundakunda's writings and adopted the method of distinction between the practical and the real point of view as suitable to his own purpose. Since our author has used the word *Anārya* in the sense of the foreigner, it must be noted that there is no race-superiority implied by the term as is ordinarily assumed. In Vedic literature the term *Ārya* is used exclusively to denote the immigrant clan of Āryans as contrasted with the people of the land who are described with the sinister name of *Dāsas*. This racial distinction ultimately led to the Hindu social organisation of four *varṇas* in which the Dāsas were assigned the fourth name or the Śūdra caste. The Jaina conception of social organisation is different from this Hindu conception. Here the distinction is based more upon profession and qualification than upon birth, as is clearly evident from the Jaina tradition that such a social organisation was originally established by Lord Ṛṣabha. Commenting upon the Sūtra *āryā mlecchāsca* (36 II. of *Tattvārtha Sūtra)*, the commentators, both Pūjyapāda and Akalaṅka, speak of five different classes of Āryas, Kśetra Āryas, Jāti-Āryas, Karma Āryas, Cāritra Āryas, and Darśana Āryas. The first class includes all those who live in the countries of Kāsi, Kosala, etc.; the second class includes those who belong to the Ikṣvāku clan; the third class includes all those who are engaged in the six kinds of professions such as defence, agricuture, trade, art, etc.; the fourth class refers to all those persons who ennoble themselves by moral conduct and spiritual discipline; and the fifth class, to all those who adopt the right faith as the basis of their religious discipline. In speaking about the *anāryas* or *mlecchas* they refer to two classes of *Mlecchas*, *Antardvīpaja*, and *Karma-bhūmija*, those that are born in foreign continents and those that are born in Bharatakhaṇḍa, called Karmabhūmi.

The Śakas, Yavanas, Śabaras, and Pulindas, etc. are *anāryas* living in the land. This description of Āryas and Anāryas is quite clear. All the people of the land irrespective of their birth and profession are included under the class *ārya.* The Śūdras engaged in agriculture, the blacksmith, the goldsmith and the sculptor are all designated by the honorific term of *āryas*. The illustration given of non-Āryans, such as Śākas, and Yavanas clearly indicates that the term is used to designate foreigners. It is in this sense that our author uses the term in the above *gāthā*, when he says that when you talk to an *anārya* you must talk to him in his language, that is in his *anārya* language, the foreigner's tongue.

जो हि सुदेणभिगच्छइ अप्पाणमिणं तु केवलं सुद्धं।
तं सुयकेवलिमिसिणो भणंति लोयप्पदीवयरा॥ ९॥

jo hi sudeṇabhigacchai appāṇamiṇam tu kevalaṁ suddhaṁ
taṁ suyakevalimisiṇo bhaṇaṁti loyappadīvayarā (9)

यो हि श्रुतेनाभिगच्छति आत्मानमिमं तु केवलं शुद्धम्।
तं श्रुतकेवलिनमृशयो भणन्ति लोकप्रदीपकरा:॥ ९॥

9. Whoever realises the absolute and pure nature of this Self through the knowledge of the scripture, him, the Ṛṣis, the light of the world, call an all-knowing Master of Scripture.

Commentary : This *gāthā* refers to *Niścaya Śrutakevalī* as contrasted with *Vyavahāra Śrutakevalī* referred to in the next *gāthā.* This real all-knowing Master of the Scripture, by the complete acquisition of the scriptural knowledge, is able to realise the Self as that which illuminates itself and the other and, hence, is of the nature of knowledge or *Jñāna*, an experience independently obtained by the *Kevala-jñāna*, as the result of *tapas*. Since almost the same result is obtained in these two cases, one through *tapas* and the other through the knowledge of the scripture, the *Śrutakevalī* is designated as *niścaya Śrutakevalī. The author describes the Vyavahāra Śrutakevalī in the next gāthā.*

जो सुयणाणं सव्वं जाणइ सुयकेवलिं तमाहु जिणा।
णाणं अप्पा सव्वं जम्हा सुयकेवली तम्हा ॥ १० ॥

jo suyaṇāṇaṁ savvaṁ jāṇaï suyakevaliṁ tamāhu jiṇā
ṇāṇaṁ appā savvaṁ jamhā suyakevalī tamhā (10)

यः श्रुतज्ञानं सर्वं जानाति श्रुतकेवलिनं तमाहुर्जिनाः।
ज्ञानमात्मा सर्वं यस्मात् श्रुतकेवली तस्मात् ॥ १० ॥

10. The Jinas call him a (*Vyavahāra*) *Śrutakevalī* who has full knowledge of the scripture; as all scriptural knowledge ultimately leads to the knowledge of the Self, therefore the (knower of the Self) is called *Śrutakevalī.*

Commentary : The person who masters completely the scripture comprising the twelve *aṅgas,* is referred to as Vyavahāra-*śrutakevalī*, since he distinguishes himself by his study of the scripture, the *dravya śruta* or the different works constituting the *aṅgas* or the *āgams.* Even with the complete study of the scripture he has not reached that stage of realising the *Ātmā* as the pure Self, though he may reach that stage ultimately. Hence he is designated as *Vyavahāra-śrutakevalī*, as contrasted with the other who, through the acquisition of *bhāva-śruta,* is able to realise the real Self for which reason he is designated as *Niścayaśrutakevalī.* The former has knowledge of all the reals, for which he is called Kevalī, and since his knowledge of all the reals is through the scriptures, he is called Śrutakevalī. And since his knowledge is obtained through the description of the reals given in the scripture, he is called *Śrutakevalī.* And since his knowledge is obtained through the description of the reals given in the scripture, he is called *Vyavahāraśrutakevalī.* The latter, through his knowledge obtained through the scripture, is able to immediately realise the *Niścayaśrutakevalī.* These two are contrasted with the omniscient, *par exellence,* one who obtains *Kevala-jñāna,* through *tapas.*

ववहारो अभूदत्थो भूदत्थो देसिदो दु सुद्धणओ।
भूदत्थमस्सिदो खलु सम्मादिट्ठी हवदि जीवो॥ ११॥

vavahāro abhūdattho bhūdattho desido du suddhaṇayo
bhūdatthamassido khalu sammādiṭṭhī havadi jīvo (11)

व्यवहारोऽभूतार्थो भूतार्थो देशितस्तु शुद्धनयः।
भूतार्थमाश्रितः खलु सम्यग्दृष्टिर्भवति जीवः॥ ११॥

11. The practical stand-point does not reveal the reals; the pure point of view is said (to relate to) the real; verily, the soul that takes refuge in the real is one of right vision.

Commentary : The *vyavahāra* point of view, since it is based upon practical interest, need not and does not take into consideration the reality as it is. Only that aspect of reality which is considered useful by the practical view in the context is taken into consideration by the *vyavahāra* point of view. Both the commentators explain this first through an illustration. An ordinary illiterate person, when he feels thirsty, may freely drink muddy water if it is immediately available to him. He wants water to quench his thirst and does not wait to enquire whether it is pure or impure. But in the case of an enlightened person the behaviour will be slightly different. If he is thirsty and if he can't get pure water, he would try to purify the muddy water by the application of the cleaning net, thus separating the pure water from the muddy deposit before using it. Exactly similar is the attitude of a man towards the nature of reality. The ordinary unenlightened person goaded on by practical interest may behave with the assumption that what is called Self is that which is in association with *karmic* impurities and thus gets on in life trying to obtain as much satisfaction as possible; but an enlightened individual will not thus be satisfied. He will try to distinguish between the Self as a pure entity and the various impurities ordinarily associated with it. With this discriminative knowledge, he will try to guide his life as far as possible, thus basing his whole conduct on the true knowledge of reality as it is. It is the latter class of persons that deserve to be called *Samyagdṛṣṭi* or right believer.

सुद्धो सुद्धादेसो णादव्वो परमभावदरिसीहिं।
ववहारदेसिदो पुण जे दु अपरमे ट्ठिदा भावे॥ १२॥

suddho suddhādeso ṇādavvo paramabhāvadarisīhiṁ
vavahāradesido puṇa je du aparame ṭṭhidā bhāve (12)

शुद्धः शुद्धादेशो ज्ञातव्यः परमभावदर्शिभिः।
व्यवहारदेशितः पुनर्ये त्वपरमे स्थिता भावे॥ १२॥

12. The pure stand-point which reveals the pure substance should be adopted by (those whose object is to be) the seers of the supreme state of the soul; but the practical one by those who are satisfied with a lower status.

Commentary : Thus it is emphasised that the point of view adopted depends upon the object of the investigator. The commentators again elucidate this point with an illustration. A person whose aim is to obtain pure gold without any impurities will go on melting it a number of times till all the impurities completely disappear; but in the case of a person who does not want gold of such purity for making certain ornaments will not bother himself with such repeated processes of purifying it in the fire. He may be satisfied with two or three times of fire-purification since his aim is not to obtain gold of the sixteen-touch purity. Thus the object of the person determines the process of purification in the matter of gold. The analogy is applied in the context to the purification of the Self. Whether he adopts the pure point of view or the practical point of view depends upon the purpose in life adopted by the individual.

Here ends the *pīṭhikā* or Indroduction.

The author then proceeds to describe the nine *padārthas* or categories according to Jaina metaphysics.

भूदत्थेणाभिगदा जीवाजीवा य पुण्णपावं च।
आसवसंवरणिज्जरबंधो मोक्खो य सम्मत्तं ॥ १३ ॥

bhūdattheṇābhigadā jīvājīvā ya puṇṇapāvaṁ ca
āsavasaṁvaraṇijjarabaṁdho mokkho ya sammataṁ (13)

भूतार्थेनाभिगता जीवाजीवौ च पुण्यपापं च।
आस्रवसंवरनिर्जरा बन्धो मोक्षश्च सम्यक्त्वम्॥ १३ ॥

13. Right belief is constituted by a clear comprehension, from the real point of view of the nature of the following categories : *Jīva* (soul), *Ajīva* (non-soul), *Puṇya* (virtue), *Pāpa* (Vice), *Āsrava* (inflow of *karmas*), *Saṁvara* (stoppage of *karmas*), *Nirjarā* (shedding of *karmas*), *Bandha* (bondage), and *Mokṣa* (emancipation).

Commentary : The nine *padārthas* or categories are important because of their relevancy for understanding the life-history of the soul. Of these, the first two, *jīva* and *ajīva*, the soul and the non-soul, are fundamental categories and associated with each other from beginningless time. The other seven categories, though they are enumerated on a par with the first two, according to the doctrine of *nava-padārthas,* must be recognised as resultant categories due to the interaction of the first two. In spite of the subsidiary nature of these seven categories, they are equally important as the first two inasmuch as their knowledge is quite essential to the process of self-development leading to the self-liberation which is the last of these nine categories and which is also the goal aimed at by spiritual development. Every one of these categories has a dual aspect. Externally it implies the material operative condition constituting the *karmic upādhi.* Internally it also implies the psychic modification in the self caused by the corresponding *karmic upādhi.* Thus each one of these seven categories has a two-fold nature, material and psychical, which are designated respectively by the terms *dravya* and *bhāva.* Thus we have in each case, *dravya puṇya,* and *bhāva puṇya, dravya āsrava* and *bhāva āsrava,* etc. These various categories in the life-history of the soul are objects apprehended by right belief. These various categories which are objects of right belief are identified by our author with right belief itself because there is really no fundamental distinction between belief and objects of belief. As has been pointed out above, these categories though considered as real entities because of their importance in the life-career of the soul, it must not be forgotten, are but the various aspects resulting from the interaction of the fundamental reals, *jīva.* and *ajīva.* Recognition of this fact would naturally imply that it is the same unitary Self that is present through these categories which are but the modifications of the same Self caused by the operation of the non-self *upādhis.* Thus it is possible to eliminate the modifications caused by external conditions since they do not form part of the real nature of the Self. Thus after eliminating all those modifications alien to the nature of the self caused by external conditions, it is possible to contemplate upon the nature of the pure Self. Such a realisation of the Self brought about by the discriminative knowledge of the true nature of the Self, as distinct from the operating external conditions, would ultimately reduce the categories which are considered real and important to a status of unreality and unimportance. Such a knowledge of the true Self present through-out these categories and yet transcending all these modifications is called *ātmakhyāti,* knowledge of the Self *par exellence,* a name introduced by Amṛtacandra in his commentary on this *gāthā*. This term, *ātmakhyāti* or Self-knowledge, is also used by him to designate the whole of his commentary on *Samayasāra.*

जो पस्सदि अप्पाणं अबद्धपुट्ठं अणण्णयं णियदं।
अविसेसमसंजुत्तं तं सुद्धणयं वियाणीहि॥ १४॥

jo passadi appāṇaṁ abaddhapuṭṭhaṁ aṇaṇṇayaṁ ṇiyadaṁ
avisesamasaṁjuttaṁ taṁ suddhaṇayaṁ viyāṇīhi (14)

यः पश्यति आत्मानं अबद्धस्पृष्टमनन्यकं नियतम्।
अविशेषसंयुक्तं तं शुद्धनयं विजानीहि॥ १४॥

14. He who perceives the *Ātmā* as not bound, not touched, not other than itself; steady, without any difference and not-combined, know ye him, as *śuddha-naya* or the pure point of view.

Commentary : The person who has the pure point of view is himself called the pure point of view according to this *gāthā,* as it is not altogether incorrect to equate the person with his intellectual attitude.

Not bound, not touched : though the *Ātmā* is associated with matter, *karmic* and *no-karmic*, it is neither bound by that matter nor contaminated by it. Really it retains its pristine purity just as a lotus leaf in water remains untouched by it.

Karmic matter means the subtle particles of matter suitable to constitute the subtle *karmic* body which continues to be in association with the soul throughout its transmigratory existence of births and deaths till the Self obtains liberation by the destruction of *karma* when the *karmic* body vanishes. *No-karmic* matter refers to the material molecules constituting the organic body of each individual being, the body which appears at birth and disintegrates after death.

No other than itself : though the soul is subject to different modifications in its roaming about in different *gatis* as a man or a deva, etc., the soul throughout retains its identity just as clay remains clay while it is shaped into different forms over the potter's wheel.

Steady : The soul inspite of its several psychic modifications remains steady in itself, unperturbed just as the sea which remains steady inspite of the disturbance caused on its surface by the waves.

Without any difference : the different qualities such as weight, colour, and malleability do not in any way interfere with the nature of gold. Similarly the possession of the psychic qualities like knowledge, perception, etc., does not in any way differentiate the *Ātmā*. It remains undifferentiated in spite of the qualities.

Not combined : this quality refers to the impossibility of the accidental emotional characteristics such as desire and aversion, combining with the true nature of the soul. This implies that the Self cannot be identified with the various emotions which are accidental characteristics.

जो पस्सदि अप्पाणं अबद्धपुट्ठं अणण्णमविसेसम्।
अपदेससुत्तमज्झं पस्सदि जिणसासणं सव्वं॥ १५॥

jo passadi appāṇaṁ abaddhapuṭṭaṁ aṇaṇṇamavisesaṁ
apadesasuttamajjhaṁ passadi jiṇasāsaṇaṁ savvaṁ (15)

यः पश्यति आत्मानं अबद्धस्पृष्टमनन्यमविशेषम्।
अपदेशसूत्रमध्यं पश्यति जिनशासनं सर्वम्॥ १५॥

15. He who perceives the Self as not bound, not touched, not other than self, steady and without any difference, understands the whole Jaina doctrine which is the kernel of the Scripture.

Commentary : The author emphasises the fact that complete realisation of the full Self is identical with the perception of the whole reality, which is the topic discussed in the Jaina Scripture. Knowledge of the Knower is also the Knowledge of the known.

दंसणणाणचरित्ताणि सेविदव्वाणि साहुणा णिच्चं।
ताणि पुण जाण तिण्णि वि अप्पाणं चेव णिच्छयदो॥ १६॥

daṁsaṇaṇāṇacarittāṇi sevidavvāṇi sāhuṇā ṇiccaṁ
tāṇi puṇa jāṇa tiṇṇi vi appāṇaṁ ceva ṇicchayado (16)

दर्शनज्ञानचारित्राणि सेवितव्यानि साधुना नित्यम्।
तानि पुनर्जानीहि त्रीण्यपि आत्मानं चैव निश्चयतः॥ १६॥

16. Faith, Knowledge, and Conduct should always be cherished by saints from the *vyavahāra* point of view. Know that, in reality, these three are the Self.

Commentary : Just as knowledge, belief, and conduct of a person called Devadatta, cannot have separate and independent existence apart from that person, so also knowledge, belief, and conduct realting to the Pure Self cannot have any independent existence apart from it and hence may be identified with its true nature. The three jewels above referred to, when cherished as the ideal to be aimed at, constitute *vyavahāra-ratna-traya.* But when they are realised as identical with the Self, they constitute the *niścaya-ratna-traya.* Thus the *niścaya* and *vyavahāra* points of view in the case stand in the relation of *sādhya* and *sādhana,* the ideal to be achieved and the method of achievement.

जह णाम कोवि पुरिसो रायाणं जाणिऊण सद्दहदि।
तो तं अणुचरदि पुणो अत्थत्थीओ पयत्तेण ॥ १७॥

jaha ṇāma kovi puriso rāyāṇaṁ jāṇiūṇa saddahadi
to taṁ aṇucaradi puṇo atthatthio payatteṇa (17)

यथा नाम कोऽपि पुरुषो राजानं ज्ञात्वा श्रद्दधाति।
ततस्तमनुचरति पुनरर्थार्थिकः प्रयत्नेन ॥ १७॥

एवं हि जीवराया णादव्वो तह य सद्दहेदव्वो।
अणुचरिदव्वो य पुणो सो चेव दु मोक्खकामेण॥ १८॥

evaṁ hi jīvarāyā ṇādavvo taha ya saddahedavvo
aṇucaridavvo ya puṇo so ceva du mokkhakāmeṇa (18)

एवं हि जीवराजा ज्ञातव्यस्तथैव श्रद्धातव्यः।
अनुचरितव्यश्च पुनः स चैव तु मोक्षकामेन॥ १८॥

17 and 18. As a man knowing the king believes in him and with the object of gain serves him with resourcefulness, even so should the king, the soul, be known, believed in and attended to with the object of emancipation.

Commentary : The nature of *ratna-traya* is explained by a simile. Any person who is desirous of obtaining presents from the king must first of all find out who the king is through the royal paraphernalia of the royal umbrella, *cāmara,* etc. Then he must have faith in the benevolent nature of the king; then he must approach him and serve him whole-heartedly in order to attain his end. Similarly one who desires *mokṣa* or liberation should obtain the knowledge of the true Self, should have faith in the possibility of realisation and finally make an effort to reach the goal. The approach towards the spiritual sovereign is compared to the approach towards a temporal king.

Thus it is emphasised that right knowledge is the indispensable condition of the attempt to successfully achieve liberation or *mokṣa*

Next, the author points out that the view which identifies the Self with the body, etc. is the mark of *ajñāna* or wrong knowledge.

कम्मे णोकम्मम्हि य अहमिदि अहयं च कम्मणोकम्मं।
जा एसा खलु बुद्धी अप्पडिबुद्धो हवदि ताव॥ १९॥

kamme ṇokammamhi ya ahamidi ahayaṁ ca kammaṇokammaṁ
jā esā khalu buddhī appaḍibuddho havadi tāva (19)

कर्मणि नोकर्मणि च अहमिति अहकं च कर्म नोकर्म।
यावदेषा खलु बुद्धिरप्रतिबुद्धो भवति तावत्॥ १९॥

19. *Karmic* matter and non-*karmic* body-matter constitute the I, and (conversely) I am identical with *karmic* matter and non-*karmic* matter. So long as this belief persists in the Self, it is said to be *aprati-buddha,* one lacking in discriminative knowledge.

Commentary : This *gāthā* emphasises the fact that it is sheer *ajñāna* or ignorance to identify the Self with the various types of non-self. *Karma,* here, refers to the subtle matter constituting the various kinds of *karma,* such as *jñānāvaraṇīya,* etc., and therefore implies the various psychic states such as delusion, desire, etc. *Non-karma* refers to the physical molecules constituting the organic body. One who recognises that the Self is by nature entirely distinct from the internal impure psychic states such as delusion, desire, and the external body, is said to be *prati-buddha* or one with discriminative knowledge. Therefore, one who believes that the *Ātmā* is identical with the various impure psychic states caused by the subtle *karmic* matter or with the gross organic body is called *aprati-buddha,* one devoid of discriminative knowledge. Such an *aprati-buddha,* is called *bahir-ātmā* or one who identifies himself with external objects.

अहमेदं एदमहं अहमेदस्स हि अत्ति मम एदं।
अण्णं जं परदव्वं सचित्ताचित्तमिस्सं वा॥ २०॥

ahamedaṁ edamahaṁ ahamedassa hi atti mama edaṁ
aṇṇaṁ jaṁ paradavvaṁ sacittācittamissaṁ vā (20)

अहमेतदेतदहमहमेतस्य ह्यस्ति ममैतत्।
अन्यद्यत्परद्रव्यं सचित्ताचित्तमिश्रं वा॥ २०॥

आसि मम पुव्वमेदं एदस्स अहं पि आसि पुव्वं हि।
होहि पुणो वि मम एदं अहमेदं चापि होस्सामि॥ २१॥

āsi mama puvvamedaṁ edassa ahaṁ pi āsi puvvaṁ hi
hohi puṇo vi mam edaṁ ahamedaṁ cāpi hossāmi. (21)

आसीन्मम पूर्वमेतदहमेतत् चापि पूर्वं हि।
भविष्यति पुनरपि ममैतत् अहमेतत् चापि भविष्यामि॥ २१॥

एदं तु असंभूदं आदवियप्पं करेदि संमूढो।
भूदत्थं जाणंतो ण करेदि दु तं असंमूढो॥ २२॥

edaṁ tu asambhūdaṁ ādaviyappaṁ karedi saṁmūḍho
bhūdatthaṁ jāṇanto ṇa karedi du taṁ asaṁmūḍho (22)

एतत्त्वसद्भूतमात्मविकल्पं करोति संमूढः।
भूतार्थं जानन् न करोति तु तमसंमूढः॥ २२॥

20 to 22. "I am other substance, animate, inanimate, or mixed; it is myself; I am its and it is mine; it was mine in past time and I was its; even again it shall be mine and I shall be its." Such erroneous notions about the Self (as identifying it with alien objects such as body, etc. (only the deluded one) *bahir-ātmā* entertains. But one who knows the real nature of the Self, non-deluded (*antar-ātmā*) never entertains (such erroneous notions about the Self).

Commentary : These *gāthās* refer to the erroneous belief of identifying one-self with one's own body as well as the environmental objects. These alien objects such as wife and children, cattle and gold and land constitute one's home and property. Wife and children and cattle are designated as *sacitta-paradravya,* living objects in the environment. Gold ornaments, house and landed property constitute *a-citta-paradravya,* inanimate objects in the environment. Wife and children wearing ornaments and costly dress would be *miśra-paradravya,* combined animate and inanimate objects of the environment. There is a tendency in the householder to identify himself with his wife and children and other properties. The identification may be as intimate as his relation to his own body. Just as he is interested in maintaining his own body free from injury or disease, so also he is interested in maintaining his property and possession free from damage by promoting the integrity and welfare of his relatives and property. Such an identification of one's self with the environmental objects is considered as an impediment to the realisation of the true Self. Such an illusory feeling of one-ness with the environmental objects, feeling elated when they increase and grow, feeling dejected when they decrease and decay, are all characteristics of self-delusion which must be got rid of by one who pursues the path of self-realisation.

Such a self-delusion, may also be present in an ascetic. Though he renounces his house and property, still he retains a few things such as *piccha* and *kamaṇḍalu* which constitute the insignia of an ascetic. For him these constitute the environmental objects and he shall not entertain the feeling that they are his personal property, lest he should be troubled by the characteristic emotions of joy in possessing them and sorrow in getting them damaged or lost. When the householder or the ascetic is enjoined not to identify himself even with his own body, it is much more important that he should be entirely uninfluenced by environmental objects—by the dear and near ones and by wealth and property.

अण्णाणमोहिदमदी मज्झमिणं भणदि पुग्गलं दव्वं।
बद्धमबद्धं च तहा जीवे बहुभावसंजुत्ते॥ २३॥

aṇṇāṇamohidamadī majjhamiṇaṁ bhaṇadi puggalaṁ davvaṁ
baddhamabaddhaṁ ca tahā jīve bahubhāvasaṁjutte (23)

अज्ञानमोहितमतिर्ममेदं भणति पुद्गलद्रव्यम्।
बद्धमबद्धं च तथा जीवे बहुभावसंयुक्ते॥ २३॥

23. In the case of the soul that is characterised by various emotions (such as desire, etc.), there are physical objects some (of which are) intimately bound to it (like the body) and some not so intimately bound (such as wealth). "These material objects are mine" so declares one (the *bahir-ātmā*) whose intellect is deluded by wrong knowledge.

सव्वण्हुणाणदिट्ठो जीवो उवओगलक्खणो णिच्चं।
किह सो पोग्गलदव्वीभूदो किं भणसि मज्झमिणं ॥ २४॥

savvaṇhuṇāṇadiṭṭho jīvo uvaogalakkhaṇo ṇiccaṁ
kiha so poggaladavvībhūdo kiṁ bhaṇasi majjhamiṇaṁ

सर्वज्ञज्ञानदृष्टो जीव उपयोगलक्षणो नित्यम्।
कथं स पुद्गलद्रव्यीभूतो यद्भणसि ममेदम्॥ २४॥

24. The nature of the soul as seen by the Omniscient, is permanently associated with its quality called *upayoga* (which comprises knowledge and perception, *par excellence).* How can such a spiritual entity become a physical object? Then how can you say, "this physical object is mine?"

जदि सो पुग्गलदव्वीभूदो जीवत्तमागदं इदरं।
तो सक्को वुत्तुं जं मज्झमिणं पुग्गलं दव्वं॥ २५॥

jadi so puggaladavvībhūdo jīvattamāgadaṁ idaraṁ
to sakko vuttuṁ jaṁ majjhamiṇaṁ puggalaṁ davvaṁ

यदि स पुद्गलद्रव्यीभूतो जीवत्वमागतमितरत्।
तच्छक्तो वक्तुं यन्ममेदं पुद्गलं द्रव्यं॥ २५॥

25. If the soul becomes matter and if the matter becomes the soul then it is possible for you, Oh! *bahir-ātmā,* to say "this physical object is mine."

Commentary : (23 TO 25) These gāthās also deal with the illusion of identifying the Self with the physical objects. The physical object may be intimately related to the soul as its own body or indirectly related to the soul as one's own wealth and property. In any case, identifying one's Self with these material objects is but a mark of the lack of knowledge as to the real nature of things. But if you say that the soul and the physical objects are not so very different in nature as to exclude all possible relations between the two, then you have to remember that your view would be in conflict with the Divine Word of the Sarvajña, or the Omniscient. According to the pravacana, the soul is fundamentally different in nature from pudgala (matter). Its nature is characterised by perfect knowledge and perfect perception, whereas matter is non-living, acetena, a characteristic which is contradictory to that of the soul. With such an imcompatability of nature, how can they be reasonably identified with each other? If your predication, "This is mine" is maintainable, it must be only on this condition, which is impossible, viz., that the soul can be transmuted into matter and matter into the soul. It is clear that the author addresses a deluded person, (*bahir-ātmā*) who is incapable of discriminating between soul and matter, and points out to him the fundamental differences between the two. It is the clear perception of this difference, vivekajñāna that forms the foundation of Right Faith.

Next the author states the possible defects which may be pointed out against the view that the Self and the body are absolutely distinct from each other.

जदि जीवो ण सरीरं तित्थयरायरियसंथुदी चेव।
सव्वावि हवदि मिच्छा तेण दु आदा हवदि देहो॥ २६ ॥

jadi jīvo ṇa sarīraṁ titthayarāyariya-saṁthudi ceva
savvāvi havadi micchā teṇa du ādā havadi deho (26)

यदि जीवो न शरीरं तीर्थंकराचार्यसंस्तुतिश्चैव।
सर्वापि भवति मिथ्या तेन तु आत्मा भवति देहः॥ २६॥

26. If the soul is not the body then the hymns praising (the bodily excellence, *rūpastava,* of) the Tīrthaṅkara or the Ācārya will all be false. Therefore the soul must indeed be the body.

Commentary : The Tīrthaṅkara as distinguished from *Siddha* has a body. *Siddha* is described as *aśarīrī*, without a body, *arūpī*, not perceivable, and so on; whereas the Tīrthaṅkara or *Arhat Parameṣṭhī* has still a body even after attaining Omniscience or Kevala-Jñāna. It is with the help of this body that He is able to preach the *dharma* (Truth) to the people, because His main function is *dharma-prabhāvanā* or proclaiming the Dharma. His worshippers both human and divine praise His body in their adoration. The adoration of an Arhat consists in the enunciation of the marvellous characteristics of His body— such as its beauty and excellence, its freedom from natural impurities and defects, and that it is the cynosure of attraction and grace, that it is the fountain source of peace and harmony, that it is the physical embodiment of the eternal values of Truth, Goodness and Beauty. The term Ācārya implies the master of a Saṁgha who in his turn transmits the divine message to his disciples and through them to the whole world. It is not necessary to emphasise the fact that in his case also adoration very often implies praising the beauty of his body as the embodiment of a great soul.

The bewildered and the doubting disciple naturally asks his master : "If the soul is of supreme importance and if the body being *acetana* is without any spiritual grace and hence to be discarded as worthless, how can we justify the various songs of devotion of *Arhanta* and Ācārya, songs which are but the praise of their physical beauty and grace. If the songs in adoration are valid, would it not be proper to infer that after all, the soul and the body are not so fundamentally different?"

The author clears the doubt expressed above by explaining the doctrine of *naya* or points of view.

ववहारणओ भासदि जीवो देहो य हवदि खलु एक्को।
णदु णिच्छयस्स जीवो देहो य कदावि एक्कट्ठो॥ २७॥

vavahāraṇao bhāsadi jīvo deho ya havadi khalu ekko
ṅadu ṇicchayassa jivo deho ya kadāvi ekkaṭṭho (27)

व्यवहारनयो भाषते जीवो देहश्च भवति खल्वेकः।
न तु निश्चयस्य जीवो देहश्च कदाप्येकार्थः॥ २७॥

27. The *vyavahāra* point of view indeed declares that body and soul are one, but according to the *niścaya* point of view, the soul and body are never identical.

Commentary : Thus the devotional songs in praise of the bodily beauty of the Lord are justified from the *vyavahāra* point of view, because the beauty of the body is but the expression of the inner beauty of the soul with which it is found in union. Though considered as one from the *vyavahāra* point, because of their association, still soul and body do not lose their intrinsic characteristics. They are really distinct in nature. The soul has its intrinsic characteristic of *upayoga (darśana and jñāna)* which characteristic is not present in matter. This fact clearly brings out their intrinsic difference. The commentators explain this combination of different things to constitute a unitary whole by a practical illustration. Gold and silver, both being precious metals, may be used in combination for certain purposes such as ornament-making, etc. Though they go together to constitute the whole so manufactured, still they do not lose their respective qualities. Gold is gold and silver is silver. One is yellow and the other is white. Hence the two can never become one in nature really. In the same way, soul and body, though found together in an embodied individual, the unity must be taken to be true from the practical point of view and not from the absolute point of view.

इणमण्णं जीवादो देहं पोग्गलमयं थुणित्तु मुणी।
मण्णादि हु संथुदो वंदिदो मए केवली भयवं॥ २८॥

iṇamaṇṇaṁ jīvāḍo dehaṁ poggalamayaṁ thuṇittu muṇī
maṇṇadi hu saṁthudo vaṁdido mae kevalī bhayavaṁ

इदमन्यत् जीवाद्देहं पुद्गलमयं स्तुत्वा मुनिः।
मन्यते खलु संस्तुतो वन्दितो मया केवली भगवान्॥ २८॥

28. By adoring the body which is different from the soul and which is constituted of matter, the saint believes, "The Omniscient Lord is thus adored and worshipped by me."

Commentary : His assumption is justified from the *vyavahāra* point of view because the praise of the body is but the praise of the personality. But in reality, the bodily characteristics, however beautiful and adorable, cannot be the genuine characteristics of the *Paramātmā*.

तं णिच्छये ण जुज्जदि ण सरीरगुणा हि होंति केवलिणो।
केवलिगुणो थुणदि जो सो तच्चं केवलिं थुणदि॥ २९॥

taṁ ṇicchaye ṇa jujjadi ṇa sarīraguṇā hi hoṁti kevaliṇo
kevaliguṇo thuṇadi jo so taccaṁ kevaliṁ thuṇadi (29)

तन्निश्चये न युज्यते न शरीरगुणा हि भवन्ति केवलिनः।
केवलिगुणान् स्तौति यः स तत्त्वं केवलिनं स्तौति॥ २९॥

29. That (body adoration is adoration of the *Paramātmā*) is not right from the *niścaya* point of view for the properties of the body are not the properties of the Omniscient Lord. One who worships the *Kevalin,* the Omniscient Lord, must do so by adoring His genuine characteristics.

णयरम्मि वण्णिदे जह ण वि रण्णो वण्णणा कदा होदि।
देहगुणो थुव्वंते ण केवलिगुणा थुदा होंति॥ ३०॥

ṇayarammi vaṇṇide jaha ṇa vi raṇṇo vaṇṇaṇā kadā hodi
dehaguṇo thuvvaṁte ṇa kevaliguṇā thudā hoṁti (30)

नगरे वर्णिते यथा नापि राज्ञो वर्णना कृता भवति।
देहगुणे स्तूयमाने न केवलिगुणाः स्तुता भवन्ति॥ ३०॥

30. As the description of a city does not constitute the description of its ruler, in the same way, the adoration of his body is not the adoration of the attributes of the Omniscient Lord.

Commentary : The same point that adoring the body can by no means amount to the adoration of the *Paramātmā* is emphasised by the example of a king and his capital.

Next the author describes the nature of adoration from the real point of view.

जो इंदिए जिणित्ता णाणसहावाधिअं मुणदि आदं।
तं खलु जिदिंदियं ते भणंति जे णिच्छिदा साहू ॥ ३१॥

jo iṁdiye jiṇittā ṇāṇasahāvādhiaṁ muṇadi ādaṁ
taṁ khalu jidiṁdiyaṁ te bhaṇaṁti je ṇicchidā sāhū (31)

यः इन्द्रियाणि जित्वा ज्ञानस्वभावाधिकं मनुते आत्मानम्।
तं खलु जितेन्द्रियं ते भणन्ति ये निश्चिताः साधवः ॥ ३१॥

31. He who, subjugating the senses, realises that the Self is of the nature of real knowledge is verily called a conqueror of the senses by the saints who know reality.

Commentary : This is given as an illustration of the true worship of the Jina through praising His qualities. Control of the senses implies three things. Control of the sense-organs or *dravyaindriyas;* control of sense-perception which is *bhāva-indriya* and, finally, the control of the perceived environmental objects or *indriya-viṣaya*. The sense-organs and sense-perception, though serving as instruments of knowledge to the soul, do only present the world of environmental objects and thus divert the attention of the soul to a world other than itself. Conquest of these senses therefore implies the acquisition of freedom from the influence of environmental objects. When such an intellectual attitude is secured through *yoga or tapas,* the attention thus liberated is directed inwards leading to the contemplation of the Pure Self. Contemplation of the Pure Self leads to becoming one with it. One who reaches this goal of self-realisation is known as Jina. This is the *summum bonum* of life to be achieved according to the Jaina faith.

जो मोहं तु जिणित्ता णाणसहावाधियं मुणदि आदं।
तं जिदमोहं साहुं परमट्ठवियाणया विंति॥ ३२॥

jo mohaṁ tu jiṇittā ṇāṇasahāvādhiyaṁ muṇadi ādaṁ
taṁ jidamohaṁ sāhuṁ paramaṭṭhaviyāṇayā viṁti (32)

यो मोहं तु जित्वा ज्ञानस्वभावाधिकं मनुते आत्मानम्।
तं जितमोहं साधुं परमार्थविज्ञायका ब्रुवन्ति॥ ३२॥

32. The saints who know the nature of absolute reality, call him *Jita-moha* or conqueror of delusion who, by subjugating the delusion, realises that the self is intrinsically of the nature of knowledge.

Commentary : This is given as an illustration of the second type of adoration through the praise of quality. Conquest of delusion is the quality praised in this *gāthā*. The term *moha* implies the various gross emotions such as anger, pride, deceitfulness, avarice, etc. These emotions naturally create undesirable excitment in the consciousness. These various emotional disturbances and the consciousness which is so disturbed are all unwarrantedly identified with the real self. This identification of the higher Self with the empirical consciousness characterised by baser emotions is certainly an evil to be got rid of. One who is able to realise this higher Self as distinct from the empirical Self and to concentrate upon one's higher Self by the conquest of the baser emotions constituting what is called *moha* or delusion, is called *Jitamoha,* the Conqueror of Delusion.

जिदमोहस्स दु जइया खीणो मोहो हविज्ज साहुस्स।
तइया दु खीणमोहो भण्णदि सो णिच्छयविदूहिं॥ ३३॥

jidomohassa du jaiyā khīṇo moho havijja sāhussa
taiyā du khīṇamoho bhaṇṇadi so ṇicchayavidūhiṁ (33)

जितमोहस्य तु यदा क्षीणो मोहो भवेत्साधोः।
तदा खलु क्षीणमोहो भण्यते स निश्चयविद्भिः॥ ३३॥

33. The Ṛsi who, after conquering *moha* or delusion, further completely eradicates *moha* (the root cause of baser emotions) is called by the Seers of Reality, the Destroyer of Delusion.

Commentary : This is the third example of worshipping the Lord by praising His qualities. Conquest of *moha* implies merely the suppression of the baser emotions and pushing aside the empirical consciousness from the focus of attention in order to obtain the undisturbed contemplation of the higher self. But in the case of *kṣīṇamoha,* the destruction of delusion, the baser emotions, and the association of the empirical Self, are completely eliminated leaving the higher Self as the unchallenged and undisturbed sovereign of the spiritual realm.

णाणं सव्वे भावे पच्चक्खादि य परेत्ति णादूण।
तम्हा पच्चक्खाणं णाणं णियमा मुणेदव्वं॥ ३४॥

ṇāṇaṁ savve bhāve paccakkhādi ya paretti ṇādūṇa
tamhā paccakkhāṇaṁ ṇāṇaṁ ṇiyamā muṇedavvaṁ (34)

ज्ञानं सर्वान् भावान् यस्मात् प्रत्याख्याति च परानिति ज्ञात्वा।
तस्मात् प्रत्याख्यानं ज्ञानं नियमात् मन्तव्यम्॥ ३४॥

34. The discriminative knowledge of the Self leads to discarding all alien dispositions, knowing them to be entirely foreign to the nature of the self; therefore in reality, this discriminative knowledge of the Self shall be known as *pratyākhyāna* or repulsion.

Commentary : The alien characteristics of the empirical Self, since they are foreign to the nature of the Self, get rejected by one who knows the true nature of the Self. This knowledge of the true nature of the indispensable condition of self-purification by the process of discarding all the foreign elements present in the Self. This process known as *pratyākhyāna* is the great renuciation or rejection of foreign encumbrances. Since the discriminative knowledge of the Self is the real and indispensible condition for *pratyākhyāna* which is the process of self-purification, such knowledge of Self is called the *pratyākhyāna*, renunciation itself, according to the principle of justificable identification of cause and effect.

जह णाम कोवि पुरिसो परदव्वमिणं ति जाणिदुं चयदि।
तह सव्वे परभावे णाऊण विमुंचदे णाणी॥ ३५॥

jaha ṇāma kovi puriso paradavvamiṇaṁ ti jāṇiduṁ cayadi
taha savve parabhāve ṇāūṇa vimuṁcade ṇāṇī (35)

यथा नाम कोऽपि पुरुषः परद्रव्यमिदमिति ज्ञात्वा त्यजति।
तथा सर्वान् परभावान् ज्ञात्वा विमुञ्चति ज्ञानी ॥ ३५॥

35. As a person rejects a thing brought to him as his own, when he realises through certain marks that it belongs

to somebody else, so also, does the sage discard all alien dispositions, as they are foreign to him.

Commentary : The author explains this fact with a practical illustration which is well brought out by the commentators. For example; a person may accept as his own a cloth brought by his washerman which might really belong to somebody else. Due to the ignorance of the real fact, he may put on the cloth. but when the real owner claims it as his pointing to his proper washerman's mark, the mistake may be recognised and the cloth may be given up as not his own. Similarly a person due to ignorance may call as his own the various emotional features of the empirical Self. But when his attention is drawn to the error of such false identification by his spiritual master, he certainly realises his mistake and is bound to discard the alien features as not his own.

णत्थि मम को वि मोहो बुज्झदि उवओग एव अहमेक्को।
तं मोहणिम्ममत्तं समयस्स वियाणया विंति॥ ३६॥

ṇatthi mama ko vi moho bujjhadi uvaoga eva ahamekko
taṁ mohaṇimmamattaṁ samayassa viyāṇayā viṁti (36)

नास्ति मम कोपि मोहो बुध्यते उपयोग एवाहमेक :।
तं मोहनिर्ममत्वं समयस्य विज्ञायकाः ब्रुवन्ति॥ ३६॥

36. I am unique inasmuch as I am of the nature of *upayoga;* hence no delusion whatever is related to me. He who thinks like this the knowers of the true Self call "one free from delusion."

Commentary : *Nirmamatva :* without any personal interest, emphasises the former characteristic of *nir-mohatva*, freedom from delusion. This *gāthā* reiterates the necessity for discarding all alien features of the empirical consciousnes. "These are not mine. I am but the light that illuminates the inner Self as well as the outer cosmos, being all-illuminating pure consciousness. I certainly have no personal interest in things resulting from self-delusion." One who thinks like that is said to be free from delustion.

णत्थि मम धम्मआदी बुज्झदि उवओग एव अहमेक्को।
तं धम्मणिम्ममत्तं समयस्स वियाणया विंति॥ ३७॥

natthi mama dhamma ādī bujjhadi uvaoga eva ahamekko
taṁ dhammaṇimmamattaṁ samayassa viyāṇayā viṁti (37)

नास्ति मम धर्मादिर्बुध्यते उपयोग एवाहमेकः।
तं धर्मनिर्ममत्वं समयस्य विज्ञायकाः ब्रुवन्ति॥ ३७॥

37. I am unique inasmuch as I am of the nature of *upayoga.* Hence *dharma* etc., are not related to me. Hence, he who thinks like this, the knowers of the true Self call, "one unrelated to *dharma,* etc."

Commentary : Previously the author has emphasised the fact that it is erroneous to identify the true Self with the empirical Self characterised by various emotions. Here he turns his attention to the outer cosmos consisting of *dharma, adharma, pudgala, ākāśa, kāla,* and other *jīvas*—the principle of motion, the principle of rest, matter, space, time, and other souls—respectively. Hence he wants to emphasise the fact that it is equally erroneous to identify oneself with these objects of the external world. The constituent objects of the cosmos have their own intrinsic inalienable nature and can by no means be derived from the nature of the Self. No doubt the *upayoga* nature of the Self in its twin aspect of knowledge and perception can completely comprehend the cosmos so that the various objects of the external world, living and non-living, may get immersed in the ocean of light that proceeds from the Perfect Knowledge of the Self. But this fact of being comprehended does not in any way interfere with the intrinsic individual reality of the objects themselves which are related to knowledge. As was already explained in a previous *gāthā*, the physical body and the Self have each an immutable and independent nature of their own, non-trasmutable one into the other. This assertion relating to matter and soul is applied to the whole of the cosmos consisting of the various objective reals such as *dharma, adharma,* etc. Here we have to note one important point that one's Self is not only distinct from the various non-living objects of the environment but also from the various personalities which are present in the outside world in the human society and the various living organisms of the biological kingdom. To talk of a mass consciousness or world-consciousness, offering only a subsidiary existence to the personalities which are but chips of the particular adjectives of the Whole would be incompatible with Jaina metaphysics.

अहमेक्को खलु सुद्धो दंसणणाणमइओ सदारूवी।
णवि अत्थि मज्झ किंचिवि अण्णं परमाणुमित्तं पि॥ ३८॥

ahamekko khalu suddho daṁsaṇaṇāṇamaio sadārūvī
ṇavi atthi majjha kiṁcivi aṇṇaṁ paramāṇumiitaṁ pi (38)

अहमेकः खलु शुद्धो दर्शनज्ञानमयः सदारूपी।
नाप्यस्ति मम किंचिदप्यन्यत् परमाणुमात्रमपि॥ ३८॥

38. Absolutely pure, having the nature of perception and knowledge, always non-corporeal, I am indeed unique. Hence not even an atom of alien things whatsoever (whether living or non-living) is related to me as mine.

Commentary : *Aham :* the Self implies this : The soul from beginningless eternity associated with ignorance and delusion forgets its true nature, gets identified with alien features and characteristics till he is roused from slumber by a benevolent spiritual master who repeatedly strives to wake him up to his true nature. Just as a person who has lost his jewel feels a joy and surprise when it is brought and placed in his hands, so also the *jīva* wakes up as a result of the master's effort to realise that his Self is the *Parameśvara,* that his nature is pure and unsullied by alien features, shedding the pure light of pure consciousness all around.

Ekaḥ : the undivided unity implies that in spite of the several psychic states, emotional, cognitive and conative, experienced by the Self, it is an indivisible unity.

Śuddhaḥ : pure. The Self, in spite of its *gati,* modification, such as human and divine and in spite of the nine types of psycho-physical midifications called *nava-padārthas,* never loses its intrinsic pure nature and hence he is *śuddha.*

Arūpī : non-corporeal. Since the pure soul has no other nature except *upayoga,* the pure knowledge and perception, and since it transcends the sense-perception of vision, taste, touch, etc., it is always non-corporeal. The Self having this nature and illuminating all things around through its light of knowledge remains absolutely uninfluenced by alien psychic states and physical objects so that not even an iota of the alien things it can call its own.

Thus ends the *jīva-padārtha* or category of Soul. The author takes up next the *ajīva-padārtha* for discussion.

The Sanskrit commentators use the term *raṅga.* Here ends the first Scene, *pūrva-raṅgaḥ samāptaḥ,* thereby suggesting that the whole work is a Cosmic Drama in which the chief hero is the Self who appears on the stage in different characters and in association with different actors—certainly a beautiful metaphor in depicting the career of the *Ātmā*.

Chapter II

AJĪVA OR NON-SOUL

Thus after describing the category of *jīva*, the author takes up now the category of *ajīva* or non-soul for discussion. First he states the *pūrvapakṣa* or the *prima facie* agrument of those *(bahirātmavādins)* who believe that there is no soul besides and beyond the various psychic activities characteristic of the empirical Self.

अप्पाणमयाणंता मूढा दु परप्पवादिणो केई।
जीवं अज्झवसाणं कम्मं च तहा परूविंति॥ ३९॥

appāṇamayāṇaṁtā mūḍhā du parappavādiṇo keī
jivaṁ ajjhavasāṇaṁ kammaṁ ca tahā parūviṁti (39)

आत्मानमजानन्तो मूढास्तु परमात्मवादिन: केचित्।
जीवमध्यवसानं कर्म च तथा प्ररूपयन्ति॥ ३९॥

39. Some of those ignorant people who maintain that the Self is but the non-Self, not knowing the true nature of the Self, assert that the Self is identical with such psychic states as desire, etc. In the same way some others state that the Self is indentical with Karmic matter.

अवरे अज्झवसाणेसु तिव्वमंदाणुभावयं जीवं।
मण्णंति तहा अवरे णोकम्मं चावि जीवो त्ति॥ ४०॥

avare ajjhavasāṇesu tivvamaṁdāṇubhāvayaṁ jīvaṁ maṇṇaṁti tahā avare ṇokammaṁ cāvi jīvotti (40)

अपरेऽध्यवसानेषु तीव्रमन्दानुभागकं जीवं।
मन्यन्ते तथापरे नोकर्म चापि जीव इति॥ ४०॥

40. Others believe the psychic potency which determines the intensity or mildness of conscious states to be the soul. Still others identify the soul with *no-karmic* matter which forms the constituent elements of the various kinds of organic bodies.

कम्मस्सुदयं जीवं अवरे कम्माणुभायमिच्छंति।
तिव्वत्तणमंदत्तणगुणेहिं जो सो हवदि जीवो॥ ४१॥

kammasudayaṁ jīvaṁ avare kammāṇubhāyamicchaṁti tivvattaṇamaṁdattaṇaguṇehiṁ jo so havadi jīvo (41)

कमर्ण उदयं जीवमपरे कर्मानुभागमिच्छन्ति।
तीव्रत्वमन्दत्वगुणाभ्यां यः स भवति जीवः॥ ४१॥

41. Some consider the manifestation of karma (resulting in pleasure or pain) to be the Self; some others believe that what determines the intensity or mildness of the *edonic* state (which is the fruit of karma) is the Self.

जीवो कम्मं उहयं दोण्णिवि खलु केवि जीवमिच्छंति।
अवरे संजोगेण दु कम्माणं जीवमिच्छंति॥ ४२॥

jīvo kammaṁ uhayaṁ doṇṇivi khalu kevi jīvamicchaṁti avare saṁjogeṇa du kammāṇaṁ jīvamicchaṁti (42)

जीवकर्मोभयं द्वे अपि खलु केऽपि जीवमिच्छन्ति।
अपरे संयोगेन तु कर्मणां जीवमिच्छन्ति॥ ४२॥

42. Some others state the Self to be *jīva* and *karma*

taken variously or together; still others consider the self to be the product of the combination of the various *karmas.*

एवंविहा बहुविहा परमप्पाणं वदंति दुम्मेहा।
ते ण दु परप्पवादी णिच्छयवादीहिं णिद्दिट्ठा ॥ ४३ ॥

evaṃvihā bahuvihā paramappāṇaṁ vadaṁti dummehā
te ṇa du parappavādī ṇicchayavādīthiṁ ṇiddiṭṭhā (43)

एवंविधा बहुविधाः परमात्मानं वदन्ति दुर्मेधसः।
ते न तु परात्मवादिनः निश्चयवादिभिः निर्दिष्टाः ॥ ४३ ॥

43. Thus in many ways perverse-minded people identify the Self with the non-Self; therefore, by believers in reality, they are declared to be not *parātmavādins* (those who do not believe in the identity of *jīva* and *paramātmā).*

Commentary : Discussing the nature of *ajīva-padārtha* or the non-living substance the author introduces first that type of *ajīva-padārtha* or non-living substance which is intimately associated with *jīva* or soul. This type of non-living substance which is associated with life is of two kinds, *karmic* matter and matter called non-*karma* which constitutes the various types of body associated with *jīva* other than the *karmic* body. *Karmic* matter constitutes the *karmic* body and is inseparable from the soul throughout its *sāmsāric* pilgrimage from one birth to another, till the soul liberates itself in the pure state by breaking all shackles of *karma.* Besides this *karmic* body which is extremely minute and imperceptible, there are other types of organic bodies in association with the *jīva* or Soul. Birth, growth, decay, and death characteristic of organic beings, man and animals, are all characteristics of grosser bodies which form the physical associates of the Self. The Self in association with these corresponding changes in its conscious nature. These changes may manifest in three different forms of experience : cognitive, pertaining to perception and knowledge; conative; pertaining to voluntary activity; and affective, pertaining to the various affective states of emotions, pleasant and unpleasant. All these conscious characteristics of the empirical Self are in reality unconnected with the real nature of the Self. These characteristics of the empirical Self in the embodied form, are the result of the Self with the various material tabernacles in which it resides. Hence there is the possibility of mistaking these characteristics to be the real nature of the Self. These *gāthās* refer to the various errors of identifying the Self with the various types of material bodies and with the consequential changes in his consciousness due to his association with such bodies.

एदे सव्वे भावा पोग्गलदव्वपरिणामणिप्पण्णा।
केवलिजिणेहिं भणिया किह ते जीवो त्ति उच्चंति॥ ४४॥

ede savve bhāvā poggala-davva-pariṇāma-ṇippaṇṇā
kevalijiṇehiṁ bhaṇiyā kiha te jīvo tti uccaṁti (44)

एते सर्वे भावाः पुद्गलद्रव्यपरिणामनिष्पन्नाः।
केवलिजिनैर्भणिताः कथं ते जीवा इत्युच्यन्ते॥ ४४॥

44. It is said by Jina, the All-knowing, that the various characteristics referred to above are all the result of the manifestation of *karmic* matter. How can they be then attributed to the Pure Self?

Commentary : This *gāthā* refutes the various erroneous positions stated in the previous *gāthās* as believed by the various Ekāntavādins. No doubt it is true that the embodied Self is associated with attributes such as desire, and aversion;

so also gold, as found in nature in the form of mineral ore, is found in association with various mineral impurities. Similarly fire is usually found in association with smoke. Neverthless fire in itself is not smoke, nor gold is the same as the impure mineral ore. In the same way the Self cannot be identified with various psychic manifestations to which it is subject because of its association with impurities. In spite of the forms in which they are found in nature, gold in its pure conditions is distinct from the impure ore, and the pure self is distinct and different from the embodied *jīva*. No doubt the self is found always in associations with its body throughout the cycle of births and deaths, but on that score it cannot be identified with the body since the Self (as distinct and different from the body) is realised in its pure form. No doubt the *karmic* body may be an inevitable condition of the transmigration of the Self in this *sāṁsāric* cycle; neverthless this *non-cetana* material condition, because of its invariable association with the Self, cannot be identified with it, as they are different in nature and hence distinct from each other. In short, what is found in association with a thing need not necessarily be identical with its true nature. The realisation of the true Self will obviously expose the alien nature of the various attributes, physical and psychical, with which it is associated in its impure state— an association which leads the uninstructed to erroneous conclusions.

अट्ठविहं पि य कम्मं सव्वं पुग्गलमयं जिणा विंति।
जस्स फलं तं वुच्चइ दुक्खं ति विपच्चमाणस्स॥ ४५॥

aṭṭhavihaṁ pi ya kammaṁ savvaṁ puggalamayaṁ jiṇā viṁti
jassa phalaṁ taṁ vuccai dukkhaṁ ti vipaccamāṇassa

अष्टविधमपि च कर्म सर्वं पुद्गलमयं जिना ब्रुवन्ति।
यस्य फलं तदुच्यते दुःखमिति विपच्यमानस्य ॥ ४५ ॥

45. The *Jinas* declare that all the eight kinds of *karmas* are material in nature; and also suffering which is the effect of *karmic* fruition (is said) to be material.

Commentary : According to Jaina metaphysics the various *karmas* are intrinsically material though of subtle form. Since they are material in nature they are quite distinct from *jīva* whose characteristic is *cetana*. The *karmic* matter which is *acetana* in nature while operating, interferes with the pure consciousness of the *jīva*. On account of this interference the various psychic states present in the empirical Self are really the effect of the operative cause of the *karmic* matter. These psychic states constitute the suffering associated with *saṁsārī jīva*. These unpleasant psychic states, as they are the effects of *karmic* matter, are considered to be material, since the cause and the effect are ultimately identical. If these psychic states, since they are produced by *karmic* matter, are also to be considered material in nature, what is the justification for referring these states of consciousness as the attributes of the *jīva*? The answer is given in the *gāthā*.

ववहारस्स दरीसणमुवदेसो वण्णिदो जिणवरेहिं।
जीवा एदे सव्वे अज्झवसाणादओ भावा॥ ४६॥

vavahārassa darīsaṇamuvadeso vaṇṇido jiṇavarehiṁ
jīvā ede savve ajjhavasāṇādao bhāvā (46)

व्यवहारस्य दर्शनमुपदेशो वर्णितो जिनवरैः।
जीवा एते सर्वेऽध्यवसानादयो भावाः॥ ४६॥

47. It is only from the *vyavahāra* point of view that these various psychic states are declared by the *Jinas* to be of the nature of the Self.

Commentary : Though these mental states have nothing to do with real Self, the attention of the ordinary man must be drawn to the fact that from the practical point of view, they are characteristic of the empirical ego. The practical point of view is an important method of instructing the unenlightened ordinary man. Otherwise there will be an extremely disastrous effect on his conduct. Waiving the practical point of view and presenting only the absolute and real nature of the Self, may result in the perverse conduct of the ordinary man. Directing his attention to the ultimate nature of the *jīva,* he may forget altogether the difference between the vegetable kingdom and the animal kingdom, the difference between the *sthāvara jīva* and *trasa jīva.* Man has to live on cereals and fruits, products of the vegetable kingdom. Since the product of the vegetable kingdom is indispensable for his life, the ordinary man may unwillingly adopt a similar attitude to the animal kingdom and hence he may not care to appreciate the importance of *Ahiṁsā* Dharma. If you can eat with impurity the products of the vegetables kingdom, you may also eat meat, the product of the animal kingdom. This undesirable result in the conduct of the ordinary man is the result of not emphasising the *vyavahāra* point of view and the intrinsic difference between the vegetable and the animal kingdoms, though the ultimate nature of *jīva* in both is the same. Similarly if the ultimate and real nature of the Self is emphasised without describing the nature of the empirical ego, the Self as a *saṁsārī jīva,* it will create an undesirable attitude in the ordinary man's life. If the ultimate nature of the Self is pure and unsullied, if it is identical with the liberated Self or *Mukta jīva,* then the ordinary man may argue, why should I unnecessarily worry myself about *mokṣa-mārga,* or the path to salvation, when my soul is already pure and liberated in nature. Both ethics and religion would appear to him superfluous and unnecessary. Presenting an ultimate ideal and prescribing a course of conduct for realising the same would all be vain and useless, because the ideal is already there. This perverse moral attitude is also to be avoided and this could be achieved only by emphaising the *vyavahāra* point. The ordinary man must be made to realise that though he has the element of divinity in him, still it is found in association with impurity while he is in the concrete world of experience. It is not enough to realise that his ultimate nature is pure. He must also realise that this pure nature is clouded and contaminated by *karmas*. This latter knowledge is possible only when his attention is directed to the *vyavahāra* point of view. Only when he realises that he has fallen from a high stage, he will make a genuine effort to regain his lost glory and eminence. Hence is the need for and the importance of the *vyavahāra* point of view. Therefore it would be unwise to come to the hasty conclusion that *vyavahāra naya* and niścaya naya, the practical point of view and the real point of view, are mutually contradictory and hence incompatible with each other.

राया हु णिग्गदो त्ति य एसो बलसमुदयस्स आदेसो।
ववहारेण दु उच्चदि तत्थेक्को णिग्गदो राया॥ ४७॥

rāyā hu ṇiggado tti ya eso balasamudayassa ādeso
vavahāreṇa du uccadi tatthekko ṇiggado rāyā (47)

राजा खलु निर्गत इत्येष बलसमुदयस्यादेशः।
व्यवहारेण तूच्यते तत्रैको निर्गतः राजा॥ ४७॥

47. At the sight of the military procession, one may exclaim : "The king has started." This statement is made from the *vyavahāra* point of view, because only one person is the king in the whole procession.

एमेव य ववहारो अज्झवसाणादि-अण्णभावाणं।
जीवो त्ति कदो सुत्ते तत्थेक्को णिच्छिदो जीवो॥ ४८॥

emeva ya vavahāro ajjhavasāṇādi-aṇṇabhāvāṇaṁ
jīvo tti kado sutte tatthekko ṇicchido jīvo (48)

एवमेव च व्यवहारोऽध्यवसानाद्यन्यभावानाम्।
जीव इति कृत: सूत्रे तत्रैको निश्चितो जीव:॥ ४८॥

48. In the same way, from the *vyavahāra* point of view, the various psychic states such as desire, aversion, etc., may be said to be the ego. But the real Self is none of these states but remains as the unitary substratum of which these are empirical modifications.

Commentary : Ordinary people, when they see the military procession marching alone, speak of the king going out. The military procession may be really very long, but really the whole of it is not the king however important; he is only one person in the whole procession. Similarly the series of psychic states and modifications may be spoken of as the Self. The whole series is not the Self. Really the Self is the underlying unitary existence whose manifestation appears in the various conscious states from which the Self is distinct and independent. The author employs a popular example to illustrate the relation between the ever-changing series of conscious states and the permanent unitary real self.

अरसमरूवमगंधं अव्वत्तं चेदणागुणमसद्दं।
जाण अलिंगग्गहणं जीवमणिद्दिट्ठसंठाणं॥ ४९॥

arasam-arūvam-agaṁdhaṁ avvattaṁ cedaṇāguṇa-masaddaṁ
jāṇa aliṁgaggahaṇaṁ jīvamaṇiddiṭṭhasaṁṭhāṇaṁ (49)

अरसमरूपमगन्धमव्यक्तं चेतनागुणमशब्दम्।
जानीहि अलिङ्गग्रहणं जीवमनिर्दिष्टसंस्थानम्॥ ४९॥

49. Know ye that the pure Self is without taste, colour, without smell, imperceptible to touch, without sound, not an object of *anumāna* or inferential knowledge, without any definite bodily shape and is characterised by *cetanā* (consciousness).

Commentary : Taste is a distinct quality of matter or *pudgala*. This attribute is not found anywhere else. Since the nature of the Pure Self or *śuddha jīva* is entirely distinct from that of matter, it is described tasteless, in order to distinguish Self from matter. Similarly colour is an intrinsic attribute of matter. It is not found as an attribute of anything else. So the Pure Self which is distinct from *acetana* matter, is described as colourless. Again smell is an attribute of physical objects and it cannot be associated with anything else The Self being distinct from matter is therefore said to be smell-less. Similarly being perceptible to touch is a characteristic of material objects and cannot be attributed to anything else. Since the nature of the Self is transcending sense-perception, it cannot be an object of contact sensation. Hence it is described as beyond touch. In the same way, sound, since it is the effect of concussion between material particles, is associated with matter alone and with nothhing else. That which sounds must be a material object as a non-material entity cannot produce sound. Hence the Self also is soundless because it is non-material in nature. Thus the Self is entirely beyond the scope of sense-perception. Can it be approached by inference or *anumāna*? No, because *anumāna* or inference entirely depends upon what must necessarily be obtained by sense-perception. Perception of smoke may lead to the inference that there is fire. But smoke must be obtained by sense perception and then only it is possible to infer that there is fire. An entity which is quite beyond the scope of sense-perception cannot be approached by inferential knowledge either. Hence *śuddha-jīva* is said to be *aliṅga-grahaṇa,* not approached by inference. In the organic world *jīva* is always found in association with its characteristic body. These characteristic bodies are classified according to their various shapes which are called *saṁsthānas.* Since these shapes of the organic body are entirely determined by the physical structure, they are purely bodily qualities and cannot be transferred to the Self associated with body. Hence the Self is without definite shape or structure. In short the pure Self whose intrinsic nature is *cetanā* is entirely different from the whole external world and hence the characteristics of the external world cannot be predicated of the Self. It is entirely devoid of the physical qualities of colour, taste, etc., It is also devoid of the characteristics of the other external entities such as space, time, etc. Resting on its own intrinsic nature, infinite knowledge, infinite vision, and infinite bliss, the pure Self is not to be associated with the various *varṇāśrama* distinctions such as Brahmaṇa, Kṣatriya etc. Since these distinctions rest on the birth of the body. It is not only distinct from the characteristics of the external world, it also remains distinct from the various inner psychic qualities which are produced by its association with *acetana* material enviroment. Neither the characteristics of the material world nor the indirect effect of the same can rightly be associated with the Pure Self.

जीवस्स णत्थि वण्णो णवि गन्धो णवि रसो णवि य फासो।
णवि रूवं ण सरीरं णवि संठाणं ण संहणणं॥ ५०॥

jīvassa ṇatthi vaṇṇo ṇavi gandho ṇavi raso ṇavi ya phāso
ṇavi rūvaṁ ṇa sarīraṁ ṇavi saṁṭhāṇaṁ ṇa saṃhaṇaṇaṁ

जीवस्य नास्ति वर्णो नापि गन्धो नापि रसो नापि च स्पर्शः।
नापि रूपं न शरीरं नापि संस्थानं न संहननम्॥ ५०॥

50. In the (pure) soul there is no colour, no smell, no taste, no touch, no visible form, no body, no bodily shape and no skeletal structure.

जीवस्स णत्थि रागो णवि दोसो णेव विज्जदे मोहो।
णो पच्चया ण कम्मं णोकम्मं चावि से णत्थि॥ ५१॥

jīvassa ṇatthi rāgo ṇavi doso ṇeva vijjade moho
ṇo paccayā ṇa kammaṁ ṇokammaṁ cāvi se ṇatthi (51)

जीवस्य नास्ति रागो नापि द्वेषो नैव विद्यते मोहः।
नो प्रत्ययः न कर्म नोकर्म चापि तस्य नास्ति॥ ५१॥

51. In the (pure) soul there is neither desire nor aversion. No delusion is found therein. There is no *karmic* condition, nor *karmic* matter, nor *no-karmic* matter in it.

जीवस्य णत्थि वग्गो ण वग्गणा णेव फड्ढया केई।
णो अज्झप्पट्ठाणा णेव य अणुभायठाणा वा॥ ५२॥

jīvassa ṇatthi vaggo ṇa vaggaṇā ṇeva phaḍḍhayā keī
ṇo ajjhappaṭṭhāṇā ṇeva ya aṇubhāyaṭhāṇā vā (52)

जीवस्य नास्ति वर्गो न वर्गणा नैव स्पर्द्धकानि कानिचित्।
नो अध्यवसानानि नैव चानुभागस्थानानि वा॥ ५२॥

52. In the (pure) soul there is no *varga* (atomic potency), no *vargaṇā* (molecules or group of atoms), no *spardhaka* (aggregates of molecules). There is no ego-consciousness of

different types and no *(karmic)* manifestations (resulting in pleasure-pain experience).

जीवस्य णत्थि केई जोग्गट्ठाणा ण बंधठाणा वा।
णेव य उदयट्ठाणा णो मग्गणट्ठाणया केई॥ ५३॥

jīvassa ṇatthi keī jogaṭṭhāṇā ṇa baṁdhaṭhāṇā vā
ṇeva ya udayaṭṭhāṇā ṇo maggaṇaṭṭhāṇayā keī (53)

जीवस्य न सन्ति कानिचिद्योगस्थानानि न बन्धस्थानानि वा।
नैव चोदयस्थानानि न मार्गस्थानानि कानिचित्॥ ५३॥

53. In the (pure) soul there is no activity of *yoga* (through *manas, vacana, kāya*), no *karmic* bondage, no effective manisfestation of *karma* bondage, no effective manifestation *karma,* and no variations according to method of inquiry into the nature of the soul (based upon the principle of classification).

णो ठिदिबंधट्ठाणा जीवस्स ण संकिलेसट्ठाणा वा।
णेव विसोहिट्ठाणा णो संजमलद्धिठाणा वा॥ ५४॥

ṇo ṭhidi -baṁdhaṭṭhāṇā jīvassa ṇa saṁkilesaṭṭhāṇā vā
ṇeva visohiṭṭhāṇā ṇo saṁjamaladdhiṭhāṇā vā (54)

नो स्थितिबन्धस्थानानि जीवस्य न संक्लेशस्थानानि वा।
नैव विशुद्धिस्थानानि नो संयमलब्धिस्थानानि वा॥ ५४॥

54. In the (pure) soul there is no stage of the duration of bondage, or of emotional excitement or of self-purification or of the acquisition of self-control.

णेव य जीवट्ठाणा ण गुणट्ठाणा य अत्थि जीवस्स।
जेण दु एदे सव्वे पोग्गलदव्वस्स परिणामा॥ ५५॥

neva ya jīvaṭṭhāṇā ṇa guṇaṭṭhāṇā ya atthi jīvassa
jeṇa du ede savve poggaladavvassa pariṇāmā (55)

नैव च जीवस्थानानि न गुणस्थानानि वा सन्ति जीवस्य।
येन तु एते सर्वे पुद्गलद्रव्यस्य परिणामा: ॥ ५५ ॥

55. The classification of the organic beings (according to the biological development) and the classification of man (according to the principle of ethico-spiritual development) are not applicable to the pure soul, since all the above-mentioned differences are the result of the manifestation of the material conditions.

Commentary : *Varṇa* or colour, such as black, green, yellow, red and white, are qualities of physical objects and physical objects alone, and hence they cannot be predicated of *jīva* which is entirely non-physical and spiritual in nature.

Gandha or smell is of two kinds pleasant odour and unpleasant odour. These are also characteristics of physical objects and hence cannot be predicated of the soul.

Rasa or taste is as follows : Sweet, bitter, acid, pungent, and astringent. These tastes are also associated with material things and hence cannot be transfered to the soul because of the intrinsic difference between the two.

Sparśa or contact sensation consists of smooth or rough, cold, hot, heavy or light, and hard or soft sensations. These different contact sensations are all again associated with physical objects. Hence these physical qualities cannot be predicated of *jīva* or soul.

Śarīra or body. The body associated with *jīva* is of five different kinds : *audārika śarīra* body given birth by the mother; *vaikrīyaka śarīra,* various bodily forms, magical and hallucinatory in nature assumed by a yogi because of his yogic powers *āhāraka sarīra* is the body drawn out of the physical body in the form of plasma by the magic powers of the yogi with the object of carrying out something which is beyond the reach of the physical body. *Taijasa śarīra* refers to the brilliant form of halo which shines forth from the physical body under certain spiritual conditions. Lastly, *kārmaṇa śarīra* is the body constituted by *karmic* matter, which is extremely subtle and which is inseparable from the soul throughout its *saṁsāric* career. Since all these different bodies are constituted by matter either gross or subtle, these cannot be identified with *jīva* or soul.

Saṁsthāna refers to the different shapes of the organic bodies. These are *samacatura saṁsthāna,* body that is symmetrically developed; *nyagrodha parimaṇḍala saṁsthāna,* body that is top-heavy like the banyan-tree; *swāti saṁsthāna,* body that is long and thin like a sword, *kubja saṁsthāna,* hunch-backed body, *vāmana saṁsthāna,* dwarfish body, and *huṇḍa saṁsthāna,* an ugly mass of flesh. All these shapes of organic bodies are nothing but the different manifestations of matter in the organic world. Hence these physical forms which are of material origin cannot be attributed to the soul.

Saṁhanana, the assemblage of bones of the skeletal structure. This refers to six types of bony joints which pertain to vertibrate animals. It is obvious that these varieties of bone-joints cannot be applicable to *jīva* which is *asarīra* by nature, a bodiless spiritual entity.

Rāga, the pleasant feeling of desire, and *dveṣa* the unpleasant experience of aversion, all these, being products of *karmic* matter, cannot be attributed to the soul.

Moha or delusion which clouds the knowing faculty and prevents its apprehension of reality, is also an effect of *karmic* matter and hence cannot be attributed to the soul.

The different kinds of *pratyaya* or *karmic* condition such as *mithyātva* false faith, *avirati,* absence of moral discipline, *kaṣāya* soul-soiling gross emotions, and *yoga*, activity of thought, speech and body, all being effects of matter either direct or indirect have no relation to the soul.

Karmas are of eight different kinds, such as *jñānāvaraṇiya, darśanāvaraṇīya,* etc. These are also mainly material in nature. Hence these *karmas* cannot be spoken of as belonging to the soul. *Non-karma* refers to the various physical molecules that build up the three types of grosser bodies of fully developed biological species. Since these body-building molecules are material they have nothing to do with *jīva* or Soul.

Varga refers to the bundle of potencies incorporated in a single indivisible atom which forms the basis of *karmic* matter.

Vargaṇā refers to the type of *karmic* molecules constituted by a number of *vargas* or *karmic* atoms.

Spardhaka refers to aggregates of *vargaṇās* or *karmic* molecules.

All these three refer to the development of *karmic* matter from the subtle type to the grosser type. These types of *karmic* matter cannot be predicated of *jīva.*

Adhyavasāna-sthāna. On account of the ignorance of its true nature, the ego may identify itself with the various objects and persons of the external world. This false feeling of one-ness with external things has nothing to do with the Pure Self, since the confusion is due to the interference of the physical objects. Similary *anubhāgasthānas,* the various types of pleasure-pain consciousness resulting from the manifestation of corresponding *karmas,* cannot be spoken of as belonging to the soul.

Yogasthānas, the different grades of activity relating to thought speech, and body which form the condition for attracting *karmic* molecules towards the soul are also mainly physical in nature and hence cannot be spoken of as of the soul. Similarly *bandhasthāna*, various kinds of *karmic* bondage and *udayasthāna*, fruit-yielding manifestation of *karmas* are also not of the soul.

*Marganā*ṣthāna, an inquiry into the nature of *jīva*, is based upon the method of classification according to various principles which are fourteen in number, such as *gati, indriya*, etc. These different principles of classification are distinctly material, since they pertain to the nature of the organic bodies, and hence they are not of the soul.

Similarly the different classifications of *jīvas* or *jīvasthāna* and the classification of man according to spiritual development or *guṇasthāna*, are all ultimately traceable to the different manifestations of matter. The nature of the Pure Self must therefore be understood to be entirely different from the above-mentioned various physical modes.

If the material characteristics, physical and psycho physical, are thus summarily disposed of either as qualities and modes of matter or as psychical effects produced thereby, then how can it be justified that the *jīva* is described in the scripture in terms of the very same attributes which are dismissed as being alien to its nature. The answer to this apparent self-contradiction is given in the next *gāthā*.

ववहारेण दु एदे जीवस्स हवंति वण्णमादीया।
गुणठाणंता भावा ण दु केई णिच्छयणयस्स॥ ५६॥

vavahāreṇa du ede jīvassa havaṁti vaṇṇamādīyā
guṇaṭhāṇaṁtā bhāvā ṇa du keī ṇicchayaṇayassa (56)

व्यवहारेण त्वेते जीवस्य भवन्ति वर्णाद्याः।
गुणस्थानान्ता भावा न तु केचिन्निश्चयनयस्य॥ ५६॥

56. These characteristics beginning from *varṇa* (colour) and ending with *guṇasthāna* or stages of spiritual development are (predicated) of the soul from the *vyavahāra* point of view; but from the point of view of reality, no one of these can be predicated of the soul.

Commentary : *Vyavahāra* or the practical point of view is taken for emphasising the *jīva-paryāya* or modifications of the soul. Emphasis of *paryāya* or modification naturally implies diversion of attention from *dravya,* the real substance. These *jīva-paryāyas* or modifications of the soul are the results of immemorial association of the soul with matter. Just as cotton cloth puts on the colour of the dyeing substance, so also the *jīva* puts on the characteristics of the associated matter. Since the empirical Self is so coloured in ordinary life, it is described in those terms though in reality it is alien to those characteristics.

The next *gāthā* explains why from the real point of view the characteristics of colour, etc. cannot be predicated of the *jīva.*

एदेहि य संबंधो जहेव खीरोदयं मुणेदव्वो।
णय हुंति तस्स ताणि दु उवओगगुणाधिगो जम्हा॥ ५७॥

edehi ya saṁbaṁdho jaheva khīrodayaṁ muṇedavvo
ṇaya huṁti tassa tāṇi du uvaogaguṇādhigo jamhā (57)

एतैश्च सम्बन्धो यथैव क्षीरोदकं मन्तव्यः।
न च भवन्ति तस्य तानि तूपयोगगुणाधिको यस्मात्॥ ५७॥

57. The association of these characteristics with soul must be understood to be like the mixture of milk and water. They are not certainly present in the soul since it is mainly characterised by *upayoga* (cognitive activity of knowledge and perception.)

Commentary : The relation of one thing to another may be in the form either of a mixture or in the form of substance and its qualities. Milk-cum-water is given as an example of mixture. Fire-cum-heat is given as an example of substance and its quality. The different things constituting the mixture can be seperated from each other. But the substance and its quality cannot be seperated at any time. Quality without substance and substance without quality will be empty abstractions incapable of independent existence. But a mixture is not so, because the inter- mixing substance in the mixture will give its colour to the mixture. Thus in the case of milk and water which is compared to the inter-mixture of soul and its material *upādhis,* the dominant substance being milk it is still called milk, when diluted with water. Exactly similar is the relation between *jīva* and its *upādhis.* Though their inter-mixture is from time immemorial, they can be separated from each other, as when the *jīva* attains *mokṣa* or liberation. Since the dominant factor in this mixture is *jīva,* the characteristics of the mixture from colour onwards to stages of spiritual development are considered as the attributes of the soul from the *vyavahāra* point of view. From the real point of view, the soul must be described in terms of *upayoga* (cognitive activity of knowledge and perception) which quality is inseparable from *jīva.* Even when the *jīva* becomes perfect through self-realisation this quality of *upayoga* will be inseparably present in it, in its complete form as *Kevala-jñāna* and *Kevaladarśana.*

The reconciliation between the *vyavahāra* point of view and the real point of view is effected by bringing in a popular illustration.

पंथे मुस्संतं पस्सिदूण लोगा भणंति ववहारी।
मुस्सदि एसो पंथो ण य पंथो मुस्सदे कोई॥ ५८॥

paṁthe mussaṁtaṁ passidūṇa logā bhaṇaṁti vavahārī
mussadi eso paṁtho ṇa ya paṁtho mussade koī (58)

पथि मुष्यमाणं दृष्ट्वा लोका भणन्ति व्यवहारिण:।
मुष्यते एष: पन्था न च पन्था मुष्यते कश्चित्॥ ५८॥

58. Seeing some one robbed on a road, ordinary people adopting the *vyavahāra* point of view, say "this road is robbed." But really what is robbed is not the road.

तह जीवे कम्माणं णोकम्माणं च पस्सिदुं वण्णं।
जीवस्स एस वण्णो जिणेहि ववहारदो उत्तो॥ ५९॥

taha jīve kammāṇaṁ ṇokammāṇaṁ ca passiduṁ vaṇṇaṁ
jīvassa esa vaṇṇo jiṇehi vavahārado utto (59)

तथा जीवे कर्मणां नोकर्मणा च दृष्ट्वा वर्णम्।
जीवस्यैष वर्णो जिनैर्व्यवहारत उक्त:॥ ५९॥

59. Similarly perceiving the colour which belongs to the material entities of *karma* and non-*karma*, which are found in association with *jīva*, the all-knowing jina describes it from the *vyavahāra* point of view, as the quality of the soul.

एवं गंधरसफासरूवा देहो संठाणमाइया जे य।
सव्वे ववहारस्स य णिच्छयदण्हू ववदिसंति॥ ६०॥

evaṁ gaṁdharasaphāsarūvā deho saṁṭhāṇamāiyā je ya
savve vavahārassa ya ṇicchayadaṇhū vavadisaṁti (60)

एवं गन्धरसस्पर्शरूपाणि देह: संस्थानादयो ये च।
सर्वे व्यवहारस्य च निश्चयद्रष्टारो व्यपदिशन्ति॥ ६०॥

60. Thus are smell, taste, touch, figure etc., predicated (of the soul) from the *vyavahāra* point of view by the All-knowing.

Why there is no intrinsic identity between *jīva* and *varṇa*, soul and colour, is explained next.

तत्थभवे जीवाणं संसारत्थाण होंति वण्णादी।
संसारपमुक्काणं णत्थि दु वण्णदओ केई ॥ ६१॥

tatthabhave jīvāṇaṁ saṁsāratthāṇa hoṁti vaṇṇādī
saṁsārapamukkāṇaṁ ṇatthi du vaṇṇādao keī (61)

तत्र भवे जीवानां संसारस्थानां भवन्ति वर्णादयः।
संसारप्रमुक्तानां न सन्ति खलु वर्णादयः केचित्॥ ६१॥

61. So long as *jīvas* have embodied existence in the world of *saṁsāra*, attributes of colour etc., are present in them. The moment they liberate themselves from the *saṁsāric* bondage, these characteristics such as colour, etc., have absolutely no relation to them.

Commentary : This *gāthā* emphasises the fact that the relation between soul and colour is one of mere association and not of identity. If in spite of this, it is obstinately mainteined that there is an intrinsic identity between *jīva* and *varṇa* it will lead to an erroneous attitude as is indicated next.

जीवो चेव हि एदे सव्वे भाव त्ति मण्णसे जदि हि।
जीवस्साजीवस्स य णत्थि विसेसो दु दे कोई ॥ ६२॥

jīvo ceva hi ede savve bhāva tti maṇṇase jadi hi
jīvassājīvassa ya ṇatthi viseso du de koī (62)

जीवश्चैव ह्येते सर्वे भावा इति मन्यसे यदि हि।
जीवस्याजीवस्य च नास्ति विशेषस्तु ते कोऽपि॥ ६२॥

62. If you maintain that all these modes pertain to the soul itself, then according to you there would be no difference whatsoever between soul and non-soul.

Commentary : *Dravya* and *guṇa*, substance and quality, have been described to be inseparable from each other and intrinsically identical. What differentiates one substance from another is the difference of qualities. Colour, taste, smell, etc. are the intrinsic qualities of matter, just as cognitive qualities are the intrinsic qualities of *jīva* or soul. If it is perversely maintained that the qualities of colour, taste, etc., are also the qualities of *jīva*, then there will be no fundamental difference between *jīva* and *pudgala,* a soul and matter. Since the qualities are identical in both, the underlying substance will become the same in nature, that is *jīva* having identical physical qualities and hence, becoming identical with matter, will cease to be an independent category as a *jīva* or soul. The whole scheme of things will then become all-devouring materialistic monism.

But if it is maintained that the identity between colour, taste, etc., and *jīva* or soul is true only in the case of the *saṁsāri jīva* or empirical Self, even then it will lead to an erroneous position which is pointed out next.

अह संसारत्थाणं जीवाणं तुज्झ होंति वण्णादी।
तम्हा संसारत्था जीवा रूवित्तमावण्णा॥ ६३॥

aha saṁsāratthāṇaṁ jīvāṇaṁ tujjha hoṁti vaṇṇādī
tamhā saṁsāratthā jivā rūvittamāvaṇṇā (63)

अथ संसारस्थानां जीवानां तव भवन्ति वर्णादयः।
तस्मात् संसारस्था जीवा रूपित्वमापन्नाः॥ ६३॥

63. If, as you maintain, the *saṁsārī-jīvas*, the empirical egos, are identical with the characteristics of colour, etc., then these empirical souls will be endowed with physical forms.

एवं पोग्गलदव्वं जीवो तह लक्खणेण मूढमदी।
णिव्वाणमुवगदो वि य जीवत्तं पोग्गलो पत्तो॥ ६४॥

evaṁ poggaladavvaṁ jīvo taha lakkhaṇeṇa mūḍhamadī
nivvāṇamuvagado vi ya jīvattaṁ poggalo patto (64)

एवं पुद्गलद्रव्यं जीवस्तथा लक्षणेन मूढमते:।
निर्वाणमुपगतोऽपि च जीवत्वं पुद्गलः प्राप्तः॥ ६४॥

64. If, according to thy philosophy, O Thou deluded one, (soul gets physical form) then it is matter that assumes the form of *jīva* in *saṁsāra* and it is again the very same matter that figures in *nirvāṇa*, the state of liberation of the soul.

Commentary : Thus it is maintained that even in the *saṁsāric* state, there is no identity between the soul and the physical qualities of colour, etc.

If there is no identity between *jīva* and the qualities of colour etc., then how is it possible to describe *jīva* according to the different stages of sense-development as *ekendriya-jīva* or one-sensed organism, etc. The point is cleared up in the next two *gāthās*.

एक्कं च दोण्णि तिण्णि य चत्तारि य पंच इंदिया जीवा।
बादरपजत्तिदरा पयडीओ णामकम्मस्स॥ ६५॥

ekkaṁ ca doṇṇi tiṇṇi ya cattāri ya paṁca indiyā jīvā
bādarapajjattidarā payaḍīo ṇāmakammassa (65)

एकं वा द्वे त्रीणि च चत्वारि च पञ्चेन्द्रियाणि जीवा:।
बादरपर्याप्तेतरा: प्रकृतयो नामकर्मण: ॥ ६५॥

65. Living beings with one, two, three, four, and five senses, gross and fully developed and their opposites (minute

and undeveloped) are all determined by the nature of *nāma karma* or body-building *karma*.

एदेहि य णिव्वत्ता जीवट्ठाणा दु करणभूदाहिं।
पयडीहिं पोग्गलमईहिं ताहिं कह भण्णदे जीवो॥ ६६॥

edehi ya nivvattā jīvaṭṭhāṇā du karaṇabhūdāhiṁ
payaḍīhiṁ poggalamaīhiṁ tāhiṁ kaha bhaṇṇade jīvo (66)

एताभिश्च निवृत्तानि जीवस्थानानि करणभूताभिः।
प्रकृतिभिः पुद्गलमयीभिस्ताभिः कथं भण्यते जीवः॥ ६६॥

66. These classes of living beings are the result of *karmic* matter which constitute their operative cause. How can these physical products be identified with soul?

Commentary : In reality there is no fundamental difference between cause and effect; for example, gold-leaf which is made of gold is of the nature of gold and nothing else. Similarly the various *jīvasthāna* or classes of living beings are the result of *nāma karmas,* the physical conditions which determine the building up of the body. Since the causal conditions are physical in nature, their products must also be physical. Hence they cannot be really identified with the nature of the soul.

पज्जत्तापज्जत्ता जे सुहुमा बादरा य जे चेव।
देहस्स जीवसण्णा सुत्ते ववहारदो उत्ता॥ ६७॥

pajjattāpajjattā je suhumā bādarā ya je ceva
dehassa jīvasaṇṇā sutte vavahārado uttā (67)

पर्याप्तापर्याप्ता ये सूक्ष्मा बादराश्च ये चैव।
देहस्य जीवसंज्ञाः सूत्रे व्यवहारतः उक्ताः॥ ६७॥

67. Completely developed, incompletely developed, minute and gross, all these modifications pertaining only to the body are given the applellation of *jiva* in the scripture from the *vyavahāra* point of view.

Commentary : *Paryāpta* and *aparyāpta* are terms applied to organisms, fully developed or incompletely developed. These attributes apply to all organisms in general. *Sūkṣma* and *bādara,* minute and gross, are attributes applicable only to *ekendriya jīvas* or one-sensed organisms. *Sūkṣma ekendriya jīvas* are the microscopic organisms present in earth, water, air, etc. *Bādara ekendriya jīvas* are the plants and trees of the whole botanical world. These two types of *ekendriya jīvas* are also called *sthāvara jīvas,* living organism incapable of locomotion or stationary beings. The types of organisms beginning with the two-sensed organisms are called *trasa jīvas,* organisms capable of locomotion. All these are various terms describing the bodily differences and yet they are used as names of *jīvas.* The commentators explain this from practical point of view with a popular illustration. Ordinarily, a vessel containing ghee is called a ghee-pot. The pot is made of clay and it is called a ghee-pot because it is used to keep ghee in it. The name of the contained article is transferred to the container, the pot of clay from the practical point of view in order to distinguish it from a water jug or a milk jug. In the same practical way, the various organic bodies get the name of the *jīvas,* which are associated with them. This transfer of nomenclature of the *jīva* to the body is only from the *vyavahāra point of view.*

मोहणकम्मस्सुदया दु वण्णिदा जे इमे गुणट्ठाणा।
ते कह हवंति जीवा जे णिच्चमचेदणा उत्ता॥ ६८॥

mohaṇakammassudayā du vaṇṇidā je ime guṇaṭṭhāṇā
te kaha havaṁti jīvā je ṇiccamacedaṇā uttā (68)

मोहनकर्मण उदयात्तु वर्णितानि यानीमानि गुणस्थानानि।
तानि कथं भवन्ति जीवा यानि नित्यमचेतनान्युक्तानि ॥ ६८ ॥

68. The stages of spiritual growth are stated to be due *to the (mohanīya)* deluding *karma* which are permanently *(acetana)* non-intelligent. How can they be identified with soul?

Commentary : The various stages of spiritual development called *guṇasthānas* are based upon the varying influence of *mohanīya karma* which manifests in two different ways. One method of its influence is to interfere with the correct perception of reality on account of which is called *darśana mohanīya,* deluding the right perception. The other way of its influence is perverse conduct on account of which it is called *cāritra mohanīya.* The various *guṇasthānaṣ* which are the results of the varying operations of this *mohanīya karma,* must maintain the relation of cause and effect. As already mentioned, cause and effect must be identical in nature. Wheat when sown will produce wheat alone and not paddy. In the same manner, the operative cause being material, the effect it produces must also be material. Hence the *guṇasthānas* must be recognised to be distinctly material in nature. Hence these cannot be taken as attributes of the soul. Neither the characteristics of the body nor the emotions and feelings of inner consciousness of the empirical Self can really be attributes of *śuddha jīva* or Pure Self.

Thus ends the Chapter on *Ajīva Padārtha*

The two previous chapters constitute the two different scenes of the First Act of the great Cosmic Drama, in which the two actors *Jīva* and *Ajīva* appear on the stage. The Ego, the living and intelligent, and the non-Ego, non-living and non-intelligent, first appear on the stage forgetting their self-identity, clasp each other as infatuated lovers and behave as if they were identical with each other. But after recognising their distinctness and of difference in nature, they become chastened from their delusion of false identity and depart from the stage.

Thus ends the First Act.

CHAPTER III

KARTĀ AND KARMA
THE DOER AND THE DEED

Dealing with the remaining seven *padārthas* such as (*puṇya, pāpa*, etc.) virtue, vice, etc., the author wants to emphasise once again that these seven *padārthas* are but the resultant secondary *padārthas* of the interaction of the two primary *padārthas, jīva* and *ajīva*, which are dealt with already. These two reappear again on the stage in different forms as agent and his action, *kartā* and *karma*.

जाव ण वेदि विसेसंतरं तु आदासवाण दोण्हं पि।
अण्णाणी ताव दु सो कोहादिसु वट्टदे जीवो॥ ६९॥

jāva ṇa vedi visesaṁtaraṁ tu ādāsavāṇa doṇahaṁpi
aṇṇāṇī tāva du so kohādisu vattade jīvo (69)

यावन्न वेत्ति विशेषान्तरं त्वात्मास्रवयोर्द्वयोरपि।
अज्ञानी तावत्स क्रोधादिषु वर्तते जीवः॥ ६९॥

69. As long as the *jīva* or soul does not recognise that the entities, *ātmā* and *āsrava*—self and *karmic* inflow—are absolutely different from each other, so long will he remain devoid of knowledge and will identify himself with baser emotions of anger, etc.

कोहादिसु वट्टंतस्स तस्स कम्मस्स संचओ होदि।
जीवस्सेवं बंधो भणिदो खलु सव्वदरसीहिं॥ ७०॥

kohādisu vaṭṭaṁtassa tassa kammassa saṁcao hodi
jīvassevaṁ baṁdho bhaṇido khalu savvadarasīhiṁ (70)

क्रोधादिषु वर्तमानस्य तस्य कर्मणः संचयो भवति।
जीवस्यैवं बन्धो भणितः खलु सर्वदर्शिभिः॥ ७०॥

70. That *jīva* which thus indulges in anger, etc., will only have an increased inflow of *karmas* and finally end with *karmic* bondage. Thus was it truly declared by the All-knowing.

Commentary : Ignorance of the distinction of the true nature of the Self and of the other alien entities is the root-cause of the trouble. The Self forgetting its pure nature imagines himself to be other than what he really is. He identifies himself with baser emotional experiences such as, "I am angry." This vitiated state of experience leads to the attraction and deposit of *karmic* molecules in the Self. The Self behaves like a person besmeared with oil all over the body walking through a cloud of dust. Dust particles get easily deposited all over the oily surface of his body. So the Self, ignorant of his own nature, provides the necessary condition for attracting the *karmic* particles which, when accumulated, permeate the whole nature of the soul thus clouding the intrinsic spiritual luminosity of the Self. This means *karmic* bondage. This *karmic* bondage in its turn produces the *saṁsāric* cycle of births and deaths, which is the inevitable career of the unenlightened Ego. Thus the unenlightened Ego imagines himself to be the agent of all disturbances which take place in the inner series of consciousness and outer scheme of things. Thus appears the drama of the deluded Self in the form of *kartā* and his *karma*, agent and his action.

जइया इमेण जीवेण अप्पणो आसवाण य तहेव।
णादं होदि विसेसंतरं तु तइया ण बंधो से॥ ७१॥

jaiyā imeṇa jīveṇa appaṇo āsavāṇa ya taheva
ṇādaṁ hodi visesaṁtaraṁ tu taiyā ṇa bandho se (71)

यदानेन जीवेनात्मनः आस्रवाणां च तथैव।
ज्ञातं भवति विशेषान्तरं तु तदा न बन्धस्तस्य॥ ७१॥

71. As soon as the absolute difference between *Ātmā* and *āsrava* is appreciated by *jīva*, bondage ceases to be.

Commentary : Just as the absence of discriminative knowledge is the root-cause of bondage in *saṁsāra*, the appearance of true knowledge has the opposite result of dissolution of bondage and disappearance of *saṁsāra*.

णादूण आसवाणं असुचित्तं च विवरीयभावं च।
दुक्खस्स कारणं ति य तदो णियत्तिं कुणदि जीवो॥ ७२॥

ṇādūṇa āsavāṇāṁ asucittaṁ ca vivarīyabhāvaṁ ca
dukkhassa kāraṇaṁ ti ya tado ṇīyattiṁ kuṇadi jīvo. (72)

ज्ञात्वा आस्रवाणामशुचित्वं च विपरीतभावं च।
दुःखस्य कारणानीति च ततो निवृत्तिं करोति जीवः॥ ७२॥

72. Knowing that the *āsravas* are impure, of contrary nature to Self, and the cause of misery, the soul abstains from them.

Commentary : Just as water gets muddy through association with clay, the *āsravas*, because of association with impurities, are impure. But the *Bhagavān Ātmā*, because of his eternal association with the absolutely clear nature of *cit* or intelligence, is perfectly pure. *Āsravas* being physical modes are non-intelligent and hence of contrary nature. But the

Lord *Ātmā* is eternally of the nature of knowledge and hence uncontaminated by an alien characteristic. *Āsravas,* because they always are productive of unpleasant experience, cause misery. But *Bhagavān Ātmā,* in his state of eternal bliss, cannot be the causal agent of any thing else and much less be the cause of misery. Hence *āsrava* is impure, *acetana* and the cause of eternal bliss. Their natures thus being fundamentally different, the *jīva* that possesses the discriminative knowledge naturally abstains from the *āsravas,* such as anger, etc. The discriminative knowledge thus leading to abstention from the *āsravas* is emphasised here, for otherwise, the Jaina point of view would be indistinguishable from that of the Sāṁkhyās. According to the Sāṁkhyas, *vivekajñāna,* the discriminative knowledge, constitutes the *summum bonum* of life. But according to the Jaina thought right knowledge must necessarily lead to right conduct, and only then it will lead to *mokṣa* or liberation.

अहमेक्को खलु सुद्धो णिम्ममओ णाणदंसणसमग्गो।
तम्हिट्ठिदो तच्चित्तो सव्वे एदे खयं णेमि॥ ७३॥

ahamekko khalu suddho ṇimmamao ṇāṇadaṁsaṇa-samaggo
tamhiṭṭhido taccitto savve ede khayaṁ ṇemi (73)

अहमेक: खलु शुद्ध: निर्ममश्च ज्ञानदर्शनसमग्र: ।
तस्मिन् स्थितस्तच्चित्त: सर्वानेतान् क्षयं नयामि॥ ७३॥

73. I am really one, pure, without the sense of ownership or mine-ness and full of complete knowledge and perception. Firmly resting in the true consciousness of such a Self, I shall lead all these *āsravas* such as anger, etc., to destruction.

Commentary : The Pure Self provided with discriminative knowledge resting on its own innate perfection of consciousness is able to destroy all those *āsravas,* alien psycho-physical characteristics with which he identified himself in the empirical state. Next it is stated that the *āsravas* which are intrinsically the products of evil should be abstained from.

जीवणिबद्धा एदे अधुव अणिच्चा तहा असरणा य।
दुक्खा दुक्खफला त्ति य णादूण णिवत्तदे तेहिं ॥ ७४॥

jīvaṇibaddhā ede adhuva aṇiccā tahā asaraṇā ya
dukkhā dukkhaphalā tti ya ṇādūṇa ṇivattade tehiṁ (74)

जीवनिबद्धा एते अध्रुवा अनित्यास्तथा अशरणाश्च।
दुःखानि दुःखफलानीति च ज्ञात्वा निवर्तते तेभ्यः ॥ ७४॥

74. Knowing them, bound as they are to the soul, to be impermanent, evanescent, unprotected and misery in their nature and also to be misery as their fruit in future (the Self) abstains from them.

Commentary : The realisation of the Self and the disappearance of the *āsravas* are inter-dependent and simultaneous. The moment the Self realises its true nature, the cloud of *āsravas* gets dispersed. The moment this cloud of *āsravas* gets dispersed, the Self shines in all its glory. Thus both are causally inter-dependent and the events occur simultaneously.

Adhruva means impermanent and extremely momentary like a flash of lightening. The *āsravas* may appear at one moment and disappear at the next. This characteristic is indicated by the word *adhruva,* non-persisting.

The term *anitya* implies the quality of vanishing like temperature in a fever-patient which may vary and finally disappear altogether. As against these attributes of *āsravas,* the *śuddha jīva* or the Pure Self is *dhruva* constant and permanent, and *nitya,* unchanging and eternal. Similary the *āsravas,* since they are produced in the soul by alien conditions, are really *aśaraṇa* or unprotected, since they are dependent upon something other than themselves. Not so is the *śuddha jīva* or Pure Self, since it is self-conditioned and hence undisturbed by anything else. The *āsravas* such as desire and hatred, constitute the misery in life. They are not only misery by nature, they carry with them the misery-producing potency through their association with *saṁsāric jīva* which has to experience the same misery even in its future birth. But the *śuddha jīva,* the Pure Self, not only shines with its intrinsic brilliance of knowledge but also rests in its own inalienable state of eternal bliss. Certainly the Self who knows his greatness and glory will never think of identifying himself with the impure and misery-producing *āsravas.*

कम्मस्स य परिणामं णोकम्मस्स य तहेव परिणामं।
ण करेदि एदमादा जो जाणइ सो हवदि णाणी॥ ७५॥

kammassa ya pariṇāmaṁ ṇokammassa ya taheva pariṇāmaṁ
ṇa karedi edamādā jo jāṇai so havadi ṇāṇi (75)

कर्मणश्च परिणामं नोकर्मणश्च तथैव परिणामम्।
न करोत्येनमात्मा यो जानाति स भवति ज्ञानी॥ ७५॥

75. The Self does not produce any modification in *karmic* matter nor in the *no-karmic* matter. He who realises this is the real knower.

Commentary : Cause or *kāraṇa* is mainly of two kinds : *upādāna kāraṇa* – substantive cause, the *nimitta kāraṇa* – external causal agency. Thus in the making of a pot, clay is the *upādāna kāraṇa* and the potter is the *nimitta kāraṇa.* In the same manner modification in *karma* and modifications in *no-karma* and modifications in have both, as their *upādāna kāraṇa,* causal substance, the material particles. These modifications are built by material particles like the pot which is made of clay. This *gāthā* therefore emphasises the fact that the various modifications of the *karmic* and *no-karmic* matter, cannot be explained as the result of the causal agency of *Ātmā,* which by its *cetana* nature cannot be the *upādāna kāraṇa* of the *acetana* material modifications.

Next the author points out that, though the *Ātmā* perceives matter, it does not become identical with the object.

णवि परिणमदि ण गिण्हदि उप्पज्जदि ण परदव्वपज्जाए।
णाणी जाणन्तो वि हु पोग्गलकम्मं अणेयविहं॥ ७६॥

ṇavi pariṇamadi ṇa giṇhadi uppajjadi ṇa paradavvapajjāe
ṇāṇī jāṇanto vi hu poggalakammaṁ aṇeyavihaṁ (76)

नापि परिणमति न गृह्णात्युत्पद्यते न परद्रव्यपर्याये।
ज्ञानी जानन्नपि खलु पुद्गलकर्मानेकविधम्॥ ७६॥

76. Material *karmas* are of various kinds. While in the process of knowing these, the knower neither manifests in, nor identifies with, nor causes the appearance of modifications of alien substance.

Commentary : The *karmic* modifications which are of various kinds are really the result of the manifestations of *karmic* matter. *Ātmā* or Self because of its *cetana* nature cannot in any way be responsible for the *karmic* modifications. These cannot be described as the result of manifestations of the Self. Nor can they be identified with Self; nor their appearances be taken to be the result of this causal agency of the *Ātmā*. In short, the Self cannot be the causal agent or *kartā* of the various *karmas*. Thus the author emphasises that the relation between the knower and the object known is quite analogous to the relation between the light and the object illuminated. That is, the knower in the process of knowing the object does not transform himself into the nature of the object known. This refutes the idealistic theory of knowledge which maintains that the process of knowing creates the object known.

णवि परिणमदि ण गिण्हदि उप्पज्जदि ण परदव्वपज्जाए।
णाणी जाणंतो वि हु सगपरिणामं अणेयविहं॥ ७७॥

ṇavi pariṇamadi ṇa giṇhadi uppajjadi ṇa paradavva-pajjāye
ṇāṇi jāṇaṁto vi hu sagapariṇāmaṁ aṇeyavihaṁ (77)

नापि परिणमति न गृह्णात्युत्पद्यते न परद्रव्यपर्याये।
ज्ञानी जानन्नपि खलु स्वकपरिणाममनेकविधम्॥ ७७॥

77. Modifications in the Self (as the result of *karmic* influence) are of various kinds. While in the process of knowing these the knower neither manifests in, nor identifies with, nor causes the appearance of modifications of alien substance.

Commentary : The changes appearing in the consciousness of the empirical Self though different from the *karmic* materials, are really produced by the *karmic* influence, though indirectly. Hence the Pure Self cannot consider these psychical modes to be the direct manifestations of his own nature. They must be traced to alien influence and hence cannot be identified with the nature of the Pure Self, though he is aware of them as objects of knowledge.

णवि परिणमदि ण गिण्हदि उप्पज्जदि ण परदव्वपज्जाए।
णाणी जाणंतो वि हु पोग्गलकम्मफलमणंतं॥ ७८॥

ṇavi pariṇamadi ṇa giṇhadi uppajjadi ṇa paradavvapajjāe
ṇāṇi jāṇaṁto vi hu poggalakammaphalamaṇaṁtaṁ (78)

नापि परिणमति न गृह्णात्युत्पद्यते न परद्रव्यपर्याये।
ज्ञानी जानन्नपि खलु पुद्गलकर्मफलमनन्तम्॥ ७८॥

78. The (pleasant and the unpleasant) fruits of *karmic* materials are really infinite. While in the process of knowing these, the knower neither manifests in, nor is identified with, nor causes the appearance of these modifications of alien substance.

Commentary : Pleasant and unpleasant experience of the empirical Self are really the fruits of *karmic* influence which is material in nature. Thus realising the true origin of the fruits of *karma,* the Pure Self cannot call these his own. Nor can he identify himself with these. Here also it is emphasised that the knower is in no way causally related to the objects known.

Thus after rejecting the doctrine from the real standpoint that the *Ātmā* or the Self is the causal agent in relation to modification of alien things as well as of the various impure psychic states, the author goes to establish a similar relation with reference to the matter that it also cannot stand as causal agent in relation to modification in the *cetana* entity, Self.

णवि परिणमदि ण गिण्हदि उप्पज्जदि ण परदव्वपज्जाए।
पोग्गलदव्वं पि तहा परिणमदि सएहिं भावेहिं॥ ७९॥

ṇavi pariṇamadi ṇa giṇhadi uppajjadi ṇa paradavvapajjāe
poggaladavvaṁ pi tahā pariṇamadi saehiṁ bhāvehiṁ

नापि परिणमति न गृह्णात्युत्पद्यते न परद्रव्यपर्याये।
पुद्गलद्रव्यमपि तथा परिणमति स्वकैर्भावैः॥ ७९॥

79. In the same way, matter also manifests in characteristic material modifications. In reality it neither manifests in, nor is identical with, nor causes the appearance of modifications in (*jīva*) whose substance is of alien nature.

Commentary : Just as the Self cannot be related to physical modifications as the *upādāna kāraṇa* or substantial cause, so also matter cannot be related to psychical changes as their *upādāna kāraṇa.* Neither *jīva* is the *kartā* of *karmas*, nor matter is the *kartā* of changes in the *jīva*. Thus there can be no identity between Self and matter, *cetana dravya* and *acetana dravya*.

Next it is pointed out that though Self and matter cannot be related to each other as material cause, still both may be related to each other as instrumental causes.

जीवपरिणामहेदुं कम्मत्तं पोग्गला परिणमंति।
पोग्गलकम्मणिमित्तं तहेव जीवो वि परिणमदि॥ ८०॥

jīvapariṇāmahedum̐ kammattam̐ poggalā pariṇamam̐ti
poggalakammaṇimittam̐ taheva jīvo vi pariṇamadi (80)

जीवपरिणामहेतुं कर्मत्वं पुद्गलाः परिणमन्ति।
पुद्गलकर्मनिमित्तं तथैव जीवोऽपि परिणमति॥ ८०॥

80. As conditioned by the modifications of *jīvas*, the material particles get modified into *karmas*. Similarly, conditioned by the *karmic* materials, *jīva* also undergoes modifications.

णवि कुव्वदि कम्मगुणे जीवो कम्मं तहेव जीवगुणे।
अण्णोण्णणिमित्तेण दु परिणामं जाण दोण्हं पि॥ ८१॥

ṇavi kuvvadi kammaguṇe jīvo kammaṁ taheva jīvaguṇe
aṇṇoṇṇaṇimitteṇa du pariṇāmaṁ jāṇa doṇhaṁ pi (81)

नापि करोति कर्मगुणान् जीवः कर्म तथैव जीवगुणान्।
अन्योन्यनिमित्तेन तु परिणामं जानीहि द्वयोरपि॥ ८१ ॥

81. *Jīva* does not produce changes in the qualities of *karma* nor does *karma* similarly in the qualities of *jīva.* The modifications of those two, know ye, are the result of one conditioning the other as *nimitta kāraṇa* or instrumental cause.

एदेण कारणेण दु कत्ता आदा सएण भावेण।
पोग्गलकम्मकदाणं ण दु कत्ता सव्वभावाणं॥ ८२॥

edeṇa kāraṇeṇa du kattā ādā saeṇa bhāveṇa
poggalakammakadāṇaṁ ṇa du kattā savvabhāvāṇaṁ (82)

एतेन कारणेन तु कर्ता आत्मा स्वकेन भावेन।
पुद्गलकर्मकृतानां न तु कर्त्ता सर्वभावानाम्॥ ८२॥

82. For this very reason the Self is the substantial cause of his own modifications (both pure and impure); but is not the substantial cause of any of the modifications of *karmic* matter.

Commentary : As the modifications of *jīva* operate as the instrumental cause, material particles get modified as *karmic* molecules. Similarly when the material particles operate as instrumental cause, *jīva* undergoes modifications. Thus the modifications of *jīva* and the modifications of matter indirectly condition each other. The relation between the two groups cannot be interpreted as a sort of causal identity that holds good between an immanent cause and its corresponding effect. Hence the relation between the two groups of modifications is not one of *karta* and *karma,* agent and action, for instrumental cause is quite different from substantive cause. Just as clay is the cause of a pot and cannot be the cause of a cloth, so *jīva* is the causal agent of all his modifications and matter is the causal agent of all its modifications.

Next it is pointed out that from the real point of view the Self is the *kartā* (agent) producing its own modifications and *bhoktā* (enjoyer) of its own states.

णिच्छयणयस्स एवं आदा अप्पाणमेव हि करेदि।
वेदयदि पुणो तं चेव जाण अत्ता दु अत्ताणं॥ ८३॥

ṇicchayaṇayassa evaṁ ādā appāṇameva hi karedi
vedayadi puṇo taṁ ceva jāna attā du attāṇaṁ (83)

निश्चयनयस्यैवमात्मात्मानमेव हि करोति।
वेदयते पुनस्तं चैव जानीहि आत्मा त्वात्मानम्॥ ८३॥

83. Thus from the real point of view the Self produces only his own Self. Again, know ye, that the Self enjoys his own Self.

Commentary : When wind blows over the surface of water in the sea, it will produce waves on its surface, waves constituted by the rise and fall of water on the surface. These waves on the surface of water, though caused by the blow of wind are really modifications of the water surface and certainly are not of the air which produces it. Air is only the *nimitta kāraṇa* of the waves, while water is the *upādāṇa kāraṇa*. Hence it is the ocean surface that undergoes modifications in the form of waves though indirectly determined by the blow of wind. Similarly *karmic* matter may operate as the instrumental cause and produce modifications in the Self. These modifications, though indirectly conditioned by *karmic* material, are really the result of the manifestation of the Self either pure or empirical. The empirical Self as an embodied entity in the world of *saṁsāra* may undergo modifications of experience, pleasant or unpleasant, accordingly as the *karmic* conditions are good or bad. Since experience-changes are confined to the nature of consciousness, though indirectly determined by *karmic* materials, they are really the result of the manifestations of the Self. In other words, the Self is the agent who produces all these changes in his own nature. Even when the determining *karmic* materials completely disappear leaving the Self free to realise his true glory and brilliance, it is the Self alone again that is the causal antecedent of the liberated Self. The consequential experience of pleasure-pain in the empirical state and his eternal bliss in the liberated state are also the manifestations of the Self. Thus it is the Self that makes his own nature whether empirical or pure, as an agent or *kartā* and it is again his own Self either empirical or pure that is enjoyed by the Self as *bhoktā* or enjoyer.

Next from the *vyavahāra* point of view the Self is described as *kartā* and *bhoktā*.

ववहारस्स दु आदा पोग्गलकम्मं करेदि अणेयविहं।
तं चेव य वेदयदे पोग्गलकम्मं अणेयविहं॥ ८४॥

vavahārassa du ādā poggalakammaṁ karedi aṇeyavihaṁ
taṁ ceva ya vedayade poggalakammaṁ aṇeyavihaṁ (84)

व्यवहारस्य त्वात्मा पुद्गलकर्म करोति अनेकविधम्।
तच्चैव पुनर्वेदयते पुद्गलकर्मानेकविधम्॥ ८४॥

84. But from the vyavahāra point of view, the Self produces various types of *karmic* modifications in matter. Similarly the various fruits of *karmic* materials, the self enjoys.

Commentary : Though the pot is really made of clay, in ordinary parlance it is made by the potter and is used for the purpose of bringing water. Thus the potter figures as the agent in making the pot and enjoyer by making use of it for different purposes. Similarly from the *vyavahāra* point of view, the Self is the agent who produces the various modifications of *karmas* out of the available material atoms. Having produced the *karmic* modification in the matter, the hedonic consequences of these *karmic* materials are enjoyed by the Self as *Bhoktā*. Thus the relationship to *karmic* materials of *kartā* and *bhoktā,* the Agent and the Enjoyer, which was denied of the Self from the real point of view, is reasserted from the *vyavahāra* point of view.

Next the author refutes *dvikriyāvāda,* the doctrine that the same cause can produce two distinct effects.

जदि पोग्गलकम्ममिणं कुव्वदि तं चेव वेदयदि आदा।
दोकिरियावादित्तं पसजदि सो जिणावमदं॥ ८५॥

jadi poggalakammamiṇaṁ kuvvadi taṁ ceva vedayadi ādā
dokiriyāvādittaṁ pasajadi so jiṇāvamadaṁ (85)

यदि पुद्गलकर्मेदं करोति तच्चैव वेदयते आत्मा।
द्विक्रियावादित्वं प्रसजति तत् स जिनावमतम्॥ ८५॥

85. If the *Ātmā* or Self produces these *karmic* materials (operating as *upādāna kartā* or substantive cause) and enjoys the consequences thereof in the same manner, it will lead to the doctrine of a single cause producing two different effects, which will be in conflict with the Jaina faith.

Commentary : If what is taken to be true from the *vyavahāra* point of view, that the *Ātmā* is the agent and enjoyer of his own *karmas*, is also taken to be true from the absolute point of view, it will lead to a metaphysical error. *Ātmā* is a *cetana dravya* or thinking substance, *karma-pudgala,* *karmic* materials, are as *acetana dravya,*—non-thinking substance. The Jaina faith is distinctly a dualistic one. *Jīva* and *pudgala,* thinking thing and non-thinking thing, are entirely distinct from each other, intransmutable one to the other and completely self-subsistent. If the Self, as an agent, is capable of producing modification not only in himself but also in *karmic* materials, operating identically in the same manner as *upādāna kartā,* then this causal agent must be credited with a potency to produce entirely two different effects and this doctrine of causation is what is called *dvikriyāvāda*—the doctrine which is rejected by the Jaina philosophy. According to Jaina metaphysics, two distinct and conflicting effects cannot be produced by identically the same cause nor, conversely, can the identically same effect be produced by two entirely distinct causes. The attempts to derive both *cetana* and *acetana* entities from the same cause would result in making the original cause in itself to be either *cetana* or *acetana.* If it is identified with the *acetana* effect, the *cetana* Self will cease to be. If it is identified with the *cetana* entity, then matter *acetana* will cease to be. In either case it would be a metaphysical error. The Vedānta doctrine which tries to derive both the Self and the external objects from the same source of *cetana dravya, Ātmā* or Brahma, must end in *māyāvāda,* which condemns objective reality as unreal and illusory.

Conversely, the attempt to derive the Self from the operation of the *acetana* matter as the Cārvākas do, must enthrone the physical world in the sovereignty of reality and dismiss the *Ātmā, cetana dravya,* as the fictitious and unreal. Neither of the conclusions is acceptable to the Jainas.

The same doctrine of *dvikriyāvāda* is again condemned with reasons.

जम्हा दु अत्तभावं पोग्गलभावं च दोवि कुव्वंति।
तेण दु मिच्छादिट्ठी दोकिरियावादिणो होंति॥ ८६ ॥

jamhā du attabhāvaṁ poggalabhāvaṁ ca dovi kuvvaṁti
teṇa du micchādiṭṭhī dokiriyāvādiṇo hoṁti. (86)

यस्मात्त्वात्मभावं पुद्गलभावं च द्वावपि कुर्वन्ति।
तेन तु मिथ्यादृष्टयो द्विक्रियावादिनो भवन्ति॥ ८६॥

86. Because they make the modifications of Self as well as modifications of matter to be effects of the same identical *Ātmā* or the Self (operating as *upādāna* cause), the believers in that doctrine of causation (which derives the conflicting effects from the same source) are said to be of erroneous faith.

Next the author describes the two-fold nature of *karma*. 1. *Dravya-karma* of which material *karmic* particles form the *upādāna* cause. 2. *Bhāva- karma* of which Self is the *upādāna* cause.

मिच्छत्तं पुण दुविहं जीवमजीवं तहेव अण्णाणं।
अविरदि जोगो मोहो कोहादीया इमे भावा॥ ८७॥

micchattaṁ puṇa duvihaṁ jīvamajīvaṁ taheva aṇṇāṇaṁ
aviradi jogo moho kohādīyā ime bhāvā (87)

मिथ्यात्वं पुनर्द्विविधं जीवोऽजीवस्तथैवाज्ञानम्।
अविरतिर्योगो मोहः क्रोधाद्या इमे भावाः॥ ८७॥

87. Erroneous faith is of two kinds. One pertaining to *jīva* or Soul and the other pertaining to *ajīva* or non-soul. Similarly the following modes are also of two kinds. Nescience, non-discipline, *yoga* (of thought, word and deed) delusion, anger, etc.

Commentary : The doctrine of *karma* according to Jaina philosophy implies two different aspects. The various modifications of *karmic* materials cloud the nature of the soul by getting entangled with it. Consequently upon this *karmic* entanglement, the soul gets vitiated and thus manifests itself in various impure psychic modes corresponding to the *karmic* materials. The *karmic* materials are called *dravya-karmas* and the consequent psychic changes, *bhāva karmas*. Since the *karmas* are consituted by material particles, they are *ajīva* and acetana, non-living and non-thinking. Since the *bhāva-karmas* are modifications in the consciousness of the Self, they pertain to *jīva* and *cetana,* and hence living and thinking. This distinction between *dravya* and *bhāva* is considered very important and it is applied to the various forms of experiences narrated in this *gāthā*. Thus *mithyātva,* which means erroneous belief, not merely implies the psychic activity which results in erroneous thought but also the physical *karmic* conditions of a particular type capable of producing erroneous belief in consciousness. This two-fold nature is present in other modes also. Thus we have *dravya ajñāna* and *bhāva ajñāna,* the former referring to the *karmic* material of a particular kind capable of interfering with the process of right cognition, and the latter the consequential effect produced in the consciousness. This distinction of *dravya-karma* and *bhāva-karma* is to be applied similarly in the other cases also.

This two-fold nature of *karma* should not be confounded with the doctrine of *dvikriyāvāda* which has been rejected though there is an apparent similarity between the two. *Karma* in the forms of *dravya- karma* and *bhāva-karma,* the material and psychical respectively, may be erroneously assumed to be two different effects of the same causal substance, *karma.* But in reality there is no such common substance called *karma* capable of producing the two kinds of *karmic* effect. As a matter of fact *dravya-karma* has matter as its *upādāna* cause, and *bhāva-karma* has the Self as the *upādāna* cause. Hence the two *karmas* have two different causes. Hence this doctrine of *karma* is distinct from the *dvikriyāvāda*.

In relation to the duality of *karma* the author explains next what is related to *jīva* and what is related to *ajīva*.

पोग्गलकम्मं मिच्छं जोगो अविरदि अण्णाणमज्जीवं।
उवओगो अण्णाणं अविरदि मिच्छं च जीवो दु॥ ८८॥

poggalakammaṁ micchaṁ jogo aviradi aṇṇāṇamajjīvaṁ
uvaogo aṇṇāṇṇaṁ aviradi micchaṁ ca jivo *'du (88)*

पुद्गलकर्म मिथ्यात्वं योगोऽविरतिरज्ञानमजीवः।
उपयोगोऽज्ञानमविरतिर्मिथ्यात्वं च जीवस्तु॥ ८८॥

88. Being of the nature of *karmic* matter, erroneous faith, *yoga* (of thought, word and deed), non-discipline, and nescience, pertain to *ajīva*—non-soul. Being of the nature of Self *(upayoga)* nescience, non-discipline, erroneous faith, pertain to soul.

Commentary : Because of this two-fold aspect of the *Karmas*, each must be called by different names, *jiva-mithyātva* when the *bhāva* aspect is emphasised, and the *ajīva-mithyātya* when the *dravya* aspect is emphasised. Similarly such different names are to be applied to the rest of the modes from the different aspects.

उवओगस्स अणाई परिणामा तिण्णि मोहजुत्तस्स।
मिच्छत्तं अण्णाणं अविरदि-भावो य णादव्वो॥ ८९॥

uvaogassa aṇāī pariṇāmā tiṇṇi mohajuttassa
micchattaṁ aṇṇāṇaṁ aviradi -bhāvo ya ṇādavvo (89)

उपयोगस्यानादयः परिणामास्त्रयो मोहयुक्तस्य।
मिथ्यात्वमज्ञानमविरतिभावश्च ज्ञातव्यः॥ ८९॥

89. The Selfed of the nature *of upayoga* (pure thought and perception) associated with delusion from beginningless

eternity undergoes three different kinds of (corrupt) modifications. Let it be understood that these three are wrong faith, wrong knowledge, and wrong conduct.

Commentary : The Self by itself is perfectly pure and flawless like a clear crystal. But this clear crystal will put on the colour of the object which is attached to its surface. Its surface will appear blue or green are yellow accordingly as a betel leaf, a plantain leaf, or a golden leaf is tacked on to it. The clear crystal appears coloured in different ways because of the associated objects. Similarly the Self in itself pure and clear puts on the characteristic of the associated objects in this case, *mohanīya karma.* The *karmic* association is throughout the beginningless infinity of time. On account of this association, the nature of the Self is corrupted and this corrupt nature appears in three forms, wrong faith, wrong knowledge, and wrong conduct. This must go on so long as the association of the alien matter persists; when the tie to the alien characteristics is broken, when the corrupt modifications disappear, the Self will regain its flawless nature and shine in its pristine purity and glory.

एदेसु य उवओगो तिविहो सुद्धो णिरंजणो भावो।
जं सो करेदि भावं उवओगो तस्स सो कत्ता ॥ ९० ॥

edesu ya uvaogo tiviho suddho ṇiraṁjaṇo bhāvo
jaṁ so karedi bhāvaṁ uvaogo tassa so kattā (90)

एतेषु चोपयोगस्त्रिविधः शुद्धो निरञ्जनो भावः।
यं स करोति भावमुपयोगस्तस्य स कर्ता॥ ९० ॥

90. The Self of the nature of *upayoga,* in himself, pure and flawless, when influenced by these three different forms of *karmic* materials, operating as *nimitta* cause, undergoes correspondingly three different impure modifications for which

the Self in impure form figures as *upādāna* (or substantive cause).

Commentary : The Self as influenced by foreign *karmic* materials has corresponding psychic modifications, for which he maintains the relationship of agent or *kartā*. The relationship of *kartā* and *karma*, thus holds good between the empirical and the impure experiences associated with it. Thus once again the author emphasises that the three-fold corrupt modifications, though started by the operation of *karmic* materials as *nimitta kāraṇa*, are still due to the empirical Self as *upādāna kāraṇa*.

जं कुणदि भावमादा कत्ता सो होदि तस्स भावस्स।
कम्मत्तं परिणमदे तम्हि सयं पोग्गलं दव्वं॥ ९१॥

jaṁ kuṇadi bhāvamādā kattā so hodi tassa bhāvassa
kammattaṁ pariṇamade tamhi sayaṁ poggalaṁ davvaṁā

यं करोति भावमात्मा कर्ता स भवति तस्य भावस्य।
कर्मत्वं परिणमते तस्मिन् स्वयं पुद्गलं द्रव्यम्॥ ९१॥

91. Whatever impure modifications the Self engenders (by relinquishing his own pure nature) to those modifications he becomes the *kartā* or the agent. These impure psychic modifications operating as instrumental cause, matter assumes, of its own accord, the corresponding *karmic* modifications.

Commentary : Thus it is emphasised that *Ātmā* or Self is only an instrumental cause, *nimitta kāraṇa,* and not the substantive cause, *upādāna kāraṇa,* of the various material *karmas.*

परमप्पाणं कुव्वं अप्पाणं पिय परं करंतो सो।
अण्णाणमओ जीवो कम्माणं कारगो हादि॥ ९२॥

paramappāṇaṁ kuvvaṁ appāṇaṁ piya paraṁ karaṅto so aṇṇāṇamao jīvo kammāṇaṁ kārago hodi (92)

परमात्मानं कुर्वन्नात्मानमपि च परं कुर्वन् सः।
अज्ञानमयो जीवः कर्मणां कारको भवति॥ ९२॥

92. That ignorant Self which makes non-self, Self, and the Self, non-self, becomes *kartā* or causal agent of those various *karmas*.

Commentary : The Self ignorant of his true nature is incapable of differentiating himself from the external objects. He readily assumes the qualities of the external objects and equally transfers his own attributes to the external objects. On account of this transposition of the attributes or *adhyāsa*, the Self puts on the qualities which really belong to matter. For example the temperature variation of the environment of being hot and cold is transferred to himself by an ordinary man who will say I am hot or I am cold. Similarly the feelings of affection and hatred are attributes relating to *karmic* matter, and yet the ignorant ego will feel identical with these attributes and say, "I desire," "I hate," "I am angry, etc." Thus vitiated by ignorance the Self figures as the *kartā* or the agent in relation to the various alien characteristics.

परमप्पाणमकुव्वं अप्पाणं पिय परं अकुव्वंतो।
सो णाणमओ जीवो कम्माणमकारगो होदि॥ ९३॥

paramappāṇamakuvvaṁ appāṇaṁ piya paraṁ akuvvanto so ṇāṇamao jīvo kammāṇamakārago hodi (93)

परमात्मानमकुर्वन्नात्मानमपि च परमकुर्वन्।
स ज्ञानमयो जीवः कर्मणामकारको भवति॥ ९३॥

93. That knowing Self which does not make non-self, Self and the Self, non-self, does not become the *kartā* or

causal agent of those various *karmas.*

Commentary : This *gāthā* emphasises the importance of discriminative knowledge. Realisation of the true characteristics of the Self as different from those of non-self, results from the disappearance of *ajñāna.* That is identical with *samyak jñāna or* Right knowledge, and this *samyak jñāna* or Right knowledge leads to *mokṣa* or liberation of the Self. In short *ajñāna,* is said to be the cause of bondage, and *samyak jñāna,* the cause of *mokṣa.*

तिविहो एसुवओगे अप्पवियप्पं करेदि कोधोहं।
कत्ता तस्सुवओगस्स होदि सो अत्तभावस्स॥ ९४॥

tiviho esuvaoge appaviyappaṁ karedi kodhohaṁ
kattā tassuvaogassa hodi so attabhāvassa (94)

त्रिविधि एष उपयोग आत्मविकल्पं करोति क्रोधोऽहम्।
कर्ता तस्योपयोगस्य भवति स आत्मभावस्य॥ ९४॥

94. Thus the Self whose nature is *upayoga,* manifests (as conditioned by corresponding *karmic pratyayas*) in three different impure forms (of wrong faith, wrong knowledge, and wrong conduct) and produces false identity (of Self with impure emotions) such as 'I am angry'. He becomes the *upādāna kartā* or the causal agency for those impure experiences of that empirical ego.

Commentary : This statement is equally applicable to the other grosser emotions as pride, delusion, etc.

तिविहो एसुवओगो अप्पवियप्पं करेदि धम्मादी।
कत्ता तस्सुवओगस्स होदि सो अत्तभावस्स॥ ९५॥

tiviho esuvaogo appaviyappaṁ karedi dhammādī
kattā tassuvaogassa hodi so attabhāvassa (95)

त्रिविध एष उपयोग आत्मविकल्पं करोति धर्मादिकम्।
कर्ता तस्योपयोगस्य भवति स आत्मभावस्य॥ ९५॥

95. Thus the Self whose nature is *upayoga*, manifests (as conditioned by corresponding *karmic pratyayas)* in three different impure forms (of wrong faith, wrong knowledge, and wrong conduct) produces false identity (of Self with external objects) such as "I am *dharmāstikāya* (principle of motion)". He becomes the *upādāna kartā* or the causal agency for those impure experiences of that empirical ego.

Commentary : The Self, on account of ignorance, imagines himself to be identical with alien characteristics which may be of two kinds, 1. internal relating to empirical consciousness, 2. External relating to the objective world. The Self, forgetting his pure nature may identify himself with either of these groups. The previous gathā describes the false identity of the Self with the inner impure and other psychic states relating to the empirical consciousness. This *gāthā* refers to the relation of the Self to the external world of things and persons. The external world according to Jaina metaphysics consists of other *jīvas, pudgala, dharma, adharma, ākāśa,* and *kāla. Jīva* and *pudgala,* Soul and Matter, being the chief actors in the *drama,* their various alliances have been already dealt with in their different aspects. Hence the author uses the word *dharmādī, dharma* etc., merely to indicate the objective world as distinguished from the subject or the ego. A glance at the Upaniṣadic literature will provide a sufficiently large number of illustrations of identifying the Self erroneously with the external objects and persons. There the *Ātmā* and the Brahma are used synonymously and this *Ātmā* or Brahma is identified with the Sun and the Moon and the rest of the bhūtas such as Earth, Air, Fire and Water. Such false identifications of *Ātmā* with *non-Ātmā* was prevalent and in abundance in the

Upaniṣadic period. Evidently the author is thinking of such metaphysical doctrines when he speaks of the Self identifying with *dharmādi.* Saṅkara who appears in the field several centuries later adopts exactly a similar attitude and condemns such identification as examples of *adhyāsa*[1] or erroneous transposition of attributes.

One other point we have to note here which is of epistemological interest is the relation of the knower to the object of knowledge. According to Jaina theory, though the object known is related to the Knower, still it is entirely independent and self-subsistent. Its nature can by no means be interfered with. The idealistic systems both in India and Europe maintain that the object of knowledge is not only known by the agent, but is also constructed by the knowing agent in the act of knowing. Thus the object of knowledge is practically derived from the creative activity of the knowing agent. The knowing Self or ego is thus credited with the capactiy of producing the external world out of itself in the process of knowing. Such an idealistic monism is incompatible with Jaina metaphysics. Probably the author was thinking of this erroneous metaphysical doctrine when he condemned the false identity of the Self with the external objects.

एवं पराणि दव्वाणि अप्पयं कुणदि मंदबुद्धीओ।
अप्पाणं अवि य परं करेदि अण्णाणभावेण॥ ९६॥

evaṁ parāṇi davvāṇi appayaṁ kuṇadi maṁdabuddhio
appāṇaṁ avi ya paraṁ karedi aṇṇāṇabhāveṇa (96)

---

1. The term *Adhyāsa* is first used by Amṛtacandra, the Commentator of *Samaysāra.* This term is not found in the upaniṣads but is adopted by Śaṅkara in his *Bhāṣya.*
अज्ञानान्मृगतृष्णिकां जलधिया धावंति पातुं मृगा अज्ञानात्तमसि द्रवंति भुजगाध्यासेन रज्जौ जनाः।

एवं पराणि द्रव्याणि आत्मानं करोति मन्दबुद्धिस्तु।[१]
आत्मानमपि च परं करोति अज्ञानभावेन ॥ ९६ ॥

96. Thus a person of dull intellect (*bahirātman*) takes alien things to be Self and through sheer ignorance takes the Self also to be alien things.

Commentary : The Self out of ignorance, not realising its own pure nature, may identify *itself* either with the impure emotions and ideas of inner consciousness or with the external objects of knowledge. In both these cases the ignorant Self figures as the agent. It may either imagine that anger, love, fear, etc., are its own attributes or that the external things such as *dharma,* etc. are of its own nature. The commentators explain both these erroneous beliefs through illustrations. A possessed person identifies himself with the spirit possessing him and behaves exactly as if that spirit is acting. He is able to carry out certain extraordinary deeds such as carrying a heavy stone or a heavy log of timber through the influence of the spirit, and yet he thinks that he performs all these deeds. Anger, fear, affection, etc. are all emotions due to alien influence and yet an ignorant person takes these to be his own just as a possessed individual imagines himself to be the agent of the extraordinary feats of strength exhibited by him. Secondly a person concentrating his attention upon an object of thought very intensely may end up in identifying himself with that object, he may forget to notice the difference between the Self attending to and the object attended to. He may cry in illusory joy, "I am that object" "I am Mahāmahiṣa; the great and powerful animal (Buffalo) "I am Garuḍa, the king of Birds; I am Kāmadeva, the god of Love; I am Agni, the fire (evidently taken from Vedic mantras)." This false identification of the Knower and the object known as the result of intense concentration is given as an illustration for the ignorant identification of the Self with the external categories such as space, time, *dharma*, *adharma*, etc. Both these notions of identity are condemned as erroneous, since they are alien to the pure nature of the Self.

एदेण दु सो कत्ता आदा णिच्छयविदूहिं परिकहिदो।
एवं खलु जो जाणदि सो मुंचदि सव्वकत्तित्तं॥ ९७॥

edeṇa du so kattā ādā ṇicchayavidūhiṁ parikahido
evaṁ khalu jo jāṇadi so muṁcadi savvakattittaṁ (97)

एतेन तु स कर्त्तात्मा निश्चयविद्भिः परिकथितः।
एवं खलु यो जानाति सः मुञ्चति सर्वकर्तृत्वम्॥ ९७॥

97. The Self on account of ignorance, figures as the agent of the various *karmas*. Thus it is declared by the knowers of reality. Whoever realises this truth gives up all causal agency (relating to alien things).

Commentary : This gāthā emphasises that it is ignorance which is the cause of making the Self kartā, an agent causing all alien characteristics, and conversely, it is knowledge that leads to complete severance of the Self from alien activities and attributes.

Thus from the real point of view after denying that the Self is the *kartā* of alien states, the author next asserts that it can be so from the *vyavahāra* point of view.

ववहारेण दु आदा करेदि घडपडरहादिदव्वाणि।
करणाणि य कम्माणि य णोकम्माणीह विविहाणि॥ ९८॥

vavahāreṇa du ādā karedi ghaḍapaḍarahādidavvāṇi
karaṇāṇi ya kammāṇi ya ṇokammāṇiha vivihāṇi (98)

व्यवहारेण त्वात्मा करोति घटपटरथादिद्रव्याणि।
करणानि च कर्माणि च नोकर्माणीह विविधानि॥ ९८॥

98. From the *vyavahāra* point of view, the self constructs external objects such as a pot, a cloth, and a chariot. In the same manner he builds within himself the various types of sense-organs, *karmic* materials and (body-building) non-*karmic* materials.

Commentary : The self in reality neither constructs any external objects nor produces internal modifications. The belief that he does so is associated with the ordinary man who thinks so from the *vyavahāra* point of view.

जदि सो परदव्वाणि य करेज्ज णियमेण तम्मओ होज्ज।
जम्हा ण तम्मओ तेण सो ण तेसिं हवदि कत्ता॥ ९९॥

jadi so paradavvāṇi ya karejja ṇiyameṇa tammao hojja
jamhā ṇa tammao teṇa so ṇa tesiṁ havadi kattā (99)

यदि स परद्रव्याणि च कुर्यान्नियमेन तन्मयो भवेत्।
यस्मान्न तन्मयस्तेन स न तेषां भवति कर्ता॥ ९९॥

99. If the Self were in reality the producer (as *upādāna kartā* or substantive cause) of those alien substances, then he must be of the same nature; as it is not so, he cannot be their author.

Commentary : *Jīva* and *pudgala*, Self and matter are two distinct substances, so different in nature that one cannot be derived from the other as a result of manifestation. If the *karmic* matter could be obtained as a result of the manifestations of *jīva*, then there must be complete identity between the evolving entity and the evolved product. Since it is not so in this case, the relation of causal manifestations cannot be predicated between *jīva* and *pudgala*. Thus it is denied that the Self can be the *upādāna kartā* or substantive cause of material things.

In the next *gāthā* it is pointed out that he cannot be even the immediate instrumental cause of material things.

जीवो ण करेदि घडं णेव पडं णेव सेसगे दव्वे।
जोगुवओगा उप्पादगा य सो तेसिं हवदि कत्ता॥ १००॥

jīvo ṇa karedi ghaḍaṁ ṇeva paḍaṁ ṇeva sesage davve
joguvaogā uppādagā ya so tesiṁ havadi kattā (100)

जीवो न करोति घटं नैव पटं नैव शेषकानि द्रव्याणि।
योगोपयोगावुत्पादकौ च तयोर्भवति कर्ता॥ १००॥

100. The Self (even as an instrumental cause or *nimitta kartā*) does not directly make a pot, nor cloth, nor other things; they are produced by *yoga* and *upayoga* (operating as *nimitta kartā* or instrumental cause) of which he is the cause.

Commentary : The term *yoga* is used to denote bodily activity and *upayoga* mental activity. In a former *gāthā* the Self was described as the maker of a pot, cloth, etc. from the *vyavahāra* point of view. Even this position is rejected here. The Self has no direct relation to the pot or the cloth. The potter or the weaver or the carpenter must use his hands for making a pot, a cloth, or a chariot and must make use of his mind for constructing designs before executing them. Thus the external objects are the direct result of the bodily and mental activity of the maker. Hence what makes the pot or the cloth is not the spiritual entity, the Self. The Self is directly related to the bodily and mental activities, *yoga* and *upayoga*, which in their turn are able to make external objects operating as *nimitta kartā*, instrumental cause. Thus it is pointed out that the Self cannot even be the *nimitta kartā* of external objects except through the instrumentality of his own body and mind.

जे पोग्गलदव्वाणं परिणामा होंति णाणआवरणा।
ण करेदि ताणि आदा जो जाणदि सो हवदि णाणी॥ १०१॥

je poggaladavvāṇaṁ pariṇāmā hoṁti ṇāṇa āvaraṇā
ṇa karedi tāṇi ādā jo jāṇadi so havadi ṇāṇī (101)

ये पुद्गलद्रव्याणां परिणामा भवन्ति ज्ञानावरणानि।
न करोति तान्यात्मा यो जानाति स भवति ज्ञानी॥ १०१॥

101. Those material modifications which become *jñānāvaraṇa*, knowledge-obscuring *karma*, the Self does not make. He who knows this is the Knower.

Commentary : *jñānāvaraṇa,* the knowledge-obscuring *karma,* is here taken as a type of *karma.* What is true of this *karma,* must be taken as true in the case of the remaining *karmas* also. What is asserted here is that the knowledge-obscuring *karma, jñānāvaraṇa karma,* is but modification of the material particles which are suitable to build up the structure of *karma.* Such particles of matter are called *karma-prayogya-pudgala-paramāṇus*—the primary atoms fit to make the *karmic* particles. Thus the various *karmas* are but the modifications of matter of which the Self, the Knower, cannot in any way be the substantive cause. For example milk may get transformed into curd, butter etc. The person who supervises the dairy operations is only the spectator of the various modifications of milk. Similarly, the Self is only a spectator of the various processes by which the material particles get transformed into *karmic* particles. One who knows these material changes and the nature of the pure Self, who is only a spectator of these changes is the real Jñānī, the Knower *par excellence.*

जं भावं सुहमसुहं करेदि आदा स तस्स खलु कत्ता।
तं तस्स होदि कम्मं सो तस्स दु वेदगो अप्पा॥ १०२॥

jaṁ bhāvaṁ suhamasuhaṁ karedi ādā sa tassa khalu kattā
taṁ tassa hodi kammaṁ so tassa du vedago appā (102)

यं भावं शुभमशुभं करोत्यात्मा स तस्य खलु कर्ता।
तत्तस्य भवति कर्म स तस्य तु वेदक आत्मा॥ १०२॥

102. Of whatever psychic disposition, good or bad, the Self is produced, he is certainly the (substantive) cause. That disposition becomes his *karma* or action and the Self enjoys the fruits thereof.

Commentary : Psychic disposition or *bhāva* is of three kinds. *śubha bhāva, aśubha bhāva,* and *śuddha bhāva,* good disposition, bad disposition, and pure disposition beyond good and evil. The first two are the characteristics of the empirical Self which is subject to *karmic* bondage, and the third refers to the Self in his pristine purity. *Śubha bhāva* is associated with virtuous conduct or *puṇya,* and *aśubha bhāva* is associated with evil or *pāpa.* The former may lead to happiness and the latter to misery. The third being beyond good and evil, transcends the worldly pleasure or pain and implies eternal bliss, characteristic of the transcendental Self. The psychic disposition both good and evil are modifications in the empirical Self, according to its ethical nature. Whether the Self be good or bad, it can only manifest in corresponding psychic dispositions and have nothing to do with *karmic* material modifications.

The author next explains the reasons why the Self cannot be the causal agent producing modifications in alien things.

जो जम्हि गुणो दव्वे सो अण्णम्हि दु ण संकमदि दव्वे।
सो अण्णमसंकंतो कह तं परिणामए दव्वं॥ १०३॥

jo jamhi guṇo davve so aṇṇamhi du ṇa saṁkamadi davve so aṇṇamasaṁkaṁto kaha taṁ pariṇamae davvaṁ (103)

यो यस्मिन् गुणो द्रव्य सोऽन्यस्मिंस्तु न संक्रामति द्रव्ये।
सोऽन्यदसंक्रान्तः कथं तत्परिणामयति द्रव्यम्॥ १०३॥

103. Whatever be the essential quality of a particular substance it cannot be transported to another substance of a different nature. Thus being non-transportable, how can the quality of one substance manifest as the quality of another substance.

Commentary : Jaina metaphysics recognises various *dravyas* or substances each with its own proper *guṇas* or qualities. Thus *jīva,* the Self has its peculiar quality of *cetana,* and *pudgala* or matter its own quality *acetana.* The former is conscious and the latter is non-conscious. Similarly with the other *dravyas.* Since the quality of a substance is the result of the manifestations of the intrinsic nature of that substance neither the quality nor the substance can be separated from each other. Since the *dravya* and its *guṇas* are so inseparably united the *guṇa* of one *dravya* cannot be transferred to another *dravya.* Thus the *guṇas* are non-transferrable, and the *dravyas* are non-transmutable. Thus the *cetana dravya,* the Self, cannot manifest as *acetana dravya* or matter. Conversely matter cannot manifest as Self.

दव्वगुणस्स य आदा ण कुणदि पोग्गलमयम्हि कम्मम्हि।
तं उभयमकुव्वंतो तम्हि कहं तस्स सो कत्ता॥ १०४॥

davvaguṇassa ya ādā ṇa kuṇadi poggalamayamhi kammamhi
taṁ ubhayamakuvvaṁto tamhi kahaṁ tassa so kattā

द्रव्यगुणस्य च आत्मा न करोति पुद्गलमयानि कर्माणि।
तदुभयमकुर्वंस्तस्मिन् कथं तस्य स कर्ता॥ १०४॥

104. The Self does not influence the substance or the attributes of *karma* which are of material nature. Thus being incapable of influencing these two (aspects) of *karmas,* how can he be their *upādāna kartā* (substantive causal agent)?

Commentary : The clay out of which a pot is made has its distinct quality. The potter in making the pot, makes use of this substance with its own quality. In making the pot, he cannot be said to manifest in the form of pot. He is not the *kartā* in that sense, though he makes the pot. He being a conscious spiritual entity, can in no way become *acetena* material pot. Similarly the Self, being a *cetana* entity cannot manifest into *karmic* forms of material nature. He is not the *kartā* nor the causal agent producing those *karmas.* This indirectly refutes the metaphysical doctrine which derives the whole of the physical universe, as a manifestation of Paramātmā or Brahma, who is by nature a pure *cetana dravya.*

जीवम्हि हेदुभूदे बंधस्स य पस्सिदूण परिणामं।
जीवेण कदं कम्मं भण्णदि उवयारमत्तेण॥ १०५॥

jīvamhi heduhbūde baṁdhassa ya passidūṇa pariṇāmaṁ
jīveṇa kadaṁ kammaṁ kammaṁ bhaṇṇadi
uvayāramatteṇa (105)

जीवे हेतुभूते बन्धस्य च दृष्ट्वा परिणामम्।
जीवेन कृतं कर्म भण्यते उपचारमात्रेण॥ १०५॥

105. When it is perceived that while the Self remains as the ground, the modification of *karmic* bondage appears (as consequence), it is figuratively sạid that the *karmas* are produced by the Self.

Commentary : The presence of the Self is merely a *nimitta* condition which produces in the *karmic* materials the various modifications of *karma* such as *jñānāvaraṇīya*, *darśanāvaraṇīya*, etc. Noticing this relation, the popular mind describes by a figure of speech that the Self is the *kartā* or the agent of those *karmic* modifications. The commentators give an illustration. The presence of the sun in a particular position with reference to clouds may result in the formation of the rainbow. This rainbow is associated with the clouds, though its appearance is consequent upon the sun remaining in a particular position. Similarly the presence of the Self results in the modification of several *karmas* out of *karmic* material present therein. In both the cases the causal agency is only figuratively true.

The author emphasises the same point by citing a popular illustration,

जोधेहिं कदे जुद्धे राएण कदं ति जप्पदे लोगो।
तह ववहारेण कदं णाणावरणादि जीवेण॥ १०६॥

jodhehiṁ kade juddhe rāeṇa kadaṁ ti jappade logo
taha vavahāreṇa kadaṁ ṇāṇāvaraṇādi jīveṇa (106)

योधैः कृते युद्धे राज्ञा कृतमिति जल्पते लोकः।
तथा व्यवहारेण कृतं ज्ञानावरणादि जीवेन॥ १०६॥

106. When a war is waged by warriors, ordinary people say that the king is engaged in the war, from the practical point of view. Similarly *jñānāvaraṇīya*, etc., is said to be produced by the *jīva* or Self.

Commentary : *Karmas* like *jñānāvaraṇīya* are the result of the operation of *karmic* materials. The Self or *Ātmā* is not directly responsible for these operations and yet he is spoken of as the causal agent producing these *karmas*. This statement is purely from the practical standpoint, and hence it should not be taken to be true from the absolute point of view. The practical point of view is explained by a simile which is obvious.

उप्पादेदि करेदि य बंधदि परिणमएदि गिण्हदि य।
आदा पोग्गलदव्वं ववहारणयस्स वत्तव्वं॥ १०७॥

uppādedi karedi ya baṁdhadi pariṇamaedi giṇhadi ya
ādā poggaladavvaṁ vavahāraṇayassa vattavvaṁ (107)

उत्पादयति करोति च बध्नाति परिणमयति गृह्णाति च।
आत्मा पुद्गलद्रव्यं व्यवहारनयस्य वक्तव्यम्॥ १०७॥

107. It is stated from the practical point of view that the Self produces, shapes, binds, causes to modify, and assimilates (*karmic)* matter.

Commentary : *Utpādayati* implies the different formations of the different types of *karmic* matter out of the material particles suitable to such formations.

Karoti implies the shaping of these types in different intensity.

Badhnāti implies determining the duration of bondage and their capacity to produce pleasure-pain experience.

Pariṇamayati implies modifications in their nature on account of which they may appear and produce effects or get withered after having produced the results.

Gṛhṇāti implies the process of attraction through which the *karmic* materials are assimilated so as to fill the whole of the self. The Self himself being pure is not responsible for any of these operations and yet he is credited with these activities only from the practical point of view.

जह राया ववहारा दोसगुणुप्पादगो त्ति आलविदो।
तह जीवो ववहारा दव्वगुणुप्पादगो भणिदो॥ १०८॥

jaha rāyā vavahārā dosaguṇuppādago tti ālavido
taha jīvo vavahārā davvaguṇuppādago bhaṇido (108)

यथा राजा व्यवहाराद्दोषगुणोत्पादक इत्यालपितः।
तथा जीवो व्यवहाराद् द्रव्यगुणोत्पादको भणितः॥ १०८॥

108. As a king is said to be, from the practical point of view, the producer of vice or virtue (in his subjects), so also from the practical point of view, the Self is said to be the producer of *kaṛmic* materials and their properties.

Commentary : *Puṇya* or *pāpa*, virtue or vice, are considered to be different material modifications of *karmic* matter. Though they correspond to the normal characteristics of the individual still they cannot be considered to be produced by the Self, since the Self, being a *cetana* entity, cannot produce *acetana karmic* material forms. If he is spoken of as a causal agent it is only metaphorically true.

सामण्णपच्चया खलु चउरो भण्णंति बंधकत्तारो।
मिच्छत्तं अविरमणं कसायजोगा य बोद्धव्वा॥ १०९॥

sāmaṇṇapaccayā khalu cauro bhaṇṇaṁti baṁdhakattāro
micchattaṁ aviramaṇaṁ kasāyajogā ya boddhavvā (109)

सामान्यतप्रत्ययाः खलु चत्वारो भण्यन्ते बन्धकर्तारः।
मिथ्यात्वमविरमणं कषाययोगौ च बोद्धव्याः॥ १०९॥

109. The general *karmic* conditions, *pratyayas,* are primarily four in number. They are said to be the immediate agents bringing about *karmic* bondage. These must be understood to be wrong belief, non-discipline, gross emotions, and *yoga* or psycho-physical structure, conditioning the activity of thought, word, and deed.

तेसिं पुणोवि य इमो भणिदो भेदो दु तेरसवियप्पो।
मिच्छादिट्ठी आदी जाव सजोगिस्स चरमंतं॥ ११०॥

tesiṁ puṇovi ya imo bhaṇido bhedo ḍu terasaviyappo
micchādiṭṭi ādī jāva sajogissa caramaṁtaṁ (110)

तेषां पुनरपि चायं भणितो भेदस्तु त्रयोदशविकल्पः।
मिथ्यादृष्ट्यादिर्यावत्सयोगिनश्चरमान्तः ॥ ११०॥

110. Of these *pratyayas,* thirteen further subdivisions of secondary conditions (based upon *āsravas*) are mentioned, which are the various *guṇasthānas* (stages of spiritual development) beginning from *mithyādṛṣṭi* or wrong believer, and ending with *sayogi kevalī* (the perfect being still with *yoga* or psycho-physical structure) conditioning the activity of thought, word and deed.

एदे अचेदणा खलु पोग्गलकम्मुदयसंभवा जम्हा।
ते जदि करंति कम्मं णवि तेसिं वेदगो आदा॥ १११॥

ede acedaṇā khalu poggalakammudayasaṁbhavā jamhā
te jadi karaṁti kammaṁ ṇavi tesiṁ vedago ādā (111)

एते अचेतना खलु पुद्गलकर्मोदयसम्भवा यस्मात्।
ते यदि कुर्वन्ति कर्म नापि तेषां वेदक आत्मा॥ १११॥

111. These stages (brought about by *uttara pratyayas* or subsidiary conditions) are really *acetana,* non-conscious, because they are brought about by the manisfestation of material *karmas;* if really they are the immediate causal conditions producing the *karmas,* then the Self cannot enjoy their fruits.

गुणसण्णिदा दु एदे कम्मं कुव्वंति पच्चया जम्हा।
तम्हा जीवो अकत्ता गुणा य कुव्वंति कम्माणि॥ ११२॥

guṇasaṇṇidā du ede kammaṁ kuvvaṁti paccayā jamhā
tamhā jīvo akattā guṇā ya kuvvaṁti kammaṇi (112)

गुणसंज्ञितास्तु एते कर्म कुर्वन्ति प्रत्यया यस्मात्।
तस्माज्जीवोऽकर्ता गुणाश्च कुर्वन्ति कर्माणि॥ ११२॥

112. Because these conditions called *gaṇasthānas* produce *karmas,* therefore the Self is not their author. Only the conditions called *guṇasthānas* produce the *karmas.*

Commentary : The conditions which bring about bondage are of two kinds : *mūlapratyaya* or primary conditions, and *uttarapratyaya* or secondary conditions. The former is of the four sorts and the latter, of thirteen as enumerated above. The *pratyayas* or conditions are material in nature, and hence *acetana,* non-conscious. They are mainly responsible for the various *karmic* modifications. Hence they constitute the *kartā of the various karmas,* and not the Self. Thus the Self, being in no way the causal agent of the *karmas,* cannot be spoken of as the *bhoktā* or the enjoyer of the fruits thereof. Thus these *pratyayas* are said to be the immediate cause of the *karmic* modifications. Though the pure Self is not in any way responsible for these *karmic* modifications, the impure Self in *saṁsāra* may be said to be the remote causal agent of these *karmas.* Thus from the absolute point of view, the pure Self is neither *kartā* nor *bhoktā,* neither the actor nor the enjoyer, whereas the impure empirical Self is both *kartā* and *bhoktā,* doer and the enjoyer. Thus the Sāṁkhya conception of *puruṣa,* that he is only the enjoyer and not the doer of *karmas,* is rejected here. He who enjoys the *karmas* must also be its agent. If he is not the one, he cannot be the other. In his pure nature, the Self has neither aspects but in his impure form he has both the aspects.

Next the author states that *jīva* and *pratyayas,* the Self and *karmic* conditions, are not absolutely identical.

जह जीवस्स अणण्णुवओगो कोहो वि तह जदि अणण्णो।
जीवस्साजीवस्स य एवमणण्णत्तमावण्णं॥ ११३॥

jaha jīvassa aṇaṇṇuvaogo koho vi taha jadi aṇaṇṇo
jīvassājīvassa ya evamaṇṇattamāvaṇṇaṁ (113)

यथा जीवस्यानन्य उपयोगः क्रोधोऽपि तथा यद्यनन्यः।
जीवस्याजीवस्य चैवमनन्यत्वमापन्नम्॥ ११३॥

113. If anger is non-different from the Self, just as *upayoga,* then it must result in the identity of the Self with the non-self.

एवमिह जो दु जीवो सो चेव दु णियमदो तहा जीवो।
अयमेयत्ते दोसो पच्चयणोकम्मकम्माणं ॥ ११४॥

evamiha jo du jīvo so ceva du ṇiyamado tahā jīvo
ayameyatte doso paccayaṇokammakammāṇaṁ (114)

एवमिह यस्तु जीवः स चैव तु नियमतस्तथाजीवः।
अयमेकत्वे दोषः प्रत्ययनोकर्मकर्मणाम्॥ ११४॥

114. If the *pratyayas* or the *karmic* conditions, *karmas (karmic* modifications) and *no-karmas* (body building material particles) are identified with the Self (in an unqualified form) it will lead to the erroneous conclusion that whatever is Self is in reality non-self.

अह पुण अण्णो कोहो अण्णुवओगप्पगो हवदि चेदा।
जह कोहो तह पच्चय कम्मं णोकम्ममवि अण्णं॥ ११५॥

aha puṇa aṇṇo koho aṇṇuvaogappago havadi cedā
jaha koho taha paccaya kammaṁ ṇokammamavi aṇṇaṁ

अथ पुनः अन्यः क्रोधोऽन्य उपयोगात्मको भवति चेतयिता।
यथा क्रोधस्तथा प्रत्ययाः कर्म नोकर्माप्यन्यत्॥ ११५॥

115. And if (you agree that) anger is one thing and the conscious Self is entirely a different one, then like anger, the *pratyayas* (or conditions), *karmas* (*karmaic*-modifications), and *non-karmas* (body-building material particles) must also be admitted to be different (from the conscious Self).

Commentary : The intrinsic attribute of the Self is *upayoga*, cognitive activity. This intrinsic quality is therefore inseparable from the *ātmā* or the Self. But this Self loses its nature when it is in association with the *acetana* matter in *saṁsāra*. As a result of this combination, several psycho-physical modifications appear. Anger is one such modification. Since it is the result of association with matter, it is said to retain the attributes of its origin of being non-conscious. This non-conscious experience of the emotion of anger must be entirely distinct from the pure Self characterised by *upayoga*. Without noticing this fundamental difference, if anger or *krodha* is elevated to the privileged position of *upayoga* and is considered as an intrinsic attribute of the Self, then the Self will be endowed with an *acetana* attribute and the fundamental distinction between *jīva* and *ajīva* will vanish and with that *jīva* itself will disappear. In order to avoid such an inconvenient conclusion of denying the existence of the Self altogether if you hold that *krodha* or anger is entirely distinct from *jīva*, then you must consistently maintain a similar attirude with regard to the other material modifications such as *pratyayas*, *karmas* and *no-karmas*, since there is no difference in nature between these and *krodha*. If *krodha* and *pratyaya* are absolutely different from the Self then there could be no possibility of association of the Self with *upādhis*. Therefore the author emphasises here that the *karmic upādhis* and the impure psychic states generated thereby are only partially different from the Self (and not absolutely).

Next the author points out what absurdity would result

from maintaining that *pratyayas*, etc. are absolutely different from *jīva*.

जीवे ण सयं बद्धं ण सयं परिणमदि कम्मभावेण।
जदि पोग्गलदव्वमिणं अप्परिणामी तदा होदि॥ ११६॥

jīve ṇa sayaṁ baddhaṁ ṇa sayaṁ pariṇamadi kammabhāveṇa
jadi poggaladavvamiṇaṁ appariṇāmī tadā hodi (116)

जीवे न स्वयं बद्धं न स्वयं परिणमते कर्मभावेन।
यदि पुद्गलद्रव्यमिदमपरिणामि तदा भवति॥ ११६॥

116. If matter, in the form of *karma,* is not of its own accord bound with the Self, nor of itself evolves into modes of *karma,* then it becomes immutable.

कम्मइयवग्गणासु य अपरिणमंतीसु कम्मभावेण।
संसारस्स अभावो पसज्जदे संखसमओ वा॥ ११७॥

kammaiyavaggaṇāsu ya apariṇamaṁtīsu kammabhāveṇa
saṁsārassa abhāvo pasajjade saṁkhasamao va (117)

कार्मणवर्गणासु चापरिणममानासु कर्मभावेन।
संसारस्याभावः प्रसज्जति सांख्यसमयो वा॥ ११७॥

117. If the primary *karmic* molecules do not transform themselves into various *karma* modes (associated with *jīva)* then it will lead to the non-existence of *saṁsāra* as in the case of the Sāṁkhya system.

जीवो परिणामयदे पोग्गलदव्वाणि कम्मभावेण।
ते समयपरिणमंते कहं णु परिणामयदि चेदा॥ ११८॥

jīvo pariṇāmayade poggaladavvāṇi kaṃmabhāveṇa
te samayapariṇamaṁte kahaṁ ṇu pariṇāmayadi cedā

जीवः परिणामयति पुद्‌गलद्रव्याणि कर्मभावेन।
तानि स्वयमपरिणममानानि कथं नु परिणामयति चेतयिता॥ ११८॥

118. If you maintain that it is the Self that transforms the primary *karmic* molecules into various *karmic* modes, then how is it possible for the Self who is a *cetana* entity to cause transformation in a thing which is by nature non-transformable.

अह सयमेव हि परिणमदि कम्मभावेण पोग्गलं दव्वं।
जीवो परिणामयदे कम्मं कम्मत्तमिदि मिच्छा॥ ११९॥

aha sayameva hi pariṇamadi kammabhāveṇa poggalaṁ davvaṁ
jīvo pariṇāmayade kammaṁ kammattamidi micchā (119)

अथ स्वयमेव हि परिणमते कर्मभावेन पुद्‌गलत्वद्रव्यम्।
जीवः परिणामयति कर्म कर्मत्वमिति मिथ्या॥ ११९॥

119. Then it follows that matter of its own accord transforms itself into various modes of *karmas*. Hence it is false to maintain that *jīva* causes this transformation into *karmic* modes.

णियमा कम्मपरिणदं कम्मं चि य होदि पोग्गलं दव्वं।
तह तं णाणावरणाइपरिणदं मुणतु तच्चेव॥ १२०॥

ṇiyamā kammapariṇadaṁ kammaṁ ci ya hodi poggalaṁ davvaṁ
taha taṁ ṇāṇāvaraṇāipariṇadaṁ muṇatu tacceva (120)

नियमात् कर्मपरिणतं कर्म चैव भवति पुद्‌गलं द्रव्यम्।
तथा तज्ज्ञानावरणादिपरिणतं जानीत तच्चैव॥ १२०॥

120. The primary *karmic* molecules which undergo transformation as various *karmic* modes are in reality material in nature. Know ye, then that the *karmic* modifications such

as *jñāṇāvaraṇīya*, knowledge-obscuring *karmas*, etc., are also of similar nature.

Commentary : *Saṁsāra* or concrete life implies embodied nature of the Self. This embodied existence of the empirical Self is primarily due to the association with *karmic* matter. This association with *karmic* matter is present through the career of the empirical Self. This *karmic* material which is associated with the Self throughout its *saṁsārī* life is made up of minute material particles. These minute material particles must constitute various types of material aggregates or types of *karma*. These various types or modes of *karma* get inextricably bound with the nature of the Self and this intimate association of Self with matter is called *karmic* bondage. These two processes of forming *karmic* aggregates from primary *karmic* molecules, and these aggregates binding themselves with the Self, are entirely the result of the manifestation of *karmic* molecules. If this tendency of matter to manifest itself into *karmic* modes is denied then there will be no *karmas*. When there are no *karmas* there is no *karmic* bondage, and when there is no *karmic* bondage, the Self must remain pure and unsullied as in the case of the *puruṣa* in the Sāṁkhya philosophy. If the Self remains perfectly pure in himself, there is no chance for his embodied existence and no scope for *saṁsāra*. This is absurd as it is contrary to our experience. If in order to avoid this inconvenient conclusion, it is maintained that the Self by his own intrinsic potency, produces the transformation of *karma* types from primary material molecules and ties himself to these types of his own accord, then this leads to an equally impossible position. Matter itself being incapable of transformation cannot be forcibly made to undergo transformation by any alien influence. Hence it must be maintained that matter by nature is capable of transformation and it is this process of transformation which matter undergoes that results in the formation of various types of *karmas* such as *jñānāvaraṇīya*.

Thus in order to refute the Sāṁkhya point of view, the tendency to manifest is predicated of matter. Similarly the same attribute is said to be true of the Self in the following *gāthās*.

ण सयं बद्धो कम्मे ण सयं परिणमदि कोहमादीहिं।
जदि एस तुज्झ जीवो अप्परिणामी तदा होदि॥ १२१॥

ṇa sayaṁ baddho kamme ṇa sayaṁ pariṇamadi kohamādīhiṁ
jadi esa tujjha jīvo appariṇāmī tadā hodi (121)

न स्वयं बद्धः कर्मणि न स्वयं परिणमते क्रोधादिभिः।
यद्येषः तव जीवोऽपरिणामी तदा भवति॥ १२१॥

121. If according to your view the Self by himself is not bound by *karmas* and does not have emotional modifications such as anger, etc., then he must by nature remain non-manifesting.

The next *gāthā* says what is wrong if the Self remains incapable of manifestation.

अपरिणमंतेहि सयं जीवे कोहादिएहि भावेहिं।
संसारस्स अभावो पसज्जदे संखसमओ वा॥ १२२॥

aparinamaṁtehi sayaṁ jīve kohādiehi bhāvehiṁ
saṁsārassa abhāvo pasajjade saṁkhasamao vā (122)

अपरिणममाने हि स्वयं जीवे क्रोधादिभिः भावैः।
संसारस्याभावः प्रसजति सांख्यसमयो वा॥ १२२॥

122. If the Self does not of his own accord undergo emotional modifications such as anger, then empirical life or

saṁsāra will cease to be. This would result in the Sāṁkhya view.

पोग्गलकम्मं कोहो जीवं परिणामएदि कोहत्तं।
तं सयमपरिणमंतं कहं णु परिणामयदि कोहो॥ १२३॥

poggalakammaṁ koho jīvaṁ pariṇāmaedi kohattaṁ
taṁ sayamapariṇamaṁtaṁ kahaṁ ṇu pariṇāmayadi koho

पुदगलकर्म क्रोधो जीवं परिणामयति क्रोधत्वम्।
तं स्वयमपरिणमन्तं कथं नु परिणामयति क्रोधः॥ १२३॥

123. If you maintain that it is *karmic* matter, by its own potency, that causes in the Self emotional modifications such as anger, then how is it possible for matter to produce any modification in the Self which is by nature incapable of manifestation.

अह सयमप्पा परिणमदि कोहभावेण एस दे बुद्धी।
कोहो परिणामयदे जीवं कोहत्तमिदि मिच्छा॥ १२४॥

aha sayamappā pariṇamadi kohabhāveṇa esa de buddhī
koho pariṇāmayade jīvaṁ kohattamidi micchā (124)

अथ स्वमात्मा परिणमते क्रोधभावेन एषा तव बुद्धिः।
क्रोधः परिणामयति जीवं क्रोधत्वमिति मिथ्या॥ १२४॥

124. If it is your belief that the Self, without any extraneous influence, undergoes emotional modifications such as anger, then Oh disciple! your statement, "*karmic* matter of anger produces in the Self the emotion of anger," becomes false.

कोहुवजुत्तो कोहो माणुवजुत्तो य माणमेवादा।
माउवजुत्तो माया लोहुवजुत्तो हवदि लोहो॥ १२५॥

kohuvajutto koho māṇuvajutto ya māṇamevādā
māuvajutto māyā lohuvajutto havadi loho (125)

क्रोधोपयुक्तः क्रोधो मानोपयुक्तश्च मान एवात्मा।
मायोपयुक्तो माया लोभोपयुक्तो भवति लोभः॥ १२५॥

125. The Self in association with *karmic* material condition of anger, has the emotion of anger, of pride, has the emotion of pride; of deceipt, has the emotion of deceipt; of greed, has the emotion of greed.

Commentary : The argument employed in the case of matter that it is capable of modification is repeated in the case of *jiva.* If the Self is by himself incapable of *karmic* bondage and is incapable of emotional modification of anger, he must remain pure and unchanging like the Sāṁkhya *puruṣa.* Hence there is no scope for *saṁsāra.* In order to avoid this conclusion, if matter is credited with potency to cause emotional modification in the Self, then this problem will remain unanswered. How can matter in any way produce changes in an alien entity, the Self, which is taken to be unchangeable in-nature. Hence it must be accepted that the Self is capable of undergoing emotional modifications when influenced by *karmic* materials operating as *nimitta* conditions.

जं कुणदि भावमादा कत्ता सो होदि तस्स भावस्स।
णाणिस्स दु णाणमओ अण्णाणमओ अणाणिस्स॥ १२६॥

jaṁ kuṇadi bhāvamādā kattā so hodi tassa bhāvassa
ṇāṇissa du ṇāṇamao aṇṇāṇamao aṇāṇissa (126)

यं करोति भावमात्मा कर्त्ता स भवति तस्य भावस्य।
ज्ञानिनस्तु ज्ञानमयोऽज्ञानमयोऽज्ञानिनः॥ १२६॥

126. Into whatever mode the Self manifests himself, he is the *upādāna kartā* substantial agent of that mode. If the manifesting agent is the Self with the right knowledge, then the corresponding mode will also be of the same nature, i.e. right knowledge. If the manifesting Self is of wrong knowledge, the corresponding mode in this case will be wrong knowledge.

Commentary : If the Self is incapable of manifestation, then it is not possible to speak of psychic modifications either pure or impure.

अण्णाणमओ भावो अणाणिणो कुणदि तेण कम्माणि।
णाणमओ णाणिस्स दु ण कुणदि तम्हा दु कम्माणि॥ १२७॥

aṇṇāṇamao bhāvo aṇāṇiṇo kuṇadi teṇa kammāṇi
ṇāṇamao ṇāṇissa du ṇa kuṇadi tamhā du kammāṇi (127)

अज्ञानमयो भावोऽज्ञानिनः करोति तेन कर्माणि।
ज्ञानमयो ज्ञानिनस्तु न करोति तस्मात्तु कर्माणि॥ १२७॥

127. The Self ignorant of his true nature, manifests in the form of wrong knowledge and through this wrong knowledge, he makes *karmas.* But the Self aware of his true nature has the manifestation of right knowledge and because of this right knowledge he does not make any *karmas.*

Commentary : Thus it is made evident that the Self, who is ignorant of his true nature, identifies himself with alien objects and characteristics. Because of this erroneous identification or *adhyāsa,* he develops various impure dispositions which finally end in *karmic* bondage. But the Self with right knowledge realises his nature to be entirely distinct from alien things and attributes, and hence never has any impure psychic experience. Thus remaining pure in himself, *karmas* do not approach him and hence no *karmic* bondage for him. He remains pure and perfect untouched by *karmas.* In short, wrong knowledge makes the Self wander in *saṁsāra* whereas right knowledge leads to *mokṣa*.

णाणमया भावाओ णाणमओ चेव जायदे भावो।
जम्हा तम्हा णाणिस्स सव्वे भावा दु णाणमया॥ १२८॥

ṇāṇamayā bhāvāo ṇāṇamao ceva jāyade bhāvo
jamhā tamhā ṇāṇissa savve bhāvā du ṇāṇamayā (128)

ज्ञानमयाद् भावाद् ज्ञानमयश्चैव जायते भावः।
यस्मात्तस्माज्ज्ञानिनः सर्वे भावाः खलु ज्ञानमयाः॥ १२८॥

128. If right knowledge alone can produce the mode or disposition of right knowledge, then it follows that every manifestation of the Self knowing his true nature must be of the nature of right knowledge.

अण्णाणमया भावा अण्णाणो चेव जायदे भावो।
जम्हा तम्हा सव्वे भावा अण्णाणमया अणाणिस्स॥ १२९॥

aṇṇāṇamayā bhāvā aṇṇāṇo ceva jāyade bhāvo
jamhā tamhā savve bhāvā aṇṇāṇamayā aṇāṇissa (129)

अज्ञानमयाद् भावादज्ञानमयश्चैव जायते भावः।
यस्मात्तस्मात्सर्वे भावा अज्ञानमया अज्ञानिनः॥ १२९॥

129. If wrong knowledge alone can produce the mode or disposition of wrong knowledge, then it follows that every manifestation of the Self ignorant of his true nature, must be of the nature of wrong knowledge.

The same point is emphasised through an illustration.

कणयमया भावादो जायंते कुंडलादयो भावा।
अयमययाभावादो जह जायंते दु कडयादि॥ १३०॥

kaṇayamayā bhāvādo jāyaṁte kuṁdalādayo bhāvā
ayamayayā bhāvado jaha jāyaṁte du kaḍayādi (130)

कनकमयाद् भावाज्जायन्ते कुण्डलादयो भावाः।
अयोमयाद्भावाद्यथा जायन्ते तु कटकादयः॥ १३०॥

अण्णाणमया भावा अणाणिणो बहुविहावि जायंते।
णाणिस्स दु णाणमया सव्वे भावा तहा होंति॥ १३१॥

aṇṇāṇamayā bhāvā aṇṇāṇiṇo bahuvihāvi jāyaṁte
ṇāṇissa du ṇāṇamayā savve bhāvā tahā hoṁti (131)

अज्ञानमया भावा अज्ञानिनो बहुविधा अपि जायन्ते।
ज्ञानिनस्तु ज्ञानमयाः सर्वे भावास्तथा भवन्ति॥ १३१॥

130 and 131 : From gold only golden ornaments like earings etc. can be produced, and from iron only iron chains etc., can be produced. In the same manner, all modifications of the knowing Self, must be of the nature of right knowledge, whereas the various modifications of the Self ignorant of his true nature would be the nature of wrong knowledge.

The various modifications of the impure Self are described next.

अण्णाणस्स स उदओ जा जीवाणं अतच्चउवलद्धी।
मिच्छत्तस्स दु उदओ जं जीवस्स असद्दहाणत्वम्॥ १३२॥

जो दु कलुसोवओगो जीवाणं सो कसाउदओ।
उदओ असंजमस्स दु जं जीवाणं हवेइ अविरमणम्॥ १३३॥

aṇṇāṇassa sa udao jā jīvāṇaṁ ataccauvaladdhī
micchattassa du udao jaṁ jīvassa asaddahāṇattaṁ (132)

jo du kalusovaogo jīvāṇaṁ so kasāudao
udao asaṁjamassa du jaṁ jīvāṇāṁ havei aviramaṇaṁ

अज्ञानस्य स उदयो या जीवानामतत्त्वोपलब्धिः।
मिथ्यात्वस्य तूदयो यं जीवस्याश्रद्दधानत्वम्॥ १३२॥

यस्तु कलुषोपयोगो जीवानां स कषायोदयः।
असंयमस्य तु उदयो यज्जीवानां भवेदविरमणम्॥ १३३॥

तं जाण जोगउदयं जो जीवाणं तु चिट्ठउच्छाहो।
सोहणमसोहणं वा कायव्वो विरदिभावो वा॥ १३४॥

taṁ jāṇa jogaudayaṁ jo jīvāṇāṁ tu ciṭṭhaucchāho
sohaṇamasohaṇaṁ vā kāyavvo viradibhāvo vā (134)

तं जानीहिं योगोदयं यो जीवानां तु चेष्टोत्साहः।
शोभनोऽशोभनो वा कर्त्तव्यो विरतिभावो वा॥ १३४॥

एदेसु हेदुभूदेसु कम्मइयवग्गणागयं जं तु।
परिणमदे अट्ठविहं णाणावरणादिभावेहिं॥ १३५॥

edesu hedubhūdesu kammaiyavaggaṇāgayaṁ jaṁ tu
pariṇamade aṭṭhavihaṁ ṇāṇāvaraṇādibhāvehiṁ (135)

एतेषु हेतुभूतेषु कार्मणवर्गणागतं यत्तु।
परिणमतेऽष्टविधं ज्ञानावरणादिभावैः॥ १३५॥

तं खलु जीवणिबद्धं कम्मइयवग्गणागयं जइया।
तइया दु होदि हेदू जीवो परिणामभावाणं॥ १३६॥

taṁ khalu jīvaṇibaddhaṁ kammaiyavaggaṇāgayaṁ jaiyā
taiyā du hodi hedū jīvo pariṇāmabhāvāṇaṁ (136)

तत्खलु जीवनिबद्धं कार्मणवर्गणागतं यदा।
तदा तु भवति हेतुर्जीवः परिणामभावानाम्॥ १३६॥

132 to 136. Know ye, that if there is in the Self knowledge of things that are not real, it is due to the operation of nescience (*karmic* materials interfering with right

knowledge); absence of belief in the reals is due to the operation of *mithyātva karma;* impure cognitive activity in the Self is due to the rise of *kaṣāya* (soul-soiling *karmas*), non-discipline in the Self is due to the rise of conduct perverting *karmas;* the tendency to act through thought, word, and deed is due to the rise of *yoga* (or the psycho-physical structure). Know ye, that everything that ought to be done is good and everything that ought to be discarded is bad. Thus conditioned by the primary *karmic* materials, are produced the eight types of *karmic* psychic dispositions such as *jñānavaraṇīya* (knowledge-obscuring). And thus when the eight types of *karmic* materials bound to the Self begin to operate, there arise in the Self corresponding psychic dispositions of which the Self is the causal agent.

Commentary : Thus it is emphasised once again that the various psychic modifications in the Self are caused by nescience and that these impure modifications can be got rid of only by true knowledge.

Next it is said from the real point of view that the various manifestations of the Self are entirely different from those of material *karmas*.

जीवस्स दुं कम्मेण य सह परिणामा हु होंति रागादी।
एवं जीवो कम्मं च दोवि रागादिमावण्णा॥ १३७॥

jīvassa du kammeṇa ya saha pariṇāmā hu homti rāgādī
evaṁ jīvo kammaṁ ca dovi rāgādimāvaṇṇā (137)

जीवस्य तु कर्मणा च सह परिणामाः खलु भवन्ति रागादयः।
एवं जीवः कर्म च द्वे अपि रागादित्वमापन्ने॥ १३७॥

एकस्स दु परिणामो जायदि जीवस्स रागमादीहिं।
ता कम्मोदयहेदूहि विणा जीवस्स परिणामो ॥ १३८॥

ekassa du pariṇāmo jāyadi jīvassa rāgamādīhiṁ
tā kammodayhedūhi viṇā jīvassa pariṇāmo (138)

एकस्य तु परिणामो जायते जीवस्य रागादिभिः।
तत्कर्मोदयहेतुभिर्विना जीवस्य परिणामः॥ १३८॥

137 and 138. If attachment and other emotions are really produced by the Self and the *karmas* co-operating together as *upādāna* causal conditions, then both the Self and the *karmic* matter will be able to appear in the form of the psychic mode of attachment. If the Self manifesting by himself is capable of producing attachment and other psychic modifications, then it must follow that even the pure Self without the influence of *karmic* materials must be able to manifest into impure forms of psychic modes such as attachment.

Commentary : In the first case when both *jīva* and *karma* co-operate to produce the psychic mode of attachment, both operating as *upādāna kāraṇa,* then according to the principle of the identity of cause and effect, even *karmic* matter which cooperates with *jīva* must be assumed to be psychical in nature, because the result produced, attachment, is psychical. Thus matter will become a *cetana* entity which is untrue. If in order to get over this difficulty, the Self is assumed to produce the psychic modifications of an impure nature without any alien influence, then this tendency must be present even in the pure Self. That is since the nature of the Self contains a latent form the tendency to produce impure psychic modifications. There can be no such thing called pure Self. This means complete denial of the possibility of *mokṣa.*

जइ जीवेण सह च्चिय पोग्गलदव्वस्स कम्मपरिणामो।
एवं पोग्गलजीवा हु दोवि कम्मत्तमावण्णा॥ १३९॥

jai jīveṇa saha cciya poggaladavassa kammapariṇāmo
evaṁ poggalajīvā hu dovi kammattamāvaṇṇā (139)

यदि जीवेन सह चेव पुद्गलद्रव्यस्य कर्मपरिणामः।
एवं पुद्गलजीवौ खलु द्वावपि कर्मत्वमापन्नौ॥ १३९॥

एक्कस्स दु परिणामो पोग्गलदव्वस्स कम्मभावेण।
ता जीवभावहेदूहिं विणा कम्मस्स परिणामो॥ १४०॥

ekkassa du pariṇāmo poggaladavvassa kammabhāveṇa
tā jīvabhāvahedūhiṁ viṇā kammassa pariṇāmo (140)

एकस्य तु परिणामः पुद्गलद्रव्यस्य कर्मभावेन।
तज्जीवभावहेतुभिर्विना कर्मणः परिणामः॥ १४०॥

139 and 140. If *dravya karmic* modes are really produced by matter in co-operation with *jīva,* as *upādāna* condition. then matter and Self will both become *dravya karmas* (matter). If matter manifesting by itself is capable of producing *karmic* modes without the influence of self, then all matter as such must be able to manifest as *karmic* modes.

Commentary : Here in the first case *jīva* (one of the co-operating causes) will become *acetana dravya,* because the effect *(dravya karma)* is *acetana.* In the second case all matter as such must be capable of manifesting as *karmic* modes. Both the conclusions are impossible.

जीवे कम्मं बद्धं पुट्ठं चेदि ववहारणयभणिदं।
सुद्धणयस्स दु जीवे अबद्धपुट्ठं हवइ कम्मं॥ १४१॥

jīve kammaṁ baddhaṁ puṭṭhaṁ cedi vavaharaṇaya-bhaṇidaṁ
suddhaṇayassa du jīve avaddhapuṭṭhaṁ havai kammaṁ

जीवे कर्म बद्धं स्पृष्टं चेति व्यवहारनयेन भणितम्।
शुद्धनयस्य तु जीवे अबद्धस्पृष्टं भवति कर्म॥ १४१॥

141. From the *vyavahāra* point of view, it is said that *karmas* bind and are in contact with the Self; but from the pure (absolute) point of view, *karmas* neither bind nor are in contact with the Self. Thus from the different points of view the Self is said to be either bound or free according as it is associated with *upādhis* or free from them.

After stating that bondage and freedom are predicated of the Self according to different points of view the author next points out that *samayasāra,* or Ego-in-itself, is beyond the view points.

कम्मं बद्धमबद्धं जीवे एदं तु जाण णयपक्खं।
पक्खातिक्कंतो पुण भण्णदि जो सो समयसारो॥ १४२॥

kammaṁ baddhamabaddhaṁ jīve edaṁ tu jāṇa ṇayapakkhaṁ
pakkhātikkaṁto puṇa bhaṇṇadi jo so samayasāro (142)

कर्म बद्धमबद्धं जीवे एवं तु जानीहि नयपक्षम्।
पक्षातिक्रान्तः पुनर्भण्यते यः स समयसारः॥ १४२॥

142. That the Self is bound with *karmas* and that it is not bound with *karmas* are statements made from different points of view. But the essence of the Self transcends these aspects, so it is said.

Next the author describes the nature of the transcendental Self.

दोण्हवि णयाण भणिदं जाणइ णवरिं तु समयपडिबद्धो।
ण दु णयपक्खं गिण्हदि किंचिवि णयपक्खपरिहीणो॥

doṇhavi ṇayāṇa bhaṇidaṁ jāṇai ṇavariṁ tu samayapaḍibaddho
ṇa du ṇayapakkhaṁ giṇhadi kiṁcivi ṇayapakkhaparihīṇo

द्वयोरपि नययोर्भणितं जानाति केवलं तु समयप्रतिबद्धः ।
न तु नयपक्षं गृह्णाति किंचिदपि नयपक्षपरिहीनः ॥ १४३ ॥

143. It is the Self whose attention is inwardly directed on himself that really knows the two natures, pure and impure, which are described by two points of view (real and practical). But the transcendental Self who is beyond these points of view does not apprehend them.

Commentary : Jaina metaphysics recognises three kinds of Self—*bahirātmā, antarātmā,* and *paramātmā*—the outer self, the inner Self, and the transcendental Self respectively. The first kind of self on account of ignorance identifies himself with the body and other external objects, cetainly an attitude which ought to be discarded; the second kind certainly recognises that his nature is quite different from material objects, including the body. This discriminative knowledge leads to the further investigation of the nature of the Self. Research into the nature of any reality, according to the Jaina philosophy, is undertaken from different *nayās* or points of view. Thus the study of the true nature of the self is undertaken by the *antarātman,* the inner self whose attention is concentrated upon his own nature. The nature of the Self so investigated appears either in bondage or free from bondage. Both these descriptions are from the relative points of view of *antarātman* whose sole aim is to discover the nature of the Self through *srutajñāna* or scriptural knowledge. In the third case these .two relational aspects have no relevancy. *Paramātma svarūpa* refers to the Perfect Self, which state is the result of Self-realisation through *tapas* or *yoga*. Naturally therefore this absolute transcendental Self is quite beyond the relational aspects and represents the highest nature of reality which ought to be the goal of all.

सम्मद्दंसणणाणं एसो लहदि त्ति णवरि ववदेसं।
सव्वणयपक्खरहिदो भणिदो जो सो समयसारो॥ १४४॥

sammaddaṁsaṇaṇāṇaṁ eso lahadi tti ṇavari vavadesaṁ
savvaṇayapakkharahido bhaṇido jo so samayasāro (144)

सम्यग्दर्शनज्ञानमेष लभत इति केवलं व्यपदेशम्।
सर्वनयपक्षरहितो भणितो यः स समयसारः॥ १४४॥

144. That the Self is really characterised by Right Perception and Right knowledge is an assertion (made by those who adopt the different points of view) and what transcends all points of view is said to be *samayasāra*. (See Appendix)

Commentary : The term *samaysāra* means the essential nature of the Self. This Absolute ultimate Unity is transcendental in nature. Hence the various appellations based upon different points of view really have no relevancy in that state.

The two characters, *jīva* and *ajīva*, which appeared on the stage as *kartā* and *karma*, each realising its true nature, exit from the stage.

Thus ends the Second Act.

CHAPTER IV

PUṆYA AND PĀPA

VIRTUE AND VICE

The single actor *Karma* enters the stage putting on the garb of two different characters, *Puṇya* and *Pāpa*, Virtue and Vice.

कम्ममसुहं कुसीलं सुहकम्मं चावि जाणह सुसीलं।
कह तं होदि सुसीलं जं संसारं पवेसेदि॥ १४५॥

kammamasuhaṁ kusīlaṁ suhakammaṁ cāvi jāṇaha susīlaṁ
kaha taṁ hodi susīlaṁ jaṁ saṁsāraṁ pavesedi. (145)

कर्माशुभं कुशीलं शुभकर्म चापि जानीहि सुशीलम्।
कथं तद् भवति सुशीलं यत्संसारं प्रवेशयति॥ १४५॥

145. Know ye, that the *karma* leading to wrong conduct is bad, that leading to right conduct is good. How can that be right conduct which pushes *jīva* into *saṁsāra* (cycle of births and deaths).

Commentary : The distinction of *karmas* into good and bad is based upon practical morality. What is good may lead one to the pleasures of *svarga* and what is evil may lead one to the miseries of Hell. Even the life of a *deva* in *svarga*, is only a life in *saṁsāra*. *Svarga* or *naraka* is merely a branch of *saṁsāra*, the cycle of births and deaths. The ultimate ideal set up transcends both good and evil and is beyond *saṁsāra*. Hence whatever leads to *saṁṣāra* is undesirable from this ultimate point of view. Hence the interrogation, "How can that be right conduct which pushes *jīva* into *saṁsāra*?"

Next the same point is elucidated by an example.

सोवण्णियं पि णियलं बंधदि कालायसं च जह पुरिसं।
बंधदि एवं जीवं सुहमसुहं वा कदं कम्मं॥ १४६॥

sovaṇṇiyaṁ pi ṇiyalaṁ baṁdhadi kālāyasaṁ ca jaha purisaṁ
baṁdhadi evaṁ jīvaṁ suhamasuhaṁ vā kadaṁ kammaṁ

सौवर्णिकमपि निगलं बध्नाति कालायसं च यथा पुरुषम्।
बध्यात्येवं जीवं शुभमशुभं वा कृतं कर्म॥ १४६॥

146. A shackle made of gold is as good as one made of iron for the purpose of chaining a man. Similarly *karma* whether good or bad equally binds the *jīva*.

Commentary : The distinction between good *karma* and bad *karma* is meaningless since the effect in both is identically the same.

तम्हा दु कुसीलेहि य रायं मा काहि मा व संसग्गं।
साहीणो हि विणासो कुसीलसंसग्गरायेण॥ १४७॥

tahmā du kusīlehi ya rāyaṁ mā kāhi mā va saṁsaggaṁ
sāhīṇo hi vaṇāso kusīlasaṁsaggarāyeṇa (147)

तस्मात्तु कुशीलैः रागं मा कुरु मा वा संसर्गम्।
स्वाधीनो हि विनाशः कुशीलसंसर्गरागेण॥ १४७॥

147. Therefore do not have attachment for or association with undesirable *karmas* whether good or bad; by such attachment for or association with undesirable *karmas* the

destruction will be inevitable.

Commentary : Both the *karmas* are to be avoided as they lead to the same undesirable result.

The author emphasises the same point through an analogy.

जह णाम कोवि पुरिसो कुच्छियसीलं जणं वियाणित्ता।
वज्जेदि तेण समयं संसग्गं रायकरणं च॥ १४८॥

jaha ṇāma kovipuriso kucchiyasīlaṁ jaṇaṁ viyāṇittā
vajjedi teṇa samayaṁ saṁsaggaṁ rāyakaraṇaṁ ca (148)

यथा नाम कश्चित्पुरुषः कुत्सितशीलं जनं विज्ञाय।
वर्जयति तेन समकं संसर्गं रागकरणं च॥१४८॥

एमेव कम्मपयडी सीलसहावं च कुच्छिदं णादुं।
वज्जंति परिहरंति यं तं संसग्गं सहावरदा॥ १४९॥

emeva kammapayadī sīlasahāvaṁ ca kucchidaṁ ṇāduṁ
vajjaṁti parihaṁti ya taṁ saṁsaggaṁ sahāvaradā (149)

एवमेव कर्मप्रकृतिशीलस्वभावं च कुत्सितं ज्ञात्वा।
वर्जयन्ति परिहरन्ति च तत्संसर्गं स्वभावरताः॥ १४९॥

148 and 149. As a person knowing certain people to be of bad character gives up association with and attachment for them, even so, those desiring to realise the Pure Self and knowing the nature and character of *karmic prakṛtis* to be evil, prevent the approach of *karmic* particles (*saṁvara*) and root out the already existing ones. (*nirjarā*).

Commentary : The Commentator, Amṛtacandra, gives an additional illustration. A clever wild male elephant, sees a decoy-female elephant—with pleasant looks or otherwise approaching him with flattering gestures with the object of chaining him. Learning her evil purpose, he does not evince any affection towards her nor does he associate with her. In the same manner an enlightened Self, knowing that the approach of *karmas,* whether pleasant or unpleasant, is for the purpose of binding him, avoids them and gives up any association with them.

That the two *karmas* should be rejected is further emphasised on the authority of *āgama* or Scripture.

रत्तो बंधदि कम्मं मुंचदि जीवो विरागसंपण्णो।
एसो जिणोवदेसो तम्हा कम्मेसु मा रज्ज॥ १५०॥

ratto baṁdhadi kammaṁ muṁcadi jīvo virāgasaṁpaṇṇo
eso jiṇovadeso tamhā kammesu mā rajja (150)

रक्तो बध्नाति कर्म मुच्यते जीवो विरागसम्पन्नः।
एष जिनोपदेशः तस्मात् कर्मसु मा रज्यस्व॥ १५०॥

150. The self with attachment gets bound by *karmas* but the one with detachment remains free from *karmas.* So has the Jina declared. Therefore do not evince attraction towards *karmas.*

Commentary : Thus attachment and detachment are shown to be the causes of bondage and liberation respectively.

परमट्ठो खलु समओ सुद्धो जो केवली मुणी णाणी।
तम्हिट्ठिदा सहावे मुणिणो पावंति णिव्वाणं॥ १५१॥

paramaṭṭho khalu samao suddho jo kevalī muṇī ṇāṇī
tahmiṭṭhidā sahāve muṇiṇo pāvaṁti ṇivvāṇaṁ (151)

परमार्थः खलु समयः शुद्धो यः केवली मुनिर्ज्ञानी।
तस्मिन् स्थिताः स्वभावे मुनयः प्राप्नुवन्ति निर्वाणम्॥ १५१॥

151. Verily, the supreme real, the Self, the Pure, the Omniscient, the Seer, and the Knower (all mean the *paramātmā).* Thus with the contemplation fixed on the Pure Self, the *Ṛṣis* attain *nirvāṇa.*

Commentary : Paramātmā is described in the following terms for the corresponding reasons. He is said to be *paramārtha* because he is the hightest reality; he is *samaya* as he is the Self manifesting in pure qualities and modes; he is *śuddha* the pure, as he is free from *karmas* both material and psychical; he is *kevalī* because his nature of omniscience is unaided by any extraneous means such as sense-perception; he is *muni* because of the intuitive perception of reality; he is *jñānī* because he is of the nature of *jñāna* or knowledge. Though these are different names, they all refer to the same reality.

परमट्ठम्मिय अठिदो जो कुणदि तवं वदं च धारयदि।
तं सव्वं बालतवं बालवदं विंति सव्वण्हु॥ १५२॥

paramaṭṭhammiya aṭhido jo kuṇadi tavaṁ vadaṁ ca dhārayadi
taṁ savvaṁ bālatavaṁ balavadaṁ viṁti savvaṇhu (152)

परमार्थे चास्थितः करोति यः तपो व्रतं च धारयति।
तत्सर्वं बालतपो बालव्रतं विंदन्ति सर्वज्ञाः॥ १५२॥

152. If one performs austerities (*tapas*) or observes vows (*vratas*) without fixed contemplation on the Supreme Self, the all-knowing call that childish austerity (*bālatapa*) and childish vow (*bālavrata*).

Commentary : *jñāna* is the ultimate cause of *mokṣa* or liberation. Whatever is done without the background of right knowledge will not achieve its end. Imitation is a characteristic of the child. Whatever is done through imitation is certainly lacking in the inner background of knowledge. Hence imitative behaviour in the child cannot have the same effect as in the case of an adult individual. Such an imitative behaviour may be an amusing play and cannot have any real significance. Similarly the performance of *tapas* and observance of *vratas* without the necessary background of correct knowledge will be merely imitative behaviour on the part of an ignorant person; hence would not produce the desired goal or ideal. In order to expose the futility of imitative behaviour without the background of correct knowledge, the author calls them *bālatapas* and *bālavratas*.

वदणियमाणि धरंता सीलाणि तहा तवं च कुव्वंता।
परमट्ठबाहिरा जेण तेण ते होंति अण्णाणि॥ १५३॥

vadaṇiyamāṇi dharaṁtā sīlāṇi tahā tavaṁ ca kuvvaṁtā
paramaṭṭhabāhirā jeṇa teṇa te homti aṇṇāṇī (153)

व्रतनियमान् धारयन्तः शीलानि तथा तपश्च कुर्वाणाः।
परमार्थबाह्या येन तेन ते भवन्त्यज्ञानिनः॥ १५३॥

153. Those who are outside the presence of *paramārtha* or Supreme Self, even though they observe vows, restraints, and rules of conduct and practice austerities, are devoid of right knowledge. (See Appendix).

Commentary : True knowledge is the condition for *mokṣa* or liberation. When that is absent, mere external activities such as strict observance of rules of conduct and performance of severe austerities will be of no avail. They by themselves cannot lead to *nirvāṇa*. Absence of true knowledge will certainly lead to *karmic* bondage.

परमट्ठबाहिरा जे ते अण्णाणेण पुण्णमिच्छन्ति।
संसारगमणहेदुं विमोक्खहेदुं अयाणंता॥ १५४॥

paramaṭṭhabāhirā je te aṇṇāṇeṇa puṇṇamicchaṁti
saṁsāragamaṇaheduṁ vimokkhaheduṁ ayāṇaṁtā (154)

परमार्थबाह्या ये ते अज्ञानेन पुण्यमिच्छन्ति।
संसारगमनहेतुं विमोक्षहेतुमजानन्तः॥ १५४॥

154. Those who are outside the presence of *paramārtha* or Supreme Self, through their ignorance—not knowing that—virtue leads to *saṁsāra,* desire the same with the belief that it will lead to *mokṣa*.

Commentary : Those who observe all the rules of conduct imagining that they are walking the path which leads to *mokṣa* are entirely mistaken. Even good conduct leads to *karmic* bondage. An ignorant person who is not aware of this truth and who boastingly exclaims, "I have kept up all the commandments, what more shall I do to enter into kingdom of Good", will soon be disillusioned.

Thus ends the Chapter on *Puṇya.*

Next the author takes up the discussion of *pāpa* or vice. He indirectly implies that vice is the cause of *saṁsāra* by stating the opposite—*mokṣa* and its cause.

जीवादीसद्दहणं सम्मत्तं तेसिमधिगमो णाणं।
रागादीपरिहरणं चरणं एसो दु मोक्खपहो॥ १५५॥

jīvādīsaddahaṇaṁ sammattaṁ tesimadhigamo ṇāṇaṁ
rāgādīpariharaṇaṁ caraṇaṁ eso du mokkhapaho (155)

जीवादिश्रद्धानं सम्यक्त्वं तेषामधिगमो ज्ञानम्।
रागादिपरिहरणं चरणं एषः तु मोक्षपथः॥ १५५॥

155. Belief in the *padārthas* such as soul etc., is right

faith, and knowing their true nature is right knowledge; then rooting out attachment etc., is right conduct. These together constitute the path to *mokṣa.*

Commentary : These are the well-known three jewels or the *ratnatraya* which constitute the *mokṣa mārga,* according to Jainism. *Ratnatraya* or the three jewels are considered from two points of view, *vyavahāra* and *niścaya. Vyavahāra ratnatraya* gradually leads to *mokṣa,* and *niścaya ratnatrsya* directly leads to *mokṣa.*

Of these two the *Ṛṣi* must choose the direct and the immediate path to *mokṣa,* and *niścaya ratnatraya* directly leads to *mokṣa,* that is real or higher *ratnatraya.* But the other one which operates gradually in producing the fruit ought to be accepted by the ordinary mortals.

मोत्तूण णिच्छयट्ठं ववहारे ण विदुसा पवट्टंति।
परमट्ठमस्सिदाणं दु जदीण कम्मक्खओ विहिओ॥ १५६॥

mottūṇa nicchayaṭṭhaṁ vavahāre ṇa vidusā pavattaṁti
paramaṭṭhamassiḍāṇaṁ du jadīṇa kammakkhao vihio

मुक्त्वा निश्चयार्थं व्यवहारे न विद्वांसः प्रवर्तन्ते।
परमार्थमाश्रितानां तु यतीनां कर्मक्षयो विहितः॥ १५६॥

156. Since it is declared that destruction of *karmas* is possible only to those *yatis* who adopt the absolute point of view, the wise ones will not walk through *(vyavahāramārga)* the practical path leaving aside the *(niścayamārga)* absolute one (See Appendix)

Commentary : When there are two courses of action open to a person, the superior and the inferior, the wise will always choose the superior one.

Next it is pointed out how this path to salvation is obstructed by the operation of evil *karmic* conditions such as *mithyātva* or wrong belief, etc.

वत्थस्स सेदभावो जह णासेदि मलविमेलणाच्छण्णो।
मिच्छत्तमलोच्छण्णं तह सम्मत्तं खु णादव्वं॥ १५७॥

vatthassa sedabhāvo jaha ṇāsedi malavimelaṇācchaṇṇo
micchattamalocchaṇṇaṁ taha saṃṃattaṁ khu ṇādavvaṁ

वस्त्रस्य श्वेतभावो यथा नश्यति मलविमेलनाच्छन्नः।
मिथ्यात्वमलावच्छन्नं तथा च सम्यक्त्वं खलु ज्ञातव्यम्॥ १५७॥

वत्थस्स सेदभावो जह णासेदि मलविमेलणाच्छण्णो।
अण्णाणमलोच्छण्णं तह णाणं होदि णादव्वं ॥ १५८॥

vattahassa sedabhāvo jaha ṇāsedi malavimelaṇācchaṇṇo
aṇṇāṇamalocchaṇṇaṁ taha ṇāṇaṁ hodi ṇādavvaṁ (158)

वस्त्रस्य श्वेतभावो यथा नश्यति मलविमेलनाच्छन्नः।
अज्ञानमलावच्छन्नं तथा ज्ञानं भवति ज्ञातव्यम्॥ १५८॥

वत्थस्स सेदभावो जह णासेदि मलविमेलणाच्छण्णो।
तह दु कसायाच्छण्णं चारित्तं होदि णादव्वं॥ १५९॥

vatthassa sedabhāvo jaha ṇāsedi malavimelaṇācchaṇṇo
taha du kasāyācchaṇṇaṁ cārittaṁ hodi ṇādavvaṁ (159)

वस्त्रस्य श्वेतभावो यथा नश्यति मलविमेलनाच्छन्नः।
तथा तु कषायावच्छन्नं चारित्रं भवति ज्ञातव्यम्॥ १५९॥

157, 158 and 159. As the whiteness of cloth is destroyed by its being covered with dirt, so let it be known that right faith is blurred by wrong belief. As the whiteness of cloth is destroyed by its being covered with dirt, so let it be known that right knowledge is destroyed, when clouded by nescience. As the whiteness of cloth is destroyed by its being covered with dirt, so let it be known that right conduct becomes perverted when vitiated by soul-soiling passions.

Commentary : Faith, knowledge and conduct, so long as they are true constitute the path to *mokṣa.* But when they are perverted by the influence of corresponding *karmic* materials, they get deflected from the right path dragging the Self to *saṁsāra.* Thus the pure manifestations of the Self get destroyed by the influence of *karmas* just as a white cloth gets soiled by impurities.

सो सव्वणाणदरिसी कम्मरयेण णिएण ओच्छण्णो।
संसारसमावण्णो ण विजाणदि सव्वदो सव्वं॥ १६०॥

so savvaṇāṇadarisī kammarayeṇa ṇieṇa occhaṇṇo
saṁsārasamāvaṇṇo ṇa vijāṇadi savvado savvaṁ (160)

स सर्वज्ञानदर्शी कर्मरजसा निजेनावच्छन्नः।
संसारसमापन्नो न विजानाति सर्वतः सर्वम्॥ १६०॥

160. The Self who is by nature all-knowing and all-perceiving, when soiled by his own *karmas,* is dragged on towards *saṁsāra,* the cycle of births and deaths, and becomes incapable of knowing all things completely.

सम्मत्तपडिणिबद्धं मिच्छत्तं जिणवरेहि परिकहियं।
तस्सोदयेण जीवो मिच्छादिट्ठित्ति णादव्वो॥ १६१॥

sammattapaḍiṇibaddhaṁ micchattaṁ jiṇavarehi parikahiyaṁ
tassodayeṇa jīvo micchāditthitti ṇādavvo (161)

सम्यक्त्वप्रतिनिबद्धं मिथ्यात्वं जिनवरैः परिकथितम्।
तस्योदयेन जीवो मिथ्यादृष्टिरिति ज्ञातव्यः॥ १६१॥

णाणस्स पडिणिबद्धं अण्णाणं जिणवरेहि परिकहियं।
तस्सोदयेण जीवो अण्णाणी होदि णादव्वो॥ १६२॥

ṅāṇassa paḍiṇibaddhaṁ aṇṇāṇaṁ jiṇavarehi parikahiyaṁ tassodayeṇa jīvo aṇṇāṇī hodi ṇādavvo (162)

ज्ञानस्य प्रतिनिबद्धमज्ञानं जिनवरैः परिकथितम्।
तस्योदयेन जीवोऽज्ञानी भवति ज्ञातव्यः॥ १६२॥

चारित्तपडिणिबद्धं कसायं जिणवरेहि परिकहियं।
तस्सोदयेण जीवो अचरित्तो होदि णादव्वो॥ १६३॥

cārittapaḍinibaddhaṁ kasāyaṁ jiṇavarehi parikahiyaṁ tassodayeṇa jīvo acharitto hodi ṇādavvo (163)

चारित्रप्रतिनिबद्धं कषायो जिनवरैः परिकथितः।
तस्योदयेन जीवोऽचारित्रो भवति ज्ञातव्यः॥ १६३॥

161, 162 and 163. It is declared by Jina that *mithyātva karma* is adverse to Right Belief; when that begins to operate, the Self becomes a wrong believer; so let it be known. It is declared by Jina that nescience is adverse to Right Knowledge; when that begins to operate; the Self becomes *ajñāni* (one devoid of knowledge), so let it be known. It is declared by Jina that *kaṣāya* (Soul-soiling gross emotions) is adverse to Right Conduct; when this begins to operate, the Self becomes *acāritra* (devoid of Right Conduct), so let it be known.

Commentary : Just as a colourless crystal puts on the colour of the associated obejct, so the pure Self undergoes various impure modifications as determined by the various *karmas*. Thus from all points of view, all *karmas* are to be destroyed.

Thus ends the chapter on *pāpa padārtha*, the category of Vice.

The *karma* which acted the role of two characters, *puṇya* and *pāpa*, Virtue and Vice, exits from the stage.

CHAPTER V

ĀŚRAVA OR INFLOW OF KARMA

Then *Āśrava* enters the stage.

मिच्छत्तं अविरमणं कसायजोगा य सण्णसण्णा दु।
बहुविहभेया जीवे तस्सेव अणण्णपरिणामा॥ १६४॥

micchattaṁ aviramaṇaṁ kasāyajogā ya saṇṇasaṇṇā du
bahuvihabheyā jīve tasseva aṇaṇṇapariṇāmā (164)

मिथ्यात्वमविरमणं कषाययोगौ च संज्ञासंज्ञास्तु।
बहुविधभेदा जीवे तस्यैवानन्यपरिणामाः॥ १६४॥

164. *Karmas* in the empirical Self, such as wrong belief, non-discipline, soul-soiling gross emotion, and psycho-physical structure, with their various sub-species are mainly of two classes, material *(acetana)* and psychical (*cetana*), (*dravya karma* and *bhāva karma*). The psychical *karmic* modifications are inseparable from the Self.

णाणावरणादीयस्स ते दु कम्मस्स कारणं होंति।
तेसिं पि होदि जीवो रागदोसादिभावकरो॥ १६५॥

ṇāṇāvaraṇādīyassa te du kammassa kāraṇaṁ hoṁti
tesiṁ pi hodi jīvo rāgadosādibhāvakaro (165)

ज्ञानावरणाद्यस्य ते तु कर्मणः कारणं भवन्ति।
तेषामपि भवति जीवः रागद्वेषादिभावकरः॥ १६५॥

165. Those impure psychic modifications cause the material *karmas* such *jñānāvaranīya* (knowledge-obscuring), etc. To them (those psychic *karmic* modifications) the empirical Self with the characteristics of attachment and aversion is the cause.

Commentary : The inflow of *karma* is of two kinds, material and psychical (*dravyāsrava* and *bhāvāsrava*) corresponding to the two kinds of *karmas,* material and psychical. These two mutually determine each other in the form of *nimitta kāraṇa,* instrumental cause. The various psychic modifications of impure nature cause the inflow of material *karmas* towards the Self. This is *dravyāsrava.* When the material *karmas,* so flowing in, influence the Self, they give rise to fresh emotional modifications which constitute the *bhāvāsrava.* To these psychic modifications of *bhāvāsrava,* the Self is the *upādāna kāraṇa,* substantial cause.

Next it is pointed out that in the case of the Right Believer, there is neither *āsrava,* the inflow of *karma,* nor the consequential *karmic* bondage *(bandha).*

णत्थि दु आसवबंधो सम्मादिट्ठिस्स आसवणिरोहो।
संते पुव्वणिबद्धे जाणदि सो ते अबंधंतो॥ १६६॥

ṇatthi du āsavabaṁdho sammādiṭṭhissa āsavaṇiroho
saṁte puvvaṇibaddhe jāṇadi so te abaṁdhaṁto (166)

नास्ति त्वास्रवो बन्धः सम्यग्दृष्टेरास्रवनिरोधः।
सन्ति पूर्वनिबद्धानि जानाति स तान्यबध्नन्॥ १६६॥

166. To Right Believer, since he blocks the inflow of *karmas,* there is neither the incoming of *karmas* nor the consequential bondage thereby. Thus remaining free from new *karmic* bondage, he understands the previously bound *karmas* (to be different from the Self).

Commentary : Thus it is pointed out that the right believer is capable of preventing the inflow of *karmas.*

Next it is pointed out that desire, aversion, and delusion constitute the main cause of *āsrava,* the inflow of *karmas.*

भावो रागादिजुदो जीवेण कदो दु बंधगो होदि।[१]
रागादिविप्पमुक्को अबंधगो जाणगो णवरि॥ १६७॥

bhāvo rāgādijudo jīveṇa kado du baṁdhago hodi
rāgādivippamukko abaṁdago jāṇago ṇavari (167)

भावो रागादियुत: जीवेन कृतस्तु बन्धको भवति।
रागादिविप्रमुक्तोऽबन्धको ज्ञायक: केवलम्॥ १६७॥

167. The psychic states associated with desire, etc., which are the modifications of *jīva* constitute the cause of bondage; but when completely free from desire, etc., the psychic state is of the nature of pure knowledge which indeed is the cause of the destruction of *karmas.*

Commentary : The emotional states such as attachment, aversions and delusion completely disfigure the nature of the Self and thus he becomes associated with nescience. In this impure state, the Self attracts *karmic* particles which get bound with the Self just as a magnet attracts iron needles to itself. When those emotional states are absent, the Self undisturbed in his nature does not attract *karmic* particles. Hence there is no chance of bondage in his cause. Thus knowledge secures freedom from bondage and the absence of it inevitably brings about bondage.

पक्के फलम्मि पडिदे जह ण फलं बज्झदे पुणो विंटे।
जीवस्स कम्मभावे पडिदे ण पुणोदयमुवेइ॥ १६८॥

pakke phalammi paḍide jaha ṇa phalam bajjhade puṇo viṁṭe
jīvassa kammabhāve paḍide ṇa puṇodayamuvei (168)

---

१. भणिदो

पक्वे फले पतिते यथा न फलं बध्यते पुनर्वृन्तैः।
जीवस्य कर्मभावे पतिते न पुनरुदयमुपैति॥ १६८॥

168. As a ripe fruit fallen (from a tree) cannot be attached again to the stalk, so when the psychic *karmic* modifications in the Self drop off, they can no more bind the Self again nor operate.

Commentary : Thus it is emphasised that to the Self, with right knowledge, there is no *bhāvāsrava* (inflow of psychic *karmas*).

Next it is stated that to the knowing Self there is no *dravyāsrava* or material *karmic* inflow either.

पुढवीपिंडसमाणा पुव्वणिबद्धा दु पुच्चया तस्स।
कम्मसरीरेण दु ते बद्धा सव्वेवि णाणिस्स॥ १६९॥

pudhavipimḍasamāṇā puvvaṇibaddhā du paccayā tassa
kammasarīreṇa du te baddhā savvevi ṇāṇissa (169)

पृथ्वीपिण्डसमानाः पूर्वनिबद्धास्तु प्रत्ययास्तस्य।
कर्मशरीरेण तु ते बद्धाः सर्वेऽपि ज्ञानिनः॥ १६९॥

169. In the Self with right knowledge, the old *karmas* remain incorporated only with the *karmic* body, like a clod of earth without any effect on the Self.

Commentary : The previous *karmic* bondage was caused by nescience, absence of correct knowledge in the Self. Presence of nescience produces impure psychic states which facilitate the inflow of *karmic* materials. Thus in this case there are both the *bhāvāsrava* and *dravyāsrava*. But when nescience disappears the Self regains his true nature of pure knowledge, and the impure psychic states have no chance to occur; when these do not occur there is no chance for fresh *karmic* materials to flow in. Thus the Self is left with only the previous *karmic* materials which got in when favourable psychic states were present. Hence they remain only part and parcel of the *kārmaṇa śarīra,* absolutely incapable of producing any corresponding impure psychic state. Thus in the case of the knowing Self, the Self with pure knowledge, both the *āsravas,* psychic and material, are absent.

चउविह अणेयभेयं बंधते णाणदंसणगुणेहिं।
समये समये जम्हा तेण अबंधत्ति णाणी दु॥ १७०॥

cauviha aṇeyabheyaṁ vaṁdhaṁte ṇāṇdaṁsaṇaguṇehiṁ
samaye samaye jamha teṇa avaṁdhatti ṇāṇī du (170)

चतुर्विधा अनेकभेदं बध्नन्ति ज्ञानदर्शनगुणाभ्याम्।
समये समये यस्मात् तेनाबन्ध इति ज्ञानी तु॥ १७०॥

170. The four primary *karmic* conditions, with their multifarious subdivisions bind the soul every moment as determined by suitable impure qualities of knowledge and perception. Hence the Self with right knowledge is not bound by them.

जम्हा दु जहण्णादो णाणगुणादो पुणो वि परिणमदि।
अण्णत्तं णाणगुणो तेण दु सो बंधगो भणिदो॥ १७१॥

jamhā du jahaṇṇādo ṇāṇaguṇādo puṇo vi pariṇamadi
aṇṇattaṁ ṇāṇaguṇo teṇa du so baṁdhago bhaṇido (171)

यस्मात्तु जघन्यात् ज्ञानगुणात् पुनरपि परिणमते।
अन्यत्वं ज्ञानगुणः तेन तु स बन्धको भणितः॥ १७१॥

171. When the Self's cognitive quality is at its lowest stage, it is liable to alternative alien modifications whether good or bad. Therefore in either case the Self is called the binder of *karmas*.

Commentary : Knowledge is the essential quality of the Self. So long as this quality is strong and intense, the Self is unassailable by external influence; but when this quality is at its weakest point, the Self becomes easily influenced by alien conditions. In that case the Self will get modified from its own intrinsic nature according to the nature of the influence, good or bad. In either case the result will be bondage, though it is emphasised that both *śubha-bhāva* and *aśubha-bhāva* respectively lead to *puṇya* and *pāpa* which both lead to *āsrava* and *bandha*. But *śuddha-bhāva* alone avoids *āsrava* and *bandha*.

दंसणणाणचरित्तं जं परिणमदे जहण्णभावेण।
णाणी तेण दु बज्झदि पोग्गलकम्मेण विविहेण॥ १७२॥

daṁsaṇaṇāṇacarittaṁ jaṁ pariṇamade jahaṇṇbhāveṇa
ṇāṇī teṇa du bajjhadi poggala-kammeṇa viviheṇa (172)

दर्शनज्ञानचारित्रं यत्परिणमते जघन्यभावेन।
ज्ञानी तेन तु बध्यते पुद्गलकर्मणा विविधेन॥ १७२॥

172. When the manifestation of Right Belief, Right Knowledge and Right Conduct is at its lowest, the Self, the Knower, is bound by various types of (good) *karmic* materials.

Commentary : The Self here is in possession of *ratnatraya*– the three jewels. Since the three jewels are in a very low degree of efficiency, bondage is predicated of the Self, and yet the *karmas* that will bind him are only the *puṇya karmas*, *karmic* materials of the good type capable of producing happiness.

सव्वे पुव्वणिबद्धा दु पच्चया संति सम्मादिट्ठिस्स।
उपओगप्पाओगं बंधंते कम्मभावेण॥ १७३॥

savve puvvaṇibaddhā du paccayā saṁti sammādiṭṭhissa
uvaogappāogaṁ baṁdhaṁte kammabhāvena (173)

सर्वे पूर्वनिबद्धास्तु प्रत्ययाः सन्ति सम्यग्दृष्टेः।
उपयोगप्रायोग्यं बध्नन्ति कर्मभावेन॥ १७३॥

संतिवि निरुवभोज्जा बाला इत्थी जहेव पुरुसस्स।
बंधदि ते उवभोज्जे तरुणी इत्थी जह णरस्स॥ १७४॥

saṁtivi ṇiruvabhojjā bālā itthī jaheva purusassa
baṁdhadi te uvabhojje taruṇī itthī jaha ṇarassa (174)

सन्त्यपि निरुपभोग्यानि बाला स्त्री यथैव पुरुषस्य।
बध्नाति तानि उपभोग्यानि तरुणी स्त्री यथा नरस्य॥ १७४॥

173 and 174. Just as to a person, his child-wife is unfit for enjoyment, but when having become mature, she is fit for enjoyment and attracts his attention, so is also in the case of a right believer : all the previously bound *karmic* conditions, though present, begin to operate only when they become mature and then they produce corresponding psychic states through which they bind the Self.

होदूण णिरुवभोज्जा तह बंधदि जह हवंति उवभोज्जा।
सत्तट्ठविहा भूदा णाणावरणादिभावेहिं॥ १७५॥

hodūṇa ṇiruvabhojjā taha baṁdhadi jaha havaṁti uvabhojjā
sattaṭṭhavihā bhūdā ṇāṇāvaraṇādibhāvehiṁ (175)

भूत्वा निरुपभोग्यानि तथा बध्नाति यथा भवन्त्युपभोग्यानि।
सप्ताष्टविधानि भूतानि ज्ञानावरणादिभावैः॥ १७५॥

175. In the case of the right believer the previously bound *karmas* such as *jñānāvaraṇīya*, remain ineffective so long as they are latent, but when they become efficient and operative, through the instrumentality of psychic states such

as attachment, they bind the Self in seven ways, (exclusive of age-*karma*) or in eight ways.

एदेण कारणेण दु सम्मादिट्ठी अबंधगो भणिदो।
आसवभावाभावे ण पच्चया बंधगा भणिदा॥ १७६॥

edeṇa kāraṇeṇa du sammādiṭṭhī abaṁdhago bhaṇido
āsavabhāvābhāve ṇa paccayā baṁdhagā bhaṇidā (176)

एतेन कारणेन तु सम्यग्दृष्टिरबन्धको भणितः।
आस्रवभावाभावे न प्रत्यया बन्धका भणिताः॥ १७६॥

176. In the case of the right believer the *karmic* inflow of the opposite psychic state is absent. (When this is absent) the remaining *karmic* conditions, (since they are incapable of producing bondage leading to *saṁsāra)* are declared to be non-binders. On account of these reasons, the right believer is said to be non-binder.

Commentary : As a general principle it is maintained that the material *karmic* condition, even though present about the Self, are incapable of binding him, unless there is facilitating opportunity, which opportunity is provided by the appearance of psychic states such as attachment. Thus it is the psychic state that is the *sine qua non* of *karmic* bondage. In the case of the right believer this necessary condition is absent; when this is absent even the previously bound *karmas*, become ineffective. When these *karmic* conditions become ineffective and when there is no chance of fresh inflow of *karmic* particles, the Self may very well be declared to be without bondage. (In the case of *vītarāga samyakdṛṣṭi)* since he is absolutely free from *karmic* states of attachment, etc., he is necessarily called unbound but in the case of *sarāga-samyakdṛṣṭi*, since the impure psychic conditions have not been completely rooted out, the name is still applicable in a figurative sense.

रागो दोसो मोहो य आसवा णत्थि सम्मदिट्ठिस्स।
तम्हा आसवभावेण विणा हेदू ण पच्चया होंति॥ १७७॥

rāgo doso moho ya āsavā ṇatthi sammadiṭṭhissa
tamhā āsavabhāveṇa viṇā hedū ṇa paccayā homṭi (177)

रागो द्वेषो मोहश्च आस्रवा न सन्ति सम्यग्दृष्टेः।
तस्मादास्रवभावेन विना हेतवो न प्रत्यया भवन्ति॥ १७७॥

177. In the case of the right believer of the higher or (*vītarāga*) type there is no inflow of psychic states relating to desire, aversion, and delusion. Hence apart from the psychic *karmic* inflow, the material *karmic* conditions cannot produce bondage.

हेदू चदुवियप्पो अट्ठवियप्पस्स कारणं होदि।
तेसिं पि य रागादि तेसिमभावे ण बज्झंति॥ १७८॥

hedū caduviyappo aṭṭhviyappassa kāraṇaṁ hodi
tesiṁ pi ya rāgādi tesimabhāve ṇa bajjhaṁti (178)

हेतुश्चतुर्विकल्पः अष्टविकल्पस्य कारणं भवति।
तेषामपि च रागादयस्तेषामभावे न बध्यन्ते॥ १७८॥

178. The four primary *karmic* conditions are said to be the cause of eight *karmas* such as *jñānāvaraṇīya.* To these *karma* conditions the psychic states such as desire, etc. form the cause. When these psychic states are absent, the *karmic* material conditions cannot bind the Self.

जह पुरिसेणाहारो गहिदो परिणमदि सो अणेयविहं।
मंसवसारुहिरादीभावे उदरग्गिसंजुत्तो॥ १७९॥

jaha puriseṇāhāro gahido pariṇamadi so aṇeyavihaṁ
maṁsavasāruhirādī bhāve unaraggisaṁjutto (179)

यथा पुरुषेणाहारो गृहीतः परिणमदि सोऽनेकविधम्।
मांसवसारुधिरादीन् भावान्, उदराग्निसंयुक्तः ॥ १७९ ॥

तह णाणिस्स दु पुव्वं जे बद्धा पच्चया बहुवियप्पं।
बज्झंते कम्मं ते णयपरिहीणा दु ते जीवा॥ १८० ॥

taha ṇāṇissa du puvvaṁ je baddhā paccayā bahuviyap-paṁ
vajjhaṁte kammaṁ te ṇayaparihīṇa du te jivā (180)

तथा ज्ञानिनस्तु पूर्वं ये बद्धाः प्रत्यया बहुविकल्पम्।
बध्नन्ति कर्म ते नयपरिहीनास्तु ते जीवाः ॥ १८० ॥

179 and 180. Just as food eaten by a person in association with gastric heat (digestive and assimilative function) is transformed into various kinds such as flesh, fat, blood etc. so also in the case of the Self, the previously bound *karmic* condition (though of uniform material type in the beginning) gets transformed into various *karmic* modifications at the time of bondage. This is true in the case of Self devoid of the pure point of view.

Commentary : Thus it is pointed out that the giving up of the pure point of view or *śuddhanaya* causes *āsrava* or *karmic* inflow, whereas the adoption of it causes *nir-āsrava,* the cessation of the inflow.

Thus ends the chapter on *āsrava.*

Thus *āsrava* quits the stage.

CHAPTER VI

SAṀVARA

BLOCKING THE INFLOW

Now Saṁvara enters the stage.

While describing the nature of *saṁvara padārth,* the author first praises its ultimate condition, the discriminative knowledge.

उवओगे उवओगो कोहादिसु णत्थि कोवि उवओगो।
कोहो कोहे चेव हि उवओगे णत्थि खलु कोहो॥ १८१॥

uvaoge uvaogo kohādisu ṇatthi kovi uvaogo
koho kohe ceva hi uvaoge ṇatthi khalu koho (181)

उपयोगे उपयोग: क्रोधादिषु नास्ति कोऽप्युपयोग:।
क्रोध: क्रोधे चैव हि उपयोगे नास्ति खलु क्रोध:॥ १८१॥

181. The pure cognitive attributes of perception and knowledge rest upon *upayoga* or the intrinsic nature of the pure Self. The impure emotions such as anger have no relation whatsoever with *upayoga.* Anger subsists on anger itself. Certainly there is no anger in the pure cognitive attributes of perception and knowledge.

Commentary : What is predicated of anger must be taken to be equally true in the case of other emotions such as pride, etc.

Next the author deals with other facts which are also distinct from *upayoga* or the nature of the pure Self.

अट्ठवियप्पे कम्मे णोकम्मे चावि णत्थि उवओगो।
उपओगम्हि य कम्मं णोकम्मं चावि णो अत्थि॥ १८२॥

aṭṭhaviyappe kamme ṇokamme cāvi ṇatthi uvaogo
uvaogamhi ya kammaṁ ṇokammaṁ cāvi ṇo atthi (182)

अष्टविकल्पे कर्मणि नोकर्मणि चापि नास्त्युपयोगः।
उपयोगे च कर्म नोकर्म चापि नो अस्ति॥ १८२॥

182. There is no *upayoga* either in the eight types of *karma* or in the *nokarma* material particles (which go to build up the various kinds of bodies). Conversely, there are neither *karmas* nor *nokarmas* in *upayoga*.

एदं तु अविवरीदं णाणं जइया दु होदि जीवस्स।
तइया ण किंचि कुव्वदि भावं उवओगसुद्धप्पा॥ १८३॥

edaṁ tu avivarīdaṁ ṇāṇaṁ jaiyā du hodi jīvassa
taiyā ṇa kiṁci kuvvadi bhāvaṁ uvaogasuddhappā (183)

एतत्त्वविपरीतं ज्ञानं यदा तु भवति जीवस्य।
तदा न किंचित्करोति भावमुपयोगशुद्धात्मा॥ १८३॥

183. When this discriminative knowledge, free from error, arises in the Self, then the nature of the Self manifests in the form of pure *upayoga*, and he does not cause any kind of impure psychic states.

Commentary : Two things which are spatially distinct which have no relation to a common cause cannot maintain the relation of substance and substratum. Substance and substratum will be applicable to a particular manifestation and the intrinsic nature which so manifests. Thus knowing activity is related to knowledge in the form of substratum, an entity and its manifestation. An entity and its manifestation are inseparably united with each other and there is intrinsic identity between the two. So viewed, the pure cognitive activity or *upayoga,* since it is based on the intrinsic nature of the Self, is inalienably identical with it. Various impure emotional states have no such intrinsic relation to the nature of the Self, because they are accidental states of the Self, and as such can disappear without in any way affecting the nature of the Self. Essential attributes are based upon the real nature of a thing, whereas the accidental attributes are not so based. It is this truth that is emphasised in the above *gāthās*. Cognitive attributes of perception and knowledge technically called *upayoga* are the essential attributes of the Self, whereas anger, pride, etc., are only accidental attributes. That is why it is said that *upayoga* is in the self, and conversely Self is in *upayoga* and negatively, anger, etc. are not in the Self nor is the Self in anger, etc. So also *karmas* and *nokarmas* being accidental adjunts to the Self have no basis in the nature of the Self. This recognition of the Self to be distinct from the various accidental attributes, psychical and physical, enables it to shut out the impure psychical states of desire, aversion. and delusion. When these are shut out there is no inflow of *karmas* and that is just *saṁvara.*

Next it is explained how the Self, even though associated with impure *karmas,* is through discriminative knowledge, able to recognise his pure nature.

जहकणयमग्गितवियं पि कणयभावं ण तं परिच्चयदि।
तह कम्मोदयतविदो ण जहदि णाणी दु णाणित्तं॥ १८४॥

jaha kaṇayamaggitaviyaṁ pi kaṇayabhāvaṁ ṇa taṁ pariccayadi
taha kammodayatavido ṇo jahadi ṇāṇī du ṇāṇittaṁ (184)

यथा कनकमग्नितप्तमपि कनकभावं न तं परित्यजति।
तथा कर्मोदयतप्तो न जहाति ज्ञानी तु ज्ञानित्वम्॥ १८४॥

184. Just as gold, however much it is heated, never loses its intrinsic nature, so also the right knowing Self, however much it is burnt by the associated *karmas,* does not lose his intrinsic nature of pure knowledge.

एवं जाणदि णाणी अण्णाणी मुणदि रागमेवादं।
अण्णाणतमोच्छण्णो आदसहावं अयाणंतो॥ १८५॥

evaṁ jāṇadi ṇāṇī aṇṇāṇī muṇadi rāgamevādaṁ
aṇṇāṇatamocchaṇṇo ādasahāvaṁ ayāṇaṁto (185)

एवं जानाति ज्ञानी अज्ञानी मनुते रागमेवात्मानम्।
अज्ञानतमोऽवच्छन्न आत्मस्वभावमजानन्॥ १८५॥

185. Thus the Self with discriminative knowledge knows his true nature. But on lacking in this knowledge, blinded by his own nescience is unable to perceive his true nature, and thinks that the nature of the Self is identical with the impure psychic states such as attachment.

Next it is pointed out how this apprehension of the pure nature is itself *saṁvara.*

सुद्धं तु वियाणंतो सुद्धं चेवप्पयं लहदि जीवो।
जाणंतो दु असुद्धं असुद्धमेवप्पयं लहदि॥ १८६॥

suddhaṁ tu viyāṇaṁto suddhaṁ cevappayaṁ lahadi jīvo
jaṇaṁto du asuddhaṁ asuddhamevappayaṁ lahadi (186)

शुद्धं तु विजानन् शुद्धमेवात्मानं लभते जीवः।
जानंस्त्वशुद्धमशुद्धमेवात्मानं लभते॥ १८६॥

186. The Self with the discriminative knowledge, by contemplating upon the pure self, becomes himself pure. But

the Self which contemplates upon the impure nature of the Self becomes himself impure.

Commentary : Thus it is pointed out that the nature of the contemplating Self is determined by the nature of the comtemplated ideal. Hence apprehension of the pure nature of the Self means *saṁvara.*

Next the method of apprehending the pure Self is described.

अप्पाणं अप्पणो रुंभिदूण दोसु पुण्णपावजोगेसु।
दंसणणाणम्हिट्ठिदो इच्छाविरदो य अण्णम्हि॥ १८७॥

appāṇaṁ appaṇo ruṁbhidūṇa dosu puṇṇapāvajogesu
daṁsaṇaṇāṇamhiṭṭhido icchāvirado ya aṇṇamhi (187)

आत्मानमात्मना रुन्ध्वा द्वयोः पुण्यपापयोगयोः।
दर्शनज्ञाने स्थितः इच्छाविरतश्चान्यस्मिन्॥ १८७॥

जो सव्वसंगमुक्को झायदि अप्पाणमप्पणो अप्पा।
णवि कम्मं णोकम्मं चेदा चिंतेदि एयत्तं॥ १८८॥

jo savvasaṁgamukko jhāyadi appāṇamappaṇo appā
ṇavi kammaṁ ṇokammaṁ cedā ciṁtedi eyattaṁ (188)

यः सर्वसङ्गमुक्तो ध्यायत्यात्मानमात्मनात्मा।
नापि कर्म नोकर्म चेतयिता चिन्तयत्येकत्वम्॥ १८८॥

अप्पाणं झायंतो दंसणणाणमओ अणण्णमओ।
लहदि अचिरेण अप्पाणमेव सो कम्मणिम्मुक्कं॥ १८९॥

appāaṇaṁ jhāyaṁto daṁsaṇaṇāṇamao aṇaṇṇamao
lahadi acireṇa appāṇameva so kammaṇimmukkaṁ (189)

आत्मानं ध्यायन् दर्शनज्ञानमयोऽनन्यमयः।
लभतेऽचिरेणात्मानमेव स कर्मनिर्मुक्तम्॥ १८९॥

187, 188 and 189. Who so restrains, through his own effort, the Self that is immersed in the activity, whether good or bad, of *yoga* (thought, word, and deed), rests on pure perception and knowledge, has no desire whatsoever for alien objects and is free from all attachments, that Self contemplates on his own unity. Such a Self never thinks that *karmas* are of the nature of the Self, nor the *nokarmas*. Such a right knowing Self, of the nature of perception and knowledge entirely different from alien nature, contemplates upon his pure Self and very soon becomes identical with the Pure Self who is free from all *karmas*.

Commentary : Thus it is pointed out that discriminative knowledge will ultimately lead to the attainment of the pure Self by destroying all the impure *karmic* shackles.

तेसिं हेदू भणिदा अज्झवसाणाणि सव्वदरसीहिं।
मिच्छत्तं अण्णाणं अविरदिभावो य जोगो य॥ १९०॥

tesiṁ hedū bhaṇidā ajjhavasāṇāṇi savvadarasīhiṁ
micchattaṁ aṇṇāṇaṁ aviradibhāvo ya jogo ya (190)

तेषां हेतवो भणिता अध्यवसानानि सर्वदर्शिभिः।
मिथ्यात्वमज्ञानमविरतभावश्च योगश्च॥ १९०॥

हेदुअभावे णियमा जायदि णाणिस्स आसवणिरोहो।
आसवभावेण विणा जायदि कम्मस्स वि णिरोहो॥ १९१॥

hedu- abhāve ṇiyamā jāyadi ṇāṇissa āsavaṇiroho
āsava- bhāveṇa viṇā jāyadi kammassa vi ṇiroho (191)

हेत्वभावे नियमाज्जायते ज्ञानिनः आस्रवनिरोधः।
आस्रवभावेन विना जायते कर्मणोऽपि निरोधः॥ १९१॥

कम्मस्साभावेण य णोकम्माणं पि जायदि णिरोहो।
णोकम्मणिरोहेण य संसारणिरोहणं होइ॥ १९२॥

kammassābhāveṇa ya nokammāṇaṁ pi jāyadi ṇiroho
ṇokammaṇiroheṇa ya saṁsāraṇirohaṇaṁ hoi (192)

कर्मणोऽभावेन च नोकर्मणामपि जायते निरोधः।
नोकर्मनिरोधेन च संसारनिरोधनं भवति॥ १९२॥

190, 191 and 192. It is declared by the Omniscient that the psychic states corresponding to wrong belief, wrong knowledge, non-discipline, and psycho-physical activity are the causes of *karma* such as *jñānāvaraṇīya.* On account of the psychic states relating to pure perception etc., the *karmic* conditions are absent. This absence of conditions in one who has discriminative knowledge causes the blocking up of psychic inflow (*bhāvāsrava*). If the psychic inflow is blocked up, the blocking of the *karmic* inflow (*dravyāsrava*) necessarily follows. When there is no inflow of material *karmas,* the inflow of *nokarmic* materials is also stopped. When there is no inflow of *nokarmic* body-building materials the process of body-building will completely disappear which means the cessation of *saṁsāra.*

Commentary : So long as the root cause, the identification of the Self with *karmas* persists, psychic activity to wrong belief, wrong knowledge, wrong conduct, and *yoga* persists. These form the cause of the *bhāvāsrava* relating to desire, aversion, and delusion. *Bhāvāsrava* forms the cause of *dravyāsrava* or material *karmas.* Material *karmas* in their turn form the cause of body-building *nokarmas*. *Nokarma* is the cause of *śaṁsāra.* This is the causal sequence. But when discriminative knowledge appears, the Self recognises its own pure *cetana* nature. This knowledge leads to the absence of psychic activity relating to wrong belief, wrong knowledge etc. Absence of such psychic activities leads to the disappearance of *bhāvāsrava.* When that is absent *karma* naturally disappears. Disappearance of *karmas* means cessation of *saṁsāra.* This is the order of *saṁvara.*

Thus ends the Chapter on *saṁvara.*

Thus *Saṁvara* quits the stage.

CHAPTER VII

NIRJARĀ

SHEDDING OF KARMAS

Then *Nirjarā* appears on the stage.

उवभोगमिंदियेहि य दव्वाणमचेदणाणमिदराणं।
जं कुणदि सम्मदिट्ठी तं सव्वं णिज्जरणिमित्तं॥ १९३॥

uvabhogamiṁdiyehi ya davvāṇamacedaṇāṇamidarāṇaṁ
jaṁ kuṇadi sammadiṭṭhī taṁ savvaṁ ṇijjaraṇimittaṁ (193)

उपभोगमिन्द्रियैः द्रव्याणामचेतनानामितरेषाम्।
यत्करोति सम्यग्दृष्टिः तत्सर्वं निर्जरानिमित्तम्॥ १९३॥

193. Whatever affective experiences the right believer (with a neutral attitude) has in relation to sense-perceived objects, conscious and nonconscious, they only lead to the shedding of *karmas* or *nirjarā*.

Commentary : Ordinarily the enjoyment of sense-perceived objects whether animate or inanimate is said to be the cause of *karmic bondage*. But in the case of a right believer, this is supposed to lead to the very opposite result of *nirjarā* or wearing down of *karmas*. What is the meaning of this paradox? Enjoyment of sense-perceived objects in the case of the right believer is quite different from the experience present in the wrong believer. The latter, because of the lack of discriminative knowledge, identifies himself with the external objects and indulges in the enjoyment of those objects, carried away by the full force of desire, aversion and delusion. In this case the enjoyment brings about *āsrava* which leads to fresh bondage of *karmas.* But in the case of the right believer who is equipped with discriminative knowledge and who is thus able to adopt a detached view of things external, these conditions of *karmic* bondage are altogether absent. No doubt he has relations with useful and enjoyable objects of the external world such as his wife, children, wealth and property. Towards these he adopts a neutral attitude. Because of this neutral attitude, he is unaffected either by their increase or decrease. Hence there is no chance for the incoming of new *karmas.* The experiences he has therefore all relate to the previous *karmas* which are present in him already. When they begin to operate they produce corresponding psychic in the right believer who, in spite of his neutral attitude, must necessarily experience the fruits of his previous *karmas.* Thus the previously acquired *karmas* after producing their inevitable result exhaust themselves and cease to be. This is *nirjarā* or wearing down of *karmas.*

After describing the wearing down of material *karmas* the author next describes the consequential *bhāvanirjarā,* the corresponding psychic result.

दव्वे उवभुज्जंते णियमा जायदि सुहं च दुक्खं वा।
तं सुहदुक्खमुदिण्णं वेददि अह णिज्जरं जादि॥ १९४॥

davve uvabhujjaṁte ṇiyamā jāyadi suhaṁ ca dukkhaṁ vā
taṁ suhadukkhamudiṇṇaṁ vedadi aha ṇijjaraṁ jādi (194)

द्रव्ये उपभुज्यमाने नियमाज्जायते सुखं च दु:खं वा।
तं सुखदु:खमुदीर्णं वेदयते अथ निर्जरां याति॥ १९४॥

194. Useful and enjoyable objects of the perceptual world when they are enjoyed by the right believer, inevitably produce pleasure or pain as determined by good or bad *karma*. Since these pleasant or painful feelings are indifferently experienced by the right believer, they wear themselves down and this is *nirjarā*.

Next the power of knowledge is extolled.

जह विसमुवभुज्जंता विज्जापुरिसा ण मरणमुवयन्ति।
पोग्गलकम्मस्सुदयं तह भुंजदि णेव वज्झदे णाणी॥ १९५॥

jaha visamuvabhujjaṁtā vijjāpurisā ṇa maraṇamuvayaṁti
poggalakammassudayaṁ taha bhuṁjadi ṇeva vajjhade ṇāṇī (195)

यथा विषमुपभुंजानाः विद्यापुरुषा न मरणमुपयान्ति।
पुद्गलकर्मण उदयं तथा भुङ्क्ते नैव बध्यते ज्ञानी॥ १९५॥

195. Just as a person who is an expert in anti-poison lore, even though he takes poison, does not meet with death; even so when the *karmic* materials become mature and produce their inevitable results of pain and pleasure, the knowing Self with a neutral attitude experiences these but remains unbound.

Commentary : The very conditions, which lead the unenlightened towards bondage are counteracted by the power of knowledge, become defunct and disappear, in the case of the enlightened one.

जह मज्जं पिवमाणो अरदिभावेण मज्जदि ण पुरिसो।
दव्वुवभोगे अरदो णाणी वि ण बज्झदि तहेव॥ १९६॥

jaha majjaṁ pivamāṇo aradibhāveṇa majjadi ṇa puriso
davvuvabhoge arado ṇāṇī vi ṇa bajjhadi taheva (196)

यथा मद्यं पिबन् अरतिभावेन माद्यति न पुरुषः।
द्रव्योपभोगे अरतो ज्ञान्यपि न बध्यते तथैव॥ १९६॥

196. Just as a person who takes wine (as medicine) without any special longing for it, does not get intoxicated, so also the enlightened Self, while he enjoys external objects without any special longing towards them, does not get bound.

Commentary : Thus is explained the extraordinary potency of the attitude of non-attachment in keeping the enlightened Self free from *karmic* bondage, even while he enjoys the objects of the external world.

सेवंतो वि ण सेवइ असेवमाणो वि सेवगो कोवि।
पगरणचेट्ठा कस्सवि ण य पायरणोत्ति सो हादि॥ १९७॥

sevaṁto vi ṇa sevai asevamāṇo vi sevago kovi
pagaraṇaceṭṭhā kassavi ṇa ya pāyaraṇnotti so hodi (197)

सेवामानोऽपि न सेवते, असेवमानोऽपि सेवकः कश्चित्।
प्रकरणचेष्टा कस्यापि न च प्राकरण इति स भवति॥ १९७॥

197. While one actually enjoys, does not really enjoy; whereas another while not enjoying does really enjoy. Just as one who plays a part does not really become that character.

Commentary : An actor on a stage may represent a particular character in a drama which may be either tragic or comic. The actor may very successfully play his part without actually suffering any emotional experience corresponding to the part. But a man in the audience who is merely a spectator may experience all the emotions because he identifies himself mentally with the character. In the former case such emotional experience is absent in spite of perfect dramatic action because the actor maintains complete isolation mentally from the dramatic situation. Isolation is the cause of the absence of emotion even while external action is present; whereas in the latter even though there is no action, there is emotional experience corresponding to the situation because of the mental identification with the situation. Exactly similar is the case with a person who enjoys the objects of the external world. The determining factor here also is the mental attitude and not action. A person may make use of external objects as a matter of duty without having corresponding emotion. But in the case of another person who is incapable of having the attitude of mental isolation, and who has a hankering after external objects, may have all the characteristic emotions even though he does not actually enjoy them either because of lack of opportunity or external restraint. Thus it is true that one who enjoys may not really enjoy, whereas another who does not enjoy may really enjoy according to the mental attitude of each.

उदयविवागो विविहो कम्माणं वण्णिदो जिणवरेहिं।
ण दु ते मज्झ सहावा जाणगभावो दु अहमेक्को॥ १९८॥

udayavivāgo viviho kammāṇaṁ vaṇṇido jiṇavarehiṁ
ṇa du te majjha sahāvā jāṇagabhāvo du ahamekko (198)

उदयविपाको विविध: कर्मणां वर्णितो जिनवरै:।
न तु ते मम स्वभावा: ज्ञायकभावस्त्वहमेक:॥ १९८॥

198. It has been declared by the great Jinas that the rise and fruition of *karmas* are of various kinds. But they are not (related to) my pure nature. I am certainly the (non-varying) one, the Knower by nature.

पोग्गलकम्मं रागो तस्स विवागोदओ हवदि एसो।
ण दु एस मज्झभावो जाणगभावो हु अहमेक्को॥ १९९॥

poggalakammaṁ rāgo tassa vivāgodao havadi eso
ṇa du esa majjhabhāvo jāṇagabhāvo hu ahamekko (199)

पुद्गलकर्म रागस्तस्य विपाकोदयो भवति एष:।
नत्वेष मम भाव: ज्ञायकभाव: खल्वहमेक:॥ १९९॥

199. Desire is *karmic* matter (previously bound). When this manisfests after maturity there is the emotion of desire. This psychic state is not of my nature. Certainly, I am the unruffled one, the Knower.

Commentary : This statement about desire must be taken to be true in the case of other emotions such as aversion, delusion, anger, pride deceit, greed, etc.

एवं सम्माइट्ठी अप्पाणं मुणदि जाणगसहावं।
उदयं कम्मविवागं च मुअदि तच्चं वियाणंतो॥ २००॥

evaṁ sammāiṭṭhī appāṇaṁ muṇadi jāṇagasahāvaṁ
udayaṁ kammavivāgaṁ ca muadi taccaṁ viyānaṁto

एवं सम्यग्दृष्टि: आत्मानं जानाति ज्ञायकस्वभावम्।
उदयं कर्मविपाकं च मुञ्चति तत्त्वं विजानन्॥ २००॥

200. Thus the right believer having a clear knowledge of reality apprehends his own Self to be of the nature as the knower, and rejects emotional states because they are the result of the manifestation of *karmic* matter.

Commentary : A clear understanding of the nature of reality thus enables one to accept what ought to be accepted and to reject what ought to be rejected.

परमाणुमित्तियं पि हु रागादीणं तु विज्जदे जस्स।
णवि सो जाणदि अप्पाणयं तु सव्वागमधरोवि॥ २०१॥

paramāṇumittiyaṁ pi hu rāgādīṇaṁ tu vijjade jassa
ṇavi so jāṇadi appāṇayaṁ tu savvāgamadharo vi (201)

परमाणुमात्रमपि खलु रागादीनां तु विद्यते यस्य।
नापि स जानात्यात्मानं तु सर्वागमधरोऽपि॥ २०१॥

201. Verily one in whom attachment. etc., even to the extent of an atom, is present, cannot know the Self even if one be a master of all scriptures.

अप्पाणमयाणंतो अणप्पयं चेव सो अयाणंतो।
कह होदि सम्मदिट्ठी जीवाजीवे अयाणंतो॥ २०२॥

appāṇamayāṇaṁto aṇappayaṁ ceva so ayāṇaṁto
kaha hodi sammadiṭṭhī jīvājīve ayāṇaṁto (202)

आत्मानमजानन् अनात्मानं चापि सोऽजानन्।
कथं भवति सम्यग्दृष्टिर्जीवाजीवावजानन्॥ २०२॥

202. He who does not know the real Self cannot know the non-Self. Thus being devoid of the knowledge of *jīva* and *ajīva*, soul and non-soul, how can he be one of right faith?

आदम्हि दव्वभावे अथिरे मोत्तूण गिण्ह तह णियदं।
थिरमेकमिमं भावं उवलब्भंतं सहावेण॥ २०३॥

ādamhi davvabhāve athire mottūṇa giṇha taha ṇiyadaṁ
thiramekamimaṁ bhāvaṁ uvalabbhaṁtaṁ sahāveṇa (203)

आत्मनि द्रव्यभावान्यस्थिराणि मुक्त्वा गृहाण तथा नियतम्।
स्थिरमेकमिमं भावं उपलभ्यमानं स्वभावेन॥ २०३॥

203. Giving up the impermanent physical and psychical states in the Self (which are due to *dravya karmas* and *bhāva karmas* respectively) makes one grasp this state resulting from the realisation of the true nature of the Self which is eternal,

unchanging, and indivisible unity.

Commentary : In the experience of the empirical ego, there are several psycho-physical states, brought about by the erroneous apprehension of the reals. These states are indeterminate, varying, momentary and erroneous in nature. Hence these must be discarded. But that psychical state resting upon the nature of the transcendental ego is characterised by qualities contrary to the above. This is determinate, permanent, one and free from error. Hence this is the ideal to be sought after.

आभिणिसुदोहिमणकेवलं च तं होदि एक्कमेव पदं।
सो एसो परमट्ठो जं लहिदुं णिव्वुदिं जादि॥ २०४॥

ābhiṇisudohimaṇakevaḷaṁ ca taṁ hodi ekkameva padaṁ
so eso paramaṭṭho jaṁ lahiduṁ ṇivvudiṁ jādi (204)

आभिनिबोधिकश्रुतावधिमनःपर्ययकेवलं च तद्भवत्येकमेव पदम्।
स एष परमार्थः यं लब्ध्वा निवृतिं याति॥ २०४॥

204. Knowledge through sense-perception, knowledge from scriptures, knowledge from clairvoyance, knowledge from telepathy, and supereme knowledge of reality—all these refer to one and the same state. That is the absolute. Realisation of that absolute is *mokṣa.*

Commentary : *Ātmā,* the Self is the absolute. That itself is *jñāna* or knowledge. The Self is one prime category. Hence knowledge is therefore the same as that absolute. Hence it is the means of *Nirvāṇa* or *mokṣa.* Various kinds of knowledge, such as *mati-jñāna, śruta jñāna etc.* do not in any way differentiate this unitary state of knowledge. These various kinds of knowledge refer only to this unitary state of knowledge. When the sun is hidden by clouds its light is not seen and when the clouds gradually disperse, the sunlight gradually reappers in varying degrees till it regains its full luminosity, when all the clouds completely disappear. So also the Self in the form of knowledge, remains hidden, shrouded by the layer of *karmas.* When the *karma*-cloud gradually gets dispersed, then the Self-knowledge begins to shine in varying brilliancy. This variation in knowledge which is due to the variation in the density of the *karmic* cloud does not in any way imply any differentiation in the nature of the underlying Self, that remains the same one, non-varying and permanent. That remains without any differentiation. It is identical with supreme knowledge. When that knowledge is obtained, it is Self-realisation. When nescience gets destroyed, then the Self is obtained; all that pertains to non-Self disappears; no more desire, hatred, or delusion; no more inflow of fresh *karmas;* no more *karmic* bondage; the previously bound *karmas* automatically wear out; thus when all *karmas* completely disappear, that state itself is *mokṣa.* Hence it follows that the absolute is equal to the Self which is equal to pure knowledge; and attaining this ought to be the aim of life since that is the door-way to *mokṣa.*

णाणगुणेन विहीणा एदं तु पदं बहूवि ण लहंते।
तं गिण्ह सुपदमेदं जदि इच्छसि कम्मपरिमोक्खं॥ २०५॥

ṇāṇaguṇeṇa vihīṇā edaṁ tu padaṁ bahūvi ṇa lahaṁte
tam giṇha supadamedaṁ jadi icchasi
kammaparimokkhaṁ (205)

ज्ञानगुणैर्विहीना एतत्तु पदं बहवोऽपि न लभन्ते।
तद्गृहाण सुपदमिदं यदीच्छसि कर्मपरिमोक्षम्॥ २०५॥

205. Those who are devoid of this attribute of knowledge even though their efforts be several, do not attain this state. If your desire complete liberation from bondage, you must

contemplate upon this pure state of knowledge.

Commentary : What is contemplated is the ideal. One who contemplates is the person who desires the ideal. By constant contemplation of the ideal, a person aiming at the goal comes nearer and nearer to it till he finds himself identified with that very ideal. This psychic effort of aiming at the ideal through the act of contemplation is here pointed out as the necessary means of realising the true nature of the Self. Further it is implied that the nature of the ideal contemplated upon is of great importance. The popular view, that one who contemplates with devotion upon an ideal whose nature may be anything is really contemplating upon the supreme *paramātmā,* is incompatible with the Jaina Siddhānta.

एदम्हि रदो णिच्चं संतुट्ठो होहि णिच्चमेदम्हि।
एदेण होहि तित्तो तो होहदि तुह उत्तमं सोक्खं॥ २०६॥

edamhi rado ṇiccaṁ saṁtuṭṭho hohi ṇiccamedamhi
edeṇa hohi titto to hohadi tuha uttamaṁ sokkhaṁ (206)

एतस्मिन् रतो नित्यं संतुष्टो भव नित्यमेतस्मिन्।
एतेन भव तृप्तः तर्हि भविष्यति तवोत्तमं सौख्यम्॥ २०६॥

206. Oh! Good soul, (turning away from the sense pleasures and fixing your attention always on the pure nature of the Self), always be in love with it and hence be happy and satisfied, for surely that will lead you to the future everlasting supreme bliss of *mokṣa.*

को णाम भणिज्ज बुहो परदव्वं ममभिदं हवदि दव्वं।
अप्पाणमप्पणो परिग्गहं तु णियदं वियाणंतो॥ २०७॥

ko ṇāma bhaṇijja būho paradavvaṁ mamamidaṁ havadi davvaṁ
appāṇamappaṇo pariggahaṁ tu ṇiyadaṁ viyāṇaṁto

को नाम भणेद् बुद्धः परद्रव्यं ममेदं भवति द्रव्यम्।
आत्मानमात्मनः परिग्रहं तु नियतं विजानन्॥ २०७॥

207. How can the wise man who realises that the Self alone is the property of the Self, really maintain these alien objects, such as his body, as genuinely his own property?

Commentary : Even an ignoramus cannot make the mistake of identifying his self with the external objects. Thus it is quite obvious that a wise man can never make such a mistake. He will always be able to discern the difference between his Self and non-Self.

मज्झं परिग्गहो जइ तदो अहमजीवदं तु गच्छेज्ज।
णादेव अहं जम्हा तम्हा ण परिग्गहो मज्झं॥ २०८॥

majjhaṁ pariggaho jai tado ahamjīvadaṁ tu gacchejja
ṇādeva ahaṁ jamhā tamhā ṇa pariggaho majjhaṁ (208)

मम परिग्रहो यदि ततोऽहमजीवतां तु गच्छेयम्।
ज्ञातैवाहं यस्मात्तस्मान्न परिग्रहो मम॥ २०८॥

208. External things owned by me, if they are absolutely of my nature, then I must become non-living (like them). Because I am a knowing Self, therefore the objects possessed by me are not of my nature.

छिज्जदु वा भिज्जदु वा णिज्जदु वा अहव जादु विप्पलयं।
जम्हा तम्हा गच्छदु तहावि ण परिग्गहो मज्झं॥ २०९॥

chijjadu vā bhijjadu vā ṇijjadu vā ahava jādu vippalayaṁ
jamhā tamhā gacchadu tahāvi ṇa pariggaho majjhaṁ

छिद्यतां वा भिद्यतां वा नीयतां वा अथवा यातु विप्रलयम्।
यस्मात्तस्माद् गच्छतु तथापि न परिग्रहो मम॥ २०९॥

209. It may be cut, it may be split, it may be dragged or it may be destroyed, whatever manner of deformity it undergoes even then it (the body or any other external object) does not cancern me as it is not really mine.

Commentary : The various ways of maiming the body or other external objects and the consequent suffering will not affect the Self which has realised its true nature to be distinct from that of the alien objects.

अपरिग्गहो अणिच्छो भणिदो णाणी य णिच्छदे धम्मं।
अपरिग्गहो दु धम्मस्स जाणगो तेण सो होदि॥ २१०॥

apariggaho aṇiccho bhaṇido ṇāṇī ya ṇicchadi dhammaṁ
apariggaho du dhammassa jāṇago teṇa so hodi (210)

अपरिग्रहोऽनिच्छो भणितो ज्ञानी च नेच्छति धर्मम्।
अपरिग्रहस्तु धर्मस्य ज्ञायकस्तेन स भवति॥ २१०॥

210. Non-possession is said to be non-attachment. For that reason the knower does not desire even merit. Thus being free from attachment towards merit, he thereby becomes merely the knower (of merit).

Commentary : Dharma or virtuous conduct is the same as what *puṇya is. Puṇya* also is considered to be a form of *karma* in spite of the fact that it is able to produce pleasurable results. Hence it must also be avoided by one who is bent upon realising the Pure Self. The Pure Self is of the form of *śuddhopayoga*. This is its real nature, whereas *puṇya* or Dharma is said to be the *śubha-upayoga*. Since the latter is different from the real nature of the Self, it ought to discarded by the knower, even though it is ordinarily a desirable course of conduct.

अपरिग्गहो अणिच्छो भणिदो णाणी य णिच्छदि अधम्मं।
अपरिग्गहो अधम्मस्स जाणगो तेण सो होदि॥ २११॥

apariggaho aṇiccho bhaṇido ṇaṇī ya ṇicchadi adhamaṁ
apariggaho adhammassa jāṇago teṇa so hodi (211)

अपरिग्रहोऽनिच्छो भणितो ज्ञानी तु नेच्छति अधर्मम्।
अपरिग्रहोऽधर्मस्य ज्ञायकस्तेन स भवति॥ २११॥

211. Non-possession is said to be non-attachment. For that reason the knower does not desire demerit. Thus being free from attachment towards demerit, he thereby becomes merely the knower (of demerit).

Commentary : Possession and attachment are identical. Where there is no desire, there is no possession. Desire is the psychic state born of nescience. This psychic state of the nature of nescience, therefore cannot happen in the knower. The knower must therefore have the psychic state of true knowledge. Hence he cannot have desire which is of the nature of nescience. Therefore he does not even desire that which is of the nature of nescience. Therefore he does not even desire merit or demerit, good or evil. Hence in the case of the knower there is no relation of possession of merit or demerit, *dharma* or *adharma* since real nature is beyond good and evil. What is asserted of *adharma* (demerit) is equally true of *rāga (desire), dveṣa* (aversion), *krodha* (anger), etc.

अपरिग्गहो अणिच्छो भणिदो[1] णाणी य णिच्छदि असणं।
अपरिग्गहो दु असणस्स जाणगो तेण सो होदि॥ २१२॥

apariggaho aṇiccho bhaṇido ṇāṇī ya ṇicchadi asaṇaṁ
apariggaho du asaṇassa jāṇago teṇa so hodi (212)

---

१. भणिदो णाणी दु णिच्छदे असणं।

अपरिग्रहोऽनिच्छो भणितो ज्ञानी च नेचछत्यशनम्।
अपरिग्रहस्त्वशनस्य ज्ञायकस्तेन स भवति॥ २१२॥

212. Non-possession is said to be non-attachment. For that reason the knower does not desire food. Thus being free from attachment for food, he thereby becomes merely the knower (of food).

अपरिग्गहो अणिच्छो भणिदो[१] णाणी च णिच्छदि पाणं।
अपरिग्गहो दु पाणस्स जाणगो तेण सो होदि॥ २१३॥

apariggaho aṇiccho bhaṇido ṇanī ca ṇicchadi pāṇaṁ
apariggaho du pāṇassa jāṇago teṇa so hodi (213)

अपरिग्रहो अनिच्छो भणितो ज्ञानी च नेच्छति पाणम्।
अपरिग्रहस्तु पानस्य ज्ञायकस्तेन स भवति॥ २१३॥

213. Non-possession is said to be non-attachment. For that reason the knower does not desire drink. Thus being free from attachment for drink, he thereby becomes merely the knower (of drink).

एवमादु एदु विविहे सव्वे भावे य णिच्छदि णाणी।
जाणगभावो णियदो णीरालम्बो दु सव्वत्थ॥ २१४॥

evamādu edu vivihe savve bhāve ya ṇicchadi ṇāṇī
jāṇagabhāvo ṇiyado ṇīrālaṁbo du savvattha (214)

एवमादिकास्तु विविधान् सर्वान् भावान् च नेच्छति ज्ञानी।
ज्ञायकभावो नियतो निरालम्बस्तु सर्वत्र॥ २१४॥

214. The knower has no hankering after all these various psychic states (such as desire and appetite for external objects). Since he is really of the nature of the knower he remains every where independent (of alien influences).

---

१. भणिदो णाणी दु णिच्छदे पाणं।

उप्पण्णोदयभोगे विओगबुद्धीय तस्स सो णिच्चं।
कंखामणागदस्स य उदयस्स ण कुव्वदे णाणी॥ २१५॥

uppaṇṇodayabhoge viogabuddhīya tassa so ṇiccaṁ
kaṁkhāmaṇāgadassa ya udayassa ṇa kuvvade ṇāṇī (215)

उत्पन्नोदयभोगो वियोगबुद्ध्या तस्य स नित्यम्।
काङ्क्षामनागतस्य च उदयस्य न करोति ज्ञानी॥ २१५॥

215. Thus the knower having always an attitude of renunciation towards the enjoyable environmental objects arising from the operation of *karmas,* he exhibits neither a desire for the present changes nor a longing for the future ones.

जो वेददि वेदिज्जदि समए समए विणस्सदे उहयं।
तं जाणगो दु णाणी उभयमवि ण कंखई कयावि॥ २१६॥

jo vedadi vedijjadi samae samae viṇassade uhayaṁ
taṁ jāṇago du ṇāṇī ubhayamavi ṇa kaṁkhai kayāvi

यो वेदयते वेद्यते समये समये विनश्यत्युभयम्।
तद् ज्ञायकस्तु ज्ञानी, उभयमपि न कांक्षति कदापि॥ २१६॥

216. Psychic activities corresponding to what feels and what is felt, both get destroyed every moment. One who knows this is the Knower. Never does he long for these.

Commentary : The series of conscious states consists of rapidly moving sensation, perception and idea. These elements form parts of the cognitive aspect of consciousness. Besides this cognitive aspect of series of consciousness, there is also the hedonic aspect associated with each item of the series. A sensation or a perception besides giving information about an external object, may also produce pleasurable or painful feeling. This pleasure-pain aspect is present in association with each item of the series. This again has two aspects, subjective and objective, the former indicated by the direction of attention, the latter indicated by the perception and idea attended to. These are technically called *vedaka* and *vedya bhāvas.* If the pleasure-pain aspect is negative, it produces an automatic reaction whether in man or in animals to turn away from the painful perception and idea. But if the hedonic aspect is positive and pleasurable it produces a contrary reaction in the individual. The individual strives to get at it and possess it because it is pleasurable. This behaviour which man has in common with lower animals, as the manifestation of the instinct of self-preservation, is not present in the case of an enlightened individual. He recognises the momentariness of the series rapidly passing in front of the real Self whose nature is entirely distinct from the characteristics of the passing series of conscious states. Resting upon this permanent reality, he is able to realise that even the pleasurable elements of consciousness are entirely ephemeral and fleeting in nature and hence incapable of producing any real satisfaction. Further he realises that there is no fundamental difference between the pleasurable and painful hedonic aspects of consciousness, since both are due to *karmic upādhic* conditions entirely alien to the nature of the Self. Hence his behaviour is different. He does not run after the pleasurable elements of consciousness, nor does he desire to possess them. The ordinary behaviour of avoiding the painful and pursuing the pleasurable is transformed in his case to an attitude of neutrality in which he remains merely a spectator of the panorama without in any way being affected by the hedonic elements even when they are pleasurable.

बंधुवभोगणिमित्तं अज्झवसाणोदएसु णाणिस्स।
संसारदेहविसएसु णेव उप्पज्जदे रागो॥ २१७॥

baṁdhuvabhogaṇimittaṁ ajjhavasāṇodaesu ṇāṇissa
saṁsāradehavisaesu ṇeva uppajjade rāgo (217)

बंधोपभोगनिमित्तेषु अध्यवसानोदयेषु ज्ञानिनः।
संसारदेहविषयेषु नैवोत्पद्यते रागः॥ २१७॥

217. The psychic states conditioned by *saṁsāra* lead to bondage while the psychic states conditioned by the body lead to enjoyment. Hence in the true knower, no desire for these is produced.

Commentary : Psychic states are of two kinds, one pertaining to *saṁsāra* that is the empirical world of things and persons, and the other pertaining to one's own body. The former results in bondage since it is conditioned by the emotions like desire, aversion and delusion. The latter leads to enjoyment either pleasurable or painful. The knowing Self is therefore without any attachment to any of these.

णाणी रागप्पजहो सव्वदव्वेसु कम्ममज्झगदो।
णो लिप्पदि कम्मरएण दु कद्दममज्झे जहा कणयं॥ २१८॥

ṇāṇī rāgappajaho savvadavvesu kammamajjhagado
ṇo lippadi kammaraeṇa du kaddamamajjhe jahā kaṇayaṁ

ज्ञानी रागप्रहायः सर्वद्रव्येषु कर्ममध्यगतः।
नो लिप्यते कर्मरजसा तु कर्दममध्ये यथा कनकम्॥ २१८॥

अण्णाणी पुण रत्तो सव्वसदव्वेसु कम्ममज्झगदो।
लिप्पदि कम्मरएण द कद्दममज्झे जहा लोहं॥ २१९॥

aṇṇāṇī puṇa ratto savvadavvesu kammamajjhgado
lippadi kammaraeṇa du kaddamamajjhe jahā lohaṁ (219)

अज्ञानी पुनः रक्तः सर्वद्रव्येषु कर्ममध्यगतः।
लिप्यते कर्मरजसा तु कर्दममध्ये यथा लोहम्॥ २१९॥

218 and 219. Just as gold in the midst of mire remains uncontaminated because of its non-adhesive property, so also the enlightened one, because of his complete non-attachment to the environment, remains unaffected even when immersed in a cloud of *karmas;* whereas the unenlightened one because of his attachment to external objects gets affected when in the midst of *karma,* just as a piece of iron gets contaminated when dipped in mire because of its adhesive property.

भुज्जंतस्स वि विविहे सच्चित्ताचित्तमिस्सिए दव्वे।
संखस्स सेदभावो ण वि सक्कदि किण्हगो काउं॥ २२०॥

bhujjaṁtassa vi vivihe saccittācittamissie davve
saṁkhassa sedabhāvo ṇa vi sakkadi kiṇhago kāuṁ (220)

भुञ्जानस्यापि विविधानि सचित्ताचित्तमिश्रितानि द्रव्याणि।
शंखस्य श्वेतभावो नापि शक्यते कृष्णकः कर्तुम्॥ २२०॥

तह णाणिस्स दु विविहे सच्चित्ताचित्तमिस्सिए दव्वे।
भुज्जंतस्स वि णाणं ण सक्कमण्णाणदं णेदुं॥ २२१॥

taha ṇāṇissa du vivihe saccittācittamissie davve
bhujjaṁtassa vi ṇāṇaṁ ṇa sakkamṇṇāṇadaṁ ṇeduṁ (221)

तथा ज्ञानिनोऽपि विविधानि सचित्ताचित्तमिश्रितानि द्रव्याणि।
भुञ्जानस्यापि ज्ञानं न शक्यमज्ञानतां नेतुम्॥ २२१॥

220 and 221. The conch-fish may eat and assimilate various things, animate, inanimate, and mixed, and yet the white colour of its shell cannot be changed into black by the things assimilated. In the same way the enlightened knower may enjoy various objects, animate, inanmiate, and mixed, and yet his nature of knowledge cannot be converted into nescience by the things so enjoyed.

जइया स एव संखो सेदसहावं तयं पजहिदूण।
गच्छेज्ज किण्हभावं तइया सुक्कत्तणं पजहे॥ २२२॥

jaiyā sa eva saṁkho sedasahāvaṁ tayaṁ pajahidūṇa
gacchejja kiṇhabāvaṁ taiyā sukkattaṇaṁ pajahe (222)

यदा स एव शंखः श्वेतस्वभावं प्रहाय।
गच्छेत् कृष्णभावं तदा शुक्लत्वं प्रज्यात्॥ २२२॥

तह णाणी विहु जइया णाणसहावं तयं पजहिदूण।
अण्णाणेण परिणदो तइया अण्णाणदं गच्छे॥ २२३॥

taha ṇāṇi vihu jaiyā ṇāṇasahāvaṁ tayaṁ pajahidūṇa
aṇṇāṇeṇa pariṇado taiyā aṇṇāṇadaṁ gacche (223)

तथा ज्ञान्यपि खलु यदा ज्ञानस्वभावं तकं प्रहाय।
अज्ञानेन परिणतस्तदा अज्ञानतां गच्छेत्॥ २२३॥

222 amd 223. The very same conch-fish (irrespective of the fact whether it eats other things or not) may intrinsically undergo a change of colour, when the white-shell will be changed into black one. Similarly the enlightened knower (who remained uninfluenced by the things enjoyed) may undergo deterioration in himself by which he may lose his nature of knowledge and assume one of nescience

Commentary : Thus it is clear that whether the Self retains it true form as the knower or deteriorates into its opposite is entirely determined by itself.

Next the author explains through an illustration taken from ordinary life the difference between the operation of the *karma* in the case of the wrong believer and that in the case of the right believer.

पुरिसो जह कोवि इहं वित्तिणिमित्तं तु सेवए रायं।
तो सोवि देदि राया विविहे भोगे सुहुप्पाए॥ २२४॥

puriso jaha kovi iham vittiṇimittaṁ tu sevae rāyaṁ
to sovi dedi rāyā vivihe bhoge suhuppāe (224)

पुरुषो यथा कोपीह वृत्तिनिमित्तं तु सेवते राजानम्।
तत्सोऽपि ददाति राजा विविधान् भोगान् सुखोत्पादकान्॥ २२४॥

एमेव जीवपुरिसो कम्मरायं सेवए सुहणिमित्तं।
तो सोवि देइ कम्मो विविहे भोए सुहुप्पाए॥ २२५॥

emeva jīvapuriso kammarāyaṁ sevae suhaṇimittaṁ
to sovi dei kammo vivihe bhoe suhuppāe (225)

एवमेव जीवपुरुषः कर्मरजः सेवते सुखनिमित्तम्।
तत्तदपि ददापि कर्म विविधान् भोगान् सुखोत्पादकान्॥ २२५॥

जह पुण सो चिय पुरिसो वित्तिणिमित्तं ण सेवए रायं।
तो सो ण देइ राया विविहे भोए सुहुप्पाए॥ २२६॥

jaha puṇa so ciya puriso vittiṇimittaṁ ṇa savae rāyaṁ
to so ṇa dei rāyā vivihe bhoe suhuppāe (226)

यथा पुनः स एव पुरुषो वृत्तिनिमित्तं न सेवते राजानम्।
तत्सोऽपि न ददाति राजा विविधान् भोगान् सुखोत्पादकान्॥ २२६॥

एवमेव सम्मदिट्ठी विसयत्तं सेवए ण कम्मरयं।
तो सो ण देइ कम्मं विविहे भोए सुहुप्पाए॥ २२७॥

evameva sammadiṭṭhī visayattaṁ sevaye ṇa kammarayaṁ
to so ṇa dei kammaṁ vivihe bhoe suhuppāe (227)

एवमेव सम्यग्दृष्टिः विषयार्थं सेवते न कर्मरजः।
तत्तन्न ददाति कर्म विविधान् भोगान् सुखोत्पादकान्॥ २२७॥

224 to 227. Just as whenever a person in this world, with the object of gaining his livelihood, serves his king and the king gives him by way of remuneration various pleasure-

producing objects; so also the Self, in the form of an unenlightened personality with the object of securing pleasures, devotes himself in the service of *karmas* and the *karma-raja* accordingly offers him pleasure-producing things. Whenever that very person does not serve the king for his livelihood, the king does not give him various pleasure-producing objects by way of remuneration. Similarly the right-believer, for the sake of sense-pleasures does not devote himself to the service of *karmas* and consequently the *karma* does not yield various objects as a source of enjoyment.

Commentary : Thus it is clear that in the case of the right-believer the *karma* is incapable of producing any effect.

While proceeding to describe the nature of right belief and its constituent elements, the author first states in general *niśśaṅka* or doubtlessness.

सम्मादिट्ठी जीवा णिस्संका होंति णिब्भया तेण।
सत्तभयविप्पमुक्का जम्हा तम्हा दु णिस्संका॥ २२८॥

sammādiṭṭhi jīvā ṇissaṁkā homti ṇibbhayā teṇa
sattabhayavippamukkā jamhā tamhā du ṇissaṁkā (228)

सम्यग्दृष्टयो जीवा निश्शङ्का भवन्ति निर्भयास्तेन।
सप्तभयविप्रमुक्ता यस्मात्तस्मात्तु निश्शङ्का॥ २२८॥

228. Souls with right belief are free from doubt and therefore they are free from fear. Because they are free from seven kinds of fear, they are free from doubt.

Commentary : The seven fears are—(1) fear relating to this life, (2) fear relating to future life, (3) fear of being without protection, (4) fear of the disclosure of what is kept in secret (5) feat of pain, (6) fear of accident and (7) fear of death.

The author further explains the characteristics of *niśśaṇka* or doubtlessness (one of the constituents of right belief).

जो चत्तारि वि पाए छिंददि ते कम्ममोहबाधकरे।
सो णिस्संको चेदा सम्मादिट्ठी मुणेयव्वो॥ २२९॥

jo cattāri vi pāe chiṁdadi te kammamohabādhakare
so ṇissaṁko cedā sammādiṭṭhī muṇeyavvo (229)

यश्चतुरोऽपि पादान् छिनत्ति तान् कर्ममोहबाधकरान्।
स निश्शङ्कश्चेतयिता सम्यग्दृष्टिर्मन्तव्यः॥ २२९॥

229. He who cuts the four feet (wrong-belief, non-discipline, soul-soiling gross emotions, and psycho-physical activity) of what produces *karma*, delusion, and suffering is the non-doubting right believer.

Commentary : Hence the Self which is non-doubting is free from bondage resulting from doubt. He has only to shed the *karmas* previously acquired.

Next the qualities of *niṣkāṅkṣa* or desirelessness is described.

जो दु ण करेदि कंखं कम्मफलेसु तह य सव्वधम्मेसु।
सो णिक्कंखो चेदा सम्मादिट्ठी मुणेयव्वो॥ २३०॥

jo du ṇa karedi kaṁkhaṁ kammaphalesu taha ya savvadhammesu
so ṇikkaṁkho cedā sammādiṭṭhī muṇeyavvo (230)

यस्तु न करोति काङ्क्षां कर्मफलेषु तथा च सर्वधर्मेषु।
स निष्काङ्क्षश्चेतयिता सम्यग्दृष्टिर्मन्तव्यः॥ २३०॥

230. He who evinces no desire for pleasures resulting from *karmas* or for all qualities of things must be understood

to be a desire-free right believer.

Commentary : The Self which is free from desire is *ipso facto* free from desire produced by bondage. He has only to do *nirjarā*, the shedding of the *karmas* previously acquired.

Next the characteristic of *nirvicikitsā* is mentioned.

जो ण करेदि जुगुंछं चेदा सव्वेसिमेव धम्माणं।
सो खलु णिव्विदिगिछो सम्मादिट्ठी मुणेयव्वो॥ २३१॥

jo ṇa karedi jugumcham cedā savvesimeva dhammāṇaṁ.
so khalu ṇivvidigimcho sammādiṭṭhī muṇeyavvo (231)

यो न करोति जुगुप्सां चेतयिता सर्वेषामेव धर्माणाम्।
स खलु निर्विचिकित्सः सम्यग्दृष्टिर्मन्तव्यः॥ २३१॥

231. He who does not exhibit any abhorrence or disgust towards all the (obnoxious) qualities of things, is said to be the right believer without any abhorrence.

Commentary : The characteristics in one's own body or in the environment which produce disgust or abhorrence in an ordinary man are without any influence in the case of the right believer who is aware of the nature of the things in themselves. This attitude of absolute indifference even in the midst of disgusting things is what is known as the quality of *nirvicikitsā*. This attitude of indifference does not produce any feeling of disgust or abhorrence. His attention is not diverted to the unpleasant situation in the environment. His attention is therefore fixed on the true nature of the Self. Hence there is no *karmic* bondage resulting from the emotions of disgust or abhorrence. He has only to achieve *nirjarā* or the shedding of the past *karmas*.

Next the author describes the quality of non-delusion (*amūḍadrṣṭitvam*).

जो हवइ असम्मूढो चेदा सद्दिट्ठी सव्व भावेसु।
सो खलु अमूढदिट्ठी सम्मादिट्ठी मुणेयव्वो॥ २३२॥

jo havai asammūḍho cedā saddiṭṭhī savva bhāvesu
so khalu amūḍhadiṭṭhī sammādiṭṭhi muṇeyavvo (232)

यो भवति असंमूढं चेतयिता सद्दृष्टिः सर्वभावेषु।
स खलु अमूढदृष्टिः सम्यग्दृष्टिर्मन्तव्यः॥ २३२॥

232. He who is completely devoid of delusion as to the nature of things is certainly understood to be the non-deluded right-believer.

Commentary : In this case also freedom from delusion as to the nature of things prevents the appearance of *karma* arising from delusion. Hence right believer has only *nirjarā* achieve.

Next the author describes *upagūhana* or the charitable concealment of defects in others.

जो सिद्धभत्तिजुत्तो उवगूहणगो दु सव्वधम्माणं।
सो उवगूहणकारी सम्मादिट्ठी मुणेयव्वो॥ २३३॥

jo siddhabhattijutto uvagūhaṇago du savvadhammāṇaṁ
so uvagūhaṇakārī sammādiṭṭhī muṇeyavvo (233)

यः सिद्धभक्तियुक्तः उपगूहनकस्तु सर्वधर्माणाम्।
स उपगूहनकारी सम्यग्दृष्टिर्मन्तव्यः॥ २३३॥

233. He who is filled with devotion to Siddha and who forbears in every way all kinds of defects in others is considered to be the right-believer endowed with the quality of forbearance.

Commentary : The important word in this *gāthā* is *upagūhana* which means the attitude of forbearance and charity through which the defects of helpless persons such as children and invalids are overlooked and concealed. This is the usual meaning given by the various Jaina writers for that word *upagūhana.* That is also the definition given by Samantabhadra in his *Ratnakaraṇdka Srāvakācāra* (1.15) where he explains the constituent element of *upagūhana.* Prabhāchandra's commentary on the same verse maintains the same point of view. "Children because of ignorance, and invalids because of their incapacity, may go wrong in their course of conduct prescribed for them by the religion. When they commit mistakes in that way those defects must not be made much of, but must be over-looked and concealed, and that is *upagūhana.*"

One of the commentators on *Samayasāra*, Amritacandra, evidently had before him the word *upabṛṁhaṇa* and not *upagūhana.* The word *upabṛṁhaṇa* means growing or increasing. With this reading evidently he explains the term as one who increases the powers of the Self, or *ātma-śakti* and that a right-believer is called one who has the soul-power in fullness. Hence in his case there is no *karmic bandha* produced by lack of soul-power or the weakness of Self. This same word *upabṛṁhaṇa* is included by both Pūjyapāda and Akalaṅka when they enumerate the eight consituent elements or *aṣṭāṅgas* of right belief. In commenting upon the Sutra 24 of Chapter VI of *Tattvārthasūtra, "Uttamakṣamādi-bhāvamaya-ātmano dharma-pari-vriddhi-kāraṇam upabṛṁhaṇam"*, increasing the true characteristics of the Self through the attitude of supreme forbearance, etc., means *upabṛṁhaṇam* or increase in soul-power. Jayasena, the other commentator on Samayasāra, evidently tries to combine the meaning of both the words *upabṛṁhaṇa* and *upagūhana.* "*Mithyātva-rāgādi-vibhava-dharmāṇām-upa-gūhaka-*

pracchādaka-vināśakāh." Thus he takes the word *upagūhana* to mean *vināśa* or destruction and what must be destroyed are the impure psychic states produced by wrong belief, attachment to sense-pleasures, etc. It is extremely difficult on our part to explain how this constituent element *upabṛṁhaṇa* was supplanted by the element *upa-gūhana,* from increasing to fullness the soul-power to charitably forbearing the defects in others. Akalaṅka's Rājavāritika gives us a clue to understanding this transformation. The increasing of the soul-power is affected by means of *uttamakṣamā,* supreme forbearance, etc. One who practises *uttamkṣamā,* etc., not only increases his own soul's potency to fulness, but also by the same process developes the supreme quality of love and forbearance towards others. Persons who go astray either through ignorance or incapacity are forgiven by those great personalities who realise themselves in fulness and thereby evince love and forbearance towards others. They are able to discern the element of goodness in things evil. They may condemn evil but they sympathise with and forgive the evil-doer. This attitude is beautifully illustrated in Christ's words addressed to the woman taken in the act of adultery, "Neither do I condemn thee. Go and sin no more." Thus *upagūhana* is in short the result of *upabṛṁhaṇa,* the fulness of power manifesting itself in forgiving and forbearance towards the weak.

In this case there is no *karmic* bondage, resulting from non-forbearance; *nirjarā,* or shedding of past *karmas* alone remains to be affected.

In the next *gāthā* the author gives a description of *sthitikaraṇa,* non-wavering firmness in faith.

उम्मग्गं गच्छंतं सगमपि मग्गे ठवेदि जो चेदा।
सो ठिदिकरण जुत्तो सम्मादिट्ठी मुणेयव्वो॥ २३४॥

ummaggaṁ gacchaṁtaṁ sagamapi magge thavedi jo cedā
so ṭhidikaraṇa jutto sammādiṭṭhī muṇeyavvo (234)

उन्मार्गं गच्छन्तं स्वकमपि मार्गे यः स्थापयति यश्चेदयिता।
स स्थितिकरणयुक्तः सम्यग्दृष्टिर्मन्तव्यः ॥ २३४॥

234. He who, instead of going astray, establishes himself firmly in the path of emancipation must be considered to be the right-believer who is endowed with steadfastness.

Commentary : In this case also since the right believer is firmly established in the path leading to *mokṣa,* there is no wavering in him. Hence there is no bondage due to the lack of firmness. Hence there is only *nirjarā* to be effected here also.

Next the author describes the constituent element *vātsalya,* the attitude of love and devotion.

जो कुणदि वच्छलत्तं तिण्हे साधूण मोक्खमग्गम्मि।
सो वच्छलभावजुदो सम्मादिट्ठी मुणेयव्वो॥ २३५॥

jo kuṇadi vacchalattaṁ tiṇhe sādhūṇa mokkhamaggammi
so vacchalabhāvajudo sammādiṭhī muṇeyavvo (235)

यः करोति वत्सलत्वं त्रयाणां साधूनां मोक्षमार्गे।
सः वात्सल्यभावयुक्तः सम्यग्दृष्टिर्मन्तव्यः॥ २३५॥

235. Whoever develops love and devotion to the three jewels which constitute the right path to *mokṣa,* that person is considered to be the right believer endowed with love and devotion to the true path.

Commentary : Love and devotion sustain him in the right path. Hence there is no lack of devotion and love and hence there is no *karmic* bondage, consequent thereupon. There is only *nirjarā* to be achieved.

Next is described the eighth constituent element of *prabhāvanā* or proclaiming the truth (of *pravacana* or Divine Word).

विज्जारहमारूढो मणोरहपहेसु भमइ जो चेदा।
सो जिणणाणपहावी सम्मादिट्ठी मुणेयव्वो॥ २३६॥

vijjārahamārūḍho maṇorahapahesu bhamai jo cedā
so jiṇaṇāṇapahāvī sammādiṭṭhī muṇeyavvo (236)

विद्यारथमारूढः मनोरथपथेषु भ्रमति यश्चेतयिता।
स जिनज्ञानप्रभावी सम्यग्दृष्टिर्मन्तव्यः॥ २३६॥

236. The Self, which mounted on the Chariot of knowledge roams about as it pleases (shedding the light of wisdom), is to be considered a right-believer who is engaged in propounding the Jaina faith.

Commentary : This emphasises the social aspect of religious faith. A person who is equipped with knowledge of reality and who is therefore engaged in self-realisation should not be satisfied with his own personal acquisition of the sublime wisdom. He must place the benefit of his achievement at the disposal of the other members of the society. There is no such thing as isolated personal salvation. He is bound to share the wisdom with others and he must take with him as many as are willing to walk the path with him. This necessarily implies that the enlightened person should not be confined to any particular place. He must go about from place to place carrying the torch of light and wisdom thus spreading the true knowledge and true faith in all parts of the country. This roaming about from place to place, spreading hope, wisdom and charity for the benefit of the whole society is what is called *dharma probhāvanā*, one of the essential characteristics of the right believer. This characteristic was present at its maximum in the life of every Tīrthaṅkara. The Lord after attaining *kevala-jñāna* or Omniscience, spends the remaining portion of his life-time in going about from place to place and preaching the *dharma* for the benefit of mankind.

Thus the right-believer endowed with the above eight characteristics is free from new *karmic* bondage but has only to achive *nirjarā* or the shedding of the past *karmas*.

Thus ends the chapter on *nirjarā*.

Nirjarā quits the stage like a character cured of its infatuous nature and filled with *śānta-rasa* or peace.

CHAPTER VIII

BANDHA
or
BONDAGE OF KARMAS

Then Bandha enters the stage.

जह णाम कोवि पुरिसो णेहभत्तो दु रेणुबहुलम्मि।
ठाणम्मि ठाइदूण य करेइ सत्थेहिं वायामं॥ २३७॥

jaha ṇāma kovi puriso ṇehabhatto du reṇubahulammi
ṭhāṇammi ṭhāidūṇa ya karei satthehiṁ vāyāmaṁ (237)

यथा नाम कोऽपि पुरुष: स्नेहाभ्यक्तस्तु रेणुबहुले।
स्थाने स्थित्वा च करोति शस्त्रैर्व्यायामम्॥ २३७॥

छिंददि भिंददि य तहा तालीतलकयलिवंसपिंडीओ।
सचित्ताचित्ताणं करेइ दव्वाणमुवघायं॥ २३८॥

chiṁdadi bhiṁdadi ya tahā tālītalakayalivaṁsapiṁḍīo
sacittācittāṇaṁ karei davvāṇamuvaghāyaṁ (238)

छिनत्ति भिनत्ति च तथा तालीतलकदलीवंशपिण्डी:।
सचित्ताचित्तानां करोति द्रव्याणामुपघातम्॥ २३८॥

उवघायं कुव्वंतस्स तस्स णाणाविहेहिं करणेहिं।
णिच्छयदो चिंतिज्जदु किं पच्चयगो दु रयबंधो॥ २३९॥

uvaghāyaṁ kuvvaṁtassa tassa ṇāṇāvihehiṁ karaṇehiṁ ṇicchayado ciṁtijjadu kiṁ paccayago du rayabaṁdho

उपघातं कुर्वन्तस्तस्य नानाविधैः करणैः।
निश्चयतश्चिन्त्यतां तु किं प्रत्ययकस्तु रजोवधः॥ २३९॥

जो सो दु णेहभावो तम्हि णरे तेण तस्स रयबन्धो।
णिच्छयदो विण्णेयं ण कायचेट्ठाहिं सेसाहिं॥ २४०॥

jo so du ṇehabhāvo tamhi ṇare teṇa tassa rayabaṁdho ṇicchayado viṇṇeyaṁ ṇa kāyaceṭṭhāhiṁ sesāhiṁ (240)

यः स तु स्नेहभावस्तस्मिन्नरे तेन तस्य रजोबन्धः।
निश्चयतो विज्ञेयं न कायचेष्टाभिः शेषाभिः॥ २४०॥

एवं मिच्छादिट्ठी वट्टंतो बहुविहासु चेट्ठासु।
रायाई उवओगे कुव्वंतो लिप्पइ रयेण॥ २४१॥

evaṁ micchādiṭṭhī vaṭṭaṁto bahuvihāsu ceṭṭhāsu rāyāi uvaoge kuvvaṁto lippai rayeṇa (241)

एवं मिथ्यादृष्टिर्वर्तमानो बहुविधासु चेष्टासु।
रागादीनुपयोगे कुर्वाणो लिप्यते रजसा॥ २४१॥

237 to 241 : For instance, a man smeared with oil standing in a place full of dust, performs exercises with a sword, cuts or breaks trees such as palm, *tamala,* plantain, bamboo, and *aśoka* and thus causes destruction to objects, animate and inanimate. In the case of this person who is engaged in the destructive activity by assuming various bodily postures, what is the real condition causing dust deposit on his person? Certainly it is the oil smeared on his body that must be considered to be the real cause of the dust-deposit and certainly not his various bodily activities. In the same way a wrong believer even while he is engaged in various

activities, only if he performs those activities with feeling of attachment then certainly he gets covered with *karmic* dust.

Commentary : Here is a person, smeared with oil all over the body, standing in a place which is naturally full of dust. He is engaged in sword exercise. He assumes various postures of his body in his rapid movement engaged in the destruction of objects animate and inanimate. Certainly his body is covered with dust. What is the real cause of the dust deposit on him? Certainly it is not the ground which is naturally full of dust. If that were so, another person without oil-smear on the body standing in the same place must also have the dust-deposit on his body. Is it the sword exercise? Certainly not. For, another person without the oily body perfoming the same exercise must get the dust deposit. Is it the destruction of objects animate and inanimate? This cannot be. For a person similarly engaged without the oily body must also get dust-deposit. In all these cases it is clear that the dust-deposit does not occur when the oily surface is not present and the dust-deposit occurs only when the oily surface is present. This one common factor in the antecedent circumstances must be taken to be the real cause of the dust-deposit. In the same way a wrong believer, who, having the feeling of attachment in himself and remaining in the world which is naturally full of *karmic* particles is engaged in various activities of thought, word and deed, directed to the destruction of animate and inanimate objects, gets covered with *karmic* dust. What is the real cause of this *karmic* bondage? Certainly it is not the world which is filled with *karmic* particles. If that were the cause, then even the *Siddhas*, the Perfect Souls, because of their existence in the same world must also be subjected to *karmic* bondage. Can it be the action involving thought, word and deed? Such activity is present even in the case of the Omniscient *Arhat* and in Him there must occur the *karmic* bondage. Then is it due to destruction of objects animate and inanimate? Certainly not. For such a destruction may happen even in the case of careful activities which go under the name of five *samitīs*. Here also the only common factor is the antecedent circumstances; the feelings of attachment, must be taken to be the causal condition of the *karmic* bondage. Thus it is established through a practical illustration that the feeling of attachment towards objects in the environment is the real cause of *karmic* bondage.

जह पुण सो चेव णरो णेहे सव्वम्हि अवणिये संते।
रेणुबहुलम्मि ठाणे करेइ सत्थेहि वायामं॥ २४२॥

jaha puṇa so çeva ṇaro ṇehe savvamhi avaṇiye saṁte
reṇubahulammi ṭhāṇe karei satthehi vāyāmaṁ (242)

यथा पुनः स चैव नरः स्नेहे सर्वस्मिन्नपनीते सति।
रेणुबहुले स्थाने करोति शस्त्रैर्व्यायामम्॥ २४२॥

छिंददि भिंददि य तहा तालीतलकयलिवंसपिंडीओ।
सच्चित्ताचित्ताणं करेई दव्वाणमुवधायं॥ २४३॥

chiṁdadi bhiṁdadi ya tahā tālītalakayalivaṁsapiṁdīo
saccittācittāṇaṁ karei davvāṇamuvadhāyaṁ (243)

छिनत्ति भिनत्ति च तथा तालीतलकदलीवंशपिण्डीः।
सचित्ताचित्ताणां करोति द्रव्याणामुपघातम्॥ २४३॥

उवघायं कुव्वंतस्स तस्स णाणाविहेहिं करणेहिं।
णिच्छयदो चिंतिज्जदु किं पच्चयगो ण रयबंधो॥ २४४॥

uvaghāyaṁ kuvvaṁtassa tassa ṇāṇāvihehiṁ karaṇehiṁ
ṇicchayado ciṁtijjadu kiṁ paccayago ṇa rayabaṁdho

उपघातं कुर्वतस्तस्य नानाविधैः करणैः।
निश्चयतश्चिन्त्यतां खलु किं प्रत्ययको न रजोबन्धः॥ २४४॥

जो सोदु णेहभावो तम्हि णरे तेण तस्स रयबंधो।
णिच्छयदो विण्णेयं ण कायचेट्ठाहिं सेसाहिं॥ २४५॥

jo sodu ṇehabhāvo tamhi ṇare teṇa tassa rayabaṁdho
ṇicchayado viṇṇeyaṁ ṇa kāyaceṭṭhāhiṁ sesāhiṁ (245)

यः स तु स्नेहभावस्तस्मिन्नरे तेन तस्य रजोबन्धः।
निश्चयतो विज्ञेयं न कायचेष्टाभिः शेषाभिः॥ २४५॥

एवं सम्मादिट्ठी वट्टंतो बहुविहेसु जोगेसु।
अकरंतो उवओगे रागाई ण लिप्पई रयेण॥ २४६॥

evaṁ sammādiṭṭhī vaṭṭaṁto bahuvihesu jogesu
akaraṁto uvaoge rāgāi ṇa lippai rayeṇa (246)

एवं सम्यग्दृष्टिर्वर्तमानो बहुविधेषु योगेषु।
अकुर्वन्नुपयोगे रागादीन् न लिप्यते रजसा॥ २४६॥

242 to 246. On the other hand a person entirely free from oily smear on the body, standing in a place full of dust, performs exercises with a sword, cuts or breaks trees such as palm, *tamāla*, plantain, bamboo and *aśoka* and thus causes destruction to objects, animate and inanimate. In the case of this person who is engaged in the destructive activity by assuming various bodily postures, what is the real explanation for the absence of dust-deposit on his person? Certainly it is the absence of oily surface that must account for the absence of dust-deposit on his person and not his various bodily activities. In the same way a right believer even while he is engaged in various activities. In the same way a right believer even while he is engaged in various activities of thought, word, and deed merely because of the

absence of feeling of attachment in them, is not bound by *karmic* particles.

Commentary : In the above *gāthās* the causal relation between the feeling of attachment and *karmic* bondage is established by citing positive instances on the one hand by which the presence of the cause necessarily implies the presence of the effect, and also by citing negative instances on the other hand where the absence of the cause implies the absence of the effect, thus adopting the principle which is known in Logic as the Joint Method of Agreement and Difference.

Next the author describes the thoughts characteristic of the nescient and the knowing Self.

जो मण्णदि हिंसामि य हिंसिज्जामि य परेहिं सत्तेहिं।
सो मूढो अण्णाणी णाणी एत्तो दु विवरीदो॥ २४७॥

jo maṇṇadi hiṁsāmi ya hiṁsijjāmi ya parehiṁ sattehiṁ
so mūḍho aṇṇāṇī ṇāṇī etto du vivarīdo (247)

यो मन्यते हिनस्मि च हिंस्ये च परैः सत्त्वैः।
स मूढोऽज्ञानी ज्ञान्यतस्तु विपरीतः॥ २४७॥

247. He who thinks, "I kill other beings or I am killed by other beings", is a deluded one, devoid of knowledge. But one who thinks otherwise is the Knower.

Commentary : The above-mentioned thought arises from the lack of true knowledge which is the characteristic of wrong belief. But such thoughts are absent in the case of one who knows the true nature of things and hence he is a right believer. The same idea occurs in the Bhagavad Gītā. "He who thinks of him as slayer, he who deems him slain—these both are void of judgement; he doth not slay nor is he slain." 11.19.

Next the author explains why such thoughts imply *ajñāna* or lack of true knowledge.

आउक्खयेण मरणं जीवाणं जिणवरेहिं पण्णत्तं।
आउं ण हरेसि तुमं कह ते मरणं कयं तेसिं॥ २४८॥

āukkhayeṇa maraṇaṁ jīvāṇaṁ jiṇavarehiṁ paṇṇattaṁ
āuṃ ṇa haresi tumaṁ kaha te maraṇaṁ kayaṁ tesiṁ

आयुःक्षयेण मरणं जीवानां जिनवरैः प्रज्ञप्तम्।
आयुर्न हरसि त्वं कथं त्वया मरणं कृतं तेषाम्॥ २४८॥

248. It is declared by the Jinas that the death of living beings is caused by the disappearance of their age-determining *karma.* (Since) they do not destroy their age-determining *karma,* how is their death caused by then?

आउक्खयेण मरणं जीवाणं जिणवरेहिं पण्णत्तं।
आउं ण हरंति तुह कह ते मरणं कयं तेहिं॥ २४९॥

āukkhayeṇa maraṇaṁ jīvāṇaṁ jiṇavarehiṁ paṇṇattaṁ
āuṁ ṇa haraṁti tuha kaha te maraṇaṁ kayaṁ tehiṁ

आयुःक्षयेण मरणं जीवानां जिनवरैः प्रज्ञप्तम्।
आयुर्न हरन्ति तव कथं ते मरणं कृतं तैः॥ २४९॥

249. It is declared by the Jinas that the death of living beings is caused by the disappearance of their age-determining *karma.* (Since) they do not destroy thine age-determining *karma* how can thy death be caused by them.

Commentary : Death of living beings results only when their age-determining *karmas* wear out. This wearing out of one's own age *karma* will be caused by its running its full course of duration and not by any other means. When that causal condition is absent, the result cannot be produced by any other means. Hence no one can think of causing the death of another. Therefore the thought, "I kill or I am killed" is certainly the mark of *ajñāna* or absence of knowledge of things real.

Next the author examines the statements expressing thoughts relating to life, from the same two aspects.

जो मण्णदि जीवेमि य जिविज्जामि य परेहिं सत्तेहिं।
सो मूढो अण्णाणी णाणी एत्तो दु विवरीदो॥ २५०॥

jo maṇṇadi jīvemi ya jīvijjāmi ya parehiṁ sattehiṁ
so mūḍho aṇṇāṇī ṇaṇī etto du vivarīdo (250)

यो मन्यते जीवयामि च जीव्ये च परैः सत्त्वैः।
स मूढोऽज्ञानी ज्ञान्यतस्तु विपरीतः॥ २५०॥

250. He who thinks, "I live (as caused by other beings) and I cause other beings to live" is a deluded one, devoid of knowledge. But one who thinks otherwise is the Knower.

Next the author points out how this thought is the result of *ajñāna*.

आऊदयेण जीवदि जीवो एवं भणंति सव्वण्हू।
आउं च ण देसि तुमं कहं तए जीवियं कयं तेसिं॥ २५१॥

āūdayeṇa jīvadi jīvo evaṁ bhaṇaṁti savvaṇhū
auṁ ca ṇa desi tumaṁ kahaṁ tae jīviyaṁ kayaṁ tesiṁ

आयुरुदयेन जीवति जीव एवं भणन्ति सर्वज्ञाः।
आयुश्च न ददासि त्वं कथं त्वया जीवितं कृतं तेषाम्॥ २५१॥

251. The Omniscient Ones declare that an organic being lives because of the operation of (its) age-*karma*. (Since) thou giveth not age-*karma* (to living beings) how is their life caused by thee?

आऊदयेण जीवदि जीवो एवं भणंति सव्वण्हू।
आउं च ण दित्ति तुहं कहं णु ते जीवियं कयं तेहिं॥ २५२॥

āūdayeṇa jīvadi jīvo evaṁ bhaṇaṁti savvaṇhū
āuṁ ca ṇa ditti tuhaṁ kahaṁ ṇu te jīviyaṁ kayaṁ tehiṁ

आयुरुदयेन जीवति जीव एवं भणन्ति सर्वज्ञाः।
आयुश्च न ददाति तव कथं तु ते जीवितं कृतं तैः॥ २५२॥

252. The Omniscient Ones declare that an organic being lives because of the operation of (its) age-*karma.* (Since) they do not give thee thine age-*karma,* how can thy life be caused by them?

Commentary : The life of an organic being depends upon the operation of its age-*karma.* So long as the age-*karma* persists to operate, the organic being continues to live. When that ceases to be, life also ceases to be. Since the age-*karma* is entirely self-determined in its operation, ir cannot be given by anybody else. Therefore, by no means can one make another live. Hence the thought, "I am caused by others to live or I cause others to live," is certainly due to *ajñāna* or absence of the knowledge of the reals.

Next it is pointed out that the thought of causing happiness or misery has the same significance.

जो अप्पणा दु मण्णदि दुहिदसुहिदे करेमि सत्तेति।
सो मूढो अण्णाणी णाणी एत्तो दु विवरीदो॥ २५३॥

jo appaṇā du maṇṇadi duhidasuhide karemi satteti
so mūḍho aṇṇāṇī ṇāṇī etto du vivarīdo (253)

य आत्मना तु मन्यते दुःखितसुखितान् करोमि सत्त्वानिति।
स मूढोऽज्ञानी ज्ञान्यतस्तु विपरीतः॥ २५३॥

253. He who thinks, "I cause happiness or misery to

other beings and I am made happy or miserable by others," is a deluded one, devoid of knowledge. The Knower thinks otherwise.

Next the author points out how this thought is the result of *ajñāna.*

कम्मोदयेण जीवा दुक्खिदसुहिदा हवंति जदि सव्वे।
कम्मं च ण देसि तुहं दुक्खिदसुहिदा कहं कया ते॥२५४॥

kammodayeṇa jīvā dukkhidasuhidā havaṁti jadi savve
kammaṁ ca ṇa desi tumaṁ dukkhidasuhidā kahaṁ kayāte

कर्मोदयेन जीवा दुःखितसुखिता भवन्ति यदि सर्वे।
कर्म च न ददासि त्वं दुःखितसुखिताः कथं कृतास्ते॥ २५४॥

254. If all living beings become miserable or happy only when their *karmas* begin to operate and since thou dost not give them their *karmas,* how are they made miserable or happy by thee.

कम्मोदयेण जीवा दुक्खिदसुहिदा हवंति जदि सव्वे।
कम्मं च ण दिंति तुहं कदोसि कहं दुक्खिदो तेहिं॥ २५५॥

kammodayeṇa jivā dukkhidasuhidā havaṁti jadi savve
kammaṁ ca ṇa diṁti tuhaṁ kadosi kahaṁ dukkhido tehiṁ

कर्मोदयेन जीवा दुःखितसुखिता भवन्ति यदि सर्वे।
कर्म च न ददति तव कृतोसि कथं दुःखितस्तै॥ २५५॥

255. If all living beings become miserable or happy only when their *karmas* begin to operate and since they do not give thee thy *karmas,* how art thou made miserable by them.

कम्मोदयेण जीवा दुक्खिदसुहिदा हवंति जदि सव्वे।
कम्मं च ण दिंति तुहं कह तं सुहिदो कदो तेहिं॥ २५६॥

kammodayeṇa jivā dukkhidasuhidā havaṁti jadi savve
kammaṁ ca ṇa diṁti tuhaṁ kaha taṁ suhido kado tehiṁ

कर्मोदयेन जीवा दुःखितसुखिता भवन्ति यदि सर्वे।
कर्म च न ददति तव कथं त्वं सुखितः कृतस्तै॥ २५६॥

256. If all living beings become miserable or happy only when their *karmas,* begin to operate and since they do not give thee thy *karmas*, how art thou made happy by them.

Commentary : Whether a living being is happy or miserable, is entirely determined by the operation of its *karmas.* If the causal condition is absent, the resultant experience will also cease to be. One's *karma* cannot be got as a gift from another. It is acquired only by one's own conduct in life. Hence one cannot make another happy or miserable. Hence the thought, "I make others happy or miserable or I am made happy or miserable by others" is certainly the mark of *ajñāna.* Thus through these *gāthās* the author emphasises that death and life, misery and happiness are all the result of the operation of one's own *karma.*

जो मरदि जो य दुहिदो जायदि कम्मोदयेण सो सव्वो।
तम्हा दु मारिदोदे दुहाविदो चेदि णहु मिच्छा॥ २५७॥

jo maradi jo ya duhido jāyadi kammodayeṇa so savvo
tamhā du māridode duhāvido cedi ṇahu micchā (257)

यो म्रियते यश्च दुःखितो जायते कर्मोदयेन स सर्वः।
तस्मात्तु मारितस्ते दुःखिनश्चेति न खलु मिथ्या॥ २५७॥

257. One dies or one becomes miserable while alive; all these happen as a result of the operation of one's own *karmas.* Therefore, "He is killed by me and he is made miserable by me"—is not this view of yours entirely false?

जो ण मरदि ण य दुहिदो सोवि य कम्मोदयेण चेव खलु।
तम्हा ण मारिदो ण दुहाविदो चेदि णहु मिच्छा॥ २५८॥

jo ṇa maradi ṇa ya duhido sovi ya kammodayeṇa ceva khalu
tamhā ṇa mārido ṇa duhāvido cedi ṇahu micchā (258)

यो न म्रियते न च दुःखितो सोऽपि च कर्मोदयेन चेव खलु।
तस्मान्न मारितो न दुःखितश्चेति न खलु मिथ्या॥ २५८॥

258. One does not die or one does not become miserable while alive, this also is certainly the result of the operation of one's own *karmas*. Therefore, "He is not killed by me and he is not made miserable by me"—is not this view of yours entirely false?

Next the author points out that this erroneous belief is the cause of bondage.

एसा दु जा मदी दे दुःखिदसुहिदे करेमि सत्तेति।
एसा दे मूढमई सुहासुहं बंधये कम्मं॥ २५९॥

esā du jā madī de dukkhidasuhide karemi satteti
esā de ·ıūḍhamaī suhāsuhaṁ baṁdhaye kammaṁ (259)

एषा तु या मतिस्ते दुःखितसुखितान् करोमि सत्त्वानिति।
एषा ते मूढमतिः शुभाशुभं बध्नाति कर्म॥ २५९॥

259. This false notion of thine, "I make other beings miserable or happy" is illusory. This leads to the bondage of *karmas* good or bad.

दुक्खिदसुहिदे सत्ते करेमि जं एवमज्झवसिदं दे।
तं पावबंधगं वा पुण्णस्स व बंधगं होदि॥ २६०॥

dukkhidasuhide satte karemi jaṁ evamajjhavasidaṁ te
taṁ pāvabaṁdhagaṁ vā puṇṇassa va baṁdhagaṁ hodi

दु:खितसुखितान् सत्त्वान् करोमि यदेवमध्यवसितं ते।
तत्पापबन्धकं वा पुण्यस्य वा बन्धकं भवति॥ २६०॥

260. "I make other beings miserable or happy". This thought of thine causes *karmic* bondage of the nature of vice or virtue.

मारेमि जीवावेमि य सत्ते जं एवमज्झवसिदं ते।
तं पावबंधगं वा पुण्णस्स व बंधगं होदि॥ २६१॥

māremi jīvāvemi ya satte jaṁ evamajjhavasidaṁ te
taṁ pāvabaṁdhagaṁ vā puṇṇassa va baṁdhagaṁ hodi

मारयामि जीवयामि च सत्त्वान् यदेवमध्यवसितं ते।
तत्पापबन्धकं वा पुण्यस्य वा बन्धकं भवति॥ २६१॥

261. "I kill other beings or I make them live." This thought of thine causes *karmic* bondage of the nature of vice or virtue.

Next it is pointed out that the thought to kill is the same as killing.

अज्झवसिदेण बंधो सत्ते मारेउ मा व मारेउ।
एसो बंधसमासो जीवाणं णिच्छयणयस्स॥ २६२॥

ajjhavasideṇa baṁdho satte māreu mā va māreu
eso baṁdhasamāso jīvāṇaṁ ṇicchayaṇayassa (262)

अध्यवसितेन बन्ध: सत्त्वान् मारयतु मा वा मारयतु।
एष बन्धसमासी जीवानां निश्चयनयस्य॥ २६२॥

262. The will to kill is enough to bring bondage irrepective of the fact whether animals are killed or are not killed. From the real point of view this in short is the mode of bondage in the case of *jīvas* (or empirical selves).

Again the auther points out how thought is the cause of

bondage of *pāpa* or *puṇya*, vice or virtue.

एवमलिये अदत्ते अबंभचेरे परिग्गहे चेव।
कीरइ अज्झवसाणं जं तेण दु बज्झए पावं॥ २६३॥

evamaliye adatte abaṁbhacere pariggahe ceva
kīrai ajjhavasāṇaṁ jaṁ teṇa du bajjhae pāvaṁ (263)

एवमलीकेऽदत्तेऽब्रह्मचर्ये परिग्रहे चैव।
क्रियतेऽध्यवसानं यत्तेन तु बध्यते पापम्॥ २६३॥

263. Thus (the will to kill), the will to lie, to steal, to be unchaste and to acquire property (inordinately) leads to bondage of evil *karmas.*

तहवि य सच्चे दत्ते बंभे अपरिगहत्तणे चेव।
कीरइ अज्झवसाणं जं तेण दु बज्झए पुण्णं॥ २६४॥

tahavi ya sacce datte baṁbhe aparigahattaṇe ceva
kīrai ajjhavasāṇaṁ jaṁ teṇa du bajjhae puṇṇaṁ (264)

तथापि च सत्ये दत्ते ब्रह्मणि अपरिग्रहत्वे चैव।
क्रियतेऽध्यवसानं यत्तेन तु बध्यते पुण्यम्॥ २६४॥

264. Where (the will not to kill), the will not to lie, not to steal, not to be unchaste and not to acquire property (inordinately) leads to the bondage of good *karmas.*

Commentary : The same truth is conveyed by Christ through his teachings when he emphasises the inner purity of heart, "Blessed are the pure in heart for they shall see God." This clearly implies that the realisation of the divinity in man is necessarily conditioned by the purity of heart; whereas when the heart is impure, it brings about sin. The following words of Christ make this clear. "Ye have heard that it was said by them of old time, Thou shall not commit adultery, But I say unto you, that whosoever looketh on a woman to lust after her hath committed adultery with her already in his heart." St. Matthew V. 27 & 28.

Next it is pointed out that the objects in the external world can neither be the cause of *karmic* bondage.

वत्थुं पडुच्च जं पुण अज्झवसाणं तु होदि जीवाणं।
ण य वत्थुदो दु बंधो अज्झवसाणेण बंधोत्ति॥ २६५॥

vatthuṁ paḍucca jaṁ puṇa ajjhavasāṇaṁ tu hodi jivāṇaṁ
ṇa ya vatthudo du baṁdho ajjhavasāṇeṇa baṁdhotti (265)

वस्तु प्रतीत्य यत्पुनरध्यवसानं तु भवति जीवानाम्।
न च वस्तुतस्तु बन्धोऽध्यवसानेन बन्धोऽस्ति॥ २६५॥

265. Thought in an empirical Self is always conditioned by an object in the external world. Nevertheless it is not that external object that is the cause of bondage. It is by thought that bondage is caused.

Commentary : The direct cause of bondage is thought and not any external object, though this is the cause of thought itself. Then why should external object be tabooed? It is for the purpose of condemning the thought based upon the external objects. Thought without the basis of an external object never occurs in the consciousness of Self. If it is possible to have thought without the basis of an external object, then thought corresponding to non-existing object must also appear. In the case of a person born of a real mother, you can entertain the thought, "I am going to kill her son". But in the case of a barren woman, the thought, "I am going to kill her son", would be meaningless because there can be no son born to a barren woman. Hence it is certain that there can be no thought without a basis in reality. Hence it necessarily follows that condemnation of evil thoughts leads to the condemnation of corresponding objects of reality. For it is only by preventing the cause that the effects can be prevented from occuring. Could it not be maintained that because the external object is the cause of that cause which produces bondage, therefore, the external object is itself the cause of bondage? No. For, the real causal condition of bondage, the conative idea is lacking. If the external object were by itself capable of producing *karmic* bondage, then it would have identical effect in the case of a saint who moves about with gentleness and caution actuated by the ideal of love and mercy and of a hypocrite in the garb of a saint who roams about rough and tough without any care. That is, both of them must have the same reaction in the environment which is common to both. It is not so as a matter of fact. The saint pure in heart is untouched by sin though he lives in the same environment as the false and hypocritical ascetic who, because of the absence of the purity of thought, is still attached to sensual pleasures and is thus subject to *karmic* bondage. Hence it is not the environmental object but it is the inner thought that is the cause of bondage.

Next the author points out that the thought which is said to be the cause of bondage is false because of the absence of objective evidence to carroborate it.

दुक्खिदसुहिदे जीवे करेमि बंधेमि तह विमोचेमि।
जा एसा मूढमई णिरच्छया सा हु दे मिच्छा॥ २६६॥

dukkhidasuhide jīve karemi baṁdhemi taha vimocemi
jā esā mūḍhamaī ṇiracchayā sā hu de micchā (266)

दुःखितसुखितान् जीवान् करोमि बध्नामि तथा विमोचयामि।
या एषा मूढमतिः निरर्थिका सा खलु ते मिथ्या॥ २६६॥

266. "I make living beings miserable or happy; I bind or release them." Such thought in you is meaningless. Verily it is false.

Commentary : Happiness or misery of a person is entirely dependent upon that person's nature and it cannot be due to any external influence. Hence the proposition, "I make him happy or I make him miserable" is false, because it is uncorroborated by objective reality. Mere assertion of a proposition cannot make it real. It cannot create its own objective evidence of corroboration. If it is possible for the asserted proposition to carry within itself the corroborative evidence of objective reality, then such statements must become real by the mere fact of assertion as, "I am gathering skyflowers." Hence no assertion by itself can carry its own truth-value with it.

Next it is explained how such a thought is without corroborative evidence.

अज्झवसाणणिमित्तं जीवा बज्झंति कम्मणा जदिहि।
मुच्चंति मोक्खमग्गे ठिदा य ते किं करोसि तुमं॥ २६७॥

ajjhavasāṇaṇimittaṁ jīvā bajjhaṁti kammaṇā jadihi
muccaṁti mokkhamagge ṭhidā ya te kiṁ karosi tumaṁ

अध्यवसाननिमित्तं जीवा बध्यन्ते कर्मणा यदि हि।
मुच्यन्ते मोक्षमार्गे स्थितांश्च तत् किं करोषि त्वम्॥ २६७॥

267. If their own thoughts are the real condition by which souls are bound by *karmas* or get released from them while standing on the path of salvation, then what is there that thou canst achieve?

Commentary : The proposition in thought, "I bind or I

release" in order to be true must have as its objective meaning, actual bondage or release of *jīvas*, as corroborative evidence. But as a matter of fact *jīvas* are bound or released according to their own thought– conditions. Another person's thought would be entirely ineffective, therefore, to bind or release other *jīvas*. Hence your thought, "I bind or I release other *jīvas*" is entirely false since it is not corroborated by objective evidence. Hence your claim, "I bind or release other *jīvas*" is only illusory.

Next the author describes the behaviour of one who is deluded by such ineffectual and fruitless thought.

सव्वे करेइ जीवो अज्झवसाणेण तिरियणेरइए।
देवमणुवे य सव्वे पुण्णं पावं च अणेयविहं॥ २६८॥

savve karei jīva ajjhavasāṇeṇa tiriyaṇeraie
devamaṇuve ya savve puṇṇaṁ pāvaṁ ca aṇeyavihaṁ

सर्वान् करोति जीवोऽध्यवसानेन तिर्यङ्नैरयिकान्।
देवमनुजांश्च सर्वान् पुण्यं पापं च नैकविधम्॥ २६८॥

268. The Self, by its own thought activity creates for itself the form of beings—sub-human, hellish, celestial, and human and also various types of virtue and vice.

धम्माधम्मं च तहा जीवाजीवे अलोयलोयं च।
सव्वे करेइ जीवो अज्झवसाणेण अप्पाणं॥ २६९॥

dhammādhammaṁ ca tahā jīvājīve aloyaloyaṁ ca
savve karei jīvo ajjhavasāṇeṇa appāṇaṁ (269)

धर्माधर्मं च तथा जीवाजीवौ अलोकलोकं च।
सर्वान् करोति जीव: अध्यवसानेन आत्मानम्॥ २६९॥

269. Similarly, the Self through its own thought-activity may identify itself with the categories of *dharma* or *adharma*,

soul, non-soul, the Universe and the Beyond.

Commentary : The will to do a thing makes a person the doer of that act. Thus the will to kill makes him a killer, the will to steal makes him a thief and so on. Thus a particular conative tendency in the Self makes that Self the agent of the corresponding action. Similarly thought condition determining birth as a hell-inhabitant, when ripe, will lead to the birth as a hellish being. Similarly appropriate and efficient thought conditions will make the Self, a celestial or human being. The same appropriate thought activity will cause him to do virtuous deeds or vicious deeds and enjoy happiness or misery. The very same thought activity as a process of knowledge, may bring in the categories of *dharam, adharma,* the world including animate and inanimate objects, and space beyond as objects of knowledge related to Self. But this very same thought vitiated by absence of right knowledge may lead the Self to erroneously identify itself with the various external objects. In all these cases the Self deviates from its own intrinsic nature of purity and gets vitiated by alien influences on account of which the Self through its vitiated thought activity goes astray from his own nature assuming various forms unreal, ephemeral, and impure. Thus the real *ṛṣis* are entirely free from such vicious and erroneous thought activity.

Next it is pointed out that those who are free from such thought activity are not subject to *karmic* bondage.

एदाणि णत्थि जेसिं अज्झवसाणाणि एवमादीणि।
ते असुहेण सुहेण व कम्मेण मुणी ण लिप्पंति॥ २७०॥

edāṇi ṇatthi jesiṁ ajjhavasāṇāṇi evamādīṇi
te asuheṇa suheṇa va kammeṇa muṇī ṇa lippaṁti (270)

एतानि न सन्ति येषामध्यवसानान्येवमादीनि।
तेऽशुभेन शुभेन वा कर्मणा मुनयो न लिप्यन्ति॥ २७०॥

270. The saints, in whom such thought activities are not present, are not contaminated by *karmas*, good or bad.

Commentary : The thought activities mentioned above, occur when the intrinsic nature of the Self is not realised. The realisation of the true Self implies the three aspects. Faith in the ultimate purity of the self, knowledge of the ultimate self, and being identified with that ultimate self—these three aspects constitute the *niścaya ratnatraya*, the three jewels from the higher point of view. The thought activities referred to in the preceding two *gāthās* are not based upon the experience of that Absolute Self. Therefore they are associated with the empirical Self. Empirical Self implies the opposite of the Transcendental Real Self. Therefore the activities of belief, knowledge and conduct of the empirical Self are from the real point of view, erroneous belief, erroneous knowledge and erroneous conduct. Therefore *karmic* bondage results from them. Hence it follows that in the case of a saint equipped with true knowledge of Self, these psychic activities are absent and hence there is no *karmic* bondage.

Next the term *Adhyavasāna* is explained.

बुद्धी ववसाओवि य अज्झवसाणं मदीय विण्णाणं।
एयट्ठमेव सव्वं चित्तं भावो य परिणामो॥ २७१॥

buddhī vavasāovi ya ajjhavasāṇaṁ madīya viṇṇāṇaṁ
eyaṭṭhameva savvaṁ cittaṁ bhāvo ya pariṇāmo (271)

बुद्धिर्व्यवसायोऽपि च अध्यवसानं मतिश्च विज्ञानम्।
एकार्थमेव सर्वं चित्तं भावश्च परिणामः॥ २७१॥

271. *Buddhi* (understanding), *vyavasāya* (resolving), *adhyavasāna* (conative activity), *mati* (thinking), *vijñāna*

(knowing), *citta* (consciousness), *bhāva* (conscious mode), and *pariṇāma* (conscious manifestation)—all these words have the same meaning.

Next the *vyavahāranaya* is denied by the *niścayanaya*.

एवं ववहारणओ पडिसिद्धो जाण णिच्छयणयेण।
णिच्छयणयास्सिदा पुण मुणिणो पावंति णिव्वाणं॥ २७२॥

evaṁ vavahāraṇao paḍisiddho jāṇa ṇicchayaṇayeṇa
ṇicchayaṇayāssidā puṇa muṇiṇo pāvaṁti ṇivvāṇaṁ

एवं व्यवहारनयः प्रतिषिद्धो जानीहि निश्चयनयेन।
निश्चयनयाश्रिताः पुनर्मुनयः प्राप्नुवन्ति निर्वाणम्॥ २७२॥

272. Thus know ye that the practical point of view is contradicted by the real point of view. It is by adopting the real point of view that the saints attain *Nirvāṇa* or Liberation.

Commentary : The (*niścaya*) real point of view is based upon the Self. The (*vyavahāra*) practical point of view is based upon external things. Thus from the real point of view, all the externally conditioned thought activities, because they constitute the causal condition for *karmic* bondage, have to be rejected by the saints who have renounced all. To renounce such thought activities, they have to reject the practical point of view itself since that is based upon external things. Spiritual liberation from *karmic* bondage is possible only by adopting the real point of view. Hence one who wants to reach the goal of *Nirvāṇa* has to adopt the real point of view and reject the practical point of view.

वदसमिदीगुत्तीओ सीलतवं जिणवरेहिं पण्णत्तं।
कुव्वंतो वि अभविओ अण्णाणी मिच्छादिट्ठी दु॥ २७३॥

vadasamidīguttīo sīlatavaṁ jiṇavarehiṁ paṇṇataṁ
kuvvaṁto vi abhavio aṇṇāṇī micchādiṭṭhī du (273)

व्रतसमितिगुप्तयः शीलं तपो जिनवरैः प्रज्ञप्तम्।
कुर्वन्नप्यभव्योऽज्ञानी मिथ्यादृष्टिस्तु॥ २७३॥

273. Persons incapable of spiritual liberation even though they observe vows, carefulness, restraints, rules of conduct and penance as described by the Jinas do remain without true knowledge and are of false faith.

Commentary : Various kinds of religious discipline prescribed by the Jina are from the *vyavahāra* point of view, Hence they constitute *vyavahāra cāritra,* course of conduct prescribed for the ordinary man. These rules of conduct may be observed even by *abhavyas*—persons innately unfit for spiritual salvation. Even though such an *abhavya* practises those rules of conduct, he cannot be considered to be equipped with the three jewels of the higher order which are based upon the nature of the pure Self. Hence his conduct is only of the lower order belonging to the three jewels of the lower order. Hence from the absolute point of view, since the *abhavya* is endowed with the inferior jewels, his faith and knowledge cannot be considered to be of the right kind. Therefore even the successful observance of the rules of conduct does not entitle him to be classed among those of right knowledge and right faith. Hence he must remain *ajñānī* and *mithyādrṣti*.

Even when he is well-versed in the Scriptures, is he still to be called an *ajñānī?* The answer is given in the next *gāthā*.

मोक्खं असद्दहंतो अभवियसत्तो दु जो अधीएज्ज।
पाठो ण करेदि गुणं असद्दहंतस्स णाणं तु॥ २७४॥

mokkhaṁ asaddahaṁto abhaviyasatto du jo adhīejja
pāṭho ṇa karedi guṇaṁ asaddahaṁtassa ṇāṇaṁ tu (274)

मोक्षमश्रद्दधानोऽभव्यसत्त्वस्तु योऽधीयेत।
पाठो न करोति गुणमश्रद्दधानस्य ज्ञानं तु॥ २७४॥

274. An *abhavya,* one unfit for spiritual salvation, has no faith in *mokṣa,* hence thought well-versed in all the scriptures, such a study does not endow him with right knowledge or qualification because of the lack of faith.

Commentary : The reality of *mokṣa* is not believed in by the *abhavya* because he is devoid of the right knowledge of the pure nature of the Self. Therefore he has no belief even in knowledge. Thus devoid of right knowledge and right faith, his mastery of the scriptures cannot make him the real knower and it does no good to him. Thus in spite of his learning, he remains devoid of knowledge.

Has he not, by his observance of the rules of conduct, faith at least in *dharma?* The anser is given in the *gāthā* below.

सद्दहदि य पत्तेदि य रोचेदि य तह पुणो य फासेदि।
धम्मं भोगणिमित्तं णहु सो कम्मक्खयणिमित्तं॥ २७५॥

saddahadi ya pattedi ya rocedi ya taha puṇo ya phāsedi
dhammaṁ bhogaṇimittaṁ ṇahu so
kammakkhayaṇimittaṁ (275)

श्रद्दधाति च प्रत्येति च रोचयति च तथा पुनश्च स्पृशति।
धर्मं भोगनिमित्तं न खलु स कर्मक्षयनिमित्तम्॥ २७५॥

275. No doubt he has faith in (a kind of) *dharma,* he acquires it, he delights in it and practises it. But it is all with the object of future enjoyment, certainly not for (that *dharma* which leads to the) destruction of *karmas.*

Next *mokṣa- mārga,* path of salvation is described from the *vyavahāra* and niścaya points of view, the former to be rejected and the latter to be adopted.

आयारादीणाणं जीवादीदंसणं च विण्णेयं।
[1]छज्जीवणिकायं च तहा भणइ चरित्तं तु ववहारो॥ २७६॥

āyārādīṇāṇaṁ jīvādīdaṁsaṇaṁ ca viṇṇeyaṁ
chajjīvāṇikāyaṁ ca tahā bhaṇai carittaṁ tu vavahāro

आचारादिज्ञानं जीवादिदर्शनं च विज्ञेयम्।
षट् जीवनिकायं च तदा भणति चरित्रं तु व्यवहारः॥ २७६॥

276. Let it be known that (knowledge of the scriptures such as) *Ācārāṅga* is right knowledge. (faith in the categories of) *jīva* etc., is right faith. (Protection of) the six kinds of organisms is right conduct. These, it is said, constitute *vyavahāra (mokṣamārga)*—the path of salvation from the practical point of view).

आदा खु मज्झ णाणं आदा मे दंसणं चरित्तं च।
आदा पच्चक्खाणं आदा मे संवरो जोगो॥ २७७॥

ādā khu majjha ṇāṇaṁ ādā me daṁsaṇaṁ carittaṁ ca
ādā paccakkhāṇaṁ ādā me saṁvaro jogo (277)

आत्मा खलु मम ज्ञानमात्मा मे दर्शनं चरित्रं च।
आत्मा प्रत्याख्यानं आत्मा में संवरो योगः॥ २७७॥

277. Whereas the Self is my right knowledge, the Self is my right faith, the Self again is my right conduct. The Self is renunciation, the Self is the stoppage of *karmas* and *yogic* meditation. (These constitute the *niśaya mokṣa mārga*, or Path of Salvation from the real point of view).

Emotional states such as attachment are the cause of bondage. They are alien to the nature of the pure Self. Then how do they occur in the consciousness of the Self? Do they

---

१. छज्जीवाणं च तहा

result from direct manisfestation of the Self or are they caused by alien influences? This question is answered in the succeeding *gāthās*.

जह फलियमणि सुद्धो ण सयं परिणमइ रायमाईहिं।
राइज्जदि अण्णेहिं दु सो रत्तादीहिं दव्वेहिं॥ २७८॥

jaha phaliyamaṇi suddho ṇa sayaṁ pariṇamai rāyamāīhiṁ
rāijjadi aṇṇehiṁ du so rattadīhiṁ davvehiṁ (278)

यथा स्फटिकमणिः शुद्धो न स्वयं परिणमते रागाद्यैः।
रज्यतेऽन्यैस्तु स रक्तादिभिर्द्रव्यैः॥ २७८॥

एवं णाणी सुद्धो ण सयं परिणमइ रायमाईहिं।
राइज्जदि अण्णेहिं दु सो रागादीहिं दोसेहिं॥ २७९॥

evaṁ ṇāṇī suddho ṇa sayaṁ pariṇamai rāyamāīhiṁ
rāijjadi aṇṇehiṁ du so rāgādīhiṁ dosehiṁ (279)

एवं ज्ञानी शुद्धो न स्वयं परिणमते रागाद्यैः।
रज्यतेऽन्यैस्तु स रागादिभिर्दोषैः॥ २७९॥

278-279. As a piece of crystal, itself being pure and colourless, cannot appear red-coloured of its own accord, but in association with another red-coloured object, it appears coloured-red; in the same way the Self, himself being pure cannot have emotional activities such as attachment, etc., of his own accord. But when influenced by alien impurities, he gets tainted by such impure emotions of attachments, etc.

It is next pointed out that one who knows the real nature of things realises that the Self, the Knower, is not the cause of the impure psychic states such as attachment, etc.

ण य रायदोसमोहं कुव्वदि णाणी कसायभावं वा।
सयमप्पणो ण सो तेण कारगो तेसिं भावाणं ॥ २८०॥

ṇa ya rāyadosamohaṁ kuvvadi ṇāṇī kasāyabhāvaṁ vā
sayamappaṇo ṇa so teṇa kārago tesiṁ bhāvāṇaṁ (280)

न च रागद्वेषमोहं करोति ज्ञानी कषायभावं वा।
स्वयमेवात्मनो न स तेन कारकस्तेषां भावानाम्॥ २८०॥

280. The knower does not of his own accord produce in himself attachment, aversion, delusion and such other grosser emotions. Hence he is not the causal agent for those psychic states.

Next it is pointed out that the ego devoid of the knowledge of the reals and immersed in nescience is causally responsible for such impure psychic states.

रागम्हिय दोसम्हिय कसायकम्मेसु चेव जे भावा।
तेहिं दु परिणमंतो रागादी बंधदि पुणोवि॥ २८१॥

rāgamhiya dosamhiya kasāyakammesu ceva je bhāvā
tehiṁ du pariṇamaṁto rāgādī baṁdhadi puṇovi (281)

रागे च द्वेषे च कषायकर्मसु चैव ये भावाः।
तैस्तु परिणममानो रागादीन् बध्नाति पुनरपि॥ २८१॥

281. When the material *karmas* pertaining to attachment, aversion, and grosser emotions begin to operate, the empirical ego begins to have corresponding psychic states. These psychic manifestations of attachment. etc., of which he is the causal agent, do produce in their turn fresh *karmic* bondage.

रागम्हिय दोसम्हिय कसायकम्मेसु चेव जे भावा।
[1]तेहिं दु परिणमंतो रागादी बंधदे चेदा॥ २८२॥

rāgamhiya dosamhiya kasāyakammesu ceva je bhāvā
tehiṁ du pariṇamaṁto rāgādī baṁdhade cedā (282)

रागे च दोषे च कषायकर्मसु चैव ये भावाः।
तैस्तु परिणममानो रागादीन् बध्नाति चेतयिता॥ २८२॥

282. The empirical ego which is manifesting in the psychic states of attachment, aversion, and grosser emotions and which identifies itself with those psychic states gets bound by corresponding fresh *karmic* matter.

Next the author points out that the Self is not the causal agent for the emotion of attachment, etc.

अपडिक्कमणं दुविहं अपच्चक्खाणं तहेव विण्णेयं।
एएणुवएसेण य अकारओ वण्णिओ चेया॥ २८३॥

apaḍikkamaṇaṁ duvihaṁ apaccakkhāṇaṁ taheva viṇṇeyaṁ
eeṇuvaesena ya akārao vaṇṇio ceyā (283)

अप्रतिक्रमणं द्विविधमप्रत्याखानं तथैव विज्ञेयम्।
एतेनोपदेशेन तु अकारको वर्णितश्चेतयिता॥ २८३॥

283. Non-repentance is of two kinds and non-renunciation also should be known to be similar. By such teaching the Self of the nature of consciousness is said to be not their causal agent.

अपडिक्कमणं दुविहं दव्वे भावे तहा अपच्चक्खाणं।
एएणुवएसेण य अकारओ वण्णिओ चेया॥ २८४॥

apaḍikkamaṇaṁ duvihaṁ davve bhāve tahā apaccakkhāṇaṁ
eeṇuvaeseṇa ya akārao vaṇṇio ceyā (284)

अप्रतिक्रमणं द्विवधं द्रव्ये भावे तथाप्रत्याख्यानम्।
एतेनोपदेशेन तु अकारको वर्णितश्चेतयिता॥ २८४॥

284. Non-repentance is of two kinds, physical and

psychical and so also non-renunciation; by such teaching the Self of the nature of consciousness is said to be not their causal agent.

जावं अपडिक्कमणं अपच्चक्खणं च दव्वभावाणं।
कुव्वइ आदा तावं कत्ता सो होइ णायव्वो॥ २८५॥

jāvaṁ apaḍikkamaṇaṁ apaccakkhaṇaṁ ca davvabhāvāṇaṁ
kuvvai ādā tāvaṁ kattā so hoi ṇāyavvo (285)

यावदप्रतिक्रमणमप्रत्याख्यानं च द्रव्यभावयो:।
करोत्यात्मा तावत्कर्त्ता स भवति ज्ञातव्य:॥ २८५॥

285. So long as the Self does not practise renunciation and repentance, both physical and psychical, it should be understood that he is the causal agent of *karmas*.

Commentary : *Praitikramaṇa* implies confession and repentance for past misdeeds. *Apratikramaṇa,* therefore, means instead of confession and repentance, recalling to memory the past experiences with implicit approval. This recalling to memory the past impure experience is of two kinds, psychical and physical. *Pratyākhyāna* implies restraining or abstaining from a desire for future sensual enjoyment. *Apratyākhyāna* is its opposite. It means the absence of that restraint and hence an uninhibited longing for future pleasures. This is also of two kinds material and psychical. The material *karmic* condition produces the corresponding psychic states of emotion either approving the past experience or longing for future pleasures. The causal relation therefore exists between the material aspect and the psychical aspect; and these two aspects of *apratikramaṇa* and *apratyākhyāna,* since they imply the operation of material *karmas* and the appearance of psychic *karma*, have no relation to the pure Self of the nature of consciousness. Hence the pure Self cannot be considered as the causal agent of these two types of *karma.* This is the Message of the Scriptures. But when the pure Self forgets its own real nature and identifies itself with the grosser emotions of the empirical ego, he is not able to repent for the past experiences, nor refrain from the future ones. So long as he is thus spiritually incapacitated to wipe out the past and to reject the future, he feels himself responsible for all those impure emotions caused by *karmic* materials and thus he becomes the *kartā* or the causal agent of those experiences.

How the material condition can produce psychic states operating as *nimitta* and how the Self is concerned or related to this causal process is elucidated by an example taken from ordinary life.

आधाकम्मादीया पोग्गलदव्वस्स जे इमे दोसा।
कह ते कुव्वइ णाणी परदव्वगुणाउ जे णिच्चं॥ २८६॥

ādhākammādīyā poggaladavvassa je ime dosā
kaha te kuvvi ṇīṇī paradavvaguṇāu je ṇiccaṁ (286)

अध:कर्माद्या: पुद्गलद्रव्यस्य य इमे दोषा:।
कथं तान्करोति ज्ञानी परद्रव्यगुणास्तु ये नित्यम्॥ २८६॥

286. How can the Self, the Knower, cause these defects in the material things used in the preparation of food since those are the attributes of external objects.

आधाकम्मं उद्देसियं च पोग्गलमयं इमं दव्वं।
कह तं मम हो कयं जं णिच्चमचेयणं वुत्तं॥ २८७॥

ādhākammaṁ uddesiyaṁ ca poggalamayaṁ imaṁ davvaṁ
kaha taṁ mama ho kayaṁ jaṁ ṇiccamaceyaṇaṁ vuttaṁ

अध:कर्मौद्देशिकं च पुद्गलमयमिदम् द्रव्यम्।
कथं तन्मम भवति कृतं यन्नित्यमचेतनमुक्तम्॥ २८७॥

287. Even when food is prepared by others for me, the things used are material in nature. How can these defects be considered to be caused by me when they really pertain to inanimate objects.

Commentary : In the case of the householder as well as the ascetic there are important principles prescribed in the matter of food. Only what is called *pavitra-āhāra* or pure food is fit to be eaten by them. But in the matter of preparing food there are various possibilities of defects occuring therein. The articles used may be defective and may vitiate the quality of food prepared therefrom. The necessary things used for preparing food such as water, fire, etc., because of careless selection may also vitiate the food prepared. Whether the preparation is made by yourself or by a cook under your instructions, the defects which may be present in the food prepared and which make it unfit for consumption are all defects of material articles utilised in the preparation of food. The articles used for the preparation together with the person engaged in cooking are all external conditions to you. Food prepared forms the effect of all these external causal conditions and this is also external,—the whole process of causal conditions resulting in the form of effect. The prepared food is completely external to the person who is going to consume the food. He is not concerned in the series of operating causes and the resulting effect. Therefore he is neither concerned in the production of the defects present in the food, nor is he responsible for the same. They all pertain to material inanimate objects in the external world. But if he accepts that food which is defective and unfit for consumption with the full knowledge of the fact that defective articles were used and there was carelessness in preparation thereof, he becomes responsible for those defects, and he is therefore subject to demerit thereof. But if he rejects that food, he is not responsible for the defects and therefore he will remain uninfluenced by the demerits thereof. This illustration is quite parallel to the previous case where the material *karmic* conditions produce corresponding psychic states of an impure nature. These impure psychic states, since they are produced by material *karmic* conditions which are different in nature from the Self and also external to it, both the cause and effect remain external and alien to the Self. Therefore the pure Self is not directly concerned in this causal series and hence is not responsible for the defects and impurities present in the result. He can maintain this unconcernedness and indifference only by the practice of *pratikramaṇa* and *pratyākhyāna,* disowning the past and rejecting the future occurrence of those impure psychic states. If on the other hand, the Self by abandoning the spiritual discipline imposed by *pratikramaṇa* and *pratyākhyāna,* identifies itself with the past impure emotions and readily commits himself to future similar indulgences, he becomes fully responsible for the defects thereof, and therefore gets bound by corresponding karmas. This case, is therefore analogous to the case where the person accepts the defective and impure food though he is not concerned with the preparation thereof.

Thus ends the chapter on *bandha* or Bondage.

Thus *bandha* quits the stage.

CHAPTER IX

MOKSA OR LIBERATION

Then *Mokṣa* enters the stage.

जह णाम कोवि पुरिसो बंधणयम्मि चिरकालपडिबद्धो।
तिव्वं मंदसहावं कालं च वियाणए तस्स॥ २८८॥

jaha ṇāma kovi puriso baṁdhaṇayammi cirakālapaḍibaddho
tivvaṁ maṁdasahāvaṁ kālaṁ ca viyāṇae tassa (288)

यथा नाम कश्चित्पुरुषो बन्धनके चिरकालप्रतिबद्धः।
तीव्रं मन्दस्वभावं कालं च विजानाति तस्य॥ २८८॥

जइ णवि कुणइ छेदं ण मुच्चए तेण बंधणवसो सं।
कालेण उ बहुएणवि ण सो णरो पावइ विमोक्खं॥ २८९॥

jai ṇavi kuṇai chedaṁ ṇa muccaye teṇa baṁdhaṇavaso saṁ
kāleṇa u bahueṇavi ṇa so ṇaro pāvai vimokkhaṁ (289)

यदि नापि करोति छेदं न मुच्यते तेन बन्धेनावशः सन्।
कालेन तु बहुकेनापि न स नरः प्राप्नोति विमोक्षम॥ २८९॥

इय कम्मबंधणाणं पयेसपयडिट्ठिदीयअणुभागं।
जाणंतो वि ण मुंचइ मुंचइ सो चेव जइ सुद्धो॥ २९०॥

iya kammabaṁdhaṇāṇaṁ payesapayaḍiṭṭhidīya-
aṇubhāgaṁ
jāṇaṁto vi ṇa muṁcai muṁcai so ceva jai suddho (290)

इति कर्मबन्धानां प्रदेशप्रकृतिस्थित्यनुभागम्।
जानन्नपि न मुञ्चति मुञ्चति स चैव यदि शुद्धः ॥ २९० ॥

288-290. As a person, who has been in shackles for a long time may be aware of the nature of his bondage, intense or feeble, and also its duration; still so long as he does not make any effort to break them, he does not get himself free from the chains, and may have to remain so for a long time without obtaining freedom. Similarly a person with *karmic* bondage, even if he has the knowledge of the extent, the nature, the duration, and the strength of the *karmic* bondage, does not get liberation (by this mere knowledge) but he gets complete liberation if pure in heart.

Commentary : Separating the Self and bondage from each other is called *mokṣa.* Some maintain that mere knowledge of the nature of this bondage is able to produce *mokṣa;* or liberation. But this is wrong. Just as in the case of a person in chains, mere knowledge of the chain is ineffectual in securing his freedom, so also the mere knowledge of the nature of *karmic* bondage is ineffectual in securing his spiritual liberation.

Next it is pointed out that mere thinking about the process and development of *karmic* bondage does not lead to the liberation of the Self.

जह बंधे चिंततो बंधणबद्धो ण पावइ विमोक्खं।
तह बंधे चिंततो जीवो वि ण पावइ विमोक्खं॥ २९१ ॥

jaha baṁdhe ciṁtaṁto baṁdhaṇabaddho ṇa pāvai
vımokkhaṁ
taha baṁdhe ciṁtaṁto jīvo vi ṇa pāvai vimokkhaṁ (291)

यथा बन्धं चिंतयन् बन्धनबद्धो न प्राप्नोति विमोक्षम्।
तथा बन्धं चिंतयन् जीवोऽपि न प्राप्नोति विमोक्षम्॥ २९१॥

291. As by (merely) thinking of bondage one bound in shackles does not get release, so also the Self by merely thinking of (*karmic*) bondage does not attain *mokṣha.*

Commentary : Others maintain that the concentration of mind on the idea of bondage is itself the cause of *mokṣa* or spiritual liberation. This view also is wrong. By mere concentration of thought on bondage one cannot obtain liberation, just as concentrated attention on the shackles cannot get freedom for the person in chains.

What then is the cause of liberation? The answer is given below.

जह बंधे छित्तूण य बंधणबद्धो उ पावइ विमोक्खं।
तह बंधे छित्तूण य जीवो संपावइ विमोक्खं॥ २९२॥

jaha baṁdhe chittūṇa ya baṁdhaṇabaddho u pāvai vimokkhaṁ
taha baṁdhe chittūṇa ya jīvo saṁpāvai vimokkhaṁ (292)

यथा बन्धं छित्वा च बन्धनबद्धस्तु प्राप्नोति विमोक्षम्।
तथा बन्धं छित्वा च जीवः सम्प्राप्नोति विमोक्षम्॥ २९२॥

292. As one bound in shackles gets release only on breaking the shackles, so also the Self attains emancipation only by breaking (*karmic*) bondage.

How is this to be effected? The method is shown below.

बंधाणं च सहावं वियाणिओ अप्पणो सहावं च।
बंधेसु जो विरज्जदि सो कम्मविमोक्खणं कुणइ॥ २९३॥

baṁdhāṇaṁ ca sahāvaṁ viyāṇio appaṇo sahāvaṁ ca
baṁdhesu jo virajjadi so kammavimokkhaṇaṁ kuṇai

बन्धानां च स्वभावं विज्ञायात्मन: स्वभावं च।
बन्धेषु यो विरज्यते स कर्मविमोक्षणं करोति॥ २९३॥

293. Whoever with a clear knowledge of the nature of *karmic* bondage as well as the nature of the Self, does not get attracted by bondage—that person obtains liberation from *karmas*.

Commentary : Thus the direct cause of liberation is determined to be the separation of the Self and the bondage from each other.

जीवो बंधोय तहा छिज्जंति सलक्खणेहिं णियएहिं।
पण्णाछेदणएण उ छिण्णा णाणत्तमावण्णा॥ २९४॥

jīvo baṁdhoya tahā chijjaṁti salakkhaṇehiṁ ṇiyaehiṁ
paṇṇāchedaṇaeṇa u chiṇṇā ṇāṇattamāvaṇṇā (294)

जीवो बन्धश्च तथा छिद्येते स्वलक्षणाभ्यां नियताभ्याम्।
प्रज्ञाछेदनकेन तु छिन्नौ नानात्वमापन्नौ॥ २९४॥

294. The Self and bondage are differentiated by their intrinsic and distinctive features; cut through by the instrument of discriminative wisdom, they fall apart.

Commentary : The attribute of the Self is pure consciousness and the attribute of bondage is the impure emotions of anger, etc., based upon wrong belief. These two by association get identified with each other. This identification of the Self with impure emotions due to *karmic* bondage is the foundation of the empirical Self in *saṁsāra*. These two entities, the Self and *karmic* bondage, characterised by their own intrinsic properties are linked together from time immemorial. This unholy alliance must be broken up. What is the effective instrument to cut these two apart? Such an instrument is said to be the discriminative wisdom. This discriminative wisdom fully realises the pure nature of the Self and its intrinsic difference from the impure emotions due to bondage, and aids the Self to reject the latter and to extricate itself. This process of isolating the Self *karmic* emotions, when once effected through discriminative wisdom, keeps the two entities permanently apart.

What ought to be done, after the separation of Self and bondage is effected, is indicated below.

जीवो बंधोय तहा छिज्जंति सलक्खणेहिं णियएहिं।
बंधो छेययव्वो सुद्धो अप्पाय घित्तव्वो॥ २९५॥

jīvo baṁdhoya tahā chijjaṁti salakkhaṇehiṁ ṇiyaehiṁ
baṁdho cheyayavvo suddho appāya ghittavvo (295)

जीवो बन्धश्च तथा छिद्येते स्वलक्षणाभ्यां नियताभ्याम्।
बन्धश्छेत्तव्य: शुद्ध आत्मा च गृहीतव्य:॥ २९५॥

295. When the Self and bondage which are differentiated by their intrinsic and distinctive attributes, are thus separted, then by completely casting away all bondage, the pure Self ought to be realised.

Thus it is emphasised that the very object of separating the two is to realise the pure Self by shaking of all bondage. Next it is pointed out how this object of self-realisation is to be achieved.

कह सो घिप्पइ अप्पा पण्णाए सो उ घिप्पए अप्पा।
जह पण्णाए विभत्तो तह पण्णा एव घित्तव्वो॥ २९६॥

kaha so ghippai appā paṇṇāe so u ghippae appā
jaha paṇṇāe vibhatto taha paṇṇā eva ghittavvo (296)

कथं स गृह्यते आत्मा प्रज्ञया स तु गृह्यते आत्मा।
यथा प्रज्ञया विभक्तस्तथा प्रज्ञयैव गृहीतव्य:॥ २९६॥

296. How is the Self realised? The Self is realised by discriminative wisdom. Just as he is separated by discriminative wisdom, so also by the very same discriminative wisdom he is realised.

How is the Self realised through discriminative wisdom? The answer is given below.

पण्णाए घित्तव्वो जो चेदा सो अहं तु णिच्छयदो।
अवसेसा जे भावा ते मज्झ परे त्ति णायव्वा॥ २९७॥

paṇṇāe ghittavvo jo cedā so ahaṁ tu ṇicchayado
avasesā je bhāvā te majjha pare tti ṇāyavvā (297)

प्रज्ञया गृहीतव्यो यश्चेतयिता सोऽहं तु निश्चयतः।
अवशेषा ये भावास्ते मम परा इति ज्ञातव्याः॥ २९७॥

297. That (pure) conscious being which is apprehended by discriminative wisdom is in reality the 'I'. Whatever mental states remain (besides) are all to be known to be other than 'mine'.

Just like pure consciousness, pure perception and pure knowledge are described to be the intrinsic attributes of the pure Self.

पण्णाए घित्तव्वो जो दट्ठा सो अहं तु णिच्छयदो।
अवसेसा जे भावा ते मज्झ परे त्ति णायव्वा॥ २९८॥

paṇṇāe ghittavvo jo daṭṭhā so ahaṁ tu ṇicchayado
avasesā je bhāvā te majjha pare tti ṇāyavvā (298)

प्रज्ञया गृहीतव्यो यो दृष्टा सोऽहं तु निश्चयतः।
अवशेषा ये भावास्ते मम परा इति ज्ञातंव्याः॥ २९८॥

298. That seer who is apprehended by discriminative wisdom is in reality the 'I.' Whatever mental states remain (besides) are all to be known to be other than 'mine'.

पण्णाए घित्तव्वो जो णादा सो अहं तु णिच्छयदो।
अवसेसा जे भावा ते मज्झ परे त्ति णायव्वा॥ २९९॥

paṇṇāe ghittavvo jo ṇādā so ahaṁ tu nicchayado
avasesā je bhāvā te majjha pare tti ṇāyavvā (299)

प्रज्ञया गृहीतव्यो यो ज्ञाता सोऽहं तु निश्चयतः।
अवशेषा ये भावास्ते मम परा इति ज्ञातव्याः॥ २९९॥

299. That knower, who is apprehended by discriminative wisdom is in reality the 'I'. Whatever mental states remain (besides) are all to be known to be other than 'mine'.

Commentary : If the pure Self is of the nature of conscious unity, how can he be the seer and the knower? Is not his nature transcending these two aspects? No, perception and knowledge are not attributes to be transcended by the supreme consciousness because they are the attributes of the supreme consciousness itself. If the supreme consciousness is to transcend these attributes, it will become an empty abstraction, for there can be no reality without attributes. This universal postulate, no reality without its attributes, is applicable to the supreme reality also. Hence an attributeless reality is mere nothing. Again if it is assumed for argument's sake, that a general substratum can exist even after the elimination of its attributes, even then, the position would be untenable. For consciousness devoid of the attributes of perception and knowledge will become practically a non-conscious entity which cannot be the nature of the Supreme Self. Hence perception and knowledge inasmuch as they are attributes resulting from the manifestation of pure consciousness must be considered to be the intrinsic properties of the pure Self, since manifesting entity cannot be different from the manifestation.

Thus, though the pure Self is to be considered apart from the characteristics of empirical consciousness, it should not be abstracted from all attributes as is done by the Vedāntin. The Vedāntin relying upon the fact that the characteristics and attributes of the empirical ego are entirely alien to the nature of the Supreme Self, justifiably places the Supreme Self quite beyond the empirical properties. Swāmi Kundakunda also emphasises the same fact when he says that all other mental attributes are entirely alien to 'me'. This justifiable denial of the empirical impure attributes to the Supreme Self is immediately followed by the prediction of the attributes of pure perception and knowledge which are present in the Supreme Self even after transcending the empirical nature. Of course it should not be misunderstood that these properties of perception and knowledge are the same as the process of perceiving and knowing associated with the empirical ego. In the latter case though the properties are called by the same names, they are entirely limited by physical conditions; whereas the pure perception and pure knowledge associated with the Supreme Self are the unconditioned and unlimited manifestation of the Supreme Self. Thus it should be noted that the Advaitin, though he keeps company with Bhagavān Kunda kunda to a considerable distance in the path of metaphysical investigation, ultimately parts company and walks to a different goal. Thus in short the Supreme Self of Sri Kundakunda is not the same as the Supreme Self of the other schools.

Next it is pointed out that a person who is equipped with this kind of discriminative wisdom, will not consider alien mental states to be his own.

को णाम भणिज्ज बुहो णाउं सव्वे परोयये भावे।
मज्झमिणं ति य वयणं जाणंतो अप्पयं सुद्धं॥ ३००॥

ko nāma bhaṇijja buho ṇāuṁ savve paroyaye bhāve
majjhamiṇaṁ ti ya vayaṇaṁ jānaṁto appayaṁ suddhaṁ

को नाम भणेत् बुध: ज्ञात्वा सर्वान् परोदयान् भावान्।
ममेदमिति च वचनं जानन्नात्मानं शुद्धम्॥ ३००॥

300. What wise man knowing the nature of the pure Self and understanding all the mental states caused by alien conditions would utter the words, "These are mine?"

That the Self which identifies itself with the external object, is subject to *karmic* bondage is explained by an illustration from ordinary life.

तेयाई अवराहे जो कुव्वइ सो उ संकिदो भमइ।
मा वज्झेहं केणवि चोरोत्ति जणम्मि वियरंतो॥ ३०१॥

teyāī avarāhe jo kuvvai so u saṁkido bhamai
mā vajjhehaṁ keṇavi corotti jaṇammi viyaraṁto (301)

स्तेयादीनपराधान् य: करोति स तु शङ्कितो भ्रमति।
मा बंध्ये केनापि चौर इति जने विचरन्॥ ३०१॥

301. He who commits crimes such as theft, while moving among the people, is troubled by anxiety and fear, "I may be arrested at any moment as a thief."

जो ण कुणइ अवराहे सो णिस्संको उ जणवए भमइ।
णवि तस्स वज्झिदुं जे चिंता उपज्जइ कयावि॥ ३०२॥

jo ṇa kuṇai avarāhe so ṇissaṁko u jaṇavae bhamai
ṇavi tassa vajjhiduṁ je ciṁtā uppajjai kayāvi (302)

यो न करोत्यपराधान् स नि:शङ्कस्तु जनपदे भ्रमति।
नापि तस्य बद्धुं य: चिन्तोत्पद्यते कदाचित्॥ ३०२॥

302. But one who commits no such crime freely moves among the people without any such anxiety. Because in his

case no thought of arrest ever occurs.

एवं हि सावराहो वज्झामि अहं तु संकिदो चेया।
जइ पुण णिरवराहो णिस्संकोहं ण वज्झामि॥ ३०३॥

evaṁ hi sāvarāho vajjhāmi ahaṁ tu saṁkido ceyā
jai puṇa ṇiravarāho ṇissaṁkohaṁ ṇa vajjhami (302)

एवं अस्मि सापराधो बध्येऽहं तु शङ्कितश्चेतयिता।
यदि पुनर्निरपराधो नि:शङ्कोऽहं न बध्ये॥ ३०३॥

303. Similarly the Self which is guilty always has the fear, "I may be bound," whereas if guiltless, the Self feels, "I am fearless and hence I may not be bound."

Commentary : It is the law of the State that the criminal should be detected and punished, Hence the criminal who commits theft always moves in society with a guilty conscience and ultimately he may get arrested, punished and imprisoned. Whereas a person who lives in society honourably without coveting others' property always moves about freely without fear of being arrested. The same analogy holds good in the case of Self. The Self which commits the mistake of claiming alien characteristics as his own is bound to face the consequences thereof, that is, *karmic* bondage. Whereas the Self that disowns all such impure states as alien has the privilege of remaining free from bondage.

Next the auther explains the term *aparādha* or guilt.

संसिद्धिराधसिद्धं साधियमाराधियं च एयट्ठं।
अवगयराधो जो खलु चेया सो होइ अवराहो॥ ३०४॥

saṁsiddhirādhasiddhaṁ sādhiyamārādhiyaṁ ca eyaṭṭhaṁ
avagayarādho jo khalu ceyā so hoi avarāho (304)

संसिद्धिराधसिद्धं साधितमाराधितं चैकार्थम्।
अपगतराधो य: खलु चेतयिता स भवत्यपराध:॥ ३०४॥

304. *Samsiddhi* (attainment), *rādha* (devotion to Self) *sidhi* (fulfilment), *sādhitam* (achievement), *ārādhitam* (adoration), are synonymous. When the soul is devoid of devotion to Pure Self, then he is certainly guilty.

जो पुण णिरवराहो चेया णिस्संकिओ उ सो होइ।
आराहणाए णिच्चं वट्टइ अहमिदि जाणंतो॥ ३०५॥

jo puṇa ṇiravarāho ceyā ṇissaṁkio u so hoi.
ārādaṇāe ṇiccaṁ vaṭṭai ahamidi jāṇaṁto (305)

यः पुनर्निरपराधश्चेतयिता निश्शंकितस्तु स भवतु।
आराधनया नित्यं वर्तते अहमिति जानन्॥ ३०५॥

305. When the soul is free from guilt, he is also free from fear. Thus realising the ego, he is ever engaged in adoration of the Self.

How is the pure spotless state of Self to be realised? Is it by concentrated adoration of the Pure self or by the practice of various kinds of moral discipline such as *pratikramaṇa*, etc.? The answer is given below.

पडिकमणं पडिसरणं परिहारो[१] धारणा णियत्ती य।
णिंदा गुरुहा सोही अट्ठविहो होई विसकुंभो॥ ३०६॥

paḍikamaṇaṁ paḍisaraṇaṁ parihāro dhāraṇā ṇiyattī ya
ṇiṁdā garuhā sohī aṭṭhaviho hoi visakuṁbho (306)

प्रतिक्रमणं प्रतिसरणं परिहारो धारणा निवृत्तिश्च।
निन्दा गर्हा शुद्धिरष्टविधो भवति विषकुम्भः॥ ३०६॥

306. *Pratikramaṇa* (repentance for past misconduct), *pratisaraṇaṁ* (pursuit of the good), *parihāra* (rejecting the evil), *dharaṇā* (concentration), *nivritti* (abstinance from attachment to external objects), *nindā* (self-censure), *garhā*

१. परिहारा धारणा णियत्तीय

(confessing before the master) and *śuddhi* (purification by expiation), these eight kinds constitute the pot of poison.

अपडिक्कमणं अपडिसरणं अपरिहारो अधारणा चेव।
अणियत्ती य अणिंदा अगरुहासोही अमयकुंभो॥ ३०७॥

apaḍikkamaṇaṁ apaḍisaraṇaṁ apariharo adhāraṇā ceva
aṇiyattī ya aṇiṁdā agaruhāsohi amayakuṁbho *(307)*

अतिक्रमणमप्रतिसरणमपरिहारोऽधारणा चैव।
अनिवृत्तिश्चानिन्दागर्हाशुद्धिरमृतकुम्भ: ॥ ३०७ ॥

307. Non-repentance for past misconduct, non-pursuit of the good, non-rejecting the evil, non-concentration, non abstinence from attachment to external objects, non-selfcensure, non-confessing before the master, and non-purification by expiation, these eight kinds constitute the pot of nectar.

Commentary : These two *gāthās* by their paradoxical statement, will be a shock from the ordinary point of view. In the case of an empirical Self, the uncontrolled rush of emotions must be kept under restraint For achieving this purpose, the eight kinds of discipline, *pratikramaṇa* etc., become necessary and desirable. Since they promote the achievement of the good they must be said to constitute the pot of nectar. Whereas the lack of the eight-fold discipline must constitute the opposite that is the pot of poison since there is a free vent to evil. This ordinary description is reversed in the two *gāthās* by Sri Kundakunda. He is thinking of the transcendental Self which is quite beyond the region of good and evil. Hence the question of discipline or non-discipline is meaningless. And hence in the case of the supremely pure state of the Self, to talk of *pratikramaṇa*, etc., is to drag it down to the empirical level and to postulate the possibility of occurrence of impure emotions which ought to be disciplined and controlled. Hence to talk of *pratikramaṇa,* etc., in this state will be a positive evil. Hence the revered author considers the various kinds of moral discipline to be things to be avoided and calls them poison- pot. Then what is the significance of the opposite, *apratikramaṇa* etc. which are described to constitute the pot of nectar? Here the term *aparatikramaṇa* implies not the mere opposite of *pratikramaṇa.* The mere opposite of *pratikramaṇa* would imply removing emotions towards the focus of attention. That would be positive degradation of the Self. Hence this interpretation of the term would be inapplicable to the pure Self in the transcendental region. Therefore the negative prefix in the words *apratikramaṇa,* etc. must be taken to signify the absence of necessity to practise the discipline. When the self is absorbed in its own pure nature by attaining the yogic *samādhi,* there is a full stop to the series of impure psychic states characteristic of the empirical Self. Hence there is no necessity to practise the various kinds of discipline. The very absence of those disciplinary practises produces spiritual peace that passes understanding. It is in that stage there is the pot of nectar. Such a spiritual peace necessarily implies spiritual bliss which is the characteristic of the Supreme Self.

Thus ends the chapter on *mokṣa.*

Here *mokṣa* quits the stage.

CHAPTER X

ALL-PURE KNOWLEDGE

Now Enters All-Pure Knowledge.

That the Self, from the real point of view, is not the doer of *karmas,* is explained below.

दवियं जं उप्पज्जइ गुणेहिं तं तेहिं जाणसु अणण्णं।
जह कडयादीहिं दु पज्जएहिं कणयं अणण्णमिह॥ ३०८॥

daviyaṁ jaṁ uppajjai guṇehiṁ taṁ tehiṁ jāṇasu aṇaṇṇaṁ
jaha kaḍayādīhiṁ du pajjaehiṁ kaṇayaṁ aṇaṇṇamiha

द्रव्यं यदुत्पद्यते गुणैस्तत्तैर्जानीह्यनन्यत्।
यथा कटकादिभिस्तु पर्यायैः कनकमनन्यदिह॥ ३०८॥

308. Whatever is produced from a substance, has the same attributes as those of the substance. Know ye : certainly they cannot be different, just as bangles etc. made of gold cannot be other than gold.

जीवस्साजीवस्स दु जे परिणामा दु देसिया सुत्ते।
तं जीवमजीवं वा तेहिमणण्णं वियाणाहि॥ ३०९॥

jīvassājīvassa du je pariṇāmā du desiyā sutte
taṁ jīvamajīvaṁ vā tehimaṇaṇṇaṁ viyāṇāhi (309)

जीवस्याजीवस्य तु ये परिणामास्तु दर्शिताः सूत्रे।
तं जीवमजीवं वा तैरनन्यं विजानीहि॥ ३०९॥

309. Whatever modifications of the Self and the non-Self are described in the scriptures, know ye : that these modifications are identical in nature with the Self and non-Self respectively and not different.

ण कुदोवि विउप्पण्णो जम्हा कज्जं ण तेण सो आदा।
उप्पादेदि ण किंचिवि कारणमवि तेण ण स होइ॥ ३१०॥

ṇa kuḍovi viuppaṇṇo jamhā kajjaṁ ṇa teṇa so ādā
uppādedi ṇa kiṁcivi kāraṇamavi teṇa ṇa sa hoi (310)

न कुतश्चिदप्युत्पन्नो यस्मात्कार्यं न तेन स आत्मा।
उत्पादयति न किंचिदपि कारणमपि तेन न स भवति॥ ३१०॥

310. The Self is not an effect because it is not produced by anything whatever, nor is it a cause because it does not produce anything whatever.

कम्मं पडुच्च कत्ता कत्तारं तह पडुच्च कम्माणि।
उप्पज्जंतिय णियमा सिद्धी दु ण दीसए अण्णा॥ ३११॥

kammaṁ paḍucca kattā kattāraṁ taha paḍucca kammāṇi
uppajjaṁtiya ṇiyamā siddhī du ṇa dīsae aṇṇā (311)

कर्म प्रतीत्य कर्ता कर्तारं तथा प्रतीत्य कर्माणि।
उत्पद्यन्ते च नियमात् सिद्धिस्तु न दृश्यतेऽन्या॥ ३११॥

311. The manifested effect conditions the nature of the manifesting agent and similarly the manifesting agent determines the nature of effects. This is the principle of causation that is observed to operate in the world of reality, and no other principle is evident.

Commentary : Whatever is produced by the direct self—manifestation of *jīva*, the living, being, is also of the nature of the living being, and cannot be a non-living thing. In the same manner whatever is produced by the direct manifestation of the non-living material must also be of the nature of the non-living material, and cannot certainly be of the nature of the living being. Thus all things whether animate or inanimate and their manifested products must be identical in nature just as gold and the ornaments made thereof. Thus no substance can be really responsible as a causal agent for the appearance of objects of entirely different nature. When this principle is admitted, then it necessarily follows that the inanimate effect cannot be caused by the living *jīva*. Hence it follows the *jīva* or the self is *akartā*, that is, he is not a causal agent influencing non-living *karmic* matter. It is only from the un-enlightened point of view that the Self is described as the causal agent, whereas the real and enlightened view takes him to be otherwise.

Next it is pointed out that the bondage of the Self by *karmic* materials is brought about by the wonderful potency of nescience or ajñāna.

चेयाउ पयडियट्ठं उप्पज्जइ विणस्सइ।
पयडी वि चेययट्ठं उपज्जइ विणस्सइ॥ ३१२॥

ceyāu payaḍiyaṭṭhaṁ uppajjai viṇassai
payaḍī vi ceyayaṭṭhaṁ uppajjai viṇassai (312)

चेतयिता प्रकृत्यर्थमुत्पद्यते विनश्यति।
प्रकृतिरपि चेतकार्थमुत्पद्यते विनश्यति॥ ३१२॥

312. The Self is born and dies because of the operation of *karmic prakṛti*. Similarly the *karmic prakṛti* as conditioned by the Self appears and disappears.

एवं बंधो उ दुण्हंपि अण्णोण्णपच्चया हवे।
अप्पणो पयडीए य संसारो तेण जायए॥ ३१३॥

evaṁ baṁdho u duṇhaṁpi aṇṇoṇṇapaccayā have
appaṇo payaḍīe ya saṁsāro teṇa jāyae (313)

एवं बन्धस्तु द्वयोरपि अन्योन्यप्रत्यययोर्भवेत्।
आत्मनः प्रकृतेश्च संसारस्तेन जायते॥ ३१३॥

313. Thus the association of the two, the Self and *karmic prakṛti* is brought about by their mutual determination as the instrumental cause. Thus by them, *saṁsāra* or the cycle of births and deaths, is produced.

Commentary : Birth and death are the intrinsic characteristics of organic beings. An organic being which is subject to birth and death, has two different aspects of existence, bodily and mental. The physical body of the organism is constituted by physical molecules. The other aspect of the organic being, consciousness, which may be present in varying degrees of development, is entirely different from the matter of which its body is made. Hence this element of consciousness is postulated to be the characteristic of a different entity altogether. It is called *jīva* or Soul. Thus an organism in the empirical world is brought about by the combination of two different entities—matter and soul, inanimate and animate categories. How are these two brought together; and how is the behaviour of the organism to be explained? This is the crucial problem facing psychology and metaphysics. Very often an easy solution is attempted by reducing the two categories as derived from the manifestation of one and the same principle. This method of cutting the gordian knot by the monistic metaphysician is not considered to be the correct solution by the Jaina thinkers. The thinking entity, Self, and the inanimate matter are kept distinctly apart and yet they are mutually related in the case of an organic being in the ordinary world. Psychologists in the West who accept the difference between mind and matter, have adopted the psychophysical parallelism to explain the relation between the two. The changes in the body are entirely according to the law of causation pertain to the realm of consciousness. Changes physical and chemical in the material body do not directly produce changes in consciousness and yet physical change and conscious change mysteriously determine each other, each functioning as the external determining condition of the other. An attitude similar to the modern hypothesis of parallelism is adopted by the Jaina thinkers. The body is subject to its own causal law of operation. Consciousness has also it own law of operation and yet one determines the other, operating in the form of *external nimitta* condition. Conscious changes constitute the *nimitta* condition for physical changes. Thus the two causal series, though not directly inter-related are indirectly related to each other; each determining the other only as an external *nimitta* condition. Thus the two series are brought together in the case of an embodied empirical ego who can be said to be born or to have died. The conscious Self, taken by itself in its pure nature, apart from the association of the body is not subject to birth or death. It becomes subject to birth and death only when it gets embodied. The building up of the body of an organic being is supposed to be due to its own mental activity. In the environment there are subtle material particles suitable for building the body. When the Self forgetting its own pure nature manifests in the form of impure psychic states, it causes the building of a body to itself out of the suitable particles in the environment. When once the building up of the body is completed, then begins the career of the empirical Self or *saṁsārī jīva* having a series of births and deaths.

जाएस पयडियट्ठं चेया णेव विमुंचइ।
अयाणओ हवे ताव मिच्छादिट्ठी असंजओ॥ ३१४॥

jāesa payaḍiyaṭṭhaṁ ceyā ṇeva vimuṁcai
ayāṇao have tāva micchādiṭṭhī asaājao (314)

यावदेष प्रकृत्यर्थं चेतयिता नैव विमुञ्चति।
अज्ञायको भवेत्तावन्मिथ्यादृष्टिरसंयत: ॥ ३१४॥

314. So long as the conscious Self does not break this relation to *karmic prakṛti,* he remains without enlightenment, without right belief and without discipline.

जया विमुंचइ चेया कम्मप्फलमणंतयं।
तया विमुत्तो हवइ जाणओ पासओ मुणी॥ ३१५॥

jayā vimuṁcai ceyā kammapphalamaṇaṁtayaṁ
tayā vimutto havai jāṇao pāsao muṇī (315)

यदा विमुञ्चति चेतयिता कर्मफलमनन्तकम्।
तदा विमुक्तो भवति ज्ञायको दर्शको मुनि: ॥ ३१५॥

315. But when the conscious Self breaks up this relation to the infinitely various fruits of *karma,* then the saint becomes endowed with right knowledge and right belief and freedom from *karmas*. But the enlightened one, when the fruits of *karma* begin to appear, does not enjoy them but remains merely a spectator.

Next it is pointed out that just as the real Self is not the producer of *karmas,* he is not the enjoyer of the fruits thereof.

अण्णाणी कम्मफलं पयडिसहावट्ठिओ दु वेदेइ।
णाणी पुण कम्मफलं जाणइ उदिदं ण वेदेइ॥ ३१६॥

aṇṇāṇī kammaphalaṁ payaḍisahāvaṭṭhio du vedei
ṇāṇī puṇa kammaphalaṁ jāṇai udidaṁ ṇa vedei (316)

अज्ञानी कर्मफलं प्रकृतिस्वभावस्थितस्तु वेदयते।
ज्ञानी पुन: कर्मफलं जानाति उदितं न वेदयते॥ ३१६॥

316. The unenlightened Self conditioned by and identifying himself with the nature of the *karmic prakṛti*, enjoys the fruits of *karmas*. But the enlightened one, when the fruits of *karma* begin to appear, does not enjoy them but remains merelý a spectator.

Commentary : The *ajñānī* or the unenlightened Self devoid of the knowledge of the pure nature of the Self misunderstands the Self and the non-Self as being identical, believes them to be the same and also behaves as if they were identical. Thus with the thought, "I am the same as the *karmic Prakṛti*" he enjoys the fruits of the *karma*. But the enlightened one realising the pure nature of the Self, understands the Self and the non-Self to be distinct, believes them to be different and correspondingly behaves, unconcerned with the other. Thus being uninfluenced by external *karmic* conditions, he does not enjoy the fruits thereof but remains merely aware of their occurence.

Next it is further emphasised that it is the *ajñānī*, the Self without right knowledge, that is the enjoyer.

ण मुणइ पयडिमभव्वो सुट्ठु वि अज्झाइऊण सत्थाणि।
गुडदुद्धंपि पिवंतो ण पण्णया णिव्विसा होंति॥ ३१७॥

ṇa muṇai payaḍimabhavvo suṭṭhu vi ajjhāiūṇa satthāṇi
guḍadudhaṁpi pivaṁto ṇa paṇṇayā ṇivvisā hoṁti (317)

न मुञ्चति प्रकृतिमभव्यः सुष्ठ्वप्यधीत्य शास्त्राणि।
गुडदुग्धमपि पिवन्तो न पन्नगा निर्विषा भवन्ति॥ ३१७॥

317. The *abhavya* or the unfit Self, even though well-versed in the Scriptures, does not give up his attachment to *karmic prakṛti* just as a snake by drinking sweetened milk does not become non-poisonous.

Next it is declared that the enlightened Self is not an enjoyer.

णिव्वेयसमावण्णो णाणी कम्मफलं वियाणेइ।
महुरं कडुवं बहुविहमवेयओ तेण सो होइ॥ ३१८॥

ṇivveyasamāvaṇṇo ṇāṇī kammaphalaṁ viyāṇei
mahuraṁ kaḍuvaṁ bahuvihamaveyao teṇa so hoi (318)

निर्वेदसमापन्नो ज्ञानी कर्मफलं विजानाति।
मधुरं कटुकं बहुविधमवेदकस्तेन स भवति॥ ३१८॥

318. The enlightened Self equipped with complete nonattachment (merely) knows the fruits of various *karmas*, sweet or bitter. He therefore remains the non-enjoyer.

Commentary : The knower, because he realises his own true nature, is uninfluenced by the environment, his own body or other enjoyable objects. Thus uninfluenced by these alien things and fully absorbed in the transcendental bliss of his own pure nature, he is not affected by the inferior type of pleasure-pain experience derived from sense-presented objects. Since he is unaffected by the objects of the perceptual world, he remains the *abhoktā* or the non-enjoyer, though he is fully aware of the fact that good produces pleasure and evil produces pain.

णवि कुव्वइ णवि वेदइ णाणी कम्माइ बहु पयाराइ।
जाणइ पुण कम्मफलं बंधं पुण्णं च पावं च॥ ३१९॥

ṇavi kuvvai ṇavi vedai ṇāṇī kammāi bahu payārāi
jāṇai puṇa kammaphalaṁ baṁdhaṁ puṇṇaṁ ca pāvaṁ ca (319)

नापि करोति नापि वेदयते ज्ञानी कर्माणि बहुप्रकाराणि।
जानाति पुनः कर्मफलं बन्धं पुण्यं च पापं च॥ ३१९॥

319. The knower neither produces the various kinds of *karmas* nor enjoys the fruits thereof, neverthless he knows the nature of *karmas* and their results, either good or bad as well as the bondage.

दिट्ठी सयंपि णाणं अकारयं तह अवेदयं चेव।
जाणइ य बंधमोक्खं कम्मुदयं णिज्जरं चेव॥ ३२०॥

diṭṭhī sayaṁpi ṇāṇaṁ akārayaṁ taha avedayaṁ ceva
jāṇai ya baṁdhamokkhaṁ kammudayaṁ ṇijjaraṁ ceva

दृष्टिः स्वयमपि ज्ञानमकारकं तथावेदकं चैव।
जानाति च बन्धमोक्षौ कर्मोदयं निर्जरां चैव॥ ३२०॥

320. Knowledge, too, like sight is neither the doer nor the enjoyer (*of karmas*); But only knows the bondage, the release, the operation of *karmas* and the shedding of karmas.

Commentary : It is a well-known fact in our experience that visual perception and the preceived object are not causally related to each other. Hence we cannot say that the act of perception produces the object perceived. Hence the relation of perception to perceived object is such that the perceived object is uninfluenced by the act of preception. If the two are causally related to each other then the perceiving agent, say in the case of fire perceived, must himself be combustible and burst into flame in order to produce the flame perceived, and similarly he must feel the heat of it in his own body. No such thing happens in the perceiving agent. This visual perception merely is aware of the object without in any way producing it. The behaviour of knowledge is said to be identical with that of the visual perception. The relation between knowledge and the object known is exactly identical. Knowledge is not in any way causally related to the objects known. Knowledge therefore cannot be said to produce the objects known. Hence *jñāna* is said to be *akāraka*, not a causal agent and also *avedaka*, non-enjoyer in relation to *bandha* (bondage), *mokṣa* (release), etc. which as objects of knowledge are merely known and not produced.

Those who see in the *ātmā* a creator, like ordinary people, are not sages desiring emancipation.

लोयस्स कुणइ विण्हू सुरणारयतिरियमाणुसे सत्ते।
समणाणं पि य अप्पा जइ कुव्वइ छव्विहे काए॥ ३२१॥

loyassa kuṇai viṇhū suraṇārayatiriyamāṇuse satte
samaṇānaṁ pi ya appā jai kuvvai chavvihe kāe (321)

लोकस्य करोति विष्णुः सुरनारकतिर्यङ्मानुषान् सत्त्वान्।
श्रमणानामपि च आत्मा यदि करोति षड्विधान् कायान्॥ ३२१॥

लोयसमणाण मेवं सिद्धंतं पडि ण दीसइ विसेसो।
लोयस्स कुणइ विण्हू समणाणं पि अप्पओ कुणइ॥ ३२२॥

loyasamaṇāṇa mevaṁ siddhaṁtaṁ paḍi ṇa dīsai viseso
loyassa kuṇai viṇhū samaṇānaṁ pi appao kuṇai (322)

लोकश्रमणानामेवं सिद्धान्तं प्रति न दृश्यते विशेषः।
लोकस्य करोति विष्णुः श्रमणानामप्यात्मा करोति॥ ३२२॥

एवं ण कोवि मोक्खो दीसइ लोयसमणाण दोण्हंपि।
णिच्चं कुव्वंताणं सदेवमणुआसुरे लोये॥ ३२३॥

evaṁ ṇa kovi mokkho dīsai loyasamaṇāṇa doṇhaṁpi
ṇiccaṁ kovvaṁtāṇaṁ sadevamaṇuāsure loye (323)

एवं न कोऽपि मोक्षो दृश्यते लोकश्रमणानां द्वयेषामपि।
नित्यं कुर्वतां सदेव मनुजान् सुरान् लोकान्॥ ३२३॥

321 to 323; According to the ordinary people Viṣṇu creates all creatures celestial, hellish, sub-human and human;

if according to the Śramaṇas, the soul creates his six kinds of organic bodies, then between the popular doctrine and the Śramaṇa doctrine, both being identical, no difference can be perceived. For the people it is Viṣṇu that creates and for the Śramaṇas it is the Self that creates. Thus if the ordinary people and the Śramaṇas both believe in the doctrine of perpetual creation of worlds, human and divine, then there is no such thing as *mokṣa* or liberation discernible in their doctrine.

Commentary : Creative activity also implies desire to achieve something. The moment a desire to achieve an ideal appears, there comes a train of emotions such as attachment, aversion, delusion, etc. Hence continuous creativity activity implies perpetuation of *saṁsāra* and hence there is no chance for liberation or *mukti*.

Next, when the Self and non-Self are so entirely distinct and when there is no chance of association of any kind between the two, much less the causal relation, how does the feeling of doer occur in the Self? The following *gathas* offer an explanation.

ववहारभासिएण उ परदव्वं मम भणंति विदियत्था।
जाणंति णिच्छयेण उ णय मम परमाणुमेत्तमवि किंचि॥

vavahārabhāsieṇa u paradavvaṁ mama bhaṇaṁti vidiyatthā
jāṇaṁti ṇicchayeṇa u ṇaya mama paramaṇumettamavi kiṁci (324)

व्यवहारभाषितेन तु परद्रव्यं मम भणन्ति विदितार्थाः।
जानन्ति निश्चयेन तु न च मम परमाणुमात्रमपि किंचित्॥ ३२४॥

जह कोवि णरो जंपइ अम्हा गामविसयणयररट्ठं।
णय होंति तस्स ताणि उ भणइ य मोहेण सो अप्पा॥ ३२५॥

jaha kovi ṇaro jaṁpai amhā gāmavisayaṇayararaṭṭhaṁ
ṇaya hoṁti tassa tāṇi u bhaṇai ya moheṇa so appā (325)

यथा कोऽपि नरो जल्पति अस्माकं ग्रामविषयनगरराष्ट्राणि।
न च भवन्ति तस्य तानि तु भणति च मोहेन स आत्मा॥ ३२५॥

एमेव मिच्छदिट्ठी णाणी णिस्संसयं हवइ एसो।
जो परदव्वं मम इदि जाणंतो अप्पयं कुणइ॥ ३२६॥

emeva micchadiṭṭhī ṇāṇī nissaṁsayaṁ havai eso
jo paradavvaṁ mama idi jāṇaṁto appayaṁ kuṇai (326)

एवमेव मिथ्यादृष्टिर्ज्ञानी निस्संशयं भवत्येषः।
यः परद्रव्यं ममेति जानन्नात्मानं करोति॥ ३२६॥

तम्हा ण मेति णिच्चा दोण्हं वि एयाण कत्ति ववसायं।
परदव्वे जाणंतो जाणिज्जो दिट्ठिरहियाणं॥ ३२७॥

tamhā ṇa meti ṇicchā doṇhaṁ vi eyāṇa katti vavassāyaṁ
paradavve jāṇaṁto jāṇijjo diṭṭhirahiyāṇaṁ (327)

तस्मान्न मे इति ज्ञात्वा द्वयेषामप्येतेषां कर्तृव्यवसायम्।
परद्रव्ये जानन् जानीयाद् दृष्टिरहितानाम्॥ ३२७॥

324 to 327. Those who know the nature of reality speak of non-Self as 'mine' using the language of the ordinary people, while they know really there is not even an atom of non-Self which is 'mine'. Just when a person speaks of my village, my country, my town or my kingdom, those are not really his. That person so speaks through self-delusion. In the same way, a person who (deluded by *vyavahāra* point of view) understands non-self as his and identifies himself with it, certainly becomes one of erroneous belief. There is no doubt about this. Among these two (ordinary people and Śramaṇas) if a person, knowing the truth that no object of non-self is his, still persists in thinking of the existence of a

creative will producing the external reality, he does so being devoid of right belief. Let it be understood to be the truth.

मिच्छत्तं जइ पयडी मिच्छादिट्ठी करेइ अप्पाणं।
तम्हा अचेयणा दे पयडी णणु कारगो पत्ता॥ ३२८॥

micchattaṁ jai payaḍī micchādiṭṭhī karei appāṇaṁ
tamhā aceyaṇā de payaḍī ṇaṇu kārago pattā (328)

मिथ्यात्वं यदि प्रकृतिर्मिथ्यादृष्टिं करोत्यात्मानम्।
तस्मादचेतना ते प्रकृतिर्ननु कारका: प्राप्ता:॥ ३२८॥

328, If the *karmic* material, responsible for wrong belief (by its own potency) makes the self a wrong believer, then does not your non-intelligent *prakṛti* assume the role of an intelligent doer?

अहवा एसो जीवो पोग्गलदव्वस्स कुणइ मिच्छत्तं।
तम्हा पोग्गलदव्वं मिच्छादिट्ठी ण पुण जीवो॥ ३२९॥

ahavā eso jīvo poggaladavvassa kuṇai micchattaṁ
tamhā poggaladavvaṁ micchādiṭṭhī ṇa puṇa jīvo (329)

अथवैष: जीव: पुद्गलद्रव्यस्य करोति मिथ्यात्वम्।
तस्मात्पुद्गलद्रव्यं मिथ्यादृष्टिर्न पुनर्जीव:॥ ३२९॥

329. If, on the other hand, the soul causes wrong belief in matter then it is matter that becomes a non-believer and not the soul.

अह जीवो पयडीतह पोग्गलदव्वं कुणंति मिच्छत्तं।
तम्हा दोहि कयं तं दोण्णिवि भुंजंति तस्स फलं॥ ३३०॥

aha jīvo payaḍītaha poggaladavvaṁ kuṇaṁti micchattaṁ
tamhā dohi kayaṁ taṁ doṇṇivi bhuṁjaṁti tassa phalaṁ

अथ जीवः प्रकृतिरपि पुद्गलद्रव्यं कुरुते मिथ्यात्वम्।
तस्माद्द्वाभ्यां कृतं तौ द्वावपि भुंजाते तस्य फलम्॥ ३३०॥

330. Again if soul and (inanimate) *prakrti* together create wrong belief out of *karmic* materials, then they both must enjoy the fruit of their actions.

अह ण पयडी ण जीवो पोग्गलदव्वं कुणंति मिच्छत्तं।
तम्हा पोग्गलदव्वं मिच्छत्तं तत्तु णहु मिच्छा॥ ३३१॥

aha ṇa payaḍī ṇa jīvo poggaladavvaṁ kuṇaṁti micchattaṁ
tamhā poggaladavvaṁ micchattaṁ tattu ṇahu micchā

अथ न प्रकृतिर्न जीवः पुद्गलद्रव्यं कुरुते मिथ्यात्वम्।
तस्मात्पुद्गलद्रव्यं मिथ्यात्वं तत्तु न खलु मिथ्या॥ ३३१॥

331. Further neither *karmic prakṛti* nor *jīva* is able to produce wrong belief out of *karmic* matter. Therefore it is not *karmic* materials that become wrong-belief. Such a view is entirely erroneous.

Commentary : Thus it is established that the Self is the causal agent of the *karma* which is the effect.

Next it is pointed out that nescience, etc. are all produced by *karma*.

कम्मेहिं दु अण्णाणी किज्जइ णाणी तहेव कम्मेहिं।
कम्मेहिं सुवाविज्जइ जग्गाविज्जइ तहेव कम्मेहिं॥ ३३२॥

kammehiṁ du aṇṇāṇī kijjai ṇāṇī taheva kammehiṁ
kammehiṁ savāvijjai jaggāvijjai taheva kammehiṁ (332)

कर्मभिस्तु अज्ञानी क्रियते ज्ञानी तथैव कर्मभिः।
कर्मभिः स्वाप्यते जागर्यते तथैव कर्मभिः॥ ३३२॥

कम्मेहिं सुहाविज्जइ दुक्खाविज्जइ तहेव कम्मेहिं।
कम्मेहिं य मिच्छत्तं णिज्जइ णिज्जइ असंजमं चेव॥ ३३३॥

kammehiṁ suhavijjai dukkhāvijjai taheva kammehiṁ
kammehiṁ ya micchattaṁ ṇijjai ṇijjai asaṁjamaṁ ceva

कर्मभिः सुखीक्रियते दुःखीक्रियते तथैव कर्मभिः।
कर्मभिः मिथ्यात्वं नीयते नीयतेऽसंयमं चैव॥ ३३३॥

कम्मेहिं भमाडिज्जइ उड्ढमहो चावि तिरियलोयं च।
कम्मेहिं चेव किज्जइ सुहासुहं जेत्तियं किंचि॥ ३३४॥

kammehiṁ bhamāḍijjai uḍḍhmaho cāvi tiriyaloyaṁ ca
kammehiṁ ceva kijjai suhāsuhaṁ jettiyaṁ kiṁci (334)

कर्मभिर्भ्राम्यते ऊर्ध्वमधश्चापि तिर्यग्लोकं च।
कर्मभिश्चैव क्रियते शुभाशुभं यावत्किंचित्॥ ३३४॥

जम्हा कम्मं कुव्वइ कम्मं देई हरइत्ति जं किंचि।
तम्हा उ सव्वजीवा अकारया हुंति आवण्णा॥ ३३५॥

jamhā kamaṁ kuvvai kammaṁ dei haraitti jaṁ kiṁci
tamhā u savvajīvā akāryā huṁti āvaṇṇā (335)

यस्मात् कर्म करोति कर्म ददाति हरतीति यत् किंचित्।
तस्मात्तु सर्वजीवा अकारका भवन्त्यापन्नाः॥ ३३५॥

332 to 335. It is by *karma* that the soul is nescient; it is by *karma* that he is made the Knower; it is by *karma* that he is asleep and it is by *karma* that he is awake; it is by *karma* that he is happy, it is by *karma* that he is miserable; it is by *karma* that he is led to wrong belief; and by the same he is led to non-discipline; it is by *karma* that he is made to wander in the upper, middle and nether worlds; and whatever good and evil is done, is also done by *karma;* because it is *karma* that does, it is *karma* that gives and it is *karma* that destroys,

therefoe all *jīvas* must become *akārakā or non-doer.*

पुरुसिच्छियाहिलासी इच्छीकम्मं च पुरिसमहिलसइ।
एसा आइरिय परंपरागया एरिसी दु सुई॥ ३३६॥

purusicchiyādhilāsī icchīkammaṁ ca purisamahilasai
esā āiriya paraṁparāgayā erisī du suī (336)

पुरुषः स्त्र्यभिलाषी स्त्रीकर्म च पुरुषमभिलषति।
एषाचार्यपरम्परागतेदृशी तु श्रुतिः॥ ३३६॥

तम्हा ण कोवि जीवो अबंभचारी उ तुम्हमुवएसे।
जम्हा कम्मं चेव हि कम्मं अहिलसइ जं भणियं॥ ३३७॥

tamhā ṇa kovi jīvo abaṁbhacārī u tumhamuvayese
jamhā kammaṁ ceva hi kammaṁ ahilasai jaṁ bhaṇiyaṁ

तस्मान्न कोऽपि जीवोऽब्रह्मचारी युष्माकमुपदेशे।
यस्मात्कर्मैव हि कर्माभिलषती यद् भणितम्॥ ३३७॥

336 to 337. The *karmic* material determining the male sex creates a longing for woman, and the *karmic* material determining the female sex creates a longing for man. If this is the teaching of the scripture handed down traditionally by the Ācāryas, then according to your gospel sex-desire is merely a matter of one material *karma* desiring another material *karma* as mentioned before.

जम्हा घाएदि परं परेण घाइज्जए य सा पयडी।
एएणत्थेण दु किर भण्णइ परघायणामेत्ति॥ ३३८॥

jamhā ghāedi paraṁ pareṇa ghyijjae ya sā payaḍī
eyeṇatthena du kira bhaṇṇai paraghāyaṇāmetti (338)

यस्माद्धन्ति परं परेण हन्यते च सा प्रकृतिः।
एतेनार्थेन किल भण्यते परघातनामेति॥ ३३८॥

तम्हा ण कोवि जीवो उवघायओ अत्थि तुम्ह उवएसे।
जम्हा कम्मं चेव हि कम्मं घाएदि इदि भणियं॥ ३३९॥

tamhā ṇa kovi jīvo uvaghāyao atthi tumha uvaese
jamhā kammaṁ ceva hi kammaṁ ghāedi idi bhaṇiyaṁ.

तस्मान्न कोऽपि जीव उपघातकोऽस्ति युष्माकमुपदेशे।
यस्मात्कर्म चैव हि कर्म हन्तीति भणितम्॥ ३३९॥

338 to 339. One class of *karma (prakṛti)* destroys another or is destroyed by another; that class in this sense is called '*Paraghāta*' (killing another being). Therefore no soul according to your teaching (can be considered) guilty of killing, because killing is merely a matter of one material *karma, destroying* another material *karma* as said above.

एवं संखुवएसं जेउ परूविंति एरिसं समणा।
तेसिं पयडी कुव्वइ अप्पा य अकारया सव्वे॥ ३४०॥

evaṁ saṁkhuvaesaṁ jeu parūviṁti erisaṁ samaṇā
tesiṁ payaḍi kuvvai appā ya akārayā savve (340)

एवं सांख्योपदेशे ये तु प्ररूपयन्तीदृशं श्रमणाः।
तेषां प्रकृतिः करोत्यात्मानश्चाकारकाः सर्वे॥ ३४०॥

अहवा मण्णसि मज्झं अप्पा अप्पाणमप्पणो कुणइ।
एसो मिच्छसहावो तुम्हं एयं मुणंतस्स॥ ३४१॥

ahavā maṇṇasi majjhaṁ appā appāṇamappaṇo kuṇai
eso micchasahāvo tumhaṁ eyaṁ muṇaṁtassa (341)

अथवा मन्यसे ममात्मात्मानमात्मना करोति।
एष मिथ्यास्वभावस्तवैतन्मन्यमानस्य॥ ३४१॥

340-341. If any Śramaṇas thus preach approving such a Sāṁkhya doctrine, then according to them *prakṛti* (*karmic* material) becomes the agent and all the souls would be inactive. On the other hand, if you maintain, "my soul transforms ifself by itself," the opinion of yours is wrong.

अप्पा णिच्चो असंखिज्जपदेसो देसिओ उ समयम्हि।
णवि सो सक्कइ तत्तो हीणो अहिओ य काउं जे॥ ३४२॥

appā ṇicco asaṁkhijjapadeso desio u samayamhi
ṇavi so sakkai tatto hīṇo ahio ya kāuṁ je (342)

आत्मा नित्योऽसंख्येयप्रदेशो दर्शितस्तु समये।
नापि स शक्यते ततो हीनोऽधिकश्च कर्तुं यत्॥ ३४२॥

342. In the Scripture, the soul is described to be eternal and of immeasurable extension. Hence, of its own accord, it is incapable of increasing or decreasing (its spatial form).

जीवस्स जीवरूवं वित्थरओ जाण लोयमेत्तं खु।
तत्तो सो हिं हीणो अहिओ य कहं कुणइ दव्वं॥ ३४३॥

jīvassa jīvarūvaṁ vittharao jāṇa loyamettaṁ khu
tatto so kiṁ hīṇo ahio ya kahaṁ kuṇai davvaṁ (343)

जीवस्य जीवरूपं विस्तरतो जानीहि लोकमात्रं खलु।
ततः स किं हीनोऽधिको वा कथं करोति द्रव्यम्॥ ३४३॥

343. Know ye : that the soul, from the point of view of extension, is really co-extensive with the universe. Therefore, how is this eternal substance caused to assume decreased or increased spatial form?

अह जाणओ दु भावो णाणसहावेण अत्थि इत्ति मयं।
तम्हा णवि अप्पा अप्पाणं तु सयमप्पणो कुणइ॥ ३४४॥

aha jāṇao du bhāvo ṇāṇasahāveṇa atthi itti mayaṁ
tamhā ṇavi appā appāṇaṁ tu sayamappaṇo kuṇai (344)

अथ ज्ञायकस्तु भावो ज्ञानस्वभावेन तिष्ठतीति मतम्।
तस्मान्नाप्यात्मात्मानं तु स्वयमात्मनः करोति॥ ३४४॥

344. It is accepted that the conscious principle remains of the nature of knowledge. Therefore, the Self, of its own accord, does not transform itself by itself.

Commentary : According to the Sāṅkhya doctrine the Self or *Puruṣa* is *nitya* and *akartā,* an absolutely unchanging, permanent *cetana* entity. All change and all activity proceed from *acetana prakṛti.* The Self is only aware of the activity. Thus he is only the knower, a mere spectator of the various changes physical and psychical which both are due to *prakṛti* according to the Sāṅkhya view. Though the *Puruṣa* is not responsible for any activity, he is still considered to be enjoying the fruits of the action of the *prakṛti.* Thus the *Puruṣa* is also the *bhoktā.* This Sāṅkhya description of the Self, that he is the knower, permanent, actionless, and enjoyer is incompatible with the Jaina conception of the Self. Obviously about the time of Bhagavān Kundakunda, some Jaina thinkers must have had leanings towards the Sāṅkhya view. According to these Śramaṇābhāsas, or the Jaina heretics, the *karmic* material played the part of the Sāṇkhyan *prakṛti.* Every change and every activity was credited to the operation of *karmic* material, the Self remaining an active spectator. This attitude is condemned by our author by showing the utter untenability of the Sāṅkhya doctrine. If every change and every activity is attributed to *prakṛti* and if the Self is merely an unchanging permanent spectator absolutely uninfluenced by the action of *karmas,* he must remain for ever a *mokṣa-jīva,* a liberated Self. It would mean the absence of *saṁsāra.* This conclusion is contradicted by actual experience, because in actual experience we have an empirical ego or *saṁsāra jīva* as a fact of reality which cannot be dismissed as unreal. This empirical state of existence in which *saṁsāra jīva* lives as a matter of fact certainly demands an explanation. This explanation which is not supplied by the Sāṅkhya view is offered by the Jaina doctrine which is put forth by our author as a corrective to the Sāṅkhya view. The *karmic* material is no doubt the main operative principle responsible for the physical and psychic changes produced in the being of a person. When the *karmic* material is operative, the Self does not remain an inactive spectator according to Jaina metaphysics. If the Self were so inactive, he would not be different from the Sāṅkhya *Puruṣa*. But the successful operation of the *karmic* material and the consequent psycho-physical changes are due to the attitude of the Self which has a suitable responsive reaction. Without this responsive reaction on the part of the Self, the *karmic* material would be impotent and will not be able to produce any change either in the body or in the consciousness. This attitude of responsive reaction on the part of the Self, is responsible for the psycho-physical changes when stimulated by *karmic* material. The changes in the empirical Self therefore are directly due to the activity of the empirical ego in the form of responsive reaction brought about by the operation of *karmic* material. Thus for the changes in the consciousness, the ego is responsible. Hence the empirical ego must be considered to be an active agent capable of producing modifications in his own consciousness in response to the operation of *karma*. Thus the Self must not only be active but must also be liable to change. As against the nature of Sāṇkhya *Puruṣa*, who is said to be *nitya*, a changing Self and an active agent. But to leave the position here would be untrue. This description of the Self is applicable only to the empirical ego which is the *saṁsāra jīva*. Though he is *anitya* and *kartā,* as an empirical ego, because of the absence of discriminative knowledge between the Self and the non-Self, still when he acquires this discriminative knowledge, when he realises his pure nature, unsullied by *karmic* influence, he would remain for ever without any change and without any action; at that stage, certainly he is *nitya* and *akartā.* The Jaina metaphysics combines both these aspects. From the absolute real point of view, the Self is *nitya* and *akartā,* but from the empirical or *vyavahāra* point of view he is *anitya* and *kartā.* It is because of the combination of such apparently conflicting views, that the Jaina system is said to be the *anekānta* view. All the other systems which emphasise one aspect of reality or the other exclusively are described to be *ekānta-vādas* and no *ekānta-vādī* is able to offer a complete and comprehensive solution for the problem of reality. Sāṅkhya is thus, as an *ekānta* system, refuted because of its incapacity to explain the nature of concrete reality or *saṁsāra.*

Next another *ekānta* system is taken up for consideration and refutation. The Bauddha system of metaphysics lays emphasis upon the changes in reality. This one-sided emphasis converts reality into an impermanent and everchanging stream of existence. This doctrine is also considered to be inadequate as is shown below.

केहि चिदु पज्जयेहिं विणस्सए णेव केहिं चिदु जीवो।
जम्हा तम्हा कुव्वइ सो वा अण्णो व णेयंतो॥ ३४५॥

kehiṁ cidu pajjayehiṁ viṇassaye ṇeva kehiṁ cidu jīvo
jamhā tamhā kuvvai so vā aṇṇo va ṇeyaṁto (345)

कैश्चित्तु पर्यायैर्विनश्यति नैव कैश्चित्तु जीवः।
यस्मात्तस्मात्करोति स वा अन्यो वा नैकान्तः॥ ३४५॥

345. From some point of view (*paryāyārthika naya*) the soul dies, but from another point of view (dravyārthika naya)

the soul never dies. Because of this *nitya-anitya* nature of the soul, the one-sided view that the soul (that enjoys) is the same as the doer or entirely different from this would be untenable.

केहिंचिदु पज्जयेहिं विणस्सए णेव केहिंचिदु जीवो।
जम्हा तम्हा वेददि सो वा अण्णो व णेयंतो॥ ३४६॥

kehiṁcidu pajjayehiṁ viṇassaye ṇeva kehiṁcidu jīvo
jamhā tamhā vedadi so vā aṇṇo va ṇeyaṁto (346)

कैश्चित्तु पर्यायैर्विनश्यति नैव कैश्चित्तु जीवः।
यस्मात्तस्माद्वेदयति स वा अन्यो वा नैकान्तः॥ ३४६॥

346. From some point of view (*paryāyārthika naya*) the soul dies, but from an other point of view (*dravyārthika naya*) the soul never dies. Because of this *nitya-anitya* nature of the soul, the one-sided view, that the soul (that acts) is the same as the enjoyer (of the fruits thereof), or entirely different from him would be untenable.

जो चेव कुणइ सो चेव य ण वेयए जस्स एस सिद्धंतो।
सो जीवो णायव्वो मिच्छादिट्ठी अणारिहदो॥ ३४७॥

jo ceva kuṇai so ceva ya ṇa veyae jassa esa siddhaṁto
so jīvo ṇāyavvo micchādiṭṭhī aṇārihado (347)

यश्चैव करोति स चैव न वेदयते यस्य एष सिद्धान्तः।
स जीवो ज्ञातव्यो मिथ्यादृष्टिरनार्हतः॥ ३४७॥

347. Let it be known that the person who holds the doctrine that the soul that acts is absolutely identical with the soul that enjoys (the fruits thereof) is a wrong believer and is not of the Arhata faith.

अण्णो करेइ अण्णो परिभुंजइ जस्स एस सिद्धंतो।
सो जीवो णायव्वो मिच्छादिट्ठी अणारिहदो॥ ३४८॥

aṇṇo karei aṇṇo paribhuṁjai jassa esa siddhaṁto
so jīvo ṇāyavvo micchādiṭṭhī aṇārihado (348)

अन्यः करोत्यन्यः परिभुङ्क्ते यस्य एष सिद्धान्तः।
स जीवो ज्ञातव्यो मिथ्यादृष्टिरनार्हतः॥ ३४८॥

348. Let it be known that the person who holds the doctrine that the soul, that acts is absolutely different from the soul that enjoys (the fruits thereof), is a wrong believer and is not of the Arhata faith.

Next the author explains through a practical illustration how the Self is the actor and the action, the enjoyer and the enjoyed.

जह सिप्पिओ उ कम्मं कुव्वइ ण य सो उ तम्मओ होइ।
तह जीवोवि य कम्मं कुव्वइ ण य तम्मओ होइ॥ ३४९॥

jaha sippio u kammaṁ kuvvai ṇa ya so u tammao hoi
taha jīvovi ya kammaṁ kuvvai ṇa ya tammao hoi *(349)*

यथा शिल्पिकस्तु कर्म करोति न च तन्मयो भवति।
तथा जीवोऽपि च कर्म करोति न च तन्मयो भवति॥ ३४९॥

349. As an artisan performs his work, but does not become identical with it, so also the Self produces *karma* but does not become identical with it.

जह सिप्पिओ उ करणेहिं कुव्वइ ण य सो उ तम्मओ होइ।
तह जीवो करणेहिं कुव्वइ ण य तम्मओ होइ॥ ३५०॥
jaha sippio u karaṇehiṁ kuvvai ṇa ya so u tammao hoyi
taha jīvo karaṇehiṁ kuvvai ṇa ya tammao hoi (350)

यथा शिल्पिकस्तु करणैः करोति न स तु तन्मयो भवति।
तथा जीवः करणैः करोति न च तन्मयो भवति॥ ३५०॥

350. As the artisan works with his tools, but does not

become identified with them, so also the Self acts through the instrumentality (of *trikaraṇa*– thought, word and deed) but does not become identified with them.

जह सिप्पिओ उ करणाणि गिण्हइ ण य सो उ तम्मओ होइ।
तह जीवो करणाणि उ गिण्हइ ण य तम्मओ होइ॥ ३५१॥

jaha sippio u karaṇāṇi giṇhai ṇa ya so u tammao hoi
taha jīvo karaṇāṇi u giṇhai ṇa ya tammao hoi (351)

यथा शिल्पिकस्तु करणानि गृह्णाति न च तु तन्मयो भवति।
तथा जीवः करणानि तु गृह्णाति न च तन्मयो भवति॥ ३५१॥

351. As the artisan holds his tools (while working) but does not become identified with them so also the Self makes use of his organs *tri-karaṇa* (while acting) but does not become identified with them.

जह सिप्पिओ कम्मफलं भुंजइ ण य सो उ तम्मओ होइ।
तह जीवो कम्मफलं भुंजइ ण य तम्मओ होइ॥ ३५२॥

jaha sippio kammaphalaṁ bhuṁjai ṇa ya so u tammo hoi
taha jīvo kammaphalaṁ bhuṁjai ṇa ya tammao hoi (352)

यथा शिल्पिकः कर्मफलं भुङ्क्ते न च स तु तन्मयो भवति।
तथा जीवः कर्मफलं भुङ्क्ते न च तन्मयो भवति॥ ३५२॥

352. As the artisan enjoys the fruits of his labour, but does not become one with it, so also the Self enjoys the fruit of *karma* but does not become one with it.

एवं ववहारस्स उ वत्तव्वं दरिसणं समासेण।
सुणु णिच्छयस्स वयणं परिणामकयं तु जं होइ॥ ३५३॥

evaṁ vavahārassa u vattavvaṁ darisaṇaṁ samāseṇa
suṇu ṇicchayassa vayaṇaṁ pariṇāmakayaṁ tu jaṁ hoi

एवं व्यवहारस्य तु वक्तव्यं दर्शनं समासेन।
शृणु निश्चयस्य वचनं परिणामकृतं तु यद्भवति॥ ३५३॥

353. Thus has the doctrine been stated briefly from the *vyavahāra* point of view; now listen to the statement from the *niścaya* point of view which refers to changes resulting from modifications (of the soul).

जह सिप्पिओ उ चिट्ठं कुव्वइ हवइ य तहा अणण्णो सो।
तह जीवोवि य कम्मं कुव्वइ हवइ य अणण्णो सो॥ ३५४॥

jaha sippio u ciṭṭhaṁ kuvvai havai ya tahā aṇaṇṇo so
taha jivovi ya kammaṁ kuvvai havai ya aṇaṇṇo so (354)

यथा शिल्पिकस्तु चेष्टां करोति भवति च तथानन्यस्तस्याः।
तथा जीवोऽपि च कर्म करोति भवति चानन्यस्तस्मात्॥ ३५४॥

354. As the artisan starts with the mental image (of the object to be produced) and translates it into physical form by his bodily activity and thus is one with it, so also the Self starts with the mental counterpart of *karmas* and is therefore one with it.

जह चिट्ठं कुव्वंतो उ सिप्पिओ णिच्चदुक्खिओ होइ।
तत्तो सिया अणण्णो तह चिट्ठंतो दुही जीवो॥ ३५५॥

jaha ciṭṭhaṁ kuvvaṁto u sippio ṇiccadukkhio hoi
tatto siyā aṇaṇṇo taha ciṭṭhaṁto duhī jīvo (355)

यथा चेष्टां कुर्वाणस्तु शिल्पिको नित्यदु:खितो भवति।
तस्माच्च स्यादनन्यस्तथा चेष्टमानो दु:खी जीव:॥ ३५५॥

355. As the artisan making an effort (to translate the mental image into physical form) always suffers thereby and is therefore one with that suffering, so also the Self that acts as stimulated by impure mental states undergoes suffering and becomes one with it.

Commentary : A casual observation of an artist at work will give us the following particulars. The metal or marble which he is going to shape, the instruments used therefore, his dexterity in handling those instruments and the final value which he obtains for the finished product, all these facts are external to the nature of the artist who remains distinct from all the external facts. But instead of such a casual observation if we try to understand the creative activity of the artist then we have a different account of the process. The artist starts with the vision of the object which he is going to make. His creative activity consists in shaping out of the shapeless metal or marble a figure exactly answering to his mental image. With this object in view he sets about to work. Thus looked at from the inner side of the artist's mind, his whole activity is a continuous identical process of expressing in the form of metal or marble what he has in his mind. The method of his work and the instruments employed all become auxiliary and sub-servient to this one process by which the artist transforms his idea into an objective figure. Here the artist cannot be differentiated from the continuous process of creative activity resulting in the finished product of art. At every stage of this process we have the progressive manifestation of the artist's mind and hence the process of activity is the artist himself engaged in the art of creation. The artist while thus engaged in translating his idea into an objective figure has to undergo an amount of labour and suffering peculiar to the creative activity of the artist. This feature of the artist in both of the aspects is employed to explain the creative activity of the Self according to the principle of analogy. The Self also has to deal with external *karmic* matter. To shape this *karmic* matter into various patterns, various instruments are employed. The Self, like the artist has to manipulate these instruments and after shaping the *karmic* matter into various patterns he has to experience the hedonic value of the finished product. All these external facts are quite distinct from the nature of the Self who cannot identify himself with any of these. The account corresponds to the casual observation of the artist and hence does not represent the real and true nature of the activity of the Self. When we try to probe into the inner working of the activity of the Self we have a complete parallel to the creative activity of the artist. The Self also starts with an intellectual pattern of the shape of things to be. Starting with such an intellectual pattern, he approaches the *karmic* material in order to create a material pattern exactly answering to the psychic pattern which he attempts to translate into material shape. When the process of expressing the intellectual pattern in physical form is completed, he experiences the hedonic value thereof. Here also we have an identical and continuous self-expression and the Self that expresses through this process of manifestation is identical with the process itself. The process, the product and the value thereof are but the different stages in the creative activity. Hence the Self cannot be taken to be distinct from the exertion and suffe·ing, a characteristic of the creative activity of the Self. Thus these two accounts of the activity of the Self, one from the *vyavahāra* point of view and the other from the *niścaya* point of view, are parallel and analogical to the activity of the artist described above.

Next it is pointed out that though apparently an object of reality seems to be capable of transferring its own attributes to another object, really it cannot do so.

जह सेटिया दु ण परस्स सेटिया सेटिया य सा होइ।
तह जाणओ दु ण परस्स जाणओ जाणओ सोदु॥ ३५६॥

jaha seṭiyā du ṇa parassa seṭiyā seṭiyā ya sā hoi
taha jāṇao du ṇa parassa jāṇao jāṇao sodu (356)

यथा सेटिका तु न परस्य सेटिका सेटिका च सा भवति।
तथा ज्ञायकस्तु न परस्य ज्ञायको ज्ञायकः स तु॥ ३५६॥

356. As chalk (when applied to whiten the surface of another thing) does not become that thing but remains as chalk (on the surface of that thing), so the Self (while knowing an object) remains as the knower and does not become the object known (which is other than the Self).

जह सेटिया दु ण परस्स सेटिया सेटिया य सा होइ।
तह पासओ दु ण परस्स पासओ पासओ सोदु॥ ३५७॥

jaha seṭiyā du ṇa parassa seṭiyā seṭiyā ya sā hoi
taha pāsao du ṇa parassa pāsao pāsao sodu (357)

यथा सेटिका तु न परस्य सेटिका सेटिका च सा भवति।
तथा दर्शकस्तु न परस्य दर्शको दर्शकः स तु॥ ३५७॥

357. As chalk (when applied to whiten the surface of another thing) does not become that thing but remains as chalk (on the surface of that thing), so the Self (while perceiving an object) remains as the perceiver and does not become the object perceived (which is other than the Self).

जह सेटिया दु ण परस्स सेटिया सेटिया य सा होइ।
तह संजओ दु ण परस्स संजओ संजओ सोदु॥ ३५८॥

jaha seṭiyā du ṇa parassa seṭiyā seṭiyā ya sā hoi
taha saṁjao du ṇa parassa saṁjao saājao sodu (358)

यथा सेटिका तु न परस्य सेटिका सेटिका च सा भवति।
तथा संयतस्तु न परस्य संयतः संयतः स तु॥ ३५८॥

358. As chalk (when applied to whiten the surface of another thing) does not become that thing but remains as chalk (on the surface of that thing), so the Self (while

renouncing the external possessions) remains as the disciplined abstainer and does not become one with the renounced possessions (which are other than the Self).

जह सेटिया दु ण परस्स सेटिया सेटिया य सा होइ।
तह दंसणं दु ण परस्स दंसणं दंसणं तं तु॥ ३५९॥

jaha seṭiyā du ṇa parassa seṭiyā seṭiyā ya sā hoi
taha daṁsaṇaṁ du ṇa parassa daṁsaṇaṁ daṁsaṇaṁ taṁ tu

यथा सेटिका तु न परस्य सेटिका सेटिका च सा भवति।
तथा दर्शनं तु न परस्य दर्शनं दर्शनं तत्तु॥ ३५९॥

359 As chalk (when applied to whiten the surface of another thing) does not become that thing but remains as chalk (on the surface of that thing), so right faith in the *Tattvas* remains as right faith and does not become one with the *Tattvas.*

एवं तु णिच्छयणयस्स भासियं णाणदंसणचरित्ते।
सुणु ववहारणयस्स य वत्तव्वं से समासेण॥ ३६०॥

evaṁ tu ṇicchayaṇayassa bhāsiyaṁ ṇāṇadaṁsaṇacaritte
suṇu vavahāraṇayassa ya vattavvaṁ se samāseṇa (360)

एवं तु निश्चयनयस्य भाषितं ज्ञानदर्शनचरित्रे।
शृणु व्यवहारनयस्य च वक्तव्यं तस्य समासेन॥ ३६०॥

360. From the stand point of reality, knowledge, faith and conduct have thus been described; now listen to a brief statement of the same from the *vyavahāra* point of view.

जह परदव्वं सेटदि हु सेटिया अप्पणो सहावेण।
तह परदव्वं जाणइ णाया वि सएण भावेण॥ ३६१॥

jaha paradavvaṁ seṭadi hu seṭiyā appaṇo sahāveṇa
taha paradavvaṁ jāṇai ṇāyā vi sayeṇa bhāveṇa (361)

यथा परद्रव्यं सेटयति खलु सेटिकात्मनः स्वभावेन।
तथा परद्रव्यं जानाति ज्ञातापि स्वकेन भावेन॥ ३६१॥

361. As chalk whitens another thing because of its intrinsic nature of (of whiteness), so also the knower knows other things because of his own intrinsic nature (of knowledge).

जह परदव्वं सेटदि हु सेटिया अप्पणो सहावेण।
तह परदव्वं पस्सइ जीवो वि सएण भावेण॥ ३६२॥

jaha paradavvaṁ seṭadi hu seṭiyā appaṇo sahāveṇa
taha paradavvaṁ passai jīvo vi sayeṇa bhāveṇa (362)

यथा परद्रव्यं सेटयति खलु सेटिकात्मनः स्वभावेन।
तथा परद्रव्यं पश्यति जीवोऽपि स्वकेन भावेन॥ ३६२॥

362. As chalk whitens another thing because of its intrinsic nature (of whiteness), so also the Self perceives other things because of his own intrinsic nature (of perception).

जह परदव्वं सेटदि हु सेटिया अप्पणो सहावेण।
तह परदव्वं विजहइ णाया वि सएण भावेण॥ ३६३॥

jaha paradavvaṁ seṭadi hu seṭiyā appaṇo sahāveṇa
taha paradavvaṁ vijahai ṇāyā vi saeṇa bhāveṇa (363)

यथा परद्रव्यं सेटयति खलु सेटिकात्मनः स्वभावेन।
तथा परद्रव्यं विजहाति ज्ञातापि स्वकेन भावेन॥ ३६३॥

363. As chalk whitens another thing because of its intrinsic nature (of whiteness), so also the knowing Self renounces external possessions because of his own intrinsic

nature (of non-attachment).

जह परदव्वं सेटदि हु सेटिया अप्पणो सहावेण।
तह परदव्वं सद्दहइ सम्माइट्ठी सहावेण॥ ३६४॥

jaha paradavvaṁ seṭadi hu seṭiyā appaṇo sahāveṇa
taha paradavvaṁ saddahai sammāiṭṭhī sahāveṇa (364)

यथा परद्रव्यं सेटयति खलु सेटिकात्मन: स्वभावेन।
तथा परद्रव्यं श्रद्धते सम्यग्दृष्टि: स्वभावेन॥ ३६४॥

364. As chalk whitens another thing because of its intrinsic nature (of whiteness), so also a right believer believes in the external reality because of his intrinsic nature (of right belief).

एवं ववहारस्स दु विणिच्छओ णाणदंसणचरित्ते।
भणिओ अण्णेसु वि पज्जएसु एमेव णायव्वो॥ ३६५॥

evaṁ vavahārassa du viṇicchao ṇāṇadaṁsaṇacaritte
bhaṇio aṇṇesu vi pajjaesu emeva ṇāyavvo (365)

एवं व्यवहारस्स तु विनिश्चयो ज्ञानदर्शनचरित्रे।
भणितोऽन्येष्वपि पर्यायेषु एवमेव ज्ञातव्य:॥ ३६५॥

365. Thus it has been stated the truth about knowledge, faith and conduct from the *vyavahāra* point of view; the other modes (of consciousness) should be understood similarly.

Commentary : When chalk is used to whiten an object, say a mud pot, though chalk appears to transfer its white colour to the pot, it does not become identical with the mud pot, nor does it lose its intrinsic nature. The relation is only external. The white surface on the pot consists of chalk particles. This illustration of external relation of one thing to another, where two things are related to each other without losing their respective intrinsic nature, one is *cetana* and the other *acetana*, conscious and non-conscious, and yet the two are related to each other in the process of knowledge as the knowing Self and the object known. The relation between the knower and the known is merely external. In the process of knowing the knower and the known, both retain their intrinsic nature. *Jñāna* or knowledge is compared by the Jaina metaphysicians to light. Light by illuminating the external objects, makes them visible, without in any way, interfering with their real nature, so also the external objects become known through knowledge, they themselves remaining uninfluenced by the process of knowing. This theory of knowledge according to Jainism is incompatible with two other rival doctrines which are refuted in these *gāthās,*—Brahma-Advaitic doctrine, and the Buddhistic doctrine. Since knowledge implies the relation between two entirely distinct reals, the pantheistic monism of the first school cuts the gordian knot by deriving both the Self and the non-Self from a primeval Brahman. This merely pushes the problem further without offering any real solution. How could the same identical cause produce two contradictory effects, still remains an insoluble mystery. Metaphysical monism offers an easy escape from the problem of knowledge without offering any satisfactory solution. The logical development of such a doctrine must necessarily identify the primeval Brahman with—one of the two—the *cetana dravya* and must end by condemning the external *acetana* worlds as *māyā* or illusory, an extremely inconvenient, erroneous conclusion. The solution offered by the Buddhistic metaphysics is equally unsatisfactory. The process of knowledge of *jñana* at any particular moment of its existence manifests in the dual aspect of the knower and the known. The metaphysical categories of Self and matter are treated to be purely hypothetical and unwarranted assumptions. *Jñāna* or knowledge is the only real and it manifests as objects of knowledge in the process of knowing. This solution of the problem of knowledge apparently gets rid of the difficulty of explaining the relation between two contradictory categories, the Self and the non-Self, by reducing both to a simple principle of *jñāna* or knowledge. If the object of knowledge is just the manifestaion of knowledge itself, what happens to it when there is no process of knowing. Absence of knowledge must necessarity mean the disapperance of the external world. This nihilistic conclusion or *śūnyavāda* that when knowledge ceases to be, then the Self and the external world cease to be is contradicted by our concrete experience. Hence both these theories of knowledge are refuted by our author in the above *gāthās*.

Impure emotional states such as attachment and aversion are the results of absence of clear knowledge of the exact nature of the reals. This is explained below.

दंसणणाणचरित्तं किंचिवि णत्थि दु अचेयणे विसए।
तम्हा किं घादयदे चेदयिदा तेसु विसएसु॥ ३६६॥

daṁsaṇaṇāṇacarittaṁ kiṁcivi ṇatthi du aceyaṇe visae
tamhā kiṁ ghādayade cedayidā tesu visaesu (366)

दर्शनज्ञानचरित्रं किंचिदपि नास्ति त्वचेतने विषये।
तस्मात्किं घातयति चेतयिता तेषु विषयेषु॥ ३६६॥

366. There is no faith, knowledge, or conduct whatsoever in a non-intelligent object; therefore what does the soul destroy in those objects?

दंसणणाणचरित्तं किंचिवि णत्थि दु अचेयणे कम्मे।
तम्हा किं घादयदे चेदयिदा तम्हि कमम्मि॥ ३६७॥

daṁsaṇaṇāṇa carittaṁ kiṁcivi ṇatthi du aceyaṇe kamme
tamhā kiṁ ghādayade cedayidā tamhi kammammi (367)

दर्शनज्ञानचरित्रं किंचिदपि नास्ति त्वचेतने कर्मणि।
तस्मात्किं घातयति चेतयिता तत्र कर्मणि॥ ३६७॥

367. There is no faith, knowledge, or conduct whatsoever in non-intelligent *karmic* material; therefore what does the soul destroy in those *karmas?*

दंसणणाणचरित्तं किंचिवि णत्थि दु अचेयणे काये।
तम्हा किं घादयदे चेदयिदा तेसु कायेसु॥ ३६८॥

daṁsaṇāṇācarittaṁ kiṁcivi ṇatthi du aceyaṇe kāye
tamhā kiṁ ghādayade cedayidā tesu kāyesu (368)

दर्शनज्ञानचरित्रं किंचिदपि नास्ति त्वचेतने काये।
तस्मात् किं घातयति चेतयिता तेषु कायेषु॥ ३६८॥

368. There is no faith, knowledge, or conduct whatsoever in non-intelligent body; therefore what does the soul destroy in those bodies?

णाणस्स दंसणस्स य भणिओ घाओ तहा चरित्तस्स।
णवि तम्हि पोग्गलदव्वस्स को वि घाओउ णिद्दिट्ठो॥ ३६९॥

ṇāṇassa daṁsaṇassa ya bhaṇio ghāo tahā carittassa
ṇavi tamhi poggladavvassa ko vi ghaou ṇiddiṭṭho (369)

ज्ञानस्य दर्शनस्य च भणितो घातस्तथा चारित्रस्य।
नापि तत्र पुद्गलद्रव्यस्य कोऽपि घातस्तु निर्दिष्टः॥ ३६९॥

369. Destruction of knowledge, faith and conduct (of the erroneous kind by the soul) is spoken of; but destruction of matter is never indicated.

जीवस्स जे गुणा केई णत्थि खलु ते परेसु दव्वेसु।
तम्हा सम्मादिट्ठिस्स णत्थि रागो उ विसएसु॥ ३७०॥

jīvassa je guṇā kei ṇatthi khalu te paresu davvesu
tamhā sammādiṭṭhissa ṇatthi rāgo u visaesu (370)

जीवस्स ये गुणाः केचिन्न सन्ति खलु ते परेषु द्रव्येषु।
तस्मात्सम्यग्दृष्टेर्नास्ति रागस्तु विषयेषु॥ ३७०॥

370. Whatever attributes are present in a soul, those are certainly not present in other substances; therefore in a right believer there is no attraction for sense-objects.

रागो दोसो मोहो जीवस्सेव य अणण्णपरिणामा।
एएण कारणेण उ सद्दादिसु णत्थि रागादि॥ ३७१॥

rāgo doso moho jīvasseva ya aṇaṇṇapariṇāmā
eeṇa kāraṇeṇa u saddādisu ṇatthi rāgādi (371)

रागो द्वेषो मोहो जीवस्यैव चानन्यपरिणामाः।
एतेन कारणेन तु शब्दादिषु न सन्ति रागादयः॥ ३७१॥

371. Attachment, aversion and delusion are the soul's own inalienable modes; for these reasons there is no attachment, etc. in sound, etc.

Commentary : A substance and its intrinsic property are so intimately related to each other that if the substance is destroyed, the property is also destroyed; and, conversely, when the property is destroyed the substance must also be destroyed. For example take a flame and the light proceeding from it. If the flame will be destroyed there will be no light, and if the light will be destroyed there will be no flame. But in the case of objects which do not have the intimate relations, the destruction of one need not follow the destruction of the other. For example take the case of lamp placed on a stand. The lamp may be destroyed while the stand may remain intact, and conversely the stand may break without destroying the lamp. Faith, knowledge and conduct are the intrinsic properties of the Self. In their impure form, they form the states of the impure Self which blinded by nescience is incapable of realising its pure nature. Realisation of the pure nature of the Self necessarily presupposes the destruction of these impure states of consciousness, wrong faith, wrong knowledge, and wrong conduct. These attributes of the Self are externally related to *karmic* materials. Since the psychic attributes of the Self have nothing to do with non-conscious matter which is only accidentally and externally related to psychic states, the destruction of the psychic states will not in any way result in the destruction of matter. Otherwise destruction of the properties of the Self must lead to the destruction of matter and, conversely, the destruction of the soul. This is absurd. Therefore the emotional states of attachment, aversion, and delusion are only properties of the Self brought about by *ajñāna,* and they can never be present in their objects. But when *ajñāna,* or nescience disappears, the impure emotions depending upon it will also disappear and the Self will regain its pure nature. The presence of impure emotions and their destruction leading to the consequential restoration of the purity of the Self, neither of these things can be predicated of external objects since the nature of the physical object cannot accommodate these properties of consciousness.

Next the author points out that the property of one thing cannot be produced by an entirely different thing.

अण्णदवियेण अण्णदवियस्स णो कीरइ गुणुप्पाओ।
तम्हा उ सव्वदव्वा उप्पज्जंते सहावेण॥ ३७२॥

aṇṇadaviyeṇa aṇṇadaviyassa ṇa kīrai guṇuppāo
tamhā u savvadavvā uppajjaṁte sahāveṇa (372)

अन्यद्रव्येणान्यद्रव्यस्य न क्रियते गुणोत्पादः।
तस्मात्तु सर्वद्रव्याण्युत्पद्यन्ते स्वभावेन॥ ३७२॥

372. By one substance (*dravya)* the properties of another substance are never produced. Therefore all substances are produced by their own nature. (See Appendix).

Commentary : By this *gāthā* the author once again emphasises the fact that impure conditions such as attachment and aversion being attributes of consciousness are not really produced by external objects. Hence if a person dissatisfied with his impure states of consciousness and actuated by sincere desire for self-reformation proceeds with a righteous indignation to destroy those external objects which he imagines to be the cause of his own impure emotions of attachment and aversion, he merely exhibits his own ignorance of the real nature of things and proceeds on a wrong path to achieve his goal of self-reformation. It is this point that is elaborated in the previous six *gāthās* and further emphasised in the present one.

णिंदियसंथुयवयणाणि पोग्गला परिणमंति बहुगाणि।
ताणि सुणिऊण रुसइ तूसइ पुणो अहं भणिओ॥ ३७३॥

ṇiṁdiyasaṁthuyavayaṇāṇi poggalā pariṇamaṁti bahugāṇi
tāṇi suṇiūṇa rusai tūsai puṇo ahaṁ bhaṇio (373)

निन्दितसंस्तुतवचनानि पुद्गलाः परिणमन्ति बहुकानि।
तानि श्रुत्वा रुष्यति तुष्यति च पुनरहं भणितः॥ ३७३॥

373. Words of blame or praise are (only) sound produced by material particles modified in various forms. On hearing them one gets angry or pleased thinking, "I am addressed thus."

पोग्गलदव्वं सद्दत्तपरिणयं तस्स जइ गुणो अण्णो।
तम्हा ण तुमं भणिओ किंचिवि किं रुससि अबुहो॥ ३७४॥

poggaladavvaṁ saddattapariṇayaṁ tassa jai guṇo aṇṇo
tamhā ṇa tumaṁ bhaṇio kiṁcivi kiṁ rusasi abuho (374)

पुद्गलद्रव्यं शब्दत्वपरिणतं तस्य यदि गुणोऽन्यः।
तस्मान्न त्वं भणितः किंचिदपि किं रुष्यस्यबुधः॥ ३७४॥

374. As words are really produced by modification of material particles, therefore their properties are entirely different from that of yours. Hence you are not in any way addressed by them. Why do you get angry? Oh, ignorant person.

असुहो सुहोव सुद्दो ण तं भणइ सुणसु मं ति सो चेव।
ण य एइ विणिग्गहिउं सोयविसयमागयं सद्दं॥ ३७५॥

asuho suhova saddo ṇa taṁ bhaṇai suṇasu maṁ ti so ceva
ṇa ya ei viṇiggahiuṁ soyavisayamāgayaṁ saddaṁ (375)

अशुभः शुभो वा शब्दः न त्वां भणति श्रृणु मामिति स एव।
न चैति विनिर्गृहीतुं श्रोत्रविषयमागतं शब्दम्॥ ३७५॥

375. A bad or good word does not of its own accord say to thee, "Hear me". Even when the sound reaches the organ of hearing it does not arrive to seize your attention (by force).

असुहं सुहं च रूवं ण तं भणइ पेच्छ मं ति सो चेव।
ण य एइ विणिग्गहिउं चक्खुविसयमागयं रूवं॥ ३७६॥

asuhaṁ suhaṁ ca rūvaṁ ṇa taṁ bhaṇai peccha maṁ ti so ceva
ṇa ya ei viṇiggahiuṁ cakkhuvisayamāgayaṁ rūvaṁ (376)

अशुभं शुभं वा रूपं न त्वां भणति पश्य मामिति स एव।
न चैति विनिर्गृहीतुं चक्षुर्विषयमागतं रूपम्॥ ३७६॥

376. An unpleasant or pleasant visual form does not of its own accord say to thee, "See me." Even when the visual stimulus reahces the organ of sight, it does not arrive there to seize your attention (by force).

असुहो सुहो व गंधो ण तं भणइ जिग्घ मं ति सो चेव।
ण य एइ विणिग्गहिउं घाणविसयमागयं गंधं॥ ३७७॥

asuho suho va gaṁdho ṇa taṁ bhaṇai jiggha maṁ ti so ceva
ṇa ya ei viṇiggahiuṁ ghāṇavisayamāgayaṁ gaṁdhaṁ

अशुभः शुभो वा गन्धो न त्वां भणति जिघ्र मामिति स एव।
न चैति विनिर्गृहीतुं घ्राणविषयमागतं गन्धम्॥ ३७७॥

377. Disagreeable or agreeable odour does not of its own accord say to thee, "Smell me." Even when the smell reaches the organ of smelling, it does not arrive there to seize your attention (by force).

असुहो सुहो व रसो ण तं भणइ रसय मं ति सो चेव।
ण य एइ विणिग्गहिउं रसणविसयमागयं तु रसं॥ ३७८॥

asuho suho va raso ṇa taṁ bhaṇai rasaya maṁ ti so ceva
ṇa ya ei viṇiggahiuṁ rasaṇavisayamāgayaṁ tu rasaṁ

अशुभः शुभो वा रसो न त्वां भणति रसय मामिति स एव।
न चैति विनिर्गृहीतुं रसनविषयमागतं तु रसम्॥ ३७८॥

378. Bad or good taste does not of its own accord say to thee, "Taste me." Even when the taste reaches the organ of tasting (tongue), it does not arrive there to seize your attention (by force).

असुहो सुहो व फासो ण तं भणइ फास मं ति सो चेव।
ण य एइ विणिग्गहिउं कायविसयमागयं फासं॥ ३७९॥

asuho suho va phāso ṇa taṁ bhaṇai phāsa maṁ ti so ceva
ṇa ya ei viṇiggahiuṁ kāyavisayamāgayaṁ phasaṁ (379)

अशुभः शुभो वा स्पर्शो न त्वां भणति स्पृश मामिति स एव।
न चैति विनिर्गृहीतुं कायविषयमागतं स्पर्शम्॥ ३७९॥

379. Unpleasant or pleasant touch does not of its own accord say to thee, "Touch me." When the contact stimulus reaches the organ of contact (body), it does not arrive there to seize your attention (by force).

असुहो सुहो व गुणो ण तं भणइ बुज्झ मं ति सो चेव।
ण य एइ विणिग्गहिउं बुद्धिविसयमागयं तु गुणं॥ ३८०॥

asuho suho va guṇo ṇa taṁ bhaṇai bujjha maṁ ti so ceva
ṇa ya ei viṇiggahiyuṁ buddhivisayamāgayaṁ tu guṇaṁ

अशुभः शुभो वा गुणो न त्वां भणति बुध्यस्व मामिति स एव।
न चैति विनिर्गृहीतुं बुद्धिविषयमागतं तु गुणम्॥ ३८०॥

380. The bad or good quality (of an object) does not of its own accord say to thee, "Think of me." Even when the quality reaches the organ of thinking (mind), it does not arrive there to seize your attention (by force).

असुहं सुहं व दव्वं ण तं भणइ बुज्झ मं ति सो चेव।
ण य एइ विणिग्गहिउं बुद्धिविसयमागयं दव्वं ॥ ३८१॥

asuhaṁ suhaṁ va davvaṁ ṇa taṁ bhaṇai bujjha maṁ ti so ceva
ṇa ya ei viṇiggahiyuṁ buddhivisayamāgayaṁ davvaṁ

अशुभं शुभं वा द्रव्यं न त्वां भणति बुध्यस्व मामिति स एव।
न चैति विनिर्गृहीतुं बुद्धिविषयमागतं द्रव्यम्॥ ३८१॥

381. A bad or good substance does not of its own accord say to thee, "Think of me." Even when the (idea of)

substance reaches the organ of thinking (mind), it does not arrive there to seize your attention (by force).

एवं तु जाणि दव्वस्स उपसमंणेव गच्छइ मूढो।
णिग्गहमणा परस्स य सयं च बुद्धिं सिवमप्पत्तो॥ ३८२॥

evaṁ tu jāṇi davvassa uvasamaṁṇeva gacchai mūḍho
ṇiggahamaṇā parassa ya sayaṁ ca buddhiṁ
sivamappatto (382)

एवं तु ज्ञातद्रव्यस्य उपशमनैव गच्छति मूढः।
निर्ग्रहमनाः परस्य च स्वयं च बुद्धिं शिवामप्राप्तः॥ ३८२॥

382. Thus devoid of a clear understanding of the nature of the objects of knowledge and incapable of abstaining from external influence, and himself not attaining mental happiness, the ignorant person does not go along the path of peace.

Commentary : Here is a beautiful picture of an individual perceiving agent situated in the midst of an environment abounding in sense-stimuli of various kinds. The environment is always full of sense-stimuli pertaining to sound, sight, smell, taste and touch. These stimuli proceed from physical objects situated in the environment, and hence they are also of physical nature. These stimuli of physical nature may reach the appropriate sense-organs of the individual person. Sound-stimulus may reach the ear, light may reach the eyes, odour may reach the nose, taste stimulus may reach the tongue, contact stimulus, the skin of the body. The mere presence of the stimuli in the environment and even their coming into contact with the respective sense-organs may not be effective enough to produce the psychic reaction in the consciousness of the individual. Many sound stimuli may not even cross the threshold of consciousness. One or two may appear in the field of consciousness and yet may flit away without being noticed. The same is the case with the other sense-stimuli. That particular sense stimulus which is capable of producing the corresponding psychic reaction does so because of the selective attention on the part of the individual. This selective attention on the part of the individual is prompted and directed by his own interest in the thing. It is this interest that he takes in the particular thing towards which his selective attention is directed that is mainly responsible for that particular sense-perception. Whether the sense perception is auditory or visual or of any other kind in each case the individual chooses a particular stimulus, attends to it because of his personal relation to it. Thus the immediate causal condition of the psychic fact of perception is the individual himself. Whatever interests him will be perceived by him and others which are of no interest to him will pass away unnoticed. When one psychic fact of perception is thus brought about by the selective attention on the part of the individual consciousness, the perception further brings about the hedonic reaction in the individual consciousness of pleasantness or unpleasantness. This feeling of pleasure or pain associated with the psychic fact of perception is also determined by the attitude of individual consciousness. When perception and its hedonic reaction in the consciousness are thus entirely determined by the psychological attitude of the individual, it is merely ignorance to take external objects of the perceptual world to be responsible for the hedonic reaction in one's self. The objects in the external world from which the stimuli proceed are entirely physical in nature and hence cannot be directly responsible for the psychic modification, perceptual and hedonic, occurring in the individual consciousness. It is this important psychological truth that is imparted by the author to an unenlightened person who is ignorant of the real nature of perception and the hedonic reaction thereby. If you set your mind in order, if you cease to take interest in the object of the perceptual world, if you direct your attention on your own Self and thus get absorbed in contemplation of the truth and beauty of the Pure Self, then the innumerable sense-organs constantly will be absolutely impotent to disturb you from your self-absorption, and you will remain enjoying the spiritual bliss which transcends all pleasures derivable from the sense-presented world.

Next it is pointed out that the Self which is free from the impure psychic states of attachment and aversion, which remains the pure Knower, will also be rid of the consciousness of being the agent, enjoyer of *karmas* and continue to be only the pure consciousness of the Knower.

कम्मं जं पुव्वकयं सुहासुहमणेयवित्थरविसेसं।
तत्तो णियत्तए अप्पयं तु जो सो पडिक्कमणं॥ ३८३॥

kammaṁ jaṁ puvvakayaṁ suhāsuhamaṇeyavitthara-visesaṁ
tatto ṇiyattae appayṁ tu jo so paḍikkamaṇaṁ (383)

कर्म यत्पूर्वकृतं शुभाशुभमनेकविस्तरविशेषम्।
तस्मान्निवर्तयत्यात्मानं तु यः स प्रतिक्रमणम्॥ ३८३॥

383. When a person turns his Self away from his previous *karmas*, good or bad, and of multifarious kinds, then that Self is certainly the *niścaya pratikramaṇa*, real repentance.

कम्मं जं सुंहमसुहं जम्हि य भावेहिं बज्झइ भविस्सं।
तत्तो णियत्तए जो सो पच्चक्खाणं हवइ चेया॥ ३८४॥

kammaṁ jaṁ suhamasuhaṁ jamhi ya bhāvehiṁ bajjhai bhavissaṁ
tatto ṇiyattae jo so paccakkhāṇaṁ havai ceyā (384)

कर्म यच्छुभमशुभं यस्मिंश्च भावे बध्यते भविष्यत्।
तस्मान्निवर्तते यः सः प्रत्याख्यानं भवति चेतयिता॥ ३८४॥

384. When a person keeps his Self away from future bondage likely to be caused by impure psychic states resulting from *karmas,* good or bad, then that Self is certainly the *niścaya pratyākhyāna* or real renunciation.

जं सुहमसुहमुदिण्णं संपहि य अणेयवित्थरविसेसं।
तं दोसं जो चेयइ सो खलु आलोयणं चेया॥ ३८५॥

jaṁ suhamasuhamudiṇṇaṁ saṁpahi ya aṇeyavittharavisesaṁ
taṁ dosaṁ jo ceyai so khalu āloyaṇaṁ ceyā (385)

यच्छुभमशुभमुदीर्णं संप्रति चानेकविस्तरविशेषम्।
तं दोषं यः चेतयते स खल्वालोचनं चेतयिता॥ ३८५॥

385. That soul which realises as evil all those psychic states of multifarious kinds which arise at present (in the consciousness) due to the operation of *karmas* is certainly the *niścaya ālocanā* or real confession.

णिच्चं पच्चक्खाणं कुव्वइ णिच्चं जो य पडिक्कमदि।
णिच्चं आलोचेयइ सो हु चरित्तं हवइ चेया॥ ३८६॥

ṇiccaṁ paccakkhāṇaṁ kuvvai ṇiccaṁ jo ya paḍikkamadi
ṇiccaṁ āloceyai so hu caittaṁ havai ceyā (386)

नित्यं प्रत्याख्यानं करोति नित्यं प्रतिक्रमति यश्च।
नित्यमालोचयति स खलु चरित्रं भवति चेतयिता॥ ३८६॥

386. The Self which is always engaged in the practice of these-real repentance, renunciation and confession, is certainly the *niścaya* or real right conduct.

Commentary : The Self which is thus of real pure conduct is the same as the Self which has realised his own pure nature of *jñāna* or knowledge.

वेदंतो कम्मफलं अप्पाणं कुणइ जो दु कम्मफलं।
सो तं पुणो वि बंधइ बीयं दुक्खस्स अट्ठविहं॥ ३८७॥

vedaṁto kammaphalaṁ appāṇaṁ kuṇai jo du kammaphalaṁ
so taṁ puṇo vi baṁdhai bīyaṁ dukkhassa aṭṭhavihaṁ

वेदयमानः कर्मफलमात्मानं करोति यस्तु कर्मफलम्।
स तत् पुनरपि बध्नाति बीजं दुःखस्याष्टविधम्॥ ३८७॥

387. One who experiencing the fruit of *karmas* identifies the Self with the fruit of *karma,* again sows the seeds of *karmic* bondage and misery of eight different kinds.

वेदंतो कम्मफलं मये कयं मुणइ जो दु कम्मफलं।
सो तं पुणोवि बंधइ बीयं दुक्खस्स अट्ठविहं॥ ३८८॥

vadaṁto kammaphalaṁ maye kayaṁ muṇai jo du kammaphalaṁ
so taṁ puṇovi baṁdhai bīyaṁ dukkhassa aṭṭhavihaṁ

वेदयमानः कर्मफलं मया कृतं जानाति यस्तु कर्मफलम्।
स तत पुनरपि बध्नाति बीजं दुःखस्याष्टविधम्॥ ३८८॥

388. One who experiencing the fruit of *karmas* thinks that he has brought it about, again sows the seeds of *karmic* bondage and misery of eight different kinds.

वेदंतो कम्मफलं सुहिदो दुहिदो य हवदि जो चेदा।
सो तं पुणोवि बंधइ बीयं दुक्खस्स अट्ठविहं॥ ३८९॥

vedaṁto kammaphalaṁ suhido duhido ya havadi jo cedā
so taṁ puṇovi baṁdhai bīyaṁ dukkhassa aṭṭhavihaṁ

वेदयमानः कर्मफलं सुखितो दुःखिश्च भवति यश्चेतयिता।
स तत्पुनरपि बध्नाति बीजं दुःखस्याष्टविधम्॥ ३८९॥

389. The soul that experiencing the fruit of *karmas* is made happy or miserable thereby, again sows the seeds of *karmic* bondage and misery of eight different kinds.

Commentary : The consciousness that, 'I am other than *jñāna* or pure knowledge' is *ajñāa cetanā* or nescient consciousness. That is of two kinds, *karma-cetanā*, and *karma-phala-cetanā.'* The feeling that, 'I produce all these things other than *jñāna*' is *karma-cetanā*. The consciousness that, 'I enjoy the fruits of all things other than *jñāna'* is *karma-phala-cetanā*. These two constitute the seed for *saṁsāra,* because they form really the cause of the eight kinds of *karmas* which form the causal condition of *saṁsāra*. Therefore the person who wants to attain *mokṣa* must destroy these two forms of *ajñāna-cetanā,* nescient consciousness. In order to achieve this end, he must renounce all *karmas* or action and also renounce all *karma-phala* or the fruits of his action. It is only by that method he can realise his divine nature of *(śuddha-jñāna cetanā)* pure consciousness of knowledge which will be his permanent heritage.

Next it is pointed out that the nature of knowledge is entirely distinct from that of other objects.

[१]सत्थं णाणं ण हवइ जम्हा सत्थं ण याणए किंचि।
तम्हा अण्णं णाणं अण्णं सत्थं जिणा विंति॥ ३९०॥

satthaṁ ṇāṇaṁ ṇa havai jamhā satthaṁ ṇa yāṇae kiṁci
tamhā aṇṇaṁ ṇāṇaṁ aṇṇaṁ satthaṁ jiṇā viṁti (390)

शास्त्रं ज्ञानं न भवति यस्माच्छास्त्रं न जानाति किंचित्।
तस्मादन्यज्ज्ञानमन्यच्छास्त्रं जिना वदन्ति॥ ३९०॥

१. सचमिति

390. The scripture is not knowledge, because the Scripture knows not anything. Therefore the Jinas have said that knowledge is entirely different from Scripture.

सद्दो णाणं ण हवइ जम्हा सद्दो ण याणए किंचि।
तम्हा अण्णं णाणं अण्णं सद्दं जिणा विंति॥ ३९१॥

saddo ṇāṇaṁ ṇa havai jaṁhā saddo ṇa yāṇae kiṁci
tamhā aṇṇaṁ ṇāṇaṁ aṇṇaṁ saddaṁ jiṇā viṁti (391)

शब्दो ज्ञानं न भवति यस्माच्छब्दो न जानाति किंचित्।
तस्मादन्यज्ज्ञानमन्यं शब्दं जिना वदन्ति॥ ३९१॥

391. Sound is not knowledge, because sound knows not anything. Therefore the Jinas have said that knowledge is entirely different from sound.

रूवं णाणं ण हवइ जम्हा रूवं ण याणए किंचि।
तम्हा अण्णं णाणं अण्णं रूवं जिणा विंति॥ ३९२॥

rūvaṁ ṇāṇaṁ ṇa havai jamhā rūvaṁ ṇa yāṇae kiṁci
tamhā aṇṇaṁ ṇāṇaṁ aṇṇaṁ rūvaṁ jiṇā viṁti (392)

रूपं ज्ञानं न भवति यस्माद्रूपं न जानाति किंचित्।
तस्मादन्यज्ज्ञानमन्यद्रूपं जिना वदन्ति॥ ३९२॥

392. Visual form is not knowledge, because visual form knows not anything. Therefore the Jinas have said that knowledge is entirely different from visual form.

वण्णो णाणं ण हवइ जम्हा वण्णो ण याणए किंचि।
तम्हा अण्णं णाणं अण्णं वण्णं जिणा विंति॥ ३९३॥

vaṇṇo ṇāṇaṁ ṇa havai jamhā vaṇṇo ṇa yāṇae kiṁci
tamhā aṇṇaṁ ṇāṇaṁ aṇṇaṁ vaṇṇaṁ jiṇā viṁti (393)

वर्णो ज्ञानं न भवति यस्माद्वर्णो न जानाति किंचित्।
तस्मादन्यज्ज्ञानमन्यं वर्णं जिना वदन्ति॥ ३९३॥

393. Colour is not knowledge, because colour knows not anything. Therefore the Jinas have said that knowledge is entirely different from colour.

गंधो णाणं ण हवइ जम्हा गंधो ण याणए किंचि।
तम्हा अण्णं णाणं अण्णं गंधं जिणा विंति॥ ३९४॥

gaṁdho ṇāṇaṁ ṇa havai jamhā gaṁdho ṇa yāṇae kiṁci
tamhā aṇṇaṁ ṇāṇaṁ aṇṇaṁ gaṁdhaṁ jiṇā viṁti (394)

गन्धो ज्ञानं न भवति यस्माद्गन्धो न जानाति किंचित्।
तस्मादन्यज्ञानमन्यं गन्धं जिना वदन्ति॥ ३९४॥

394. Smell is not knowledge, because smell knows not anything. Therefore the Jinas have said that knowledge is entirely different from smell.

ण रसो दु हवइ णाणं जम्हा दु रसो ण याणए किंचि।
तम्हा अण्णं णाणं रसं य अण्णं जिणा विंति॥ ३९५॥

ṇa raso du havai ṇāṇaṁ jamhā du raso ṇa yāṇae kiṁci
tamhā aṇṇaṁ ṇāṇaṁ rasaṁ ya aṇṇaṁ jiṇā viṁti (395)

न रसस्तु भवति ज्ञानं यस्मात्तु रसो न जानाति किंचित्।
तस्मादन्यज्ज्ञानं रसं चान्यं जिना वदन्ति॥ ३९५॥

395. Taste is not knowledge, because taste knows not anything. Therefore the Jinas have said that knowledge is entirely different from taste.

फासो णाणं ण हवइ जम्हा फासो ण याणए किंचि।
तम्हा अण्णं णाणं अण्णं फासं जिणा विंति॥ ३९६॥

phāso ṇāṇaṁ ṇa havai jamhā phāso ṇa yāṇae kiṁci
tamhā aṇṇaṁ ṇāṇaṁ aṇṇaṁ phāsaṁ jiṇā viṁti (396)

स्पर्शो ज्ञानं न भवति यस्मात्स्पर्शो न जानाति किंचित्।
तस्मादन्यज्ज्ञानमन्यं स्पर्शं जिना वदन्ति॥ ३९६॥

396. Touch is not knowledge, because touch knows not anything. Therefore the Jinas have said that knowledge is entirely different from touch.

कम्मं णाणं ण हवइ जम्हा कम्मं ण याणए किंचि।
तम्हा अण्णं णाणं अण्णं कम्मं जिणा विंति॥ ३९७॥

kammaṁ ṇāṇaṁ ṇa havai jamhā kammaṁ ṇa yāṇae kiṁci
tamhā aṇṇaṁ ṇāṇaṁ aṇṇaṁ kammaṁ jiṇā viṁti (397)

कर्म ज्ञानं न भवति यस्मात्कर्म न जानाति किंचित्।
तस्मादन्यज्ज्ञानमन्यत्कर्म जिना वदन्ति॥ ३९७॥

397. *Karma* is not knowledge, because *karma* knows not anything. Therefore the Jinas have said that knowledge is entirely different from *karma*.

धम्मो णाणं ण हवइ जम्हा धम्मो ण याणए किंचि।
तम्हा अण्णं णाणं अण्णं धम्मं जिणा विंति॥ ३९८॥

dhammo ṇāṇaṁ ṇa havai jamhā dhammo ṇa yāṇae kiṁci
tamhā aṇṇaṁ ṇāṇaṁ aṇṇaṁ dhammaṁ jiṇā viṁti (398)

धर्मो ज्ञानं न भवति यस्माद्धर्मो न जानाति किंचित्।
तस्मादन्यज्ज्ञानमन्यं धर्मं जिना वदन्ति॥ ३९८॥

398. Principle of motion is not knowledge, becasue the principle of motion knows not anything. Therefore the Jinas have said that knowledge is entirely different from the principle of motion.

णाणमधम्मो ण हवदि जम्हाधम्मो ण याणए किंचि।
तम्हा अण्णं णाणं अण्णमधम्मं जिणा विंति॥ ३९९॥

ṇāṇamadhammo ṇa havadi jamhā adhammo ṇa yāṇae kiṁci
tamhā aṇṇaṁ ṇāṇaṁ aṇṇamadhammaṁ jiṇā viṁti (399)

ज्ञानमधर्मो न भवति यस्मात् अधर्मो जानाति किंचित्।
तस्मादन्यज्ज्ञानमन्यमधर्मं जिना वदन्ति॥ ३९९॥

399. The principle of Rest is not knowledge, because the principle of Rest knows not anything. Therefore the Jinas have said that knowledge is entirely different from the principle of rest.

कालो णाणं ण हवइ जम्हा कालो ण याणए किंचि।
तम्हा अण्णं णाणं अण्णं कालं जिणा विंति॥ ४००॥

kālo ṇānaṁ ṇa havai jamhā kālo ṇa yāṇae kiṁci
tamhṁ aṇṇaṁ ṇāṇaṁ aṇṇaṁ kālaṁ jiṇā viṁti (400)

कालो ज्ञानं न भवति यस्मात्कालो न जानाति किंचित्।
तस्मादन्यज्ज्ञानमन्यं कालं जिना वदन्ति॥ ४००॥

400. Time is not knowledge, because time knows not anything. Therefore the Jinas have said that knowledge is entirely different from time.

आयासंपि ण णाणं जम्हायासं ण याणए किंचि।
तम्हा आयासं अण्णं णाणं अण्णं जिणा विंति॥ ४०१॥

āyāsaṁpi ṇā ṇāṇāṁ jamhāyāsaṁ ṇa yāṇae kiṁci
taṁhā āyāsaṁ aṇṇaṁ ṇāṇaṁ aṇṇaṁ jiṇā viṁti (401)

आकाशमपि न ज्ञानं यस्मादाकाशं न जानाति किंचित्।
तस्मादन्याकाशमन्यज्ज्ञानं जिना वदन्ति॥ ४०१॥

401. Space is not knowledge, because space knows not anything. Therefore the Jinas have said that knowledge is entirely different from space.

णाज्झवसाणं णाणं अज्झवसाणं अचेदणं जम्हा।
तम्हा अण्णं णाणं अज्झवसाणं तहा अण्णं॥ ४०२॥

ṇājjhavasāṇaṁ ṇāṇaṁ ajjhavasāṇaṁ acedaṇaṃ jamhā
tamhā aṇṇaṁ ṇāṇaṁ ajjhavasāṇaṁ tahā aṇṇaṁ (402)

नाध्यवसानं ज्ञानमध्यवसानमचेतनं यस्मात्।
तस्मादन्यज्ज्ञानमध्यवसानं तथान्यत्॥ ४०२॥

402. Effort is not knowledge, because, effort knows not anything. Therefore knowledge is one thing and effort quite another.

जम्हा जाणइ णिच्चं तम्हा जीवो दु जाणओ णाणी।
णाणं च जाणयादो अव्वदिरित्तं मुणेयव्वं॥ ४०३॥

Jamhā jāṇai ṇiccaṁ tamhā jīvo du jāṇao ṇāṇī
ṇāṇaṁ ca jāṇayādo avvadirittaṁ muṇeyavvaṁ (403)

यस्माज्जानाति नित्यं तस्माज्जीवस्तु ज्ञायको ज्ञानी।
ज्ञानं च ज्ञायकादव्यतिरिक्तं ज्ञातव्यम्॥ ४०३॥

403. As the characteristic of the soul is to be always knowing, therefore the soul is certainly the subject of knowledge, the Knower, *par excellence*. It should be understood that knowledge and the knower cannot be differentiated from each other.

णाणं सम्मादिट्ठि दु संजमं सुत्तमंगपुव्वगयं।
धम्माधम्मं च तहा पव्वज्जं अब्भुवंति बुहा॥ ४०४॥

ṇāṇaṁ sammādiṭṭhi du saṁjamaṁ suttamaṁgapuvva-
gayaṁ
dhammādhammaṁ ca tahā pavvajjaṁ abbhuvaṁti buhā

ज्ञानं सम्यग्दृष्टिस्तु संयमं सूत्रमंगपूर्वगतम्।
धर्माधर्मं च तथा प्रव्रज्यामभ्युपयन्ति बुधा:॥ ४०४॥

404. Knowledge is the same as right belief, discipline, Scripture consisting of *aṅgas pūrvas*, merit and demerit and

asceticism. So declare the wise.

Commentary : The investigation into the nature of Self or *samayasāra* has resulted in the above definitions of the *ātmā*. The definition is both negative and affirmative. Negatively it states what it is not and affirmatively it states what it is. All the facts which are distinct in nature from that of the Self are excluded from the scope of definition, whereas all the facts which are of the nature of Self are included. Thus the definition is logically accurate inasmuch as it is free from the usual fallacy of definition of either being too wide or too narrow. These two defects according to Indian Logic are called respectively *ativyāpti* and *avyāpti*. The former indicates the defects of including the things which do not come into the concept defined, and the latter refers to the neglect of not including the facts which should come under the scope of definition. The definition in its affirmative form therefore emphasises the intrinsic identity between the thing and its attributes, *jīva* and *jñāna*– Self and knowledge. A thing and its attributes are not different categories brought together by a third category called *samavāya,* a view maintained by other schools of thought. According to Jaina metaphysics *dravya* and *guṇa* are inseparable and indivisible unity—no *dravya* without *guṇa* and no *guṇa* without *dravya*. This leads to the fundamental proposition which states the identity of the Self with knowledge. The Self, the Knower, is identical with knowledge. *Jñāna* and *jñānī* are one and the same. The definition further implies as its corrollory that the different aspects and modifications of the Self are also identical with the Self or *ātmā*. Thus right belief, right knowledge, and right conduct, which are but different aspects of the same Self become identical with the Self. These three conjointly constitute the *mokṣa mārga*—the path to spiritual salvation, and the *mokṣa mārga* also must be located in the nature of the Self as it is identical in nature with that of the Self inasmuch as it represents a stage in the development of the Self. Thus it is clearly pointed out that the Kingdom of Heaven is within you. One who deserves to reach the goal of liberation or *mokṣa* has nothing to do with the non-conscious external things since he has within himself everything that is necessary to realise his purpose. The spiritual development therefore consists in the continuous development of the Self to a higher and higher state followed by the progressive widening of knowledge till the Self becomes perfect and knowledge becomes completely co-extensive with the reality. At this stage the Self becomes both *sarvajña* and *paramātmā,* the Omniscient and the Absolute Self. This is the end of *saṁsāra* and the goal of life from which there is no return.

If *jñāna* is thus completely different from other things, how can *jñāna* be the eater of food? The answer is given below.

अत्ता जस्स अमुत्तो णहु सो आहारओ हवइ एवं।
आहारो खलु मुत्तो जम्हा सो पोग्गलमओ उ॥ ४०५॥

attā jassa amutto ṇahu so āhārao havai evaṁ
āhāro khalu mutto jamhā so poggalamao u (405)

आत्मा यस्यामूर्तो न खलु स आहारको भवत्येवम्।
आहारः खलु मूर्तो यस्मात्स पुद्गलमयस्तु॥ ४०५॥

405. Since the Self is non-corporeal, he is certainly not the eater of food, because food being of the nature of matter is corporeal.

ण वि सक्कइ घित्तुं जं ण[१] वि मोत्तुं जं य जं परदव्वं।
सो कोवि य तस्स गुणो पाउग्गिय विस्ससो वावि॥ ४०६॥

१. णवि मोत्तं जं परं दव्वं।

ṇa vi sakkai ghittuṁ jaṁ ṇa vi mottuṁ jaṁ ya jaṁ paradavvaṁ
so kovi ya tassa guṇo pāuggiya vissaso vāvi (406)

नापि शक्यते गृहीतुं यन्न विमोक्तुं यत्परं द्रव्यम्।
स कोऽपि च तस्य गुणः प्रायोगिको वैस्रसो वापि॥ ४०६॥

406. It has no attribute either acquired or natural to enable it to grasp or give up foreign matter.

तम्हा उ जो विसुद्धो चेया सो णेव गिण्हए किंचि।
णेव विमुंचइ किंचिवि जीवाजीवाण दव्वाणं॥ ४०७॥

tamhā u jo visuddho ceyā so ṇeva giṇhae kiṁci
ṇeva vimuṁcai kiṁcivi jīvājīvāṇa davvāṇaṁ (407)

तस्मात्तु यो विशुद्धश्चेतयिता स नैव गृह्णाति किंचित्।
नैव विमुञ्चति किंचिदपि जीवाजीवयोर्द्रव्ययोः॥ ४०७॥

407. Therefore that Self which is of the nature of pure consciousness neither grasps anything nor relinquishes anything of objects, animate or inanimate.

Commentary : These *gāthās* are obviously intended to refute the Upaniṣadic doctrine that *ātmā* is *anna-maya* and *kośa-maya* for valid reasons.

Next it is pointed out that adopting any bodily insignia or mark as a means for realising *moksa* is certainly inadequate because the body is shown to be the eater of food and hence corporeal and distinct from the non-corporeal Self.

पासंडिय लिंगाणिव गिहलिंगाणि व बहुप्पयाराणि।
घित्तुं वदंति मूढा लिंगमिणं मोक्खमग्गोत्ति॥ ४०८॥

pāsaṁḍiya liṁgāṇiva gihaliṁgāṇi va bahuppayārāṇi
ghittuṁ vadaṁti mūḍhā lingamiṇaṁ mokkhamaggotti (

पाषण्डिलिङ्गानि वा गृहलिङ्गानि वा बहुप्रकाराणि।
गृहीत्वा वदन्ति मूढा लिङ्गमिदं मोक्षमार्ग इति॥ ४०८॥

408. Fools put on various types of insignia of false ascetics or householders and maintain that this outer mark constitutes the path to *mokṣa*.

णदु होइ मोक्खमग्गो लिंगं जं देहणिम्ममा अरिहा।
लिंगं मुचित्तु दंसणणाणचरित्ताणि सेवंति॥ ४०९॥

ṇadu hoi mokkhamaggo liṁgaṁ jaṁ dehaṇimmamā arihā
liṁgaṁ mucittu daṁsaṇaṇāṇacarittāṇi sevaṁti (409)

न तु भवति मोक्षमार्गो लिङ्गं यद्देहनैर्ममा अर्हन्तः।
लिङ्गं मुक्त्वा दर्शनज्ञानचारित्राणि सेवन्ते॥ ४०९॥

409. Bodily mark is not certainly the path of emancipation (as is evident from the fact that) the *Arhats* discard the bodily mark by disowning the body itself and devote their attention only to right belief, knowledge and conduct.

णवि एस मोक्खमग्गो पासंडी गिहमयाणि लिंगाणि।
दंसणणाणचरित्ताणि मोक्खमग्गं जिणा विंति॥ ४१०॥

ṇavi esa mokkamaggo pāsaṁḍī gihamayāṇi liṁgāṇi
daṁsaṇanacarittāṇi mokkhamaggaṁ jiṇā viṁti (410)

नाप्येष मोक्षमार्गः पाषण्डिगृहमयानि लिङ्गानि।
दर्शनज्ञानचरित्राणि मोक्षमार्गं जिना वदन्ति॥ ४१०॥

410. The insignia of false ascetics or householders never (constitute) the path of emancipation. The Jinas declare that faith, knowledge and conduct (together constitute) the path of emancipation.

Commentary : Thus it is further emphasised that it is not the bodily mark but the spiritual qualities that constitute the path to salvation.

जम्हा जहित्तु लिंगे सागारणगारएहिं वा गहिए।
दंसणणाणचरित्ते अप्पाणं जुंज मोक्खपहे॥ ४११॥

jamhā jahittu liṁge sāgāraṇagāraehiṁ vā gahie
daṁsaṇaṇāṇacaritte appāṇaṁ juṁja mokkhapahe (411)

यस्मात् जहित्वा लिङ्गानि सागारैरनगारिकैर्वा गृहीतानि।
दर्शनज्ञानचारित्रे आत्मानं युङ्क्ष्व मोक्षपथे॥ ४११॥

411. Therefore, giving up the insignia adopted by householders and the homeless ones, direct the Self to faith, knowledge and conduct, the path of emancipation.

Commentary : Hence the saint has to discard all bodily marks as they are useless and concentrate upon the three jewels or Right Belief, Right Knowledge and Right Conduct which are spiritual in nature and which are therefore the true path.

मोक्खपहे अप्पाणं ठवेहि तं चेव झाहि तं चेद।
तत्थेव विहर णिच्चं मा विहरसु अण्णदव्वेसु॥ ४१२॥

mokkhapahe appāṇaṁ ṭhavehi taṁ ceva jhāhi taṁ ceda
tattheva vihara ṇiccaṁ mā viharasu aṇṇadavvesu (412)

मोक्षपथे आत्मानं स्थापय तं चैव ध्यायस्व तं चैतयस्व।
तत्रैव विहर नित्यं मा विहार्षीरन्यद्रव्येषु॥ ४१२॥

412. Keep the Self on the path of emancipation, meditate on him, experience him, always move in Him, do not move among other things.

Commentary : It has already been shown that the three jewels which constitute the *mokṣa mārga* are really of the nature of the Self. Therefore the directions to establish, to experience, to meditate etc., refer to the Self. Thus it is emphasised that you are always to live, move and have your being in the Self and never to look beyond to the outer world. This is the surest method for self-realisation.

Next it is pointed out that those who are devoid of real knowledge and who put their faith on bodily garbs alone, cannot realise the Absolute Self.

पाखंडिलिंगेसु व गिहलिंगेसु व बहुप्पयारेसु।
कुव्वंति जे ममत्तं तेहिं ण णायं समयसारं॥ ४१३॥

pākhaṁdiliṅgesu va gihaliṁgesu va bahuppayāresu
kuvvaṁti je mamataṁ tehiṁ ṇa ṇāyaṁ samatasāraṁ (413)

पाषण्डिलिङ्गेषु वा गृहीलिङ्गेषु वा बहुप्रकारेषु।
कुर्वन्ति ये ममत्वं तैर्न ज्ञात: समयसार:॥ ४१३॥

413. The real Self is not seen by those who put on the garb of ascetics or householders and fancy that therefore they are the real seers.

Next it is emphasised that bodily insignia are therefore irrelevant and useless.

ववहारिओ पुण णओ दोण्णिवि लिंगाणि भणइ मोक्खपहे।
णिच्छयणओ ण इच्छइ मोक्खपहै सव्वलिंगाणि॥ ४१४॥

vavahārio puṇa ṇao doṇṇivi liṁgāṇi bhaṇai mokkhapahe
ṇicchayaṇao ṇa icchai mokkhapahe savvaliṅgāṇi (414)

व्यवहारिक: पुनर्नयो द्वे अपि लिङ्गे भणति मोक्षपथे।
निश्चयनयो नेच्छति मोक्षपथे सर्वलिङगानि॥ ४१४॥

414. Although, the *vyavahāra* point of view declares the two (classes of insignia) to be the path of emancipation, the standpoint of reality does not want any insignia whatsoever for the path of liberation.

Commentary : Those who maintain that what is obtained from the *vyavahāra* point of view is the real and ultimate truth can never realise the *samayasāra or* the Supreme Self. Realisation of *samayasāra* or True Self is possible only by adopting the *niścaya* point of view which is the only way to reach the Absolute Reality.

जो समयपाहुडमिणं पठिऊण अत्थतच्चओ णाउं।
अत्थे ठाहिदि चेया सो होहि उत्तमं सोक्खं॥ ४१५॥

jo samayapāhuḍamiṇaṁ paṭhiūṇa atthataccao ṇāuṁ
atthe ṭhāhidi ceyā so hohi uttamaṁ sokkhaṁ (415)

यः समयाप्राभृतमिदं पठित्वा अर्थतत्त्वतो ज्ञात्वा।
अर्थे स्थास्यति चेतयिता स भविष्यत्युत्तमं सौख्यम्॥ ४१५॥

415, That persom who, having read the *Samayapāhuḍa*, and having known its real meaning firmly holds to the truth thereof will attain Supreme Bliss.

Commentary : In the last *gāthā* the author indicates the benefits that will accrue to one who carefully studies the work dealing with the nature of the Supreme Self. It is a well-known fact that the value of a study depends upon the nature of the book whereas the book itself derives its value from the subject-matter dealt therein. This book by Bhagavān Kundakunda has as its contents and investigation into the nature of the Supreme Reality called *Samayasāra,* by the author which is synonymous with *paramātmā* or the *para* *brahman* or the Supreme Self. The nature of this *parama brahman* is said to be *jñānamaya,* knowledge, *par-excellence,* which illuminates the whole of reality and comprehends it within itself.This Self is the Light that illuminates the whole of reality since it has transcended completely the toil and turmoil of the world of *saṁsāra,* a world full of jarring discord, and since the Self has reached the place of Perfect Harmony and Supreme Bliss, He is also designated to be *ānanda-maya* or of the nature of Supreme Bliss. This *parama brahaman* characterised by *jñānamaya* and ānandamaya, all-knowledge and all-bliss , constitutes the subject matter of this book. Hence the book itself is therefore described as *Sabda Brahman,* the Word Divine, the name which it derives from its contents. This *Sabda Brahman* is therefore the gateway to the Realm of Ultimate Reality, the *parama brahman!* One who studies this work carefully and who comprehends clearly its meaning has therefore the privilege of entering into the promised Land of Paradise, the Realm of the Real, the place of the *Paramātmā.* This privilege which he acquires through study leads to the falling off of scales from his eyes. He sees a vision. He is face to face with the light that lights up the whole Universe. His own personality is in tune with the infinite. His whole being throbs in a responsive melody to the devine and perfect harmony. Being in that atmosphere of Supreme Bliss, He himself feels a thrill of joy unsurpassed—verily a great boon for a noble effort.

Thus ends *Samayasāra.*

GĀTHĀNUKRAMA

गाथानुक्रम

[अ]

[आ]

APPENDIX

GĀTHĀ 144

Samayasāra is the pure soul in its essence. A right believer himself becomes the soul in Essence, when he is absorbed in his own soul which is full of all its pure attributes, conation, knowledge, belief, peace, power, happiness etc. It is the association of karmic bondage which brings about the impure modifications of soul. Really, the soul is above all these impurities. It is all pure, peaceful and happy and modifier of its own pure thought-activities. One who meditates upon this again and again acquires self-absorption, which is *Samayasāra*. (cf. from *Samayasāra*, Ed. by J.L. Jaini, P. 90)

GĀTHĀ 153

Observing the vows and resolutions, and performing the subsidiary vows and austerities, they are unknowing, because they are away from (realization of) the highest Soul-purity, (cf. from *Samayasāra* by J.L. Jaini, P. 95)

GĀTHĀ 156

Mere practical conduct without realization of the pure and real nature of soul, cannot be the cause of liberation, so the learned do not neglect their own pure soul. When there is non-attachment to all non-self and absorption in the own self, then that fire of concentration is kindled up which burns karmic matter and purifies the soul. (cf. from *Samayasāra* by J.L. Jaini, P. 97)

GĀTHĀ 304

Aparādha means without rādha or self-devotion. In common parlance *Aparādha* means fault or offence. From the real point of view, Shri Kundakundachrya reduces the word to its ultimate root-meaning, making fault or offence equivalent to being devoid of devotion to the self. Real truth whether it is belief, knowledge or conduct is one, self-absorption. All else is error of one kind or the other. Our lives on earth or in heaven may be the purest and the highest. But that is of no avail. Any lapse from this condition of pure self-realisation is necessarily a fault, an *Aparādha* which becomes the cause of the inflow and bondage of karmic matter. From this pure point of view, good and bad are equally undesirable, equally mundane and worthy of renunciation.

The soul's safety lies in itself. Safety here does not lie in numbers. It lies in loneliness. The meditation of oneness of loneliness *(Ekatva Anuprekṣā)*, has this teaching for its highest meaning. The soul must realise its full independence by realising that it accomplishes its aim only when, and in so far as, it is absorbed in itself. Then alone, matter is important and the non-self stands aloof, incapable of attacking the soul or attaching itself to it. Any intermission of this self-devotion is the immediate passport to the mundane wheel going on once again. (cf. from *Samayasāra* by J.L. Jaini, P. 173)

GĀTHĀ 372

Creation and destruction only mean the change of condition of a substance. The primary attributes are not destroyed, and no fresh ones are created in any substance. Any other substance is merely an auxiliary cause for creation and destruction of any condition of another substance, but it cannot create any new attribute in another substance nor destroy any attribute of another. Therefore a person who wants to purify himself must rectify his own thought-activity. If he thinks that outward objects like women, wealth, lands, clothes, ornaments, etc., are causes of his impure thought-activity and thus by their removal only he will become pure, this view is not altogether correct. If internal attachment, etc., are not removed, this renunciation merely will not stop the advent of karmic matter. Internal attachment and external possession should both be discarded. If internal attachment is removed no inclination for external objects remains. (cf. from *Samayasāra* by J.L. Jaini, P. 193-94).

□□□

णाणं

पयासयं

वीर नि.सं. 2470

ई.सन् 1944

भारतीय ज्ञानपीठ